BRICS
An Anti-Capitalist Critique

BRICS
An Anti-Capitalist Critique

edited by
Patrick Bond and Ana Garcia

Haymarket Books,
Chicago, Illinois

First published in southern Africa by Jacana Media (Pty) Ltd in 2015
© 2015 Patrick Bond and Ana Garcia

This edition published by
Haymarket Books
P.O. Box 180165
Chicago, IL 60618
773-583-7884
info@haymarketbooks.org
www.haymarketbooks.org

ISBN: 978-1-60846-533-0

Trade distribution:
In the US through Consortium Book Sales and Distribution, www.cbsd.com
In the UK, Turnaround Publisher Services, www.turnaround-uk.com
In Canada, Publishers Group Canada, www.pgcbooks.ca
All other countries, Publishers Group Worldwide, www.pgw.com

This book was published with the generous support of the Wallace Action Fund
and Lannan Foundation.

Cover design by Josh On.

Printed in Canada by union labor.

Library of Congress CIP Data is available.

10 9 8 7 6 5 4 3 2 1

Contents

Contributors

Elmar Altvater was a Professor at the Free University of Berlin from 1970 to 2004. He coedited *PROKLA: Zeitschrift für kritische Sozialwissenschaft*. He is a member of the Scientific Council of ATTAC Germany, and an associate of the Berlin Institute for International Political Economy. His books include *Das Ende des Kapitalismus, wie wir ihn kennen* (2005), *Grenzen der Globalisierung* (with Birgit Mahnkopf) (1999) and *The Future of the Market* (1993).

Baruti Amisi is a visiting scholar in Development Studies at the University of KwaZulu-Natal's Centre for Civil Society in Durban. His PhD thesis addresses the Inga Hydropower Projects on the Congo River, the world's largest construction and energy project. He is from the eastern Democratic Republic of the Congo, and a refugee leader in Durban. He has published academic articles on xenophobia, refugee life, the Clean Development Mechanism, and water and sanitation policy.

Patrick Bond is Senior Professor of Development Studies at the University of KwaZulu-Natal in Durban, where he directs the Centre for Civil Society, and also a Professor of Political Economy at Wits University in Johannesburg. His recent books include *Elite Transition* (2014), *South Africa: The Present as Future* (with John Saul) (2014) and *Politics of Climate Justice* (2012).

Omar Bonilla Martinez is an Ecuadorian historian. He researches territorial transformation, especially the expansion of extractive frontiers of oil and mining industries. He is a member of the collective Critical Geography of Ecuador and the YASunidos Collective. He has also worked extensively with local communities situated along the proposed Manta–Manaus transport axis.

Einar Braathen is Senior Researcher in International Studies at the Norwegian Institute for Urban and Regional Research. For the last years his main work has been on Brazil, and until 2018 he heads the project 'Insurgent Citizenship in Brazil: the Role of Mega-Sports Events'.

Pedro Henrique Campos is Professor of History and International Relations at the Federal Rural University of Rio de Janeiro. His PhD in Social History at the Fluminense Federal University focused on the relationship of construction companies to the Brazilian dictatorships (1964–1988).

Ruslan Dzarasov is the Head of the Department of Political Economy at the G.V. Plekhanov Russian University of Economics, and Senior Research Fellow at the Central Institute of Economics and Mathematics within the Russian Academy of Sciences. He has written for the academic journals *Debatte: Journal of Contemporary Central and Eastern Europe* and the *Cambridge Journal of Economics*. His recent book is *The Conundrum of Russian Capitalism* (2014).

Virginia Fontes is an historian based at the Fluminense Federal University in Rio de Janeiro. Her major works include *O Brasil eo capital-imperialismo: teoria e história* (2010), *A sociedade civil no Brasil contemporâneo: lutas sociais e luta teórica na década de 1980* (2006), *Reflexões impertinentes: história e capitalismo contemporâneo* (2004), *Capitalismo, exclusões e inclusão forçada* (1997) and *História do Brasil recente: 1964–1992* (1996).

Ana Garcia is Professor of International Relations at the Federal Rural University of Rio de Janeiro and an associate of the UKZN Centre for Civil Society and the Institute of Alternative Policies for the Southern Cone of Latin America. Her doctorate was completed at the Pontifical Catholic University of Rio de Janeiro. She co-edited (with Patrick Bond) the special issue of *Tensões Mundiais: Perspectivas Críticas Sobre os BRICS* (2014).

Ho-fung Hung is Associate Professor of Sociology at the Johns Hopkins University. He researches global political economy, protest and nationalism. He is the author of *Protest with Chinese Characteristics* (2013) and *The China Boom: Origins, Global Impacts, and Demise* (2015).

Richard Kamidza holds a doctorate in Development Studies from the University of KwaZulu-Natal and is a post-doctoral research fellow at North West University.

Karina Kato is a Professor in the Department of Development, Agriculture and Society at the Federal Rural University of Rio de Janeiro and an associate of the Institute of Alternative Policies for the Southern Cone of Latin America.

Claudio Katz is Professor at the University of Buenos Aires and a researcher with the National Scientific and Technical Research Council of Argentina. His books include *Bajo el imperio del capital* (2011), *Las disyuntivas de la izquierda en América Latina (2008) and El porvenir de socialismo* (2004).

Mathias Luce is Professor of Latin American History at Federal University of Rio Grande do Sul, Porto Alegre, where he heads the research group on the Economic History of Dependent Capitalism. His writings focus on super-exploitation, sub-imperialism and dependent capitalism. He is co-editor of *Padrão de reprodução do capital: contribuições da teoria marxista da dependência* (2012).

Farai Maguwu is a PhD student at the University of KwaZulu-Natal's Centre for Civil Society in Durban, and Director of the Centre for Natural Resource Governance in Harare. He is a recipient of the Human Rights Watch Alison Des Forges Award for Extraordinary Activism based on his critique of the Marange diamond looting.

Judith Marshall is a Canadian labour educator, writer and global activist. She recently retired after 20 years in the Canadian steelworkers' union, where she coordinated Steelworkers Humanity Fund projects in southern Africa and organised global exchange programmes linking workers and community organisations affected by transnational mining companies like Vale. Her PhD at the University of Toronto was published as *Literacy, Power and Democracy in Mozambique* (1993).

Gilmar Mascarenhas is Associate Professor in Human Geography at the State University of Rio de Janeiro. Since 2004 he has published several papers and a book about the relations between mega-sports events and host cities, focusing on territorial changes, conflicts and citizenship.

Sam Moyo is Professor of Agrarian Studies and Director of the African Institute for Agrarian Studies and Honorary Professor at the University of KwaZulu-Natal's Centre for Civil Society. He has served as President of the Council for the Development of Social Research in Africa (2009–11); his books include *African*

Land Questions, Agrarian Transitions and the State (2008) and he co-edited (with KS Amanor) *Land and Sustainable Development in Africa* (2008) and (with Paris Yeros) *Reclaiming the Land: The Resurgence of Rural Movements in Africa, Asia and Latin America* (2005).

Leo Panitch is the editor of the *Socialist Register* and Distinguished Research Professor of Political Science at York University, Canada. He is co-author (with Sam Gindin) of *The Making of Global Capitalism* (2013). Other major books include *The Global Financial Meltdown and Left Alternatives* (2010) and *Social Democracy and Industrial Militancy* (1976).

Bobby Peek is Director of groundwork and Friends of the Earth South Africa. He grew up on the fenceline of south Durban's Engen oil refinery, co-founded the South Durban Community Environmental Alliance, was national campaigns coordinator for the Environmental Justice Networking Forum, and in 1998 received the Goldman Environmental Prize for Africa. He holds an honorary doctorate from the Durban University of Technology.

Gonzalo Pozo is a Lecturer in International Political Economy at King's College London and is a researcher for the 'The Visions of Eurasia' project at Södertörn University and the Baltic Sea Foundation in Stockholm. His main focus is on Russian political economy, Marxist theory, imperialism and geopolitics. He recently authored *The Geopolitics of Capitalism: New Spaces of Imperialist Rivalry* (2015).

Vijay Prashad is the George and Martha Kellner Chair in South Asian History and Professor of International Studies at Trinity College Hartford. In 2013–14, he was Edward Said Chair at the American University of Beirut. His books include *No Free Left: The Futures of Indian Communism* (2015), *Arab Spring, Libyan Winter* (2012) and *The Darker Nations: A People's History of the Third World* (2007).

Niall Reddy is a research master's candidate at the University of KwaZulu-Natal's Centre for Civil Society and a research affiliate of the Alternative Information Development Centre, Cape Town. His focus is on emerging powers, theories of sub-imperialism, financialisation and wage-led growth.

William Robinson is Professor of Sociology at the University of California, Santa Barbara. He focuses on macro and comparative sociology, globalisation and transnationalism, political economy, political sociology, development and social change, immigration, Latin America and the Third World. His books include *Global Capitalism and the Crisis of Humanity* (2014) and *Latin America and Global Capitalism: A Critical Globalization Perspective* (2008).

Susanne Soederberg is Professor of Global Political Economy at Queen's University, Kingston, Canada. Her books include *Corporate Power and Ownership in Contemporary Capitalism* (2010) and *Debtfare States and the Poverty Industry: Money, Discipline and the Surplus Population* (2014).

Celina Sørbøe is a PhD research fellow at the Norwegian Institute for Urban and Regional Research. She has a master's degree in Latin American Studies, has been a long-time international solidarity activist and recently spent two years based in Rio de Janeiro.

Achin Vanaik is retired Professor of International Relations and Global Politics at the University of Delhi. He is a founding member of the Coalition for Nuclear Disarmament and Peace, India. His latest book is *After the Bomb: Reflections on India's Nuclear Journey* (2015).

Immanuel Wallerstein is Senior Research Scholar at Yale University. He is the author of *The Modern World-System*; *Utopistics, or Historical Choices of the Twenty-first Century*; *Decline of American Power: The U.S. in a Chaotic World*; and *European Universalism: The Rhetoric of Power*.

Paris Yeros is Professor of Economics in the Federal University of ABC, São Paulo, and an affiliate of the African Institute of Agrarian Studies in Harare. He is editor of *Agrarian South: Journal of Political Economy*. His PhD in International Relations was completed at the London School of Economics and Political Science, and his research areas include Africa, North–South and South–South relations, state and development, nationalism, race, the agrarian question and social movements.

Abbreviations

ABC	Brazilian Cooperation Agency
ABS	asset-backed securitisation
AFRICOM	Africa Command
ALBA	Bolivarian Alternative for the Americas
ALCA	Free Trade Areas of the Americas
ANC	African National Congress
ASEAN	Association of South-East Asian Nations
BASIC	British American Security Information Council
BDS	boycotts, divestment and sanctions
BIT	bilateral trade and investment agreement
BJP	Bharatiya Janata Party
BNDES	National Social and Economic Development Bank of Brazil
BRICS	Brazil, Russia, India, China and South Africa
CAPES	Federal Agency for the Support and Evaluation of Graduate Education (Brazil)
CCP	Communist Party of China
CGAP	Consultative Group to Assist the Poor
CIDA	Canadian International Development Agency
CIS	Commonwealth of Independent States (ex-USSR)
CIVETS	Colombia, Indonesia, Vietnam, Egypt, Turkey and South Africa
CNOOC	China National Offshore Oil Corporation
CNPC	China National Petrol Corporation
CNPQ	National Council for Scientific and Technological Development (Brazil)
CRA	Contingent Reserve Arrangement
DBSA	Development Bank of Southern Africa
DRC	Democratic Republic of the Congo
DTZ	Development Trust of Zimbabwe
ECLA	United Nations Economic Commission for Latin America
EEU	Eurasian Economic Union
Embrapa	Brazilian Enterprise for Agricultural Research
EU	European Union
FAO	Food and Agriculture Organisation
FDI	foreign direct investment
FIFA	Fédération Internationale de Football Association
FIRJAN	Federation of Industries of the State of Rio de Janeiro
FSB	Federal Security Service (Russia)
GDP	gross domestic product
GIF	Global Infrastructure Facility
GNP	gross national product
IBGE	Institute of Geography and Statistics of Brazil
IIAM	Institute of Agricultural Research of Mozambique

IIRSA	Initiative for the Integration of the Regional Infrastructure of South America
IMF	International Monetary Fund
IOC	International Olympic Committee
IPEA	Institute of Applied Economic Research
ITT	Ishpingo–Tambococha–Tiputini
JICA	Japanese International Cooperation Agency
MAVINS	Mexico, Australia, Vietnam, Indonesia, Nigeria and South Africa
MBA	Master of Business Administration
MCMV	My House My Life programme
MDT	Marxist dependency theory
MEND	Movement for the Emancipation of the Niger Delta
Mercosur	Southern Common Market
MFI	micro-finance institution
MINT	Mexico, India, Nigeria and Turkey
MNC	multinational corporation
NAFTA	North American Free Trade Agreement
NAM	Non-Aligned Movement
NATO	North Atlantic Treaty Organisation
NDB	New Development Bank
NEP	New Economic Policy
NEPAD	New Partnership for Africa's Development
NGO	non-governmental organisation
NIEO	New International Economic Order
NMDC	National Mineral Development Corporation (India)
NSA	National Security Agency (US)
OECD	Organisation for Economic Cooperation and Development
ONGC	Oil and Natural Gas Corporation (India)
PAC	Programme for Accelerated Growth (Brazil)
PES	Payments for Ecosystem Services
POEA	Philippines Overseas Employment Administration
PPP	public–private partnership
ProSavana	Program of Triangular Co-operation for Agricultural Development of the Tropical Savannahs of Mozambique
PT	Workers Party (Brazil)
R&D	research and development
REDD	Reducing Emissions from Deforestation and Degradation
RMB	renminbi
SADC	Southern African Development Community
SENAI	National Industrial Training Service (Brazil)
SINOPEC	China Petrol and Chemical Corporation
Sodepac	Capanda Agro-industrial Complex
TAZARA	Tanzania–Zambia railway
TEEB	The Economics of Ecosystems and the Biosphere
TISA	Trade in Services Agreement
TNC	transnational corporation
TPP	Trans-Pacific Partnership
TRF	Federal Regional Tribunal (Brazil)
TTIP	Transatlantic Trade and Investment Partnership
UK	United Kingdom
UN	United Nations
UNAC	National Union of Peasants (Mozambique)
Unasul	Union of South American Nations
UNCTAD	United Nations Conference on Trade and Development

Abbreviations

UNDP	United Nations Development Programme
UPP	Units of Pacifying Police
US	United States
USAID	United States Agency for Institutional Development
USSR	Union of Soviet Socialist Republics
USW	United Steelworkers (Canada)
VISTA	Vietnam, Indonesia, South Africa, Turkey and Argentina
WHO	World Health Organisation
WSA	world system analysis
WTO	World Trade Organisation
ZANU-PF	Zimbabwe African National Union – Patriotic Front
ZIA	Zimbabwe Investment Authority
ZISCO	Zimbabwe Iron and Steel Company

1
Introduction

ANA GARCIA AND PATRICK BOND

This book addresses the prospects of imperial power from above, emerging powers from the middle and nascent popular counter-powers from below. The relative economic decline of the United States, Europe and Japan is often linked to the rise of an 'emerging' bloc comprising Brazil, Russia, India, China and South Africa (BRICS). But the latter regularly demand 'a seat at the table' in a process that some term 'antagonistic cooperation'. That means, in practice, that in areas ranging from world finance to climate change to super-exploitative relations with the periphery and even to soccer, the bloc aims not to overturn tables at the proverbial temple, but to collaborate in holding them up. Consider some recent evidence:

- After funding the International Monetary Fund (IMF) with US$75 billion in 2012, in the following year there were two meetings of BRICS leaders (in Durban and St. Petersburg) which pronounced growing dissatisfaction with the Bretton Woods Institutions.
- The BRICS' stated intention to create a New Development Bank with capital of US$50 billion, and an IMF-style Contingent Reserve Arrangement with US$100 billion, was accomplished in 2014 at the Fortaleza summit, but ultimately, given the role of neoliberal finance ministers in their conceptualisation, these were celebrated in Washington as complementary to, not competitive with, the existing multilateral financial power structure.
- A Brazilian directs the World Trade Organisation and, based on a more aggressive policy of liberalisation, tries to break persistent blockages between

1

the US and EU that hinder the growth of global trade.

- Chinese and Indian economists occupy a second tier of the bureaucracies in the World Bank and IMF.
- Climate negotiations at the global scale increasingly revolve around Washington's managed relations with BRICS countries, first through the deal done in 2009 in Copenhagen (involving four of the five BRICS) and then the US-China emissions cuts agreed to bilaterally in 2014.
- In other bilateral relations with South Africa and India, US President Barack Obama made substantial progress in trips, respectively, during 2013 (twice) and 2015.
- Soccer remains the most symbolic and profitable commercial component of sports in the imperialist project, with FIFA machinery controlling the game's World Cup in alliance with elites from host countries South Africa, Brazil and Russia from 2010 to 2018, no matter the vast social costs involved in White Elephant stadium construction and suppression of local unrest. To add insult to injury, key BRICS countries supported Blatter's continual re-election to world soccer managerial leadership, notwithstanding vast evidence of wrongdoing during his five-term reign.

But there is also countervailing evidence:

- Several members of the BRICS have resisted demands by Western countries to impose stricter intellectual property controls (in the case of medicines this has saved millions of lives, especially in South Africa).
- Geopolitically, some BRICS leaders boldly challenged Washington after revelations of espionage by whistleblower Edward Snowden and before Washington's proposed bombing of Syria in 2013. In March 2014, the BRICS implicitly supported Russia in the conflict over Crimea, for which the G7 imposed sanctions and expelled Moscow (Putin had originally been scheduled to host the G8 meeting in Sochi a few weeks later). BRICS foreign ministers even successfully threatened to withdraw from the subsequent G20 summit in Australia in late 2014, were it to have become a G19 without Russia.
- In May 2014, Russia agreed to supply gas to China using local currencies, not the US dollar, seeking to partially reduce Russia's dependence on sales to the European market as sanctions resulting from the Ukraine chaos loomed.
- In early 2015, dramatic economic developments began unfolding as this book went to press, as emerging markets faced financial stress, as the Russian rouble crashed because of sanctions and the oil price collapse, and as China initiated

an Asian Infrastructure Investment Bank, whose co-founders included the richest European countries and the Bretton Woods Institutions, leaving the Obama administration diplomatically embarrassed.

These incidents suggest the possibility that at least two of the BRICS – China and Russia – occasionally adopt 'inter-imperial' stances against Western powers, but in a stop-start way that is quite unpredictable. At the same time, however, the underlying BRICS project has much in common with the Western status quo regarding the stabilisation of the financial world, in generating additional capacities of 'lender of last resort' and in stabilising multilateral governance. BRICS still provides a sustained demand for the US dollar, despite monetary turbulence due to Federal Reserve policies; it is distressing but true that Chinese dollar purchases soared to record highs during the first half of 2014, only declining slightly a year later.

Moreover, the BRICS countries promote an extractive, high-carbon economic model which threatens to amplify the catastrophic environmental and social destruction of advanced capitalism. The role of the BRICS in the *de facto* derailing of the Kyoto Protocol to limit climate change is revealing: Russia endorsed the Treaty in 2005 but withdrew in 2012, while in 2009 the other BRICS leaders joined Barack Obama to promote the Copenhagen Accord in behind-the-scenes negotiations. That 2009 deal rejected a mandatory limit on emissions, and at subsequent UN Framework Convention on Climate Change Conferences of the Parties, BRICS countries (including host South Africa in 2011) were among those joining Washington as most resistant to binding emissions cuts and payment of climate debt. By 2011 in South Africa, they had agreed to whittle away the critical notion of 'common but differentiated responsibility' for the crisis, to the detriment of the world's poorest and lowest-emitting countries.

As for Snowden's revelations, the surveillance of citizens seems as severe in the BRICS countries as in the anglophone West, in a style reminiscent of George Orwell's *1984*, reaching even into the South African parliament in February 2015, when journalists' cellphones and Wi-Fi signals were jammed by Pretoria's security apparatus. The BRICS' criminalisation of social movements and the oppression of dissidents are even worse than in the G7. The economic and political domination of the BRICS' less-developed neighbours is a growing concern, leading critics to postulate the incorporation of sub-imperialist BRICS into world capitalism, just as Ruy Mauro Marini wrote regarding the position of Brazil more than 40 years ago.

Resistance and ideological vacillation

However, as we conclude in the last pages, the contradictions that characterise all the BRICS have created incisive forms of social resistance. These include some of the largest protests and other social convulsions in the world, though some have expressed a conservative bias (Brazil) or articulated liberal ideals (India, Russia and Hong Kong). But other resistance struggles against mega-projects are manifestations of the limits to the BRICS' pro-corporate economic growth model. Most progressive activists mistrust the rhetoric of the BRICS governments, which promise prosperity for their countries by following the current trajectory of global neoliberalism, especially in alliance with one another.

Other radical activists and Third Worldist analysts have supported the BRICS governments, though, believing that their claims of wanting to democratise the world order might do more than simply add a layer of collaborators. There is not yet a consistent approach on the left, as progressive forces in each country operate still unaware of possible concrete links with other movements in the other BRICS countries, and even in their own hinterlands which BRICS corporations are busy exploiting. The critical question for the future is whether social struggles in each of the BRICS countries will discover linkages of solidarity between peoples, on the basis of reversing the path of the elites and creating paths for another kind of development.

This connection between the struggles and collective experiences of resistance and construction of alternatives is what we call 'BRICS from below'. Considering the various stances taken towards BRICS using a class analysis, we can discern some rough ideological positions towards this bloc of countries: 'BRICS from above' (the position of government and corporate bodies), 'Brics from the middle' (the position of some academics, think tanks and NGOs), 'BRICS from below' (grassroots social movements that can create common bonds of struggle and transnational solidarity), and, finally, those looking at BRICS from a pro-Western corporate perspective. The latter are adherents of the old capitalist order based on US hegemony, and fear the rise of the BRICS. We describe these positions, with three nuanced perspectives in the main categories, within the box below, based especially on experiences in South Africa.

From this attempt to organise ideological positioning, it is possible to identify various analyses of this group of countries. Recall that the first appearance of the acronym BRIC was in 2001, offered by Jim O'Neill of Goldman Sachs to identify promising markets for financial investors. There were those who discredited the bloc as an incoherent collection, arguing that these countries have nothing in common with each other. Others have considered these countries as a possible threat to US hegemony, aspiring to have more power and participation in the international order, with demands to the traditional powers to adjust rules and standards accordingly. Others have celebrated the rise of the BRICS as the democratisation of the world order, without which it will be impossible to find solutions to the global financial crisis which began in the US.

Because of the BRICS' apparent importance, funding agencies began to allocate resources to projects and academic papers on the topic, and the BRICS states also officially supported alliances of generally pro-government, pro-business academics and think tanks. In early 2015, the Russian government established a 'Civic BRICS' to involve 500 approved representatives from the five countries plus guest countries. The strategy was in part, according to the civilbrics.ru website, 'to make decisions made at the Summit more legitimate,' which in turn led the main Brazilian civil society network (Rebrip) to formally dissociate from the process, given Putin's record of repressing Russian NGOs hostile to the Moscow regime.

Even though three of the five BRICS were suffering severe economic problems by 2015, with the end of China's boom adding to world economic dislocation, much of the analysis coming from mainstream academics and NGOs has been upbeat in tone. The texts gathered below aim to fill a gap in studies, events and documents dealing with BRICS: critical analysis of these economies and societies within the framework of a global capitalism that is increasingly predatory, exclusionary and unequal, in many cases quite explicitly so within the BRICS themselves. We take up the challenge of bringing together a set of chapters from different approaches, albeit all 'anti-capitalist', reflecting upon the uncertain rise of a 'Global South (and East)', which is sometimes cooperative with and sometimes antagonistic to the traditional powers (US, Europe and Japan, plus the main multilateral institutions).

Most importantly, the BRICS' rise occurs in the context of the expansion and deepening of capitalism in the 21st century, and also in the midst of world capitalism's worst crisis since the 1930s. The point of critical anti-capitalist analysis of this sort is to thereby strengthen understandings of where BRICS fit in the world economy and global governance, how their own companies' capital accumulation strategies are developing, how national political dynamics comply, and how networks of resistance have begun to respond. The goal is simple: contribute to building transnational solidarity towards a 'BRICS from below' that genuinely defends the interests of people, environment and sovereignty in both BRICS and their hinterlands, against the depredations of capitalism.

TEN IDEOLOGICAL STANDPOINTS IN RELATION TO THE BRICS

1. *BRICS from above* – heads of state, corporates and elite allies
   - 1.1 BRICS as *anti*-imperialist: foreign ministry *rhetoric* – 'Talk Left, Walk Right' – based upon national-liberation traditions, with some concrete actions (such as opposition to Intellectual Property applied to medicines, especially for AIDS, safe haven for US spy whistleblower Edward Snowden, and hostility to the proposed US bombing of Syria in 2013)
   - 1.2 BRICS as *sub*-imperialist: relegitimisation of 'globalisation', lubricating neoliberalism in – and exploiting – BRICS hinterlands, intensifying structural exploitation of the poor / workers / women / nature on behalf of global / local capital, ensuring maximum greenhouse gas emissions alongside BASIC / US no matter the local / continental / global consequences, and even sometimes playing a 'deputy sheriff' role to world hegemons
   - 1.3 BRICS as *inter*-imperialist: potential new internet delinked from the US; promotion of Putin v Obama in September 2013 at G20; and backing Russia in Crimea/Ukraine conflict

2. Brics from the middle – BRICS Academic Forum, intellectuals, trade unions, NGOs
   - 2.1 *pro-BRICS advocates*: most of Academic Forum, most establishment 'think tanks', the 'Civic BRICS' initiated by Russia, and others (including leftists) claiming BRICS will increasingly challenge global injustices
   - 2.2 *wait-and-see about BRICS:* most NGOs and their funders – as well as most 'Third Worldist' intellectuals – who wish for BRICS to become 'anti-impi' in the UN and Bretton Woods Institutions, using the New Development Bank and Contingent Reserve Arrangement, etc.
   - 2.3 *critics of BRICS:* those associated with BRICS-from-below networks who consider BRICS to be 'sub-impis' and sometimes also 'inter-impis'

---

3. BRICS from below – grassroots activists whose visions run local to global
- 3.1 *localist:* stuck within local or sectoral silos, including myriad momentary 'popcorn protests' (even some against BRICS corporations or projects) that are insurgent, unstrategic, at constant risk of becoming xenophobic, and prone to populist demagoguery
- 3.2 *nationally bound:* most civil society activists who are vaguely aware of BRICS and are hostile to it, yet who are so bound up in national and sectoral battles – most of which counteract BRICS' agenda – that they fail to link up even in areas that would serve their interests
- 3.3 *solidaristic-internationalist:* 'global justice movement' allies providing solidarity to allies across the BRICS when they are repressed and jointly campaigning for human and ecological rights against common BRICS enemies (such as Vale, the China Development Bank, DBSA, Transnet/mega-shipping, fossil fuel corporations and other polluters, and the coming BRICS Development Bank)

4. pro-West business – most organic intellectuals of business connected to Old Money, multinational-corporate branch plants, northern-centric institutions and political parties, all increasingly worried that BRICS may act as a coherent anti-Western bloc some day (a phenomenon mainly evident in South Africa, given its important unpatriotic bourgeoisie)

The architecture of this book

Thus, two goals were established for this collection. The first is to bring together analyses that prompt debate between social movements, organised labour and other activists in the struggle for social justice and for alternatives to the current international capitalist order; such debate was lively in counter-summits in South Africa in 2013 and Brazil in 2014, and we hope it will continue in coming years as contradictions in the world system and BRICS countries are heightened. BRICS is a new and rather tentative area of concern for many of the anti-neoliberal social movements, but we are confident that the same critical sensibilities will prevail, and that those movements and NGOs which temporarily endorsed the uncritical optimism of BRICS from above will continue reflecting upon the many downsides associated with elite practices. The second goal is to generate critical academic debate involving contemporary themes and theoretical discussions, such as whether BRICS represent cases of sub-imperialism, orthodox neo-developmentalism and what in Latin America is derisively termed 'extractivism'.

These objectives have been largely achieved. A first set of chapters considers the categories of imperialism, sub-imperialism and capital-imperialism.

- Patrick Bond discusses how sub-imperialism has emerged as a theoretical category, with a focus on the characteristics of semi-peripheral accumulation, hinterland exploitation, internal modes of super-exploitation and the reproduction of a world system based on neoliberalism and military aggression.
- Mathias Luce revisits Ruy Mauro Marini's formulations within the Marxist theory of dependency, and he develops a comprehensive theory of sub-imperialism as the 'highest stage of dependent capitalism'. This results in a new hierarchy in the world system, with intermediate links in the imperialist chain, a position held especially by Brazil, South Africa and India. According to Luce, however, China and Russia cannot be characterised similarly.
- Virginia Fontes is already working with a new category, 'capital-imperialism', in order to understand transformations of contemporary capitalism and its new economic, political and social contradictions. For Fontes, the dominance exercised by the core countries must be understood not as something external, but internalised in other countries, with BRICS countries revealing a subordinate membership within capital-imperialist expansion.
- Leo Panitch provides the perspective on imperialism which he and Sam Gindin have pioneered, in which older theories of inter-imperial rivalry and capital export have less relevance in view of the post-War centrality of US institutions. These still define the scope for all other actors, including the BRICS. If the BRICS are less easy to incorporate than Washington's G7 allies, Panitch is also interested in their internal contestations, including Chinese, Brazilian and South African class struggles.
- Claudio Katz analyses the general status of what he calls emerging, intermediate and peripheral neoliberalism. Katz scans the BRICS as well as Turkey and other countries in the process of emergence. He stresses, especially, contradictions within semi-peripheral capitalism, and considers food price inflation and the super-exploitation of labour to have great importance, perhaps setting the stage for new revolts linking production and social reproduction processes.

These attempts to set the global context lead us to a second set of chapters on corporate and political expansion of BRICS in Africa and Latin America, the sites of our utmost concern in 2013–14 due to the regional 'gateway' claims of the

BRICS hosts those years. Russia in Eastern Europe prompted similar concerns in 2015.

- From a Southern African perspective, Baruti Amisi, Patrick Bond, Richard Kamidza, Farai Maguwu and Bobby Peek expound on the role of the BRICS in Africa, especially Mozambique and Zimbabwe, mainly through investment opportunities in the extractive sector and large infrastructure projects with adverse impacts on societies and the environment. The authors fear that the BRICS New Development Bank will facilitate the 'resource curse' evident in so much of Africa. BRICS elites, both political leaders and corporations, are allies of the local ruling classes, they argue, in Africa's ongoing underdevelopment.

- Ana Garcia and Karina Kato explore Brazilian insertions in Angola and Mozambique through National Social and Economic Development Bank financing, direct investment from private and public companies, and the policies of 'development cooperation'. The authors emphasise three themes: the identification of priority sectors and their institutional arrangements; the unique role of the state in each of these countries and the ambiguous relationship and conflict with Brazilian actors and projects; and new forms of 'South–South debt' generated from these transactions, with consequences for the economies of African countries.

- In Latin America, similar maldevelopment is visible. Omar Bonilla provides an Ecuadorian perspective on oil geopolitics in relation to the Chinese companies which have adapted quickly to policy changes in the Andean region. There, little has been done to comply with national and international human rights standards. In Ecuador, Chinese companies have contributed significantly to the expansion of the extractive frontier, with special concerns about the Yasuní National Park, showing little interest in improving working conditions and the environment even in the world's most ambitious campaign site for 'leaving oil in the soil'.

- Pedro Henrique Campos considers the internationalisation of Brazilian construction conglomerates. For him, the thesis of Brazilian sub-imperialism is insufficient, since it is not the narrowness of the market that explains the performance of companies abroad, but the experience and expansive capacity of capital developed in Brazil, before and especially during the civil-military dictatorship. This is due to the state's broad support and encouragement, especially in priority regions, for Brazilian foreign policy within South America and Africa.

- Judith Marshall offers a comprehensive analysis of the overall performance of the Brazilian mining company Vale and its impacts on workers and communities in Canada, Mozambique and Brazil itself. The behaviour of Vale exemplifies the worst tendencies of large mining companies, and contributes to global tensions by increasing the gap between rich and poor, along with exacerbating environmental degradation wherever it seeks minerals. A global civil society campaign is underway to link its victims' resistances.

- Both South Africa and Brazil suffered sub-imperial soccer temptations when it came to hosting the World Cup in 2010 and 2014, and Russia's turn is in 2018. Einar Braathen, Celina Sørbøe and Gilmar Mascarenhas discuss the allocation of resources for mega-events in a country, Brazil, whose institutional capacity to protect human rights and the environment was disappointingly fragile. In the context of neoliberal global competition among countries, the authors show how what they term 'cities of exception' are sold as 'global cities'. Exemplified by Rio de Janeiro, these cities seek to build coalitions between government and companies seeking 'opportunities for urban entrepreneurialism'. The FIFA 2014 World Cup and 2016 Olympics are creating a social backlash and the social sensibility that even the poorest people have a 'right to the city'.

- Moving to Eastern Europe, Ruslan Dzarasov locates Russia within the world system. It is, 'on the one hand, dependent on the core, but on the other aspires to control its own regional periphery in the area of the former USSR'. The contradictions can be seen in the way the parasitic fractions of the bourgeoisie pothole Russia's road back to regional dominance, in part through massive capital flight.

- Gonzalo Pozo adds more detail, especially in scoping out both the neoliberal nature of the Putin regime and its inter-imperial character. These features relate closely to the character of capital accumulation involving apparatchiks and the new bourgeoisie.

Finally, a group of shorter papers explore critical and contrarian positions on the BRICS within the world system. These contributions include analyses by William Robinson, Elmar Altvater, Sam Moyo and Paris Yeros, Susanne Soederberg, Ho-fung Hung, Achin Vanaik, Vijay Prashad, Immanuel Wallerstein, Niall Reddy and ourselves. While some – by Robinson, Vanaik, Prashad and Wallerstein – are overarching in scope, we also feel that specific moments and sectors are vital for understanding the internal contradictions. Altvater tackles environment, Moyo and Yeros consider super-exploitation, Soederberg looks at strategies of financial incorporation through consumer credit, and Ho-fung Hung locates China in the World System.

Finally, along with Reddy's contribution on Fortaleza, we as editors round off the volume by briefly taking up the lessons of recent summits, especially from the standpoint of resistance. In our conclusion, we reflect upon the possibilities of building a 'BRICS-from-below' coalition to watchdog and then resist the role played by BRICS in world capitalism. During a decade in which popular rebellions have multiplied, including within each of the BRICS, it is urgent that these networks arise and generate an effective solidaristic praxis, both nationally and internationally. In our view, the BRICS New Development Bank poses the biggest future challenge for those social groups that have been resisting international financial institutions, extractivist maldevelopment and ecological destruction, and the related effects of mega-infrastructure projects. The Contingent Reserve Arrangement looks likely to smuggle in Washington Consensus ideology directly from the International Monetary Fund, along with increased Bretton Woods direct influence (thanks to a clause limiting BRICS borrowers to 30% of their borrowing quota until they agree on a formal structural adjustment programme, a problem we anticipate South Africa will suffer first as sovereign debt crisis looms). The ongoing downturn in several BRICS economies makes the extractive, export-oriented economic approach less tenable, even as BRICS corporations more desperately intensify their search for new terrains for accumulation. The potential for sane climate change management will be dashed in the process.

These chapters were mainly generated during debates about the BRICS in the two most recent summit host countries, South Africa and Brazil, in 2013–14, with updates provided in 2015 in preparation for the Russian summit. A short pamphlet was distributed to Durban BRICS counter-summit attendees in March 2013, much of which was published in the *Pambazuka* African ezines in March–April 2013 and March 2014. Then, as synthesis emerged in many critical accounts, a similar version of this book was prepared in Portuguese for the Fortaleza summit in July 2014, in partnership with the journal *Tensões Mundiais* (World Tensions) of the State University of Ceará. These publications are thanked for their willingness to test out our critique of the BRICS.

We thank greatly all authors who have contributed to this project, as they considerably raised the quality of the discussions about the BRICS. We are also grateful to Camilla Costa, from the Centre for Nationalities research network headquartered at the State University of Ceará; Bonaventure Monjane from the Centre for Civil Society, University of KwaZulu-Natal in Durban, whose work enabled the Portuguese translation of this publication; Rosemary Galli, whose careful review and translation of the Brazilian chapters enabled this English issue; and Todd Chretien who generously assisted with Spanish–English translation. Venilla Yoganathan and Megan Southey provided excellent editing assistance. Our final thanks are to the Ford Foundation which, through the 'BRICS-from-below' project at the Centre for Civil Society, financed some of this work, as well as our other core institutional supporters, including the University of KwaZulu-Natal. Our colleagues, comrades and families are warmly thanked for their patience and solidarity.

AG – Rio de Janeiro
PB – Durban
February 2015

PART 1

Sub-imperial, inter-imperial or capitalist-imperial?

2

BRICS and the sub-imperial location

PATRICK BOND

The notion of 'sub-imperialist' states that accompany and extend imperialism was originally invoked by Ruy Mauro Marini (1965) to describe the Brazilian dictatorship's role in the western hemisphere. The sub-imperialist label was then repeatedly applied during the 1970s when the Nixon Doctrine allowed Washington to outsource geopolitical policing responsibilities and accumulation opportunities to favoured regional allies, mostly pro-corporate authoritarian regimes. The idea may be on the verge of being revived, for the rise of the Brazil-Russia-India-China-South Africa (BRICS) bloc represents a potentially important force that mostly appears sub-imperialist insofar as it contributes to global neoliberal regime maintenance. Although some believe BRICS will have sufficient autonomy to become actively 'anti-imperialist' (Desai 2013; Escobar 2013; Keet 2013; Martin 2013; Shubin 2013; Third World Network 2013), at the level of global governance this bloc has tended to reinforce, not challenge, prevailing power relations. There are interesting exceptions: cases such as generic medicines (so vital to the health of tens of millions of HIV+ people) and geopolitics, as in 2013 when Syria was threatened with bombing by Washington and in 2014 when Russia invaded Crimea after losing crucial influence in Ukraine. Like other more isolated states in prior epochs of service to imperialism, the BRICS accumulation trajectory, global geopolitical-economic-environmental strategy, hegemony over hinterlands and internal dynamics of class formation collectively suggest a pattern deserving the phrase sub-imperialist.

The debate about whether imperialism *requires* sub-imperial allies has waxed and waned for decades. In the Comintern era, the phrase 'minor partner of imperialism' described the great powers' deputies. Since the 1970s, the label sub-

15

imperial has been applied to ruling elites from regional power centres – including Israel, Turkey, Indonesia and Taiwan – which have also served the military, extractive and legitimating interests of imperialism. However, this status needs regular revisiting especially because others in a similar role (e.g. Iran before 1979, Argentina before 1982) found the posture to be profoundly contradictory. Fred Halliday (1979:283) advocated the following concept of sub-imperialism, '(a) a continuing if partial strategic subordination to US imperialism on the one hand, and (b) an autonomous regional role on the other.' The volatility intrinsic in this location reflects not the strength but rather the fragility of Washington's agenda, namely, a 'doctrine designed to create a structure of sub-imperial powers', as Joseph Gerson and Bruce Birchard (1991) explained.

The term sub-imperialism has had other euphemisms, including the 'semi-periphery' coined by Immanuel Wallerstein (1974, 1997), which continues to be used by world systems analysts. Chris Chase-Dunn (2013) remarks 'that the main function of having a stratum in the middle is to somewhat depolarise the larger system analogously to a large middle class within a national society'. Alternatively, a 'secondary imperialist' role for Australia and Canada reflects a very different relationship to imperialism in these countries (Albo and Klaasen 2013). In the same spirit, the word 'sub-empire' refers 'to a lower-level empire that is dependent on an empire at a higher level in the imperialist hierarchy', according to Chen Kuan-Hsing (2013:18).

These are ideas generally favoured by left critics of imperialism. In contrast, the concept 'middle power' is so nebulous and non-threatening that its use by mainstream political scientists continues to depoliticise the art of global geopolitics (Jordaan 2003). Finally, for historians (whether radical or mainstream), the age of imperialism was the era *prior* to World War I, replete with colonial relations and the scramble for parts of the world without strong states, especially in Africa, so the concept of sub-imperial powers – especially the British colonies that came to make up South Africa in 1910 – has occasionally been invoked in this context.

Imperialism, capitalist crisis, super-exploitation and regional hegemony

The semantic differences are not important, not when compared to at least four core, lasting relations of sub-imperialism: to imperialism, to capitalist crisis tendencies, to regional hegemony and to super-exploitative processes of accumulation.

First, to define sub-imperialism properly implies a coherent definition of the systemic processes of imperialism within which it operates. There are a variety of ways to understand imperialism, but the most durable appears to be the conception which Rosa Luxemburg (1968) set out in *The Accumulation of Capital* in 1913, stressing the extra-economic coercion associated with exploitation between capitalist and non-capitalist spheres under conditions of capitalist crisis (in contrast to other accounts of the era which hinge more upon capital export, formal colonial relations and inter-imperial rivalries). Translated to the present, this is, for David Harvey (2003), a *New Imperialism* in which accumulation is increasingly based upon dispossession, and in which regional powers logically emerge to facilitate the process. This point deserves further consideration, below.

Second, as a result, capitalist crisis conditions become evident within the sub-imperial economies just as they are in the imperialist, even when accumulation is moving ahead at an apparently rapid clip. Overaccumulation of capital is a constant problem everywhere, often rising to crisis stage. As a result, in several sub-imperialist countries there are powerful impulses for local capital to both externalise and financialise. It is in this sense, again following Harvey, that the BRICS offer some of the most extreme sites of new sub-imperialism in the world today. These crisis conditions are particularly important because in the contemporary period they have shifted what had earlier been nationalist (or even 'state-capitalist') power relations imposed by patronage-oriented states, towards the neoliberal public policies practised elsewhere. They also entail intensified uneven development combined with super-exploitative (and often extra-economically coercive) systems of accumulation, as well as economic symptoms of imperialist desperation, especially financialisation.

Third, sub-imperial regimes expand these same neoliberal practices for use within their regional spheres of influence, thus legitimating the Washington Consensus in ideological and concrete terms, especially by facilitating multilateral trade, investment and financing arrangements. Indeed, sub-imperial powers often promote neoliberal institutions even when complaining (sometimes bitterly) about their indifference to poorer countries, and they sometimes establish new ones that have similar functions in regional terms. This in turn often permits the sub-imperial power to act as a regional platform for accumulation, drawing resources from the hinterland and marketing exports that typically destroy hinterland productive capacity and economic sovereignty. Usually the benefits are manifold, including trade surpluses with the hinterland (where the latter often supplies crucial raw materials on advantageous terms), the opportunity for profits to be accumulated within the sub-imperial power's financial centres, and the expansion of influence via a strengthened economy especially where trade is conducted in the sub-imperial power's currency. All of this logically entails a regional gendarme role, a division of policing labour that allows the world capitalist system to continue with expansion of binding business contracts, their enforcement and the extraction of adequate flows of materials (as well as workers) from distant sites that remain critical to the smooth functioning of the world division of labour.

Fourth, as Sam Moyo and Paris Yeros (2011:19) put it, imperialism's relations with sub-imperial allies always entailed 'the *super-exploitation* of domestic labour. It was natural, therefore, that, as it grew, it would require external markets for the resolution of its profit realisation crisis.' Concretely, to take BRICS as an example, super-exploitative relations are witnessed in the way that Chinese households are torn from rural land during the ongoing urbanisation process, and in the broader context in which rural people require special work permits to live in cities where they are paid much lower wages. Such super-exploitative relations are then readily transferred to the international scale, where China's role has been even more predatory than that of Western corporations, backed by its support of local dictators (e.g. the case of Zimbabwe where Chinese military and Zimbabwean generals conjoined as the Anjin Corporation in the world's largest diamond fields, with a resulting resource curse as extreme as any in contemporary Africa) (Maguwu 2013).

Likewise, South Africa's historical mode of apartheid super-exploitation – termed 'articulations of modes of production' by Harold Wolpe (1980) – exemplified the most extreme internal dimension of sub-imperial accumulation. Migrant male workers from rural Bantustans as well as regional hinterlands as far north as Malawi long provided 'cheap labour', thanks to black rural women's unpaid reproduction of children, sick workers and retirees generally without state support. This was not merely a matter of formal racial power. The expansion of the South African migrancy model much deeper into the Southern African region in the wake of apartheid's early 1990s demise occurred notwithstanding tragic xenophobic reactions from the local working class that continue to this day. The August 2012 Marikana massacre of striking migrant platinum mineworkers at Lonmin was another example of how far the regime's policing function would go internally so as to defend the profitability of multinational extractive corporations (Saul and Bond 2014).

But it is the inexorable regional-hinterland expansion of these processes that compels sub-imperial states to follow the logic of imperialism. This is recognised by professional geopoliticians of capital, such as the Texas intelligence firm Stratfor (2009), in an internal memo (as revealed by WikiLeaks): 'South Africa's history is driven by the interplay of competition and cohabitation between domestic and foreign interests exploiting the country's mineral resources. Despite being led by a democratically-elected government, the core imperatives of South Africa remain the maintenance of a liberal regime that permits the free flow of labour and capital to and from the southern Africa region, as well as the maintenance of a superior security capability able to project into south-central Africa.'

However, South African capital's ability to move up-continent was thrown into question in March 2013, in the Central African Republic capital of Bangui after authoritarian ruler François Bozizé was ousted by guerrillas. More than a dozen South African soldiers were killed, according to interviews with surviving troops in Johannesburg's main Sunday newspaper, while 'protecting belongings of ... businesses in Jo'burg ... We were lied to straight out ... We were told we were here to serve and protect, to ensure peace' (Hosken and Mahlangu 2013). The protected Johannesburg capitalists included firms linked to the ruling African National Congress party (ANC) (Amabhungane 2013). After the fiasco involving a couple of hundred troops in Bangui, in 2014 more than 1500 troops were deployed in the eastern Democratic Republic of the Congo replete with advanced fighter helicopters. Not far away, President Jacob Zuma's nephew Khulubuse had suspiciously acquired a US\$10 billion oil concession, and other South African firms (even Anglo American) were embarrassed by ties to warlords. At least five million people have been killed in this mineral-rich Great Lakes region since South Africa won democracy in 1994.

Dynamics of imperialism and sub-imperialism

These latter relationships, in which capitalism both exploits and corrodes non-capitalist relations through extra-economic coercive techniques, yet also maintains them through imperial power relations, were theorised originally by Rosa Luxemburg. They have been revitalised as an explanatory system by David Harvey under the rubric of accumulation by dispossession. In other words, there are theoretically derived processes which explain the logic of imperialism and sub-imperialism together, even if contingencies may change the metabolisms and the geographical places, shapes and scales within which these processes unfold.

Luxemburg's (1968:396) *Accumulation of Capital* focuses on how capitalism's extra-economic coercive capacities draw surpluses not just from formal capital–labour productive relations but also from families (especially women's role in social reproduction), the land, all forms of nature, mutual aid systems and what we have come to know as the 'commons', and the shrinking state: 'The relations between capitalism and the non-capitalist modes of production start making their appearance on the international stage. Its predominant methods are colonial policy, an international loan system – a policy of spheres of interest – and war.

Force, fraud, oppression, looting are openly displayed without any attempt at concealment, and it requires an effort to discover within this tangle of political violence and contests of power the stern laws of the economic process.'

Her core insight (1968:397), as distinct from framings by Lenin, Bukharin, Hilferding, Hobson and others of her era, was to show that 'Capital cannot accumulate without the aid of non-capitalist' relations and 'Only the continuous and progressive disintegration of non-capitalist organisation makes accumulation of capital possible'. This process, in which 'capital feeds on the ruins' of the non-capitalist social relations, amounts to 'eating it up. Historically, the accumulation of capital is a kind of metabolism between capitalism and those pre-capitalist methods of production without which it cannot go on and which, in this light, it corrodes and assimilates.'

This process is amplified during periods of desperation intrinsic to capitalist crisis, Luxemburg (1968:76) observed, drawing on Marx's classical theory about 'perpetual overproduction', characterised by 'the ceaseless flow of capital from one branch of production to another, and finally in the periodical and cyclical swings of reproduction between overproduction and crisis.' At that point, as Luxemburg (1968:327) insists, the core countries reveal 'the deep and fundamental antagonism between the capacity to consume and the capacity to produce in a capitalist society, a conflict resulting from the very accumulation of capital which periodically bursts out in crises and spurs capital on to a continual extension of the market' (see Bond, Chitonge and Hopfmann 2007 for contemporary Southern African applications of Luxemburg's thesis).

With the current renewal of this process – crisis, extension of the market, and amplified capitalist–noncapitalist super-exploitative relations – serving as the basis for renewed imperialism, Harvey (2003) adds a new layer to this argument: 'The opening up of global markets in both commodities and capital created openings for other states to insert themselves into the global economy, first as absorbers but then as producers of surplus capitals. They then became competitors on the world stage. What might be called "sub-imperialisms" arose ... Each developing centre of capital accumulation sought out systematic spatio-temporal fixes for its own surplus capital by defining territorial spheres of influence.'

The idea of the 'spatio-temporal fix' requires elaboration, again because this notion hard-wires capital's geographic needs and territorial powers within the system's very logic. Harvey (1992) identifies 'a cascading and proliferating series of spatio-temporal fixes' to persistent economic crises, which are invoked so as to extend capitalism geographically and across time, usually facilitated by dramatic financial expansion. The role of banks in core and even sub-imperial countries is to indebt poorer countries so that they can be wedged open for the sake of liberalised trade and investment or simple resource extraction. Expansion of the credit system is also the traditional way to address overproduction of goods, as debt allows these to be mopped up in the present with a promise to extract further surpluses to pay the price in future, in what amounts to a temporal fix. According to Harvey (2003:134), these fixes do not result in crisis *resolution,* but instead they displace capital's overaccumulation.

Indeed, they lead to new contradictions associated with uneven development in the form of 'increasingly fierce international competition as multiple dynamic centres of capital accumulation emerge to compete on the world stage in the face of strong currents of overaccumulation. Since they cannot all succeed in the long run, either the weakest succumb and fall into serious crises of devaluation, or geopolitical confrontations erupt in the form of trade wars, currency wars and even military confrontations.'

The territorially rooted power blocs generated by internal alliances (and conflicts) within national boundaries, or occasionally across boundaries agglomerating to regional scale, are the critical units of analysis when it comes to fending off the devalorisation of overaccumulated capital. By unveiling how these units of analysis are forged within the capital accumulation process, Harvey roots his geopolitical theory and applies it to contemporary imperialism. Sub-imperial states are critical transmission belts according to this theory, in part because the opening up of global markets in both commodities and capital created openings for other states to insert themselves into the global economy. But the sub-imperial elites are rarely patriotic, for they maintain their own personal (and sometimes corporate) accounts in the metropole, leading Harvey (2003:196) to remark,

> The benefits of this system were, however, highly concentrated among a restricted class of multinational CEOs, financiers, and rentiers. Some sort of transnational capitalist class emerged that nevertheless focused on Wall Street and other centres such as London and Frankfurt as secure sites for placements of capital. This class looked, as always, to the United States to protect its asset values and the rights of property and ownership across the globe. While economic power seemed to be highly concentrated within the United States, other territorial concentrations of financial power could and did arise.

The BRICS reflect this new relationship, for as Brazilian president Lula da Silva announced in 2010, 'A new global economic geography is born'. However, relying upon financiers such as Goldman Sachs' Jim O'Neill (originator of the 'BRIC' meme in 2001) to codify economic power is risky. What appeared as a strong bloc of BRICS countries at a leadership summit in March 2013 became, within four months, the core of the 'Fragile Five' countries, leaving O'Neill to remark that only China deserved the 'building-block' BRICS designation (Magalhaes 2013). Meanwhile, India, South Africa and Brazil lost vast amounts of their currency values and funding flows once financial capital left these markets in search of the dollar safe-haven once the US Federal Reserve's loose monetary policy – 'Quantitative Easing' – began to be 'tapered' in mid-2013. The same experience of massive capital outflow hit Russia in early 2014, first because of the loss of regional power signified by the Ukraine's government overthrow, and then when Moscow began a blunt takeover of Crimea, the threat of Western sanctions crashed its stock market. The rot continued in 2015, and the prospect of the end of China's economic miracle also loomed.

So notwithstanding the validity of the general approach Luxemburg proposed, in which ongoing capital accumulation entails imperialism reaching into the terrain of extra-economic coercion, this is not a stable outcome. Each situation must be evaluated on its own concrete terms. Dating at least a half-century to when the idea of sub-imperialism was introduced, in Brazil, the concrete settings are vital because contingencies arise that may divert from the twin logics of capital and expanding territorial power relations.

Concrete sub-imperial locations

The new concentrations of Southern power began to be evident by the 1960s when new alliances strengthened in the Cold War context. In his pioneering writing about Latin American geopolitics dating to the 1960s, Marini (1974) argued that 1970s-era Brazil was 'the best current manifestation of sub-imperialism', because of regional economic extraction, export of capital typically associated with imperialist politics, and internal corporate monopolisation, including financialisation.

There are three additional roles for these regimes today, if they are to be considered sub-imperialist. One is ensuring regional geopolitical 'stability' in areas suffering severe tensions: for example, Brasilia's army in Haiti and Pretoria's deal-making in African hotspots like South Sudan, the Great Lakes and the Central African Republic (although in West Africa, especially Côte d'Ivoire, Pretoria was far less influential). The Israeli and Saudi Arabian roles in the Middle East are comparable, and white-ruled South Africa was, likewise, a Western sub-imperial outpost during the Cold War, what with liberation struggles raging in surrounding countries during the 1960s–1980s. Extra-economic coercion in support of raw material extraction is a common feature of this power, when in many cases the role of regional 'deputy sheriff' is not just 'peace-keeping' but transferring surpluses from the hinterland to the sub-imperialist capital city, and often from there to the imperialist headquarters, as is especially evident for contemporary South Africa (Bond 2006a, 2006b).

The second is advancing the broader agenda of globalised neoliberalism, so as to legitimate deepened market access. This occurs insofar as most sub-imperial powers have been enthusiastic financial backers of the main institutions of global economic governance, especially the Bretton Woods Institutions and World Trade Organisation. For rhetorical purposes the sub-imperial powers' foreign, trade and even finance ministries may be less than flattering about global governance and, in the case of the BRICS, may even launch new multilateral initiatives with the stated aim of challenging power. But standing by the IMF even in times of crisis – e.g. the institution's recapitalisation in 2009 and 2012 occurred with notable BRICS support (US$75 billion in coordinated aid in the latter case) – reflects the overall role that sub-imperial regimes play: they lubricate, legitimise and extend neoliberal political economy deeper into their regional hinterlands.

The same has been true in the single most important long-term global governance challenge, climate management, where the BRICS (without Russia) lined up as critical allies within Washington's 'Copenhagen Accord' strategy in 2009, both avoiding emissions cuts and promoting the further financialisation of the climate strategy through extended carbon trading (Bond 2012; Böhm, Misoczky and Moog 2012). (Later, Russia cemented this function by raising its own greenhouse gas emissions and fossil fuel extraction dramatically and then reneging on Kyoto Protocol commitments and withdrawing from the main climate treaty.) This role of propping up global economic and environmental malgovernance often benefits home-based corporations in the sub-imperial countries, but it is also a marker of cooperation and collaboration with the imperialist projects of core countries' multinational corporations and states: extension of the neoliberal conception that everything can and should be commodified, *even the air* through carbon markets.

Another example of where this was not only helpful but necessary was the World Trade Organisation (WTO), which in an earlier manifestation several BRICS countries had sought to revitalise as early as the 2005 Hong Kong ministerial summit. Free-trade corporate expansion and ongoing self-interested protectionism prevail in an often uneasy mix in sub-imperial economies. But

BRICS counterhegemonic activity in the WTO has occurred well within the broader agenda of neoliberalism. According to one of the coordinators of the Our World Is Not for Sale civil society network (James 2013), the mid-2013 promotion of the Brazilian ambassador to the WTO, Roberto Azevêdo, to become the body's director-general, represented a debilitating form of co-optation, sure to lessen resistance by the South's 'G110' bloc. The cancellation of Europe–South African Bilateral Investment Treaties by South African Trade Minister Rob Davies was considered to be an inspiring case of standing up to the West, but as an exception which proved the rule. This manoeuvre also confirmed Pretoria's defence of regional domination against EU intrusion into its immediate hinterland, the Southern African Customs Union. By December 2014, the main provisions of a new South African investment law that would have protected local sovereignty were withdrawn under pressure from corporations. And indeed within the WTO, in December 2013, Azevêdo was able to arrange a WTO ministerial agreement that put the organisation back on track. This was a notable accomplishment given the failure of his predecessor, Pascal Lamy, who hailed from (and invariably supported) the European Union during prior failed efforts. On the trade front, aside from sanctions against Russia resulting in a slight reorientation to China, as well as the insistence by health professionals and activists that generic medicines production be retained in India, Brazil and South Africa, virtually all the trade-related processes involving BRICS were aimed at strengthening the global corporate agenda. The same proved true for BRICS corporate direct investments.

In this context, what may emerge from the networking of the sub-imperialist elites, as witnessed in the BRICS bloc in its initial formation period, is an agenda that more systematically confirms super-exploitative practices within their hinterlands. Just as the political carving of Africa in Berlin at the 1884–85 conference hosted by Bismarck drew the continent's irrational boundaries mainly in order to benefit extractive enterprises – mining houses and plantations as well as construction firms associated with England, France, Portugal, Belgium and Germany – BRICS appears to follow colonial and neo-colonial tracks. Identifying port, bridge, road, rail, hydropower and other infrastructure projects in the same image, the BRICS 2013 Durban summit had as its aim the continent's *economic* carve-up, unburdened – now as then – by what would be derided as 'Western' concerns about democracy and human rights. More than a dozen African heads of state were present as collaborators. The New Partnership for Economic Development and the African Peer Review Mechanism were often alleged to serve as African homegrown policing mechanisms for such infrastructure, but were ineffective (Bond 2005, 2009). The Programme for Infrastructure Development in Africa, while difficult to implement, offered systems of financing beyond the diminishing pool of Chinese credit.

However, it is also critical to concede that the forms of BRICS sub-imperialism are diverse, for as Moyo and Yeros (2011:19) remark,

> Some are driven by private blocs of capital with strong state support (Brazil, India); others, like China, include the direct participation of state-owned enterprises; while in the case of South Africa, it is increasingly difficult to speak of an autonomous domestic bourgeoisie, given the extreme degree of de-nationalisation of its economy in the post-apartheid period. The degree of participation in the Western military project is also different from one case to the next although, one might say, there is a 'schizophrenia' to all this, typical of 'sub-imperialism'.

In sum, the recent period has reignited a fruitful debate about the concept of sub-imperialism and about the truncated nature of aspirant transitions from sub- to inter-imperialism, and perhaps also one day – in the wake of future social revolutions against BRICS elites – to anti-imperialism. However, the most critical factor in making this debate real, not just a struggle over semantics between impotent leftist intellectuals, is a different process entirely, one not contingent upon rhetoric from above, but upon reality from below. That reality is increasingly tense in each of the main sub-imperialist powers currently seeking unity, the BRICS.

Such local struggles are impulsive and impossible to predict (as discussed in this book's final chapters), but much deeper class struggles against super-exploitation, ecological destruction and neoliberalism are unfolding constantly in each site. The challenge for BRICS critics from below is to link and internationalise as quickly as possible, because their interests and campaigning analyses, strategies, tactics and alliances have many points of overlap, with each other and with the world's progressive forces. Only then will a genuine global anti-imperialist project become possible, i.e. when anti-sub-imperialists of the world also unite.

References

Albo, G and J Klaasen (2013) *Empire's Ally,* Toronto, University of Toronto Press

Amabhungane (2013) Is this what our soldiers died for? *Mail & Guardian,* 28 March, http://mg.co.za/article/2013-03-28-00-central-african-republic-is-this-what-our-soldiers-died-for

Böhm, S, M Misoczky and S Moog (2012) Greening capitalism? A Marxist critique of carbon markets, *Organisation Studies,* November 2012, 33, 11

Bond, P (2005) *Fanon's Warning*, Trenton, Africa World Press

Bond, P (2006a) *Talk Left Walk Right*, Pietermaritzburg, University of KwaZulu-Natal Press

Bond, P (2006b) *Looting Africa*, London, Zed Books

Bond, P (2009) Removing neocolonialism's APRM mask: a critique of the African Peer Review Mechanism, *Review of African Political Economy*, 36, 122, pp 595–603

Bond, P (2012) *Politics of Climate Justice*, Pietermaritzburg, University of KwaZulu-Natal Press

Bond, P, H Chitonge and A Hopfmann (2007) *The Accumulation of Capital in Southern Africa*, Berlin, Rosa Luxemburg Foundation

Chase-Dunn, C (2013) Contemporary semiperipheral development, University of California-Riverside Institute for Research on World-Systems, Working Paper 78, http://irows.ucr.edu/papers/irows78/irows78.htm

Desai, R (2013) The Brics are building a challenge to Western economic supremacy, *The Guardian*, 2 April

Escobar, P (2013), Brazil, Russia, India, China and South Africa: BRICS go over the wall, *Asia Times*, 27 March

Gerson, J and B Birchard (1991) *The Sun Never Sets: Confronting the Network of Foreign U.S. Military Bases*, Boston, South End Press

Halliday, F (1979) *Iran: Dictatorship and Development*, New York, Penguin Books

Harvey, D (1992) *Limits to Capital*, Chicago, Chicago University Press

Harvey, D (2003) *The New Imperialism*, Oxford, Oxford University Press

Hosken, G and I Mahlangu (2013) We were killing kids, *Sunday Times*, 31 March

James, D (2013) personal correspondence, 19 November

Jordaan, E (2003) The concept of a middle power in international relations: distinguishing between emerging and traditional middle powers, *Politikon*, 30, 1, pp 165–181

Keet, D (2013) Perspectives and proposals on the BRICS for and from popular civil society organisations, Economic Justice Network, November

Kuan-Hsing, C (2013) *Asia as Method*, Durham, Duke University Press

Luxemburg, R (1968, 1913) *The Accumulation of Capital*, New York, Monthly Review Press

Magalhaes, L (2013) China only BRIC country currently worthy of the title – O'Neill, *Wall Street Journal*, 23 August, http://stream.wsj.com/story/latest-headlines/SS-2-63399/SS-2-308220/

Maguwu, F (2013) Marange diamonds and Zimbabwe's political transition, *Journal of Peacebuilding and Development*, 8, 1, pp 74–78

Marini, RM (1965) Brazilian interdependence and imperialist integration, *Monthly Review*, 17, 7

Marini, RM (1974) *Subdesarrollo y revolución*, Mexico City, Siglo XXI Editores, http://mrzine.monthlyreview.org/2010/bt280210p.html#_edn13

Martin, W (2013) South Africa and the 'new scramble for Africa': imperialist, sub-imperialist, or victim? *Agrarian South: Journal of Political Economy*, 2, 2, pp 161–188

Moyo, S and P Yeros (2011) Rethinking the theory of primitive accumulation, Paper presented to the 2nd IIPPE Conference, 20–22 May 2011, Istanbul

Saul, J and P Bond (2014) *South Africa: Present as History*, Oxford, James Currey

Shubin, V (2013) BRICS viewed from Russia, *Pambazuka News*, 20 March, http://www.pambazuka.org/en/category/features/86658/print

Stratfor (2009), Monography for comment: South Africa, 5 May, http://search.wikileaks.org/gifiles/?viewemailid=951571

Third World Network (2013) Whither the BRICS? *Third World Resurgence* 274, June, http://www.twnside.org.sg/title2/resurgence/2013/twr274.htm

Wallerstein, I (1974) *Semi-Peripheral Countries and the Contemporary World Crisis*, New York City, Academic Press

Wallerstein, I (1997) *The Capitalist World Economy*, New York City, Cambridge University Press

Wolpe, H (ed) (1980) *The Articulation of Modes of Production*, London, Routledge and Kegan Paul

3

Sub-imperialism, the highest stage of dependent capitalism

Mathias Luce

Based on Ruy Mauro Marini's theses developed within the Marxist Dependency Theory school of thought, this chapter uncovers the foundations for a global theory of sub-imperialism by tackling each level of abstraction that makes up the total phenomenon.[1] Sub-imperialism is considered the result of the laws of dependent capitalism in combination with the world economic system configured by post-World War II capital movements. The arrival of a few socio-economic formations at the highest stage of dependent capitalism along with the rise of intermediate links in the imperialist chain made room for a new hierarchical level in the global order. In this way these formations turn into countries that do not just transfer surplus value to imperialist centres but also succeed in appropriating weaker countries' surplus value by displacing some of the contradictions specific to dependent capitalism. And they develop a policy of antagonistic cooperation with the dominant imperialism.

Ever since imperialism's advent as the highest stage of capitalism, Marxist theorists have sought to define the nature of distinct socio-economic formations in a hierarchically differentiated world system. After the Third International's debates, Marxist vocabulary classified countries as imperialist, colonial and semi-colonial. With the transformations that capitalism underwent in the crisis brought on by the world wars and the decolonisation process, the theory of imperialism had to address the new reality. Terms such as *neo-colonialism* (Nkrumah 1966) and *imperialism without colonies* (Magdoff 1978) were used to express the new type of domination exercised by imperialist powers.

At another level of analysis – that of the historic-concrete formations subject to imperialist relations – the word *dependency,* devised by Marxist Dependency Theorists (MDTs), gained currency as an analytical category. It was thought of as a necessary complement to the theory of imperialism. Laying the bases for the study of Latin American capitalism, the Marxist dependency theorists revealed the laws of operation of this *sui generis* capitalism and shared in the effort of establishing Marxism on the continent (Ferreira and Luce 2012). Among them was Ruy Mauro Marini who, by analysing the changes in the capitalist world system during the 1960s and 1970s, identified the emergence of sub-imperialism as a new stage of dependent capitalism by means of the coming-of-age of a new type of socio-economic formation that, in Latin America, took shape in Brazil.

Today it is commonplace to use the word 'sub-imperialism' to characterise 'emerging' sub-powers' economic and political expansion into other historical and geographical contexts, for example the relationship of South Africa with its neighbours, that of India in its region, Brazil in South America and even that of China (which is beyond the category of sub-imperialism) on the African continent. The few translations of Marini's original work into other languages have difficulty amplifying and deepening the studies of the category sub-imperialism.[2]

Our purpose in this chapter is not to evaluate or review studies of the BRICS group but rather to discuss Marini's category by reflecting upon his proposal within the Marxist tradition. At the same time, it is hoped, by means of Marini's category of sub-imperialism, to introduce elements that will confer greater rigour on the analyses, which frequently erase the required differentiation between such very disparate economies and socio-economic formations as those under the umbrella of the BRICS acronym.[3] The argument is that the foundations of a global theory of sub-imperialism are discernible in Marini's books and dozens of articles on Brazilian and Latin American capitalism. If, on the one hand, these elements are dispersed in the totality of Marini's writings with no text where the author's final word on the category's significance can be found, on the other hand its systematisation can be accomplished with rigour, provided that one respects the categorial connection tying his propositions on sub-imperialism to MDT theoretical works. These include the laws of dependent capitalism (over-exploitation of the workforce, value transfer, rifts between the phases of the capital reproduction cycle) and other notions and categories developed by him and other MDT exponents, especially those of the capital reproduction pattern and antagonistic cooperation and the typology of socio-economic formations within dependent industrialisation.

Marini's writings on sub-imperialism will be discussed through the prism of each of the MDT levels of abstraction to which they belong. As we will put it, they are the distinct instances or components of the totality.[4] The phenomenon is not equal to the sum of its parts. As a totality, sub-imperialism only exists in the dialectic that arises out of the articulation of the historical determinations that constitute its essence. Lack of theoretical clarity for understanding this totality and its essence causes confusion about Marini's category not only among rival theoreticians who praise the Brazilian bourgeoisie but also other critics, including contemporary Marxist ones.

What is sub-imperialism? As we hope to show, sub-imperialism has to be understood as a hierarchical level of the world system and at the same time as a stage of dependent capitalism (its highest stage) out of which some socio-economic formations are transformed into new links in the imperialist chain without ever leaving the condition of economic dependency. Besides transferring value to imperialist centres, they also move into appropriating the surplus value of weaker nations for themselves. The socio-economic formations that ascend to the sub-imperialist condition succeed in displacing the very conditions of dependent capitalism in a way that ensures expanded reproduction and mitigates the effects of dependency through forms that are specific to the pattern of capital reproduction and a policy of antagonistic cooperation with dominant imperialism in different situations; they claim relative autonomy for the sub-imperialist state without, however, questioning the framework of dependency.

A hierarchical level of the world system

The worldwide appearance of imperialism and sub-imperialism constitutes global capitalism's coming-of-age with passage to the phase of monopoly and finance capital – a process that occurs first in the centre and then in the periphery. For this reason its examination must begin at the level of abstraction of the capitalist system framed by the entrance of capitalism into a new stage as a world system. If the historical advent of imperialism dates back to the turn of the 19th century, sub-imperialism dates from the new integrationist tendency of world capitalism that arises out of post-World War II capital movements.

> The expansion and acceleration not only of the circulation of productive capital but also of money have been shaping a new capitalist world economy that rests upon a structure of international division of labour distinct from that which ruled before the world crisis ... The era of the simple centre-periphery model characterised by the exchange of manufactures

for comestibles and raw materials has passed. We find ourselves facing an economic reality in which industry assumes an ever more decisive role ... The result has been a repositioning, a hierarchic arrangement of capitalist countries in the form of a pyramid and, consequently, the rise of intermediate centres of accumulation – that are also middle capitalist powers – which brought us to speak about the emergence of a sub-imperialism (Marini 1977a:25. Author's translation).

Both imperialism and sub-imperialism occur in a capitalist system organised into centres and peripheries, in an historical relationship that is modified over time and based on international divisions of labour that also change over time (with adjustments of the use-values that each produces, with new forms of value extraction and with the integration of production systems). At the root of sub-imperialism as a new link in the imperialist chain:

One thus observes the rise of a new international division of labour, which relocates stages of industrial production – it is worth remembering, unequally – to dependent countries while advanced countries specialise in higher stages; at the same time, financial control mechanisms and technology over the whole system are perfected. Capital's circulation on the world scale is intensified and deepened at the same time as accumulation is diversified. Meanwhile tendencies of capital accumulation concentrate and centralise progress even though now also in the interests of nations of an intermediate organic composition. *From a strictly economic perspective,* this is consistent with sub-imperialism (Marini 2012:40. Emphasis in the original).

At system level and, in strictly economic terms, the historical foundation of sub-imperialism came about in the 1960s and 1970s when a few social formations arrived at the phase of monopoly and finance capitalism and at an intermediate level of the organic composition of capital: 'Sub-imperialism corresponds with, on the one hand, the rise of intermediate points in global capitalism's organic composition as the integration of production systems intensifies – and, on the other hand, the arrival of a dependent economy at the monopoly and finance capital phase' (Marini 2012:41). This transformation at the same time explains the change in the imperialist dynamic *tout court* and the rise of sub-imperialist formations in the context of the expansion of world capital accumulation. This is a dialectical movement whereby the external (capital export) is internalised (upgrade of the level of capital's organic composition) and, as a new synthesis of many determinations is again externalised (sub-imperialist expansion), alters the way world capitalism operates.

> Sub-imperialism corresponds to the perverse manifestation of world differ-entiation as a result of capitalist internationalisation, which counterposes a much more complex system of relationships to the simple structure of a division of labour – crystallised in the centre-periphery relationship that preoccupied ECLA. In it, the spread of manufacturing elevating the average national organic composition of capital, that is, the relationship existing between the means of production and the working class gives way to economic (and political) sub-centres endowed with relative autonomy even though they remain subordinated to the global dynamic imposed by the great centres (Marini 1992:137–8).

The perverse sense to which Marini refers is the fact that relative autonomy cannot escape the global dynamic imposed by the great centres. When one or more dependent economies ascend to a new level in the world capitalist hierarchy, they take on a new character of dependency and are also converted into extractors of surplus value, appropriating a portion of the value produced in the peripheries – but without raising the general standard of living of their working class.[5] As already stated: 'capital accumulation's tendency to concentrate and centralise progresses even though now also in the interests of nations of an intermediate organic composition.' In summary, the general tendencies of the world economy and system are crystallised and take the form of certain specific social formations as much to breathe life into imperialism as into sub-imperialism.

A stage of dependent capitalism

In the same way Lenin described imperialism as the highest stage of capitalism, sub-imperialism for Marini consisted of 'the form that dependent capitalism takes when it reaches the monopoly and finance capitalism stage' (Marini 1977a:31). It is a superior level of development in which, 'due to its dependent and subordinate manner, Brazil would enter the capital-exporting stage as well as in the pillage of external energy sources such as petroleum, iron and natural gas' (Marini 1977a:32).

In this sense, a dependent country's arrival at the sub-imperialist stage establishes a sub-regional division benefiting sub-imperialist capital visible by the appropriation of the surplus value of weaker nations. These nations are shaped into the sphere of influence that serves the sub-imperialist country's capital reproduction (whether the property of the internal bourgeoisie or that of the great imperialist centres, being common to their relationship).[6] Under these conditions as part of the diversified industrial pattern of capital reproduction, Brazil's ascent to the status of manufactured goods exporter distinguishes it from other Latin American nations who witness their productive specialisation being embedded in the market of the regional division of labour that sub-imperialism engenders. According to what has been explained:

> All this influences Latin America's integration process, which develops on two planes: the renewed linking of the Latin American economy as a whole with the world economy on the basis of the development of an industrial-type exporting economy, and the re-definition of the economic relations among the very countries of the zone. Overspecialisation becomes, in this way, the counterpart of an intensification of dependency and is realised on the basis of what up until now was thought to be the key for Latin American economic emancipation: industrialisation (Marini 1976. Author's translation).

As a particular form of industrial economy liable to be adopted by the development of dependent capitalism's industrial process, Marini understood sub-imperialism as a phenomenon beyond the Brazilian political regime ruling in the years of technocratic-military dictatorship and over and above a reality that had taken place or that could only take place in Brazil.[7]

> In the broadest sense, sub-imperialism is not an essentially Brazilian phenomenon nor does it correspond to an anomaly in the evolution of dependent capitalism. Certainly the very conditions of the Brazilian economy are what allows it to carry forward its industrialisation and also to create heavy industry … but it is no less certain that this sub-imperialism is nothing more than a particular formation, which presumes an industrial economy that develops within the framework of dependent capitalism (Marini 2005:179–180).

In other words, a country's maturing to the sub-imperialist condition is beyond a specific conjuncture as well as a country narrowly considered. In truth, it corresponds to dependent capital's reaching the monopoly and finance capitalist stage, which engenders new tendencies imparted by this level of accumulation.

A type of social formation

The projection in political terms of the economic conditions presented above (development of monopolies and finance capital, and the rise of the organic composition of capital) so that they progress into engendering sub-imperialism requires other elements, such as a strong state, and a bourgeoisie with its own ambitions that converts these projects of political and economic expansion into national ones – which implies persuading or controlling other bourgeois fractions or persuading and subordinating other social classes domestically as well as internationally. As Marini argues:

> Sub-imperialism implies two basic components: on the one hand, an intermediate organic composition of national productive systems on the world scale and, on the other hand, the exercise of a relatively autonomous expansionist policy not only accompanied by a greater integration in the imperialist productive system but also maintained within the hegemonic framework exercised by imperialism on the international scene. Put in these terms, it seems to us that, independently of the efforts of Argentina and other countries to reach the sub-imperialist rank, in Latin America only Brazil fully manifests a phenomenon of this kind (Marini 1977a:31).

What does the exercise of a relatively autonomous expansionist policy within the framework of the global imperialist productive system and hegemony imply? Why is it that, in Latin America, Brazil – and not Mexico or Argentina – achieves this position? This obeys the dialectical principle that governs reality. Not all the new economic sub-centres that achieve an intermediate organic composition and also attain the status of exporter of manufactured goods and, to a lesser extent, of capital are in a condition to impose a sub-regional division of labour in the interest of their domestic bourgeoisie. In other words, in the whole of Latin American capitalism, only Brazil became a sub-imperialist social formation.

This is where the concrete conditions of socio-economic formations and the role of national states are important for sub-imperialism. Studied at the analytic level of socio-economic formations, the trajectory of different state formations reveals that in some societies the national state matures into a sub-imperialist formation.

From the viewpoint of the conditions necessary for dependent industrialisation to bring sub-imperialism into being, it is possible to identify five determining elements that make sub-imperialism's relatively autonomous expansionist policy possible through state action. The first is a dependent country's accession (among which are those of Type A in Vania Bambirra's typology of dependent industrialisation (Bambirra 2012)) to regional sub-centre status in response to global accumulation patterns through its transformation into a sub-centre of heavy industry with a certain domestic level of production and financial capitalist operation. The second element is bourgeois unity through displacing internal contradictions. The third is the formulation of a national sub-imperialist plan while the fourth involves formation of national capitalist trusts that tie the dependent economy to imperialism via state intermediation. The fifth element is the dependent economic condition that not only transfers value to imperialist economies but also appropriates the surplus value of weaker nations.

Despite having reached the monopoly and finance capitalist stage and having led in South America before Brazil ascended to industrial production, Argentina has historical characteristics that impede it from becoming a sub-imperialist formation. As seen, rifts in the heart of the Argentinian bourgeoisie stopped it from taking on a national expansionist project abroad with sufficient force. Thus the existing division between big agro-capital and big industrial capital obstructs unified projects, state enhancement and the consolidation of dominant classes.

In Mexico, economic and political subservience to the ambitions of great US imperialism blocks national capital from having its own ventures. The degree of US imperialist penetration in Mexico hampers the state from putting into practice a relatively autonomous expansionist policy. In this manner, a subordinate formation in both Argentina and Mexico has matured but not as a relatively autonomous sub-imperialism.

In Latin America, only Brazil has reunited the conditions to bring sub-imperialism into being, including national capital trusts that set into motion a new pattern of unequal exchange in which the dependent sub-imperialist economy not only transfers value but also appropriates it. Among the already enumerated conditions, domestic capitalist trusts received Marini's major analytical treatment within the sub-imperialist category.

In his article 'World capitalist accumulation and sub-imperialism', Marini incorporated aspects of Bukharin's conglomeration theory in order to examine the state's role in the sub-imperialist dynamic via the process of capital-state agglomeration, mustering capitalist trusts within the context of global capitalism's integrationist tendency. In Bukharin's work, *World Economy and Imperialism* (1986), the Russian theorist highlighted the fact that capital internationalisation cannot be achieved without its internalisation. 'By effecting greater capitalist development in subordinate regions like Latin America, integration made it possible for its counter-trends to manifest themselves with greater force also in them, in particular, the one that works towards reinforcing national states' (Marini 1977a:33. Author's translation).

In this regard, a dialectical process of internationalisation–internalisation is established in which state consolidation in sub-imperialist states acts in a way that is contradictory to the internationalisation process, as an element guaranteeing the integration of productive systems. 'If the export of capital coming from national imperialism marks the moment when the tendency for capital to expand internationally is revealed in a pure form, then its decisive transformation into productive capital within a domestic economy represents the moment of its negation when this capital begins to depend upon the capacity of this economy – and, therefore, of the state that governs it – to guarantee its reproduction' (Marini 1977a:33. Author's translation).

Given the dimension of the disadvantages existing between the imperialist bourgeoisie and that of dependent countries, the latter find themselves lacking the conditions to negotiate directly with imperialism, a position beneficial to their decision to associate with the integrationist tendency imposed by imperialist centres. Because of this they 'opt for consolidating the national state as an intermediary'. That option allows them to focus on organising their forces. This intermediation, when combined with emphasis on the capital concentration and centralisation process that has now reached dependent economies, facilitates 'the reproduction in these countries of the phenomenon of agglomeration of capital with the national state, to which Bukharin alludes, involving as much national as well as foreign capital'. The result of this agglomeration 'is not the simple and pure submission of the state to capital'. On the contrary:

> Although if it is evident that the state is transformed into what Bukharin calls a 'national capitalist trust,' the very fact that it is obliged to order and arbitrate economic life (as far as its arbitration is compatible with its subordination to imperialist states) places it in a situation in which its relative autonomy in the face of distinct capitalist groups is highlighted … It was in relation to this that the Brazilian state was able to formulate a plan that was not one with a sub-imperialist structure but was a sub-imperialist policy with a much greater degree of rationality than that which the national and foreign capital operating in Brazil could give it (Marini 1977a:34. Author's translation).

In this way, the state is there both to ensure the better reproduction of imperial capitalist investment and to preserve a relative autonomy in front of foreign capitalist groups, providing the local bourgeoisie with the means they lack to have a relatively more favourable status within the development process associated and integrated with imperialism. The formation of these 'national capitalist trusts' on the basis of the agglomeration of state and private capital was the deciding factor for the expansionist impetus that transformed Brazil into an exporter of manufactured goods and capital. In this way, the state was the basic means for these same conglomerations achieving a scale of production, just as it was the source for elaborating the national sub-imperialist project (the Brazilian Superior War College, the Foreign Ministry, etc.) and the guardian of unity among different bourgeois fractions.

A set of forms of the capital reproduction pattern

Next, as we shall see, due to the level of the capital reproduction pattern, 'the axis of the sub-imperialist structure is organised around the market problem' (Marini 2012:256). At the intermediate level of abstraction, the reproduction pattern is the synthesis of two interlocked determinations, which are: the dialectic between the world economy and dependent capitalism, which determines social formations; and the dialectic between the social-economic formations and the real motion controlling dependent capitalism in various historical conjunctures. Thus, the 'external' is internalised and the 'internal' is externalised. In this regard, the investigation of sub-imperialism as a set of forms of the reproduction pattern[8] takes the history of the succession of different patterns into account, having as its analytical benchmark the forms capital has assumed (cyclical regularities and changes considered from the point of view of the use-value produced and of the value process itself) in a socio-economic formation in which both economic and political conditions had matured, transforming it into a sub-imperialist country.

Just as in imperialism where the expansion of capitalist power and of imperialist states exercises the effect of countervailing the law of the tendency for the rate of profit to fall and other contradictions that emanate from the logic of value and class struggle, in sub-imperialism the contradictions inherent in dependent capitalism are displaced. Hence, under the angle of the reproduction pattern, sub-imperialism is located in the juxtaposition of the laws of the dependent economy and the international division of labour governing every period of the world economy. In Marini's words, sub-imperialism originates in and is defined by

(a) the restructuring of the world capitalist system that derives from the new international division of labour; (b) the very laws of the dependent economy, essentially: the super-exploitation of labour; the disjuncture between capitalist cycles; the extreme monopolisation favouring the luxury goods industry; the integration of national with foreign capital or, which is the same, the integration of production systems (and not simply the internationalisation of the domestic market as some authors state) (Marini 2012:40).[9]

The post-World War II integration of production systems into the international division of labour converted the heavy goods industry into the dynamic sector of the Brazilian economy. 'Although many products directly or indirectly derived from this, it consisted frankly of luxury goods within Latin American conditions; it was due to these goods that the productive structure was altered for the convenience of foreign capital' (Marini 1977a:27. Author's translation). Under the aegis of the diversified industrial model, Brazil thus became the leading Latin American automobile producer and the ninth in world ranking. It was the locus of the rise of a military-industrial complex that raised the country to the position of the second armaments producer in the Third World, only after Israel. The average level of capital organic composition showed the importance of the processing industry, especially heavy industry. As one of the sub-centres of the processing industry in the dependent world, the Brazilian state set about adapting a sub-regional division of labour for the export of manufactured goods and the supply of cheap raw materials in order to realise the production of commodity-capital and cheapen constant capital.

To state, as Marini does, that sub-imperialism 'is constituted by the market problem' means that, from the perspective of the capital reproduction pattern, the sub-imperialist country succeeds in reuniting the conditions to displace, through expansion, that which engenders realisation problems for the dependent economy in the second phase of circulation (C – M). It also signifies succeeding to reunite conditions that mitigate some of dependency's structural effects in the first phase of circulation (M – C) and in the accumulation process on a broader scale: finance capital operating in the country and the productive enterprises dedicated to its logic, which form national capitalist trusts – never disconnected from foreign capital, it should be noted. These trusts get to appropriate extraordinary profit either by being domestic leaders in their respective sectors or by operating in other economies that submit to sub-imperialist expansion, where they appropriate the weaker countries' surplus value. And one part of this mass of surplus value – the other is drained away through relations with imperialism – is absorbed, making possible, within the limits of a dependent economy, a certain development with some technological control in production and some presence even if subordinated in the circuits of financial appreciation. The cases of Petrobras, Embraer, Banco do Brasil, BNDES (the National Social and Economic Development Bank) and the private bank Itaú are examples of the above.

Still, what permits a dependent country to differentiate itself within the group of other countries to which it belongs and to displace, in the capital cycle, contradictions coming from the operational laws of dependent capitalism, turning itself into an economy that does not simply transfer surplus value but which appropriates a part of that value within the international division of labour? Marini attributed this role to the state. During the phase of the diversified industrial pattern, the state was responsible for 60% of gross fixed investment (Marini 1977b). This was accompanied by international monetary capital investment, which promoted the merger of banking with industrial capital through the money market (the rise of financial instruments, partnership laws and so on). This process leveraged the standard dynamic business sectors then underway and strengthened the domain of high consumption (automobiles, domestic appliances) through purchases on credit. In the second stage of circulation, luxury consumption and the external market appear as factors of realisation, both counting on state procurement: regressive income distribution increases high levels of consumption, and state incentives and subsidies stimulate the exports of manufactured goods – just as the capture of Latin American markets and those of the rest of the dependent world through foreign policy guarantees sales of produced consumption goods.

At present, under the new export model of specialised production, the extractive industries have replaced manufacturing industry in the forefront of industrial composition. And raw materials emerge again as a sector that dynamises the reproduction pattern, altering the historical form of dependency. These sectors, together with financial appreciation per se along with some few branches of the previous reproduction pattern (especially the automobile industry), are the touchstone of Brazilian capitalism at the beginning of this century. If the automobile, household appliance and armaments industry were, before, factors of realisation of use-value production in foreign, state and luxury consumption markets, today mainly agro-business exports and mineral extraction sectors mobilise foreign markets in the second phase of circulation while the automobile industry continues to find channels of realisation in luxury consumption and in the state (via tax exemptions on industrial products).

At the same time, old and new national capitalist trusts expanded their businesses with BNDES financial support and offerings on the stock exchange (the merger of banking and industrial capital). In any case, Brazilian sub-imperialism did not disappear with the end of the diversified industrial model; it only assumed new forms under the new specialised productive export pattern.[10] Why did privatisation and the de-nationalisation of export enterprises and of the banking system not make Brazil and the other countries in the region equal? Why were the local bourgeoisie and the Brazilian state not simply absorbed by foreign capital, as in other countries, but instead acted in an integrated manner as assistants – and even as protagonists – of the process of de-nationalisation on the continent? The condition of the sub-imperialist country is the key to explaining these peculiarities.

Antagonistic cooperation with imperialism through conjunctures

The category used to express state action in different conjunctures in a sub-imperialist socio-economic formation is antagonistic cooperation. It has been defined as a search for relative autonomy within the dependency framework: 'The relations between the Brazilian bourgeoisie and imperialism have to be viewed within the laws of antagonistic co-operation which is established in the course of international capitalist integration.' Antagonistic cooperation means that a sub-imperialist country never leaves the state of a dependent economy. It is not an imperialist country: 'Without being able to question imperialist dominion itself (otherwise it would mean questioning capitalism itself) the national bourgeoisie can only bargain for better relations within its subordinate status – better prices, better agreements, the appropriate areas for exploitation, etc.' (Martins, nd).

As proposed, in sub-imperialism antagonistic cooperation with centre imperialism expresses a search for relative autonomy in international politics and for control over a part of surplus value, so that the economy not only transmits but also appropriates surplus value. Not every dependent country that enters the monopoly and finance capital stage unites the conditions to practise an antagonistic cooperation policy. Besides, 'such relations [in terms of antagonistic cooperation] depend upon power relations in each situation: the economic conjuncture nationally and internationally, the political situation, the periods of détente and escalation with revolutionary forces, etc.' (Martins, nd).

Where this was not possible, the new nature of dependency reinforced subordination. Where, on the contrary, relations with dominant centres were of the antagonistic cooperation type, it was because the conditions for relative autonomy had been created, developing the sub-imperialist formation. This is the sense of Marini's weighty deliberation: 'As in Brazil, countries such as Argentina, Israel, Iran, Iraq and South Africa take on – or took on, in some moment of their recent evolution – the sub-imperialistic character along with other sub-centres in which this tendency has not manifested itself fully or has only just insinuated itself' (Marini 1992:138). 'Sub-imperialism's historical materialisation is not merely a question of economics. The existence of the right conditions for its development is not guaranteed only by the transformation of a country into a sub-imperialist centre ... In this sense, in our days [it] is Brazil [that] can be identified as the purest manifestation of sub-imperialism' (Marini 2012:41).

Conclusion

As we have tried to sustain in our analysis, Marini's category of sub-imperialism conveys a totality formed by different levels of abstraction. Confusion about these different levels of analysis or abstraction – taking the historical determinations of only one or some of them – is at the origin of many incorrect interpretations of his proposed category. As an historical phenomenon, sub-imperialism undergoes varied forms while conserving its very essence. Ignoring these two premises has given rise to many of the mistaken interpretations surrounding the concept developed by Marini.

Obviously it is much easier to point to the gaps in an analysis that is embryonic than to follow the path Marini inaugurated and to further his investigation. But selecting the first option can mean pushing a theory backwards. By contrast our option has been to show that in Marini there are the basic elements for a global theory of sub-imperialism and that it is from them that we are able to explain with due rigour the present expansionist trend of Brazilian capitalism and its foreign policy; for example, the mergers and acquisitions involving multinationals with Brazilian capital, the control over other Latin American or African countries' raw materials and energy sources, or the military occupation of Haiti.

Analyses that overestimate capitalism's and the Brazilian state's autonomy as well as those that neglect its relative autonomy within the boundaries of sub-imperialism misunderstand the significance of sub-imperialism. For the former, sub-imperialism does not make sense because it is supposed to be a mere channel of communication for the dominant imperialism. For those who adhere to the latter perspective, the category is not sustainable because it implies the notion of a second-rank imperialism. Neither connotation corresponds to the concept of sub-imperialism whose true meaning we hope to have helped restore in the course of this chapter.

Accordingly it is possible to affirm that Brazil in Latin America, South Africa in Southern Africa, Israel in the Middle East and India in Southeast Asia are examples, today, of sub-imperialist countries, whose power structures and logic demand a rigorous analysis without forgoing their complex categorial network.

Thus, among the BRICS countries, Brazil, South Africa and India are economies that demonstrate the tendencies that Marini examined on the basis of the sub-imperialist category. It is not possible to characterise China as sub-imperialist but rather as a *sui generis* imperialism of a new kind, even supplanting the United States and the European Union as the principal market for Latin American exports and as the primary investor in the region. Russia, in turn, is also not a sub-imperialist socio-economic formation but an ancient empire that until 1917 participated in inter-imperialist competition and contradictions when capitalism had reached its highest stage. The restoration of Russian capitalism with the fall of the Soviet Union reinstated it in the concert of imperialist powers. However, the comparison of the context and the nature of each of the BRICS' ascent to sub-imperialism or imperialism and their exercise of power is the theme of another essay. For now, we will underline that neither China nor Russia partakes in dependent capitalism but Brazil, South Africa and India do.

With this we are not suggesting that there are no interests and common ties among the BRICS members, among the states, classes and fractions of classes to which they respond. Nevertheless, theory and concrete social reality suggest to us a set of necessary problematisations, at the risk of obscuring global economic and political relationships and the real and present configuration of imperialist relations in which the internal contradictions and new forms of antagonistic cooperation between the dominant and subordinate links in the imperialist chain are balanced.

Concerning Brazil, we can draw attention to old and new capitalist trusts increasing their businesses in the last 15 years with BNDES financial support and share offerings (merging banking with industrial capital) that absorb neighbouring countries' wealth, just as has happened with the Vale and Votorantim mining companies, the Marfrig and JBS Friboi meat companies, Petrobras, the Odebrecht and OAS construction companies, the Gerdau group and so on. The sub-imperialist Mercosur contrasts with the large imperialist ALCA. So, too, Unasul, when it reduces itself to a forum for IIRSA implementation, plays the role that imperialism reserves for us in the international division of labour in the name of regional integration, with the difference that it seek its own sphere of influence and the relative autonomy for a dependent bourgeoisie in terms of an antagonistic cooperation with imperialist centres and at a cost for its brother neighbouring countries. Substituting China for the United States or the European Union as the principal market for exports in no way alters imperialist logic, in our view; it still plants its roots in our societies and continues to despoil the peoples of the continent with the active participation of the Brazilian governments of

Lula and Dilma, as demonstrated by the struggles over Tipnis, Bolivia, those in the Peruvian and Ecuadorian Amazon, in Uruguayan and Paraguayan lands, in African countries and so on, while the most essential conditions of life and work are denied the Brazilian working class.

If dependency means economies dedicated to responding to the needs of other economies and sub-imperialism means a dependent economy that not only transmits value but appropriates that of weaker countries, today as before Brazilian sub-imperialism plunders the working class subordinate to it in order to reproduce in an expanded form the plunder of its own working class. The biggest meat company in the world belongs to the bourgeoisie of a country that denies food to its people. One of the largest development banks in the world belongs to a country where half of the federal budget is intended for payment to the high finance bourgeoisie. Some of the world's biggest construction companies are part of the political class of a country where the working class lacks sanitation, good public transport and has to spend up to four hours a day going between their jobs and homes in metropolitan areas. All this validates the relevance of Marini's concluding remarks in *Subdesarrollo y revolución* [*Underdevelopment and Revolution*], which are: the sub-imperialist nature that the dependent bourgeoisie tries to imprint upon its domination should make continental anti-imperialist resistance team up with the class struggle that moves (and should move) the Brazilian working class.

Notes

1. This chapter is an amended and expanded version of the text by the same name published in *Crítica Marxista*, 36, 2013, pp 129–141.
2. See Luce 2011. A work that has Marini as a reference point for examining South African sub-imperialism is Coles and Cohen 1977.
3. In this chapter we present theoretical advances to the discussion found in my doctoral dissertation (Luce 2011) on Marini's category of sub-imperialism. I thank Jaime Osorio for his valuable comments on the ideas presented here.
4. They are: the capitalist mode of production, the capitalist world system, the pattern of capital reproduction, the socio-economic formation and the conjuncture (Osorio 2012a). See Cardoso and Serra 1979 and Marini's reply (2000).
5. For a discussion of its validity and even the increase of the working class's over-exploitation under other forms of contemporary Brazilian capitalism, see my article 'Brasil: nova classe média ou novas formas de superexploração da classe trabalhadora?' (Luce 2013).
6. There is no space in this chapter for an analysis of the differences between Marini's category of sub-imperialism and Wallerstein's semi-periphery. For now, very briefly and abstracting the theoretical and political differences between MDT and world system analyses, one can say that every sub-imperialist country is part of what used to be called the semi-periphery but not every semi-peripheral country is a sub-imperialist socio-economic formation.
7. Besides Brazil, Marini also considered South Africa and Israel among the countries that take on the condition of sub-imperialist socio-economic formations.
8. Marini laid the foundations for the category *capital reproduction pattern* that were taken

forward by Jaime Osorio, his disciple, who arrived at its definitive theoretical formulation. See Osorio 2012a.

9. The question of the divorce or rift between the phases of cycle of capital examined by Marini is one that has been misunderstood by different present-day authors. This category is usually confounded with the idea of a permanent realisation crisis or with the domestic market's inability to expand by means of credit or other mechanisms. I refer the reader directly to the texts, *El ciclo del capital en la economía dependiente* [*The Cycle of Capital in the Dependent Economy*] and *Plusvalía extraordinaria y acumulación de capital* [*Extraordinary Surplus Value and Capital Accumulation*], where one will be able to comprehend better the ensemble of determinations expressed in this category. The original texts can be consulted in www.marini-escritos.unam.mx.

10. For an analysis of the present-day specialised productive export pattern, see Osorio 2012b.

References

Bambirra, Vania (2012) *O capitalismo dependente latino-americano*, Florianópolis, Insular
Bukharin, Nicolai (1986) *A economia mundial e o imperialism*, São Paulo, Abril Cultural
Cardoso, Fernando Henrique and José Serra (1979) As desventuras da dialética da dependência, *Estudos Cebrap*, São Paulo, 23, pp 33–80
Coles, Jane and Robin Cohen (1977) O sub-imperialismo sul-africano. In Centro de Estudos Da Dependencia-Cedep (ed) *A África Austral em perspectiva*. Vol. 2. *A África do Sul e as ex-colônias portuguesas*, Lisboa, Iniciativas Editoriais
Ferreira, Carla and Mathias Seibel Luce (2012) Introdução. In Carla Ferreira, Jaime Osorio and Mathias Seibel Luce (eds) *Padrão de reprodução do capital: contribuições da teoria marxista da dependência*, São Paulo, Boitempo
Luce, Mathias Seibel (2011) *A teoria do sub-imperialismo em Ruy Mauro Marini. Contradições do capitalismo dependente e a questão do padrão de reprodução do capital*, Porto Alegre, Programa de Pós-Graduação em História-UFRGS, Tese de Doutorado
Luce, Mathias Seibel (2013) Brasil: nova classe média ou novas formas de superexploração da classe trabalhadora? *Revista Trabalho, Educação e Saúde*, Rio de Janeiro, Escola Politécnica de Saúde Joaquim Venâncio, 11, 1, pp 169–190
Magdoff, Harry (1978) Imperialism without colonies. In *Imperialism: From the Colonial Age to the Present*, New York, Monthly Review Press
Marini, Ruy Mauro (1976) Crisis del Pacto Andino: el fracaso del desarrollismo, *El Sol de México*, Mexico City, 14 October 1976
Marini, Ruy Mauro (1977a) La acumulación capitalista mundial y el sub-imperialismo, *Cuadernos Políticos*, Mexico City, Ediciones Era, no. 12, pp 21–39, www.marini-escritos.unam.mx/pdf/acumulacion.pdf
Marini, Ruy Mauro (1977b) Estado y crisis en Brasil, *Cuadernos Políticos*, Mexico City, Ediciones Era, no. 13, pp 76–84, www.marini-escritos.unam.mx/017_estado_crisis_es.htm
Marini, Ruy Mauro (1992) *América Latina: dependência e integração*, São Paulo, Brasil Urgente
Marini, Ruy Mauro (1992) As razões do neodesenvolvimentismo: resposta a Cardoso e Serra. In Emir Sader (ed) *Dialética da dependência: uma antologia da obra de Ruy Mauro Marini*, Petrópolis, Vozes
Marini, Ruy Mauro (2000) *Dialética da dependência: uma antologia da obra de Ruy Mauro Marini*, Petrópolis, Vozes
Marini, Ruy Mauro (2005) Dialética da dependência. In JP Stédile and R Traspadini (eds) *Ruy Mauro Marini: vida e obra*, São Paulo, Expressão Popular
Marini, Ruy Mauro (2012) *Subdesenvolvimento e revolução*, Florianópolis, Insular,Coleção Pátria Grande
Martins, Ernesto (nd) APERJ, Coleção Darf, Documento 545
Nkrumah, Kwame (1966) *Neocolonialismo: última etapa del imperialismo*, Mexico City, Siglo XXI
Osorio, Jaime (2012a) Padrão de reprodução do capital: uma proposta teórica. In Carla Ferreira,

Jaime Osorio and Mathias Seibel Luce (eds) *Padrão de reprodução do capital: contribuições da teoria Marxista da dependência*, São Paulo, Boitempo

Osorio, Jaime (2012b) América Latina: o novo padrão exportador de especialização produtiva – estudo de cinco economias da região. In Carla Ferreira, Jaime Osorio and Mathias Seibel Luce (eds) *Padrão de reprodução do capital: contribuições da teoria Marxista da dependência*, São Paulo, Boitempo

4

BRICS, capitalist-imperialism
and new contradictions

VIRGINIA FONTES

Understanding the emergence of a group of countries such as the BRICS requires a wide-ranging reflection on contemporary capitalism's transformations and the spelling out of new economic, political and, above all, social contradictions. In this chapter we briefly present a set of characteristics that we call capital-imperialism. We start from the premise that the required analysis of diverse national contexts needs to take into account not only the interaction of domestic social sectors but also their increasing internationalisation. Today the influence (and predominance) of centre countries has to be seen not just as something external but as profoundly and unequally internalised in the other countries. External obligations do not diminish as there is a strong pressure for subordinate countries – such as the BRICS – to adhere to the modes of capital-imperialist expansion. This process generates new tensions that need clarification to be overcome.

If any coherence exists among the BRICS countries – countries that are historically, culturally, geographically and economically disparate – is it manifest in an international trend on behalf of a broad humanitarian project? Or do the BRICS countries come together to guarantee themselves a place in the present international order, not to subvert it, but to secure room at the top of the pyramid for at least their dominant classes and enriched elites? A more reasonable expectation seems to be that the BRICS member-states demonstrate new contradictions.

Whatever role they come to play in spite of their inconsistency, their very emergence on the international scene as countries with intensifying capitalist relations translates into a very different historical process than that considered 'normal'. This process has been defined by a key certainty, hidden under 'pedagogical' or 'missionary' discourse, that the expansion of capitalism responds to a certain quality intrinsic to some countries/peoples (racial characteristics, history, customs, language, spirit of initiative, education and so on).[1] From the perspective of many intellectuals of late or very late capitalist countries, the assumption was that dominant nations jealously guarded their 'advances' for themselves, subjugating the rest and impeding or delaying capitalist expansion.

From this argument emerged three strategic patterns for subordinate countries which preserve contact among themselves: the first was based on the study of development 'models,' copying (or adjusting) them, in an attempt to repeat a similar trajectory. Some more radical intellectuals proposed the need for national autonomy to get out from under the yoke imposed by the dominant countries (those indeed considered autonomous), to be followed by the development of their own capitalism. The second strategy aimed at adjusting to the yoke, at incorporating the pedagogy of co-sharing in eventual benefits through the classical political-economy formula of 'comparative advantages'. Even among the most integrated intellectuals, this option left lingering doubts over the input/extent of such 'benefits' as well as over the correctness of the thesis with its explicit purpose of safeguarding the international status quo. The third revolutionary strategy involved a complete break with the capitalist dynamic and the construction of a new economic and political organisation facilitating another type of social relations. For different reasons, several of its proponents came at times close to the more radical exponents of the first strategy.

This chapter's underlying thesis – capital-imperialism (Fontes 2012) – seeks to grasp its historical process by means of the contradictions inherent in the spread of capitalism. Such contradictions result as much from its protagonists' desires and plans as from the collisions and struggles between radically different domestic projects in each country (and among countries), taking into consideration that they do not happen in a vacuum but in the context of dominant capitalist social relations whose central characteristic is to expand, not just economically. Besides presenting a historical analysis, the chapter discloses some of capital-imperialism's characteristics, which in our opinion helps to get a better measure of the BRICS 'emergence'. It emphasises some of the contemporary tensions that the mere existence of BRICS definitely tends to exacerbate.

We do not endorse the idea of a quantifiable and accountable 'economics', separate from the rest of existence, which expresses human rationality.[2] Neither is there a political 'instance' capable of defining and implementing projects as a 'rational' task, related to the idealisation of entrepreneurial activity, transferred to the activity of managers, politicians or think tanks operating nationally and internationally. Projects, clashes and struggles are the basic foundation and most concrete forms of historicity. The organising role of political and associational bodies (and of their proponents and managers) is basic to the conduct of such clashes. Nevertheless, we do not always come across clear and well-defined struggles or neat class divisions; many times class struggles occur in a subtle manner by means of innumerable quiet tensions. The result is therefore not linear; history is not teleology and even the most powerful capitalist sectors do not decide its course.[3] In fact, these sectors have many powers: they dominate, conspire, manipulate and are temporarily able to shape, accelerate as well as delay tendencies. But active contradictions arise unceasingly and social struggles assume chameleon-like and changing shapes.

Capitalism is a totalising socio-economic dynamic (involving all aspects of human existence) and has an expansive character. Its intrinsic requirement, the expansion of value, is most effectively and securely realised through the appropriation of surplus value. Increasing value involves forcing, in a compelling and disordered manner, the spread of conditions that make the appropriation of surplus value possible; the owners of capital need to invest it in whatever human activity offers possibilities for its enlargement. This is the foundation of what is commonly called the commodification of life: the permanent creation of available masses of social beings in and for the market, robbed of whatever conditions that would allow them to secure their livelihood or to confront capital. They are thus fully in the market and need – and, therefore, want – to integrate themselves in it in order to make a living. They act as (free) workers in very different occupations through employment and contracts or in various precarious circumstances. In some cases, they are constrained to integrate themselves into the market through compulsory (legal or illegal) routes. They are necessarily consumers since they are only able to get the goods essential to life through the market. Although this perspective does not grasp all the dimensions of the phenomenon, it is crucial because it does not allow us to forget the concrete reality of the social beings that we are.

In summary, capital-imperialism results from the propagation and expansion of capitalism still in its classical form of imperialism but gestated under new conditions since World War II. Capital-imperialism expresses the exacerbation – economic, social and political – of a particular, unequal and combined form through which capitalism is precariously – and we should hope never completely

– generalised[4] throughout the planet. The chapter thus attempts to capture the changes in capitalism in its imperialist form, by addressing its economic dimensions without neglecting the social, political, cultural and ideological transformations integral to it. The gigantic scope of contemporary capitalism involves new and growing contradictions in almost all dimensions of social life.

The usual dominant periodisation has an obvious centric-capitalist profile besides transmitting openly or subtly North American and European values (Eurocentrism). It presupposes a bonanza post-war period that is guaranteed by international institutions despite difficulties attributed to the Cold War. Around the 1970s, a period of crisis erupts with different outlines: economic (the end of the Bretton Woods agreements and the oil crisis), social (May 1968) and military (the US defeat in Vietnam). Despite the reduced role of labour and the new financial dominance,[5] this periodisation assumes that neoliberalism will be the response to these crises as the successor to the welfare state that has reached its limits. The death of the Soviet Union strengthened the new 'Pax Americana', which sometimes considered the US as the unique superpower, at other times as a member of a 'Triad' together with Europe and Japan.

We propose a periodisation that does not ignore these elements but is defined by different benchmarks. In our view, the period 1945–1960, more than a bonanza, corresponds to imperialism's adjustment and expansion under conditions both constructed voluntarily and the result of unplanned situations. In the period significant alterations occur, beginning with the formidable quantum leap of capitalist concentration in the productive sector and worker formation (primary and secondary expropriations and the socialisation of the work process) and in the main organisational structure of politics. Capital-imperialism is therefore capitalist expansion now completely alienated from imperialism inasmuch as its expansion has reached previously unknown proportions and, therefore, needs to face different levels of contradictions.

After the inter-imperialist military devastation generated by World War II, the characteristic that up until then marked centre states' power politics, two new types of obstacles to the continuity of the previous mould were erected: the persistence and even expansion of the former Soviet Union and the use of the nuclear bomb in 1945, the United States' prerogative for only a while because in 1949 the Soviet Union detonated its first atomic weapon. The Cold War period began.

Even if the capitalist leaders' intentions had still been filled with imperialist attitude, as Lenin brilliantly and succinctly portrayed, through open or nuanced forms of territorial control over the periphery and through pacification of popular struggles in central countries, that system would not have lasted. For at least 30 years, between 1945 and 1975, an intense process of change took place from traditional imperialism to capital-imperialism,[6] which modified some of the characteristics initially analysed by Lenin without, however, overturning them. Given that he edited the pamphlet on imperialism before the existence of the Soviet Union, Lenin could not have foreseen the first change. For the United States, the great capitalist winner, the constitution of two opposing blocs meant a dislocation of its theatre of operations and its target of hostility. From then on, new types of alliances had to be built among capitalist countries, including the support of a winning country for the defeated, never before seen or reproduced (instead of the traditional and historically legitimate – even if tragic – imposition of reparations). These alliances were tied together by a common, though nuanced, preventive anti-communist strategy.[7] This unequal interlocking of capitals is the first feature of capital-imperialism to highlight.

Leo Panitch and Sam Gindin (2012) analyse US centrality as the result of an early power project openly defined as an 'informal empire'. This has many affinities with the argument here; nevertheless, in my judgement these authors attribute too much weight to the official US position – expressed by state officials, intellectuals and big businessmen – and give little emphasis to social struggles within and outside of the United States and their unforeseen or even desired impacts. Besides, they consider Lenin's arguments wrong regarding the necessarily warlike inter-imperialist rivalry. In my opinion, the concentration of US economic and military power does not allow one to discard the possibility of new inter-imperialist wars. On the contrary, it stimulates tensions even if the wars occur under new and carefully local forms. Nevertheless, the authors' rich analysis helps to verify the hypothesis regarding the informal empire preparing and justifying the particular inter-imperialist interconnection under US predominance that results in capital-imperialism.

In my view, even though there are disparate (and conflicting) positions among entrepreneurs, intellectuals and government sectors about the strategies to adopt, capital-imperialism is not the result of a consensus or a 'decision' but rather of a particular situation derived from the already cited specific characteristics at the end of the war. Out of this situation capital's expansive pressures arose, in that special context of containing the USSR (and, in turn, China and Cuba) and of constant counterrevolution, which accelerated the take-off of the so-called multinational corporations, associating even more profoundly the principal capitalist countries under US primacy. Associations, cartels and the internationalisation of firms did not start there; rather, what did begin was their contemporary design and scope as monopolies started transferring factories to other countries. Alliances and inter-business groups, whose historical roots are diversified,[8] developed further with governmental agreements served by international institutions that guarantee capitalist property. This process was not without tensions because large areas of the planet, even though under Western dominion, resisted. It is important to remember that the great majority of people in the world still lived in rural areas and reproduced – and defended – pre-capitalist modes of existence.

It is crucial to emphasise that capitalist social relations do not only respond to pressures coming from powerful countries but go through all social formations. Derived out of varied historical combinations, subordinate (or peripheral) countries' dominant classes produce many tense pressures toward transforming existing social relations. Segments of the subaltern classes respect the thrust of 'development', which is generally thought to be the same as 'progress'. Many times social demands are confounded – even if confusedly – with support for the expansion of capitalist social relations. The dominant international dynamic influences the very formation of national social classes. Facilitated by powerful media, the creation of spaces of capitalist-type production and consumption produces acceleration as well as delay due to historical conditions. Added to this are the complex relationships between different fractions of the dominant and subordinate classes, which are already complicated by permanent external stresses (pressures and obstacles).

The integration of these countries into the multinational industrial and commercial network not only derives from external imposition but also depends upon the active behaviour of local bourgeoisies and their capacity for accumulation, organisation and control over the state.[9] They achieve a dynamic membership in capital-imperialism as well as in its institutional (through legal adjustments), social and political defence, as we shall see later. This is the second characteristic we highlight: the double – internal and external – incorporation of subordinate countries into capital-imperialism, in a process which involves not only external imposition but also the consolidation of states and local bourgeoisies. This feature requires analysis of the unequal and combined forms that constitute capitalist expansion, surely as diverse as the various countries involved. Meanwhile it is possible to state that, within the BRICS countries, there has occurred a deep and important expansion of capitalist social relations, due as much to the existence of processes of industrialisation as to the transformation of the lives of large population sectors.

The shape of multinationalisation (of enterprises and capitals) was given an enormous impetus by China's industrialisation and later the final Soviet crisis.

Finally the territorial limits imposed by the Cold War on capitalist expansion were broken. Already in the 1960s and '70s the level of capital concentration had reached new and frightening heights, breeding a few layers of large capitalists in the subaltern countries integrated with this dynamic; even though subordinate, they, in turn, need to ensure large areas for the reproduction of their capitals. We have now come to the third and fundamental characteristic of capital-imperialism: if the original model of capital concentration was that of a fusion between industry (then understood as industrial units) and large banks, the new scale generated more complex templates, including the really pornographic fusion of large property. The size of property concentration exploded the then existing segmentation frontiers (primary, secondary and tertiary sectors, in descriptive terms; or in Marxist terms, industrial capital – that which is dedicated to the appropriation of surplus value, and not merely 'manufacturing' – banking capital and commercial capital). Even though each mega-property can have one of these activities as its origin or principal centre, its dimensions tend to make it owners not only of the means of production but, above all, of the capacity to use those means in whatever space, whatever activity able to extract value (even fictitiously) and under whatever conditions. We call this form the ownership of the social resources of production, which includes as well as transcends ownership of the means of production. In other words, the effective capital is concentrated in a monetary form, making it more abstract, yet its existential condition continues to be that of urging – every day more forceful and impatient – the appropriation of value.

This capital concentration needs and urges the production of workers, the only ones who create the value that reproduces and nourishes capital. This fourth characteristic of capital-imperialism is as basic as the third one. Far from a worldwide reduction of labour,[10] worker numbers constantly increase, just as the creation of new ways to make them more dependent on the market and therefore supposedly more docile increase. Marx (1996:339–383) had already satirised economists who idyllically called 'primitive accumulation' that which in reality was the dramatic production of the social bases that permanently support capitalism: the expropriation of rural peoples, triggering large socially dispossessed masses needing to sell that which they have left, their capacity to work. He therefore denounced the condition of this liberty, which at its core was necessity leading to submission to capital.

In the last 50 years, the global expropriation of millions of peasants has accelerated, producing new 'poor people' (as they are treated by international agencies) in good measure resulting from the 'Green Revolution',[11] which –

intentionally or not – creates formidable masses of workers needing to sell their labour in the 'free' markets of Latin America, Asia, Africa and Europe. For the first time in humanity's history, the urban population in the 21st century is greater than the rural population, and the expropriation process continues unabated. From now on these conditions permit new expropriating arrangements affecting workers, already long deprived of their productive means, whose rights derived from the labour contract have now been reduced (through flexible and precarious arrangements). They also affect collective goods and conquests through the privatisation of public enterprises and the elimination of health, transport, education and media rights. They already implacably beat down all humankind by the expropriation of water resources and deprive humanity of the capacity to reproduce seeds, historically at the basis of world nourishment (rice, wheat, maize, soya).[12] This group of actions, which I call secondary expropriations, sadly reaffirm Marxist thought, according to which the social basis of capitalism demands always-increasing expropriations.

We are witnessing a profound process being experienced in a deeply unequal manner by diverse regions of the planet as well as different countries. This transformation of capitalism's scale, initiated in the post-war era and consolidated at the end of the Cold War, has also targeted politics. After 1944 a formidable strategic vision was activated in all spheres – military, business, intellectual and so on – narrating the development achieved under the intense process of social struggles; it laid the international basis for institutions that guaranteed the extraction of value in all fields and impeded any social processes that could question capital-imperialism's expansion. From the end of the 1960s, given the new global complexity, what was an embryonic form up until then transformed into a kind of political standard with great elasticity adaptable to various national conjunctures, yet extremely rigid with regard to the intransigent defence of large-scale private property.

The fifth feature of capital-imperialism focuses on the transformation of states and the democratic purpose. International relations take an interstate form based in broadly representative forums (such as the United Nations and UNESCO) plus associations with a corporate profile, under US supremacy; they joined the great powers together in dominance over the economies of the rest of the world. They aimed at ensuring the consent and adhesion of the dominant country populations to an accelerated process of international capital expansion and – given the Cold War context – in large measure dependent upon two fundamental elements present in the centre and offered as models for the remaining countries – the welfare state and democracy (reduced to representative elections).

Under US dominance, democracy was the expression of partial conquests weighed down by the contradiction of the very high degree of capital and power concentration. At the moment, the capital-imperialist partnership in progress derives and deepens socialisation processes of production much beyond those above-mentioned frontiers. If the international division of labour promotes perverse specialisations (such as the agro-exporting countries contrasted with the countries jealously controlling high technology or, more recently, with unequal degrees of productivity and of labour regimes), more intense and severe socialisation gaps are also growing as multinational companies multiply and aggregate workers from different countries in the same production line. Despite all the anticommunist apparatus put in operation, the capital-imperialist partnership under US primacy and its propaganda expand democratic and even socialist demands internationally.

The internationalised scale of the production process deepens contradictions and brings unusual possibilities such as the internationalisation of social struggles. If these struggles owe anything to the building of international worker organisations, they result much more from the emergence of new and serious issues that transcend national frontiers, such as the question of racism, feminism and, above all, environmental issues (or, in more precise terms, the aggravation of the socio-metabolic crisis). In the latter, the struggle against the nuclear apparatus has a relevant role, just as the confrontation with the ever more serious air, water and soil pollution, which is not limited to the contaminators' political territory. At the end of the 1960s, the fuse of social struggles on the international stage, lit by the French May 1968 experience, clearly showed the tendency of social struggle frontiers to expand.

From then on it became even more fundamental than before (when this seemed 'natural') to limit politics to national spaces while at the same time accepting (and in some cases stimulating) countervailing channels of international communication increasingly in line with national and international ('philanthropic') public and private financing. A 'povertology' sought to skew any analysis (even including statistics) in terms of social class and to wipe away any evidence of production modes reasserted and intensified by social inequalities.

The central forms of social, ideological, political and repressive containment of the popular masses are anchored in states; their importance expanded as the locus in which conflicts could be admitted, as long as they excluded any revolutionary possibility or popular anti-capitalist expression. These had to be de-legitimised and, when they were conducted in electoral forums, they were immediately overthrown or undermined (as exemplified by the case of Chile in

1973). The tensions involved in achieving containment were huge even though they were – and still are – temporary.[13]

It was a question of implementing political forms that were able to ensure the spread of value appropriation with a permanent supply of the newly expropriated labour force under new, highly internationalised conditions. For this, several fields of study were created to absorb and to 'specialise' disparate international tensions (for example, unemployment in the centre and super-exploitation in the periphery), maintaining state controls over popular masses.[14] Democracy is now reduced almost totally to the judicial-electoral moment, freed from every connection to 'welfare'. State enclosure of social struggles intensifies, affecting workers' autonomous capacity to organise, extending even to erasing the very perception of an ever growing, unequal, yet intimately associated working class organised on an international scale. Secondary expropriations, especially those that take away worker contractual rights (outsourcings and casualisations), act upon the material basis for reproducing life. They dilute comprehension of this process by naturalising the urgency for health, home and food. At the same time, the 'new poor' emerges without a sense of belonging to the working class.

Liberal thought labels social organisations with the term Non-Governmental Organisations (NGOs). Well, under capitalism this is the classic terrain of class struggle and, therefore, also of dominant class organisation nationally and internationally. In a rich and complex way, Antonio Gramsci analysed the private hegemonic structures, or civil society, as integrating the state and the part essential to decision-making, which the term NGO obscures and erases (Gramsci 2001; Fontes 2009). The present modifications of the political sphere not only refer to dominant sector manoeuvrings but also to a certain alteration in the clash of intense social struggles.

Both globally and in the Brazilian case, the opposition to multiplying popular demands seeks to prevent their political unity (on national and international levels) by means of stimulating a supposedly 'apolitical' specialisation, which the term NGO helps to reinforce. Its efficacy consists in actualising the conversion of popular processes of organising demands into bodies specialised in targeted social policies made possible by the 'donation' of resources controlled by business groups (national, international or mainly different associated bourgeoisies) or directly through public funding (Pereira 2011).

Grassroots political activity is dispersed, fragmented over different territories; it is economically controlled by business (or philanthropic) sectors and overburdened by combating innumerable problems, while acting locally and palliatively. Therefore, the main consequence is a section of sub-national policy aimed at popular sectors and carried out either by business groups or associations dependent upon business financing. A varying number of groups become state auxiliaries in the execution of practices aimed at lessening the impact of growing inequalities. Protagonists of a new political modality of social and public resource management, they meanwhile maintain the target group distant from the development of national policy. This is the label of origin of countless public–private partnerships.

Their international counterpart is also significant: sub-national segmentation mirrors a similar specialisation on the international scene also regarded as 'apolitical'. As can be seen, adjustments in the way capitalist states operate merit a deeper study than permitted by the space of this chapter. It is worthwhile mentioning another growing aspect of state internationalisation, which does not take away from its importance or that of the local bourgeoisie. The official international institutions originating at Bretton Woods have undergone adjustments to the extent that peripheral country bourgeoisies do not just believe capital-imperialist prescriptions and values but train their intellectuals in the new international management institutes (whose model has been the dissemination of the Masters in Business Administration – MBAs); these peripheral country intellectuals are integrated into extensive economic and political policy-formulating networks (think tanks and NGOs) and, no less important, they propagate this model domestically (Dreifuss 1986). This is without speaking about the co-participation in national and international economic enterprises of businesses from subordinate capital-imperialist countries and their establishment of local offices attached to international agencies (such as the World Bank or IMF) directly coupled with public institutions.

Subaltern yet domestically strong bourgeoisies are shaped by their own capitalist interests in value appropriation and are unequally interlocked with the capitalist-imperialist enterprise, which they embrace. They are prepared to try new economic formats on a large scale in their countries presently under 'democratic' guise. In counterpart they bring to international entities – and to the class struggles in other countries – an experience weighed down by constantly updated truculence from their historical domination. Furthermore, this owes nothing to some genetic flaw but started with the very colonisation process under which many BRICS members were constituted and of which they are the direct heirs. One cannot forget that dominant groups from the central countries decisively intervened in the use of violence, as Agamben (2004) and Arantes (2007) recalled.

The sixth and last characteristic of capital-imperialism is the dissemination of the requirements of economic expansion and political control towards subordinate or subaltern countries, in particular those that make up the BRICS. With deep internal inequalities, among which are those prevalent in the leading countries, they are submerged in blind impositions of value appropriation in the domestic sphere (in the national territorial space) and increasingly in the international sphere. In this, they not only support large multinational companies that originate in their countries but also maintain different levels of association with central country enterprises and with their respective states, thus experiencing the characteristic contradictions of inter-capitalist competition in complex situations.

Moreover, for value appropriation to occur, it is necessary – as in primary or central countries – to ensure relative stability and job training for national working classes, which are essential conditions for the subordinate capitalists and their states. New palliative modes of operation are introduced into the political system in view of the growing anarchic allocation of capitals, concentrated in pornographic proportions, as well as the massive primary and secondary expropriation that business entities have forcefully imposed, seeking to surf above the class struggle. They are considered rare and insufficient to the many but diffuse popular and worker claims, in a context in which 'development' and 'progress' for subalterns (even though they have few rights and very low incomes) have as their reverse side the brutal reduction of employment and central worker rights.

BRICS as a manifestation of the new capital-imperialist contradictions

Considered from the perspective of capital-imperialism's major characteristics, the countries under the BRICS acronym manifest the presence of powerful contradictions which the traditional solutions have no response to or even hope of overcoming. Peripheral capital-imperialist industrialisation – or combined and unequal interconnection – responded to the exigencies that have attempted to block and isolate a part of the planet under socialist experiments, fuelling preventive counter-revolutionary strategies. At that time, subaltern popular democratising claims received positive signs from the existing central social-democratic countries, which were indicated as an example and destination. The entrance of subordinate countries into the subaltern capital-imperialist category occurred, however, in the twilight of the expansion of social rights, democracy having been reduced to the electoral process and powerfully marred by the economic weight of giant enterprises.

Small and very limited gaps opened in the sense of integrating leaders from the popular classes into a process that represented something more than co-optation, by fostering the conversion of many popular leaders. Far from any substantive transformation, a left arose, set on adapting popular sectors for capitalism: with experience in guiding popular organisations and entities, with the capacity to translate this experience into votes, the left took management positions in capitalist companies, in pension funds and in private bodies that took over the administration of privatised sections of what formerly had been universal entitlement. If the more durable political traditions in the subordinate countries did not disappear, many business groups sought to combine them with new forms of belief. Analysed in depth in the Brazilian case (cf. Neves 2005; Martins 2009; Coelho 2012), this phenomenon has its parallel in the extension of the national or international voluntary sector in the BRICS member-states.

In this optic, the entrance of new competing associated members and the volume of expropriations affecting unequally all types of workers involve serious difficulties. Centre country worker losses intensify and breed political and ideological utterances, which at times are translated into arguments that get close to extreme nationalism or fascism. Large popular mobilisations, whether in centre or peripheral countries, are ignored and do not result in effective political solutions, which leads to exasperation and to proof that the democratic sphere has been reduced to an electoral game between ever more similar candidates. An extremely complex and highly unpredictable social and political era is opened on the international level. Mass commitment to claims of equality (which democracy was supposed to secure) is seen as blocked, provoking a lack of confidence in political organisations, entities and institutions. Thus workers in centre or peripheral capital-imperialist countries find fewer and fewer ways of making their demands at a time when the international division of labour links them together more intensively.

Local bourgeoisies in middle-power countries and with consolidated states were able to expand, even though as subalterns and, strictly speaking, by continuing to be subaltern. The continuing crises in primary countries produce new impasses: on the one hand, the predominant country, the United States, propagates a capital-imperialist policy (democracy as social control without social rights, capture of popular social movements and their conversion into specialised managers, national compression of class struggles and so on); on the other hand, foreign direct investments (FDI) combined with local modes of value extraction as well as ruptures accomplished by public debts. In critical junctures, therefore, in the face of the fragility of worker bodies, leading capitalists and their states tend to return to the hardest and less 'interconnected' positions, voicing more directly their military and economic dominance. With this, they threaten to curb the expansion of capital-imperialism in its 'pacific' form; that is, centred on localised wars and on the direct and indirect attack on any anti-capitalist initiative. The subordinate and subaltern capitalist-imperialist countries' room for manoeuvre shrinks; their area for expansion and operation has a tendency to replicate in more fragile countries the modalities of 'conversion' (persuasion accompanied by economic financing for the enhancement of their 'local' capitals) and of violence, including cutting off options through international agencies and institutions, thereby reopening tensions at the international level.

From labour's perspective, there is a crisis and also an expansion. The crisis, already shown, dispatches rare rights and increases their precariousness. As already seen, the general diminishing economic growth has up until now not shown any limitation to the processes of capital concentration and capitalisation, or aggravated falls in large monopoly profitability; on the contrary, inequalities deepen. There is, thus, capitalist expansion alongside social crisis with indiscriminate value extraction, taking advantage of all means of exploitation, from workers with contracts and rights to those with scarce rights. The fact that this process is invisible on national and international levels does not mean it disappears: every day the production processes demand greater connection among workers despite the enormous inequalities that separate them.

The BRICS personify the most impressive pinnacle of subaltern countries elevated – by external pressures and domestic demands and possibilities – to an industrialisation and generalisation of capitalist social relations that require outward expansion. Although there are internal differences among them, they all maintain a double position: on the one hand, assimilation and commitment to capital-imperialist values; on the other, a certain lack of confidence in the maintenance of current international rules in a crisis situation. A fear remains that centre powers, beginning with the United States, would pull back from 'integrating' capital-imperialist positions, on the military plane above all. Tensions between the great industrialised powers seem a thing of the past but can reappear as demonstrated by the recent episode in the Ukraine.

Notes

1. As is known, this is one of the foundations of Eurocentrism and was pointed out by Quijano (2005) as one of the bases of contemporary racism and machismo.
2. Max Weber (1983) analysed capitalism's different modes, and the most remembered is the Western rational, interpreted as the separation of family and enterprise, as rational accountability and the rational organisation of free labour. Many forget that, in the same classic work, Weber shows the irrationality of an existence turned toward restricting pleasure and satisfaction, based on the Protestant ethic and fundamental to what he defined as the capitalist spirit.

3. In this respect two present-day examples are interesting to ponder: the impossibility to predict and contain capitalist crises, like the recent one that exploded in 2008 in the United States and continues with devastating effects in Europe, and the practice of the National Security Agency (NSA) of the US to spy on global correspondence and activities, unveiled by Edward Snowden.
4. This generalisation does not mean egalitarian homogenisation; it is the most powerful historic way of creating inequality. This 'generalisation' signifies an international space entirely given over to reproducing value, marked by states that are unequal among themselves and stuck in ever-increasing social inequalities. As pointed out by Meszaros (2002), this assumption represents a threat to the very existence of humanity.
5. The category *financialisation* is often presented in an imprecise manner. Sometimes it is close to Lenin's formulation, which signals an intimate relation between industrial and bank capital; at other times it rejects this formulation by limiting itself to banking activity including stock exchange values and the financial, not banking, sector. We start from Lenin's premise although warning of a quantum leap in the fusion between the diverse capital sectors, as we shall see below.
6. This period, 1945–75, is often idealised as manifesting a 'normalisation' of capitalism under the generous management of the welfare state. In fact, this was the tonic for the people of Western Europe, the United States, Japan and also a small handful of nations. For a good part of the rest of the countries, this was a time of bloody anti-colonial struggles and subsequent foreign military interventions (such as in Latin America) and bloody dictatorships with US support and European complicity.
7. In that period no European country experienced the persecution of communists that McCarthyism imposed on the United States in spite of its 'model' character as well as the reach of its ideology being shaped by the cinema, above all.
8. Dreifuss (1986) studied the early beginnings of business think tanks originating in the UK and the US, disseminated to cover just about all of the continents, absorbing intellectuals and businessmen of innumerable countries. See also Gramsci's broad and far-reaching reflection on the form of capitalist state organisation from the 1920s and 1930s, when the state expanded through tight interlocking with private hegemonic apparatuses (civil society).
9. Marini early on emphasised the relative autonomy of the state in order that subaltern countries such as Brazil under the military dictatorship introduce a sub-imperialist policy (Marini 1977:20–21).
10. With varied levels of complexity, different authors argue that technology can eliminate (or reduce to tiny levels) the number of workers necessary for capital reproduction. The coherence of this reasoning ignores the fact that the general reproduction of capital has never limited itself to the relation between any particular national capital and 'its' workers. If this were true in capitalism's early beginnings, such as in the case of slavery, particularly of Africans, it becomes even truer after modern imperialist expansion at the end of the 20th century.
11. Various technologies and chemical inputs were introduced in different countries since the 1960s, aiming at a rapid industrialisation of agricultural production. Production growth was accompanied by the concentration of landed property, social inequality, water and soil pollution, and propagation of hybrid or transgenic products with risks to human health.
12. The commercialisation of seeds is not a new phenomenon and did not until recently imply large-scale expropriation. The international imposition of transgenic seeds, especially the Terminator type (which does not create new seeds except those of very short life), can colonise fields sown with native seeds (even against farmers' wishes). Disseminating these seeds on a large scale opens the terrible possibility that the historical ability of human beings to freely cultivate their food will be destroyed. It seems that a series of biological expropriations are in progress whose consequences are yet unknown.
13. Just as they are incapable of preventing economic crises, they also are unable to prevent processes of a socialist nature from implanting themselves in diverse countries. The most evident cases are those of Cuba, Venezuela and Bolivia, which resist permanent harassment. In later popular manifestations such as in the Middle East, international interference has been

explicit, combining economic plans, training politicians *ex-ante* to occupy political positions through electoral processes with immense economic resources, preventive media wars, direct and indirect military intervention. Popular struggles that emerge from this were increasingly diverted from its best intentions, disfigured and blocked.

14. In this respect, it is worth noting the importance Fukuyama gives to state-building, as a contemporary strategic necessity. See Fukuyama 2004.

References

Agamben, G (2004) *Estado de exceção*, São Paulo, Boitempo

Arantes, P (2007) *Extinção*, São Paulo, Boitempo

Coelho, E (2012) *Uma esquerda para o capital: o transformismo dos grupos dirigentes do PT (1979–1998)*, São Paulo, Xamã

Dreifuss, RA (1986) *A internacional capitalista: estratégia e táticas* do empresariado transnacional *(1919–1986)*, Rio de Janeiro, Espaço e Tempo

Fontes, V (2012) *O Brasil e o capital-imperialismo, teoria e história*, Rio de Janeiro, EPSJV-Fiocruz

Fontes, V (2009) Verbete: sociedade civil. In IB Pereira and JCF Lima (eds) *Dicionário da educação profissional em saúde*, Rio de Janeiro: EPSJV/Fiocruz

Fukuyama, F (2004) *State-Building: Governance and World Order in the 21st Century*, Ithaca, NY, Cornell University Press

Gramsci, A (2001) *Cadernos do cárcere*, Rio de Janeiro, Civilização Brasileira

Marini, RM (1977) La acumulación capitalista mundial y el sub-imperialismo, *Cuadernos Políticos*, Mexico City, Ediciones Era, no. 12, pp 21–39

Martins, AS (2009) *A direita para o social: a educação da sociabilidade no Brasil contemporâneo*, Juiz de Fora, UFJF

Marx, K (1996) *O capital*, São Paulo, Nova Cultural

Meszaros, I (2002) *Para além do capital: rumo a uma teoria da transição*, São Paulo, Boitempo

Neves, LMW (ed) (2005) *A nova pedagogia da hegemonia*, São Paulo, Xamã

Panitch, L and S Gindin (2012) *The Making of Global Capitalism: The Political Economy of American Empire*, London, Verso

Pereira, JMM (2011) *O Banco Mundial como ator político, intelectual e financeiro*, Rio de Janeiro, Civilização Brasileira

Quijano, A (2005) Colonialidade do poder, eurocentrismo e América Latina. In E Lander (ed) *A colonialidade do saber: Eurocentrismo e ciências sociais. Perspectivas latino-americanas*, Buenos Aires, Clacso

Weber, M (1983) *A ética protestante e o espírito do capitalismo*, São Paulo, Pioneira

5

BRICS, the G20 and the American Empire

LEO PANITCH

For most of the 20th century, the widespread influence of Marxism around the world had a lot to do with its explanation of the new relationship between capitalism and imperialism that gave rise to the Great War. We cannot know what Marx would have made of the way Lenin identified imperialism with 'the highest stage of capitalism', but there was unquestionably a certain symmetry between *Das Kapital*'s famous description of capital as having come 'into the world dripping from head to foot, from every pore, with blood and dirt' and Lenin's expectation that it was in the process of leaving the world in the same way. Indeed, in 1888, five years after Marx's death, Engels had explicitly raised the prospect of 'a world war of an extent and violence hitherto unimagined ... irretrievable dislocation of our artificial system of trade, industry and credit, ending in universal bankruptcy, collapse of the old states and their conventional political wisdom ... and the creation of the conditions for the ultimate victory of the working class.'[1]

Of course, we can see today just how much more time capitalism had to run, and how much more space it had yet to conquer, despite the wars, revolutions and depressions it spawned in the first half of the 20th century. But the link the Marxist theorists of imperialism made between the export of capital and the inter-imperial rivalry of those years was, in fact, problematic even in its own time.[2] It failed to give sufficient weight to the continuing role of pre-capitalist ruling classes in driving territorial expansion and militarism. It far too narrowly saw state behaviour as subject to the exclusive and direct control of capitalists. And it far too directly associated the export of capital with the old history of imperialism as an extension of rule through armed conquest of territories.

Moreover, the theory's portrayal of the dominant capitalist classes in terms of trusts directly linking industry and banking under the rubric of 'finance capital' extrapolated far too generally from Germany, whereas a much looser relationship between production and financial markets, very much along American lines, increasingly became the norm through the course of the century. And the explanation of the export of capital to peripheral regions in terms of the saturation of domestic markets in the major capitalist countries was premised on the mistaken notion that progressive immiseration rather than increasing consumerism necessarily characterised the condition of the working classes in the mature capitalist countries.[3]

After World War II, the informal American empire took responsibility for the extension and reproduction of capitalism on a world scale, with the strong support of capitalist classes abroad. The closest economic, political and military linkages were forged among the advanced capitalist states of North America, Europe and Japan rather than with the former colonies and dependencies of the so-called 'Third World'. Profits were largely realised at home through expanding working-class consumption, even while the ground was being laid for massive capital exports through multinational corporations and the extensive development of international financial markets. The US committed to creating the conditions for globalised capital accumulation to the extent that capitalists abroad as well as at home came to see the US as the ultimate guarantor of their property. What Britain had been unable to achieve – indeed hardly even to contemplate – in the 19th century was now accomplished by the American informal empire, which succeeded in integrating all the other capitalist powers into an effective system of coordination under its aegis.

In this context, a strong case was already made in the 1970s that the Marxist identification of imperialism with 'an undifferentiated global product of a certain stage of capitalism' reflected the old theory's lack of 'any serious historical or sociological dimensions'.[4] Moreover, the growth of manufacturing production and exports in a diverse range of countries – from South Korea to Brazil – was not only strongly encouraged under the rubric of American-led 'globalisation' but very much advanced by domestic capitalist classes, with their own capital outflows and MNCs actively promoted by their states. This undermined the identification of imperialism with neo-colonialism and the development of underdevelopment.[5]

Yet it is quite remarkable how widely many of its underlying premises have continued to guide analyses of imperialism in our time. Exports and capital flows from, first, Germany, then Japan and more recently China have repeatedly been read off as constituting challenges to American hegemony. And US military interventions are often still seen as assertions of a 'territorial logic' of empire along the old lines and/or as compensating for the decline of US economic power which international economic competitiveness has been taken to represent.[6]

In fact, what has characterised relations among the major capitalist states – as their response to the global economic crisis of the 1970s already showed, and is again being confirmed in the current crisis – is not a temporary and fleeting condominium among their capitalist classes such as Kautsky, much to Lenin's ire, predicted might emerge after World War I, but rather a much deeper integration. This has been marked by international networks of integrated production; the centrality of the dollar and US Treasury bonds in international trade and capital flows, with Wall Street and its satellite in London as the preeminent international financial centres; and the common elaboration of domestic, commercial and international law very much modelled along US lines, but above all designed to guarantee that foreign capital would be treated the same as domestic capital.

While this does not efface economic competition between various centres of accumulation, it does largely efface the interest and capacity of each 'national bourgeoisie' to act as the kind of coherent force directed to challenging the informal American empire, not least because they see it as the ultimate guarantor of capitalist interests globally. And while the imperial role of the American state internationally certainly has encompassed the representation of its capitalists' interests abroad, the US 'national interest' has come to be defined in terms of more fundamental concerns with the extension and defence of global capitalism.

The integration of a good many major states in the Global South over the last quarter of the century into global capitalism, often through the crucible of economic crises, has extended but also complicated the imperial responsibilities of the American state. Yet to always search for the rationale for US military interventions in either the old logic of territorial expansion or the assertion of the specific interests of some fraction of American capital remains an all too common mistake. Rather, it is important to see that the same logic of sustaining and expanding the conditions for a global capitalism that originally underlay the development and maintenance of overwhelming US military power has left the American state with the burden of deploying that power in the face of such morbid symptoms as uneven capitalist development produces.

US military interventions abroad are best understood in a manner quite analogous to what police forces at home have done in 'restoring order' when the divisions of race and class have blown up into open conflicts in American cities, from South Central Los Angeles to Ferguson, Missouri and Baltimore. In fact, the wars that America has since fought have been in places quite marginal to the dynamics of global capitalism. However much it deserves condemnation, what the Pentagon does is much less important to sustaining global capitalism than the US Treasury and Federal Reserve, which have become the pivotal institutions in coordinating the economic policies of the world's capitalist states.[7]

This has been confirmed by the global economic crisis that began in 2007–8, and is still very much with us. The Treasury and Federal Reserve's central role in global crisis management – from currency swaps to provide other states with much needed dollars, to overseeing policy cooperation among G7 central banks and finance ministries – has been front and centre, while the formerly highly-touted supranational system of European governance has proved dysfunctional in the management of global capitalism, ending all the easy ruminations about the euro displacing the dollar as the international reserve currency.

Amidst this crisis, the G20 group of capitalist states, initially called into being by the US Treasury as a means of 'failure containment' in the wake of the Asian financial crisis at the end of the 1990s has been given more prominence. The G20 was designed to get the major 'emerging market' states to take responsibility for the 'new international financial architecture'. This was seen as providing legitimacy for the continuing central role of the US in superintending a greatly expanded but increasingly volatile global capitalism.

Ever since the leaders of these states were summoned to Washington by George Bush in the ominous autumn of 2008, G20 communiqués have repeatedly renewed their 'commitment to refrain from raising barriers or imposing new barriers to investment or trade in goods and services ... [and] minimise any negative impact on trade and investment of our domestic policy actions, including fiscal policy and action to support the financial sector'.[8] This is not to say that the US has ceded much operational control to the G20. The key policy decisions are made in Washington DC where the IMF and World Bank are headquartered, but even more decisively where the Treasury and Federal Reserve are located. The coordinated G20 fiscal stimulus in 2009 was significant, but mainly because it made it easier for the US Congress to accept the Treasury's initial plan for massive deficit spending. After Congress turned its face sharply against this in 2010, the centrepiece of policy shifted to the Federal Reserve's monetary policy of 'quantitative easing', and has remained there ever since.[9] The impact of this was felt as much internationally as domestically, as the Federal Reserve effectively acted as the world's central bank through its role in setting benchmark interest rates and streaming of dollars to foreign as well as US banks.

To be sure, the crisis has brought into sharp relief the internal tensions which the American state faces between acting as both the state of the United States and as the 'indispensable' state of global capitalism. Frictions with Congress are nothing new, of course. After the baptism of fire Robert Rubin went through as soon as he became Treasury secretary during the Mexican peso crisis at the beginning of 1995, with Congress (even under a Democratic majority) initially refusing the bailout the Treasury had orchestrated, Rubin said he understood Congressional resistance as 'meant to oppose us without actually stopping us'.[10] This was again confirmed as the bitter confrontations between Congress and the Obama Administration unfolded to yield Washington's 'debt ceiling' sagas from 2011 to 2013. Notably, the appetite for Treasury bonds, far from abating, greatly increased during the course of this crisis – not least from China, which only hastened to remind American political leaders that 'political brinkmanship in Washington is dangerously irresponsible' given the US's unique responsibilities for 'the world's economic soundness'.[11]

There were, of course, widespread expectations that the 'exorbitant privilege' of the dollar would be undermined in the course of this crisis. Brazil, Russia, India and China were not so naïve as to imagine the G20 would be the venue for overseeing the demise of the dollar, and also held their own first summit meeting in Yekaterinburg in 2008. Joined by South Africa in 2010 (and thereby completing the acronym of the BRICS), they soon began hatching plans for their own international bank, autonomous from the US and the Washington-based financial institutions. These plans were reinforced when the US Congress refused to endorse the larger vote for the BRICS in the IMF and World Bank, agreed at G20 meetings, and the formation of their new bank was finally announced at the BRICS meeting in Fortaleza, Brazil, in July 2014.

For Joseph Stiglitz, the Nobel-prize winning ex-chief economist of the World Bank, the announcement of the new bank signalled a clear challenge to the US-led world order, reflecting 'a fundamental change in global economic and political power'.[12] Fidel Castro associated it with his own country's resistance to 'the most powerful empire ever to exist', and expressed his confidence that the BRICS leaders' promotion of 'cooperation and solidarity with the peoples ... in the achievement of sustainable development, and the eradication of poverty', would culminate in 'one of the greatest feats of human history'.[13]

A more sober assessment is called for. The alacrity with which the World Bank has welcomed the BRICS New Development Bank relates to the fact that its goals look not very different from the resource-depleting, export-oriented economic strategies that have heretofore governed the participation of 'emerging markets' in capitalist globalisation. Along the lines of Brazil's BNDES development bank,[14] it might promote each of the BRICS states' own multinational corporations, but this stands in sharp contrast with the cooperative socialist principles of the now defunct Latin American Bank of the South that revolutionary governments in Venezuela and Bolivia initially had in mind.[15]

Moreover, the room for manoeuvre the BRICS bank seeks to take vis-à-vis the IMF is itself distinctly limited. Indeed, to obtain the full benefit of borrowing under the BRICS 'Contingent Reserve Arrangement' would still be contingent on a country having an 'on-track arrangement' with the IMF.[16] This looks very much like the 2000 'Chiang Mai Initiative' arrangement for currency swaps among China, Japan, South Korea and ASEAN countries after the 1997–98 financial crisis, which was little used and proved largely symbolic.

The main reason for the continuing central role of the dollar has very little to do with the institutional structure of the IMF, or the greater size of its capitalisation relative to what the BRICS bank will muster. It primarily reflects the absence – even in Shanghai, where the new bank will be headquartered – of anything like the depth and range of the financial markets centred on Wall Street and its satellite in the City of London. And it is the way in which these markets are, in turn, so deeply intertwined with the US Treasury and Federal Reserve that explains the latter's dominant role in global economic management. The analogous state institutions in China, let alone in Russia or the other BRICS, have nowhere near the capacity to play such a global role, even if they had such an interest at the moment.

Notably, far from fearing that the renminbi would displace the dollar, it has been the US which has encouraged the Chinese central bank in particular to take on greater responsibility for making its currency more of a player in international currency markets. Largely unnoticed amidst all the fanfare around the BRICS Bank announcement at Fortaleza was that the week before it began, two days of talks between US and China resulted in the first joint document between the two countries wherein China committed itself to a policy of 'exchange rate flexibility as conditions permit'. China's central bank governor affirmed that this meant it would orient its policies so as to facilitate 'market supply and demand to play a bigger role'.[17]

It is of course much more difficult to integrate the states of the BRICS into the US informal empire than it was to integrate the states of the G7. This is especially the case given the absence of the deep linkages among the latter's military and security apparatuses. The regional conflicts in the South China Sea and, even more telling, in the Ukraine speak directly to what it means to be in and out of NATO in relation to the American empire. But the fact that these are only regional conflicts displays the limited character of China's and Russia's nationalism, played out in direct relation to the global role of the US empire.

In fact, the most salient conflicts in the world today are class conflicts within states, including the US, rather than conflicts between them. At both Durban and Fortaleza, 'BRICS-from-below' meetings of civil society groups stressed the extent to which the dominant classes and governments of each of the BRICS members were themselves committed to neoliberal policies, often brutally administered in their own countries.[18] They were in this respect at one with the recent L20 trade union statement, made at the Australian G20 meetings, which in criticising 'austerity policies and structural "reforms" that reduce wages and workers' protection' saw the BRICS as no model for an alternative. Indeed, the L20 noted that 'if in emerging Asian economies income distribution had not worsened over the past 20 years, the region's rapid growth would have lifted an extra 240 million people out of poverty.'[19]

This brings us back to one of the central dilemmas of Marxism today, namely the divorce between theory and practice. The working class political institutions that fostered the socialist idea in the 20th century proved unsuitable for realising it. Whether there can be a radical redefinition of socialist politics and labour organisations in the context of new working class struggles is now on the agenda as never before. This is especially so in light of the dangers posed by reactionary nationalisms in Russia and India today, on the one hand, and the promise offered by the strike waves in China, the mass protests in Brazil, and the sponsorship of a new socialist party by the metalworkers' leadership of South Africa's largest trade union. In this sense we are back to 1917, and the hope revolutionaries then entertained about the international reverberations of a break with capitalism in any one country. Even while the unmaking of global capitalism may not necessarily be initiated by radical forces in the heart of empire, the continuing central role of the American state in global capitalism only highlights the great importance today of struggles oriented to bringing about a major shift in the balance of class forces inside the US itself.

Notes

1. Quoted by Colin Leys, 'The British Ruling Class', *Socialist Register 2014*, p 132. Engels did not see such a war as inevitable, nor as necessary for working class victory. Indeed, in subsequent writings in the years up to his death in 1895 Engels was rather surprisingly unconcerned with the theoretical and political problems raised by the connections between the growing tendencies to the export of capital and the rival militarisms and the scramble for colonies, problems which, 'almost as soon as his ashes had been scattered, forced themselves on the international left in the form of the great debate on imperialism'. See Eric Hobsbawm (2011) *How to Change the*

World: Reflections on Marx and Marxism, New Haven, Yale University Press, p 81.

2. The classic texts are Buhkharin's *Imperialism and the World Economy*, originally published in 1915 with an introduction by Lenin, and Lenin's own *Imperialism: The Highest Stage of Capitalism* (1917). Both were drawing heavily on Hilferding's *Finance Capital: A Study in the Latest Phase of Capitalist Development* (1910), and influenced by Luxemburg's *The Accumulation of Capital* (1913).

3. The Marxist texts were influenced by the proto-Keynesian underconsumptionist arguments advanced in JA Hobson's famous book *Imperialism: A Study* (1902), which itself drew on writings by American business economists who were contending at the time that the domestic market was no longer able to sustain the enormous productive capacity of the new corporations or provide sufficient outlets for the capital they had accumulated. Such claims were, of course, soon to prove wildly wrong. It was not because profits could not be realised at home but to take advantage of additional opportunities that American capitalists invested abroad at the time. As Gabriel Kolko put it, in challenging William Appleman Williams's very influential revisionist history of the modern roots of American empire, which interpreted the Open Door policy in terms of the overall lack of profitable opportunities at home, it suggested a kind of 'transcendental false consciousness' whereby capital and the state 'failed to perceive where it was their main gains were to be made'. See Gabriel Kolko (1976) *Main Currents in Modern American History*, New York, Harper & Row, p 36. See also William Appleman Williams (1966) *The Contours of American History*, Chicago, Quadrangle. It is ironic in this light that mainstream non-Marxist theorists of US empire have belatedly endorsed Williams's approach. See Peter Cain (2002) *Hobson and Imperialism: Radicalism, New Liberalism and Finance 1887–1938*, Oxford, Oxford University Press, pp 111–115; Andrew J Bacevich (2002) *American Empire: The Realities and Consequences of U.S. Diplomacy*, Cambridge, MA, Harvard University Press; and Christopher Layne (2006) *The Peace of Illusions: American Grand Strategy from 1940 to the Present*, Ithaca, Cornell University Press.

4. Gareth Stedman Jones, 'The Specificity of US Imperialism', *New Left Review*, I/60, March–April 1970, p 60, n1. Giovanni Arrighi went so far as to say that what had 'once been the *pride* of Marxism – the theory of imperialism – had become a tower of Babel, in which not even Marxists knew any longer how to find their way.' *The Geometry of Imperialism*, London, NLB, 1978, p 17.

5. Especially telling in this respect, given Gunder Frank's original focus on Brazil in making the case for the 'development of underdevelopment' thesis, is the recent article by Virginia Fontes and Ana Garcia, Brazil's imperial capitalism, *Socialist Register 2014*.

6. This has been the case from Mandel's *Late Capitalism* (1974) to Arrighi's *Long Twentieth Century* (1994) to Harvey's *The New Imperialism* (2003) to Callincos's *Imperialism and Global Political Economy* (2009) to Radhika Desai's *Geopolitical Economy: After US Hegemony, Globalisation and Empire* (2013).

7. Of course, it remains conventionally thought that the Pentagon bears the greatest responsibility in the American state for containing the morbid symptoms that increasingly seem to come with globalisation. This view was perhaps most graphically expressed on the famous cover of the *New York Times Magazine* on 28 March 1999 featuring Thomas Friedman's 'Manifesto for a Fast World': superimposed over a mailed fist were the bold words: 'For globalisation to work, America can't be afraid to act like the almighty superpower that it is.' When the term 'empire' was openly embraced to characterise the American state at the time of the Bush administration's response to 9/11 (including by some of its advisors), the stress was placed, in Niall Ferguson's words, on the 'potential advantages of a self-conscious American imperialism' as against 'the grave perils of being an "empire in denial"', against the threat of 'non-state actors' like criminal organisations and terrorist cells. Niall Ferguson (2005) *Colossus: The Rise and Fall of the American Empire*, New York, Penguin, pp viii, xxvii.

8. G20 Toronto Summit communiqué, June 2010.

9. http://www.theguardian.com/business/2012/jul/05/quantitative-easing-explained.

10. Robert Rubin (2003) *In an Uncertain World*, New York, Random House, p 25.

11. BBC News, China state media agency Xinhua criticises US on debt, 29 July 2011.
12. http://www.washingtontimes.com/news/2014/aug/5/emerging-economic-powers-to-challenge-us-imf-with-/?page=all.
13. http://www.counterpunch.org/2014/07/25/it-is-time-to-know-a-little-more-about-realities/.
14. http://www.bndes.gov.br/SiteBNDES/bndes/bndes_en/.
15. http://www.theguardian.com/global-development/poverty-matters/2012/mar/16/chinese-finance-latin-america-win-win.
16. http://www.dw.de/brics-launch-new-bank-and-monetary-fund/a-17789608.
17. US hails China's shift on trade, *Financial Times*, 11 July 2014.
18. Ana Garcia, Building BRICS from below?, http://www.socialistproject.ca/bullet/1018.php.
19. L20 Trade Union Statement to the G20 Labour and Employment Ministers' Meeting, Melbourne, Australia, 10–11 September 2014, p 3, http://www.ituc-csi.org/IMG/pdf/1409t_g20-labour-melbourne-en.pdf.

References

Bacevich, Andrew J (2002) *American Empire: The Realities and Consequences of U.S. Diplomacy*, Cambridge, MA, Harvard University Press

BBC News (2011) China state media agency Xinhua criticises US on debt, 29 July

Cain, Peter (2002) *Hobson and Imperialism: Radicalism, New Liberalism and Finance 1887–1938*, Oxford, Oxford University Press

Ferguson, Niall (2005) *Colossus: The Rise and Fall of the American Empire*, New York, Penguin

Financial Times (2014) US hails China's shift on trade, 11 July

Hobsbawm, Eric (2011) *How to Change the World: Reflections on Marx and Marxism*, New Haven, Yale University Press

Kolko, Gabriel (1976) *Main Currents in Modern American History*, New York, Harper & Row

Layne, Christopher (2006) *The Peace of Illusions: American Grand Strategy from 1940 to the Present*, Ithaca, Cornell University Press

Leys, Colin (2014) The British ruling class, *Socialist Register 2014*

Rubin, Robert (2003) *In an Uncertain World*, New York, Random House

Stedman Jones, Gareth (1970) The specificity of US imperialism, *New Left Review*, I, 60

Williams, William Appleman (1966) *The Contours of American History*, Chicago, Quadrangle

6

Capitalist mutations in emerging, intermediate and peripheral neoliberalism

Claudio Katz

The emerging economies are as fascinating as they are difficult to interpret. They include countries which are neither integrated into the bloc of developed nations, nor on the marginalised periphery. They have expanded, gaining a certain space in the world market and increasing their geopolitical influence. But it is not easy to distinguish among the members of this sector. As often happens with labels made popular in the media, the term has been popularised before it has been clearly defined. It is applied indiscriminately to various economies, without differentiating China from the pack of emerging economies. This sort of generalisation stands in the way of us recognising the most important qualitative transformation of the current period: the conversion of the Asian giant into a world power.

China's road to capitalism
China is already becoming part of the core countries and has far outpaced any other emerging economy. It has become the world's workshop and enjoys an insertion into the global economy which is very different from those countries providing primary materials or subcontracting services. China's new position in the world hierarchy is crowned by the strengthening of its industrial sector. This mutation is the result of a dizzying growth which increased per capita GDP 22 times between 1980 and 2011 (from US$220 to US$4930), while purchasing power has grown by 33 times. The country's commercial volume has doubled every four years over that same period. In 2001, Chinese commercial transactions

were valued at a mere 20% when compared to those in the United States; by 2005, that figure jumped to 40%, and today, they are on a par with their rival. In 1978, only 9.8% of the economy was derived from international trade, while that figure currently stands at 65%. These transformations have completely disrupted the country's internal economy. The weight of the agricultural sector has fallen precipitously, services have expanded, and industry has become the motor force driving all economic activity.[1]

This new Asian power has sustained lofty growth rates during three complex moments along its course: the periphery's 'lost decades', the collapse of the Soviet bloc, and the recent global crisis. Throughout each of these stages, China has ploughed ahead in a historical transformation comparable to the steam revolution in England, industrialisation in the United States, and development in the Soviet Union. China's new gravitational pull has been confirmed over the last six years. Its support for the dollar and euro at the height of the crisis prevented the 2009 recession from becoming a global depression. Financial aid from Beijing was decisive in the initial rescue of US mortgage institutions, the subsequent support of bonds and treasuries, and the recent propping up of the European currency. The magnitude of savings accumulated by China underscores the dimensions of this rescue. This support was not a philanthropic act. It served to assure the continuity of its exports and avoid the devaluation of the enormous quantity of assets it has amassed in foreign currency. But the real novelty of the situation is the country's gravitational pull. In the 1970s it would have been inconceivable that the international financial system could be saved by China.

The mutation of this economy began in 1978 and, until 2007, was centred on rural emigration and an increase in productivity outpacing wage growth. This combination opened the door to the turn to exports and the capture of an increasing portion of the world market. However, this expansion was not without its costs. Wages and overall consumption fell as a proportion of total income. The export boom flourished alongside profits, giving rise to an internal social breach. China's rise illustrated the expanse in which accumulation could bloom in a continent-sized, underdeveloped economy. Yet it is also worth noting that China was not starting from zero. The aggregate value of its industry in 1980 was already much greater than Brazil's; India's remained abysmally far behind (Dic and Zhang 2011).

The crisis, in turn, tended to reinforce a turn towards greater consumption. An attempt was made to reduce dependency on the export of basic manufactured goods and to expand the internal market. With these aims in mind, various Keynesian plans to stimulate demand were introduced. But the results of the last six years have been modest. Consumption has grown slightly, wages have increased a few percentage points in terms of national income, and there has been a small decline in the percentage of exports. These changes are hardly ambitious. The biggest problem for an economy structured around extremely high returns on foreign trade is that it cannot be turned towards domestic consumption without losing its competitive edge.

China has long begun to feel the consequences of its transition to capitalism. From 1978 to 1992, this path was limited by the preeminence of a model of commercial reforms which were subordinated to central planning. Under this scheme, rural communes were converted into agro-industrial units guided by the profit principle, but without yet opening to widespread privatisations. Managers appeared with the power to reorganise industrial plants, but they did not have the power to enforce mass layoffs or to sell enterprises. Meanwhile, tax-free zones were established along the coasts which were open to foreign investment and initiated exports; however, these activities did not strategically dominate the rest of the economy. In this period, industrialisation fed back into demand and increases in consumption preserved the previous distribution of national income. This model relied on an updated version of the New Economic Policy (NEP), introduced into the USSR to overcome stagnation (Li and Piovani 2011).

The turn to capitalism was consummated at the beginning of the 1990s, starting with privatisations carried out by the old directors of state enterprises with the intention of forging a capitalist class. The members of this group were transformed into the main investors in these new companies. Private accumulation was also accelerated through exploitation of the agricultural producers. China's entry into the WTO also reinforced the intertwining of the dominant elites with transnational corporations. The tripling of per capita income and the quadrupling of growth rates signified, from this point on, enormous levels of social inequality and the rollback of the revolution's popular gains.

The revolution's most important advances were disrupted. The doubling of life expectancy (from 32 to 65 years) and a massive increase in literacy (from 15% to 80–90% of the population) were replaced with an expansion in the inequality coefficient (from a Gini coefficient of 0.27 in 1984 to 0.47 in 2009). It became very difficult for working-class families to afford common health and education costs (Chun 2009). Capitalist imbalances began to emerge in an economy which saw its average growth reduced from 9–11% per year to 6–7% as a consequence of its aging industry and increasing costs. During the 2013–14 fiscal year, the level of economic activity would record its lowest expansion in the last decade. As happened previously in Japan and South Korea, China's model led to problems with competitiveness. Wages in China remain far below those in these two countries, but in the coastal regions and in higher skilled sectors, this differential is closing.

Financial imbalances are also multiplying. A significant portion of banks are operating in the shadows, carrying risky debts which underwrite middle-class consumption. Likewise, local governments' shady operations are financed with clandestine loans. At the same time, a visible real estate bubble is expanding in the biggest cities. Inflation, which has oscillated around 2% over the last decade, has grown to 6.2%. Together with a jump in the number of millionaires (from 3 to 197 over the last ten years), a scourge of precarious jobs performed by immigrants in the cities has taken root. However, the main current imbalance stems from the sky-high rate of investment, which has remained at unsustainable levels (43.8% of GDP in 2007 and 48.3% in 2011), especially given the current conjuncture of a decelerating international economy. These levels generate a tremendous scale of over-accumulation of capital and an over-production of goods.

An economy cannot grow at 10% while consumption is only growing at 2–3%. All the Keynesian plans of recent years have only aggravated the problem, which cannot be resolved by simply increasing imports (Zhu and Kotz 2011). Chinese levels of investment are all out of proportion with any historical or international patterns. They are a consequence of an export model which requires an unsustainable use of primary materials as well as terrible ecological devastation. Once economic planning was replaced with market competition, it has not been easy to moderate this type of over-investment. The clamour for profit will impede any process seeking to reduce this excess in an orderly manner.

Internal and external conflicts

China's economic contradictions are accentuated by a conflict that sets the group of coastal leaders (associated with foreign capital) against elites in the interior of the country (who are interested in developing state capitalism). The first sector seeks to reinforce the country's integration into global capital circuits with greater external trade commitments, new acquisitions of European and US assets, and an eventual share in the design of a future global currency. On the contrary, the second sector proposes a more radical turn towards the internal market, questions excessive increases in foreign investment, and objects to big bailouts for foreign currencies and banks.

The clash between these two fractions has led to important changes in the highest echelons of the Communist Party of China (CCP), consequently strengthening the neoliberal group, which is highly concentrated in the

Gaungdong export region. Its rival sector, on the other hand, suffered the displacement of various leaders such as Bo Xilai. The conflict is ongoing, but the last Party Congress confirmed the leadership of Xi Jinping and authorised a new round of privatisations. The exporting group resists any distancing of itself from the world economy that might threaten its privileges.

These tensions within the dominant fractions have not altered the defensive geopolitical strategy which characterises the entire Chinese leadership. They seek to assure themselves international access to natural resources, guarantee the security of their conflicted borders (Tibet), and finalise national reconstruction through the reincorporation of Taiwan. In order to achieve these objectives, the elite groups rely on heterogeneous alliances and operate on a fully realpolitik set of policies. This orientation guides its naval guardianship in the Pacific and its intervention into the negotiations over the nuclear arms being built by North Korea. This emphasis on protecting its borders explains its corresponding politico-military absence abroad when compared to its international economic expansion. China inundates the planet with capital and products, but not with armies or covert operatives. It maintains a defensive attitude in the face of periodic harassment by US administrations, building up its surveillance and defensive capabilities.

Beijing's leaders know that the United States dominates the leadership of the imperialist bloc and do not aspire to assume this position. They sense that, no matter to what degree global industry shifts to the East, the Yankee gendarmerie will continue to supervise imperialist interventions. Chinese leaders do not imagine themselves taking over this role under any foreseeable scenario. But China's new status as a global economic power has upset this strategic equilibrium. Its need for natural resources and new markets pushes its leaders to adopt an ever more aggressive posture. Securing raw materials in Africa and signing free trade agreements in Latin America are two examples of this compulsion. There is widespread naivety in the belief that China can avoid capitalism's typical conflicts, returning to a tradition of Eastern pacifism as opposed to Western expansionism.[2]

This new power has joined in the global throng and in its consequent international rivalries. Its export model is not simply a contribution to the market place, nor is it inclusive. It aims to overwhelm competitors in its own Asian sphere. China's rise threatens Japan's central place and South Korea's strength. And tensions are increasing owing to the new giant's growing export of high-value goods and its location of industrial plants in the Asian periphery in order to take advantage of cheap labour costs there.

74

Scenarios and outcomes

The principal geopolitical questions revolve around Sino-US relations. Some hypotheses expect a great conflict to erupt when the Asian economy externalises the tensions inherent in its model, pressing suppliers to reduce input costs and demanding that competitors cede markets. According to these predictions, China will confront the United States and then take control over the international reserve currency. But another possibility must be kept in mind, and this has to do with the co-dependency which has developed between China and the United States in recent decades. The great Eastern exporter needs the North American market to unload its surpluses and the Great Power needs Chinese financing to cover its monumental trade imbalances. The transformation of Shanghai into a great multinational business centre illustrates how both powers' plans interact with each other. At least two central figures in imperial policy-making are betting on the stability of this relationship. They believe the United States will accept the preponderant economic position of China in exchange for its recognition as the world's sheriff.[3]

Until now, the tendencies toward conflict and cooperation have played out with similar intensity, making it very difficult to predict the outcome. Predicting an open clash between the two powers is as hazardous as envisioning an idyllic amalgam. For the moment, the Eastern giant cannot replace its Western adversary and the North American gendarmerie oscillates between conciliation and hostility toward its rival. The United States foments military tension by placing itself in the middle of Sino-Japanese territorial disputes. It is also overseeing South Korean naval exercises, reinforcing its marine base in Australia, and redoubling the pressure on North Korea to dismantle its nuclear arsenal. But these actions coexist with the extension of joint investments.

The outcome of this conflict will also help clarify the real nature of the Chinese regime. Some sympathetic commentators emphasise political autonomy and ponder over a model of national-interventionist accumulation without looking more deeply into the social nature of the current system.[4] This point of view prevents them from analysing how China's economic ascension was achieved by means of an international association with transnational corporations which, in turn, accelerated the rise of a new capitalist class. The peculiarity of this process has been the direct link between bourgeoisified groups in China with these corporations. They have not followed the classical trajectory of national accumulation based on protective barriers and rivalry with other powers for control of external markets. Rather, they have directly joined capitalism's new internationalised context. Based on this foundation, they have introduced a restoration of large-scale property, increasing privatisation, reinforcing the preeminence of profit, and assuring the supremacy of the market over planning. It can be debated whether or not this process has been concluded or is irreversible, but its depth and its regressive social consequences are plain for all to see. Authors who underline this retreat are able to present a more realistic picture than those who interpret this process as a variety of 'market socialism'.[5]

Confusion over emerging economies

Some countries remain classified along with China in the same bloc of emerging economies. India, Brazil and Russia are especially included in this column. But this grouping ignores the fact that China's economy is two-and-a-half times bigger than India's and four times bigger than that of Brazil or Russia. Moreover, its growth rates have been much higher and its accumulated reserves far surpass the sum of all three of these nations combined.[6] These distinctions are compounded by a very different insertion into the international economy. While China directly impacts the flow of the global circuit, these other countries have only a secondary influence. The decisive aid China's central bank extended to the Triad during the crisis contrasted sharply with the absence of any sort of gravitational pull displayed by the other three countries. This group is located closer to the camp seeking aid than the camp offering it. Nor have these three countries been the recipients of the general transfer of industry which has moved toward the Far East.

The most recent classifications also include Turkey and South Africa among the emerging economies. They have undergone expansion over the last decade, suffering only limited effects from the recent crisis and a milder debt problem when compared to the developed economies. Yet the growth rates for these economies have been variable and very uncertain, and they are based on relatively recent developments and not on changes accumulated over several decades. Still other countries located in the emerging sector have grown as a consequence of higher international prices for raw materials. The long-term structural, and not merely financial, changes behind this higher valorisation do not alter the vulnerability of these countries, which remain so dependent on commodity fluctuations.

Grouping all these under the same heading of emerging economies only multiplies confusion. The category itself is based on short-term financial considerations. The acronym BRICS, for example, was introduced by a trader at Goldman Sachs to point out investment opportunities. Using this same logic, other financial analysts have walked away from the BRICS and are preparing to replace them with the MINT (Mexico, Indonesia, Nigeria and Turkey), which are seen as candidates for financial speculation. In reality, potential recipients for these funds are as numerous as they are fleeting. Other recently named candidates include: Vietnam, Australia, Bangladesh, Chile, Colombia, South Korea, Egypt, the Philippines, Iran, Israel, Malaysia, Mexico, Nigeria, Pakistan, Peru, Poland, the Czech Republic, Singapore and Thailand. As there are no criteria for classifying such a wide variety of countries, the alphabet soup only multiplies (CIVETS, EAGLES, AEM, VISTA, MAVINS). It should be clear that all this terminological double talk does nothing to clarify any economic processes. Based on some financial similarity, medium-sized and peripheral or industrialised and rentier states are all mixed together.

Semi-peripheral economies

The expected increase in US interest rates has already reduced the BRICS' breathing space. Some economists consider the greatest risks in the next financial panic will be displaced onto the intermediate economies, which have higher fiscal deficits and lower growth rates.[7] Others fear a repetition of the terrible crises that similar economies fell into during the 1990s (Mexico 1994, Southeast Asia 1997, Russia 1998, or Argentina 2001). But beyond this conjunctural diagnosis, it is important to remember that the division within the old bloc of non-industrialised nations has deepened. One segment has improved its weak economic infrastructure by developing manufactured exports, integrating businesses into the circuits of international corporations, or growing productive services. The other sector retains, in turn, its old raw materials profile.

The classification of economies by their structure and their insertion into the international division of labour is favoured by authors who are critical of the vague concept of 'emerging' economies. Flowing from an analysis centred on the global productive process, these authors have clarified the content of the notion of the 'semi-periphery'.[8] This category applies to countries such as Korea, Taiwan, Turkey, Mexico, Brazil and South Africa, which have distanced themselves from the bulk of the Asian, African or Latin American periphery. This intermediate position supports the idea of a tri-polar order postulated by world systems theorists and their characterisation of the semi-periphery as a segment which serves as a buffer between the two poles of global capitalism.[9] This group is currently playing a leading role in creating the bifurcation that traditionally separates the emerging economies from their underdeveloped peers. This is how the trajectory followed by countries which, through contradictory periods, cross over from proximity to the centre to convergence with the periphery, is repeated.

This characterisation challenges the current belief in a general pattern of growth for the emerging economies. It emphasises that these economies are competing among themselves while being situated in a generally stable, overall framework, where success for one country conspires against the possibilities for its rivals who are located on the same level of development. These intermediate economies repeat the trajectory taken by previous cohorts on the semi-periphery who also sought to climb the rungs up to the centre. But global segmentation always impedes collective success. If China's expansion is consolidated, it will only go to underscore the exceptional nature of its leap. Entering the ranks of the developed countries is beyond the reach of the other BRICS, MINTs or EAGLES.

Scattered sub-powers

The regional geopolitical role of each semi-peripheral economy is crucial for its success or failure; this determines whether it is able to occupy an empty spot in the global order. Some countries included in this segment are enormous, boasting truly continental dimensions, but some have also suffered frustrated imperial intentions. They began as powers but ended up as semi-colonies and had to fall back on plans for constructing a limited, regional domination. Russia, India, and Turkey especially share these peculiarities. These nations are spread out over huge territories and control important demographic or natural resources, and they are able to negotiate directly with the Triad. Their geopolitical capacity for action directly influences their location in the semi-peripheral ranking.

Many analysts estimate that these countries will tend to converge in common blocs in order to contend with the central powers. However, clear indications of this coming together are few and far between, and the disparate treatment meted out to each by imperialism only makes this convergence less likely. For instance, the United States is hostile to Russia, but it is closely associated with Turkey and is rebuilding its relationship with India. Instead of forming a bloc, each sub-power seeks its own niche within the neoliberal order. They accept free trade, the primacy of the transnational corporations, and the continuity of cross-border financial flows. In contrast to what occurred during the 1930s, there has been no attempt to erect protectionist networks, nor to construct militarist coalitions.

All the players have agreed to work within the existing international organisations to reinforce their own influence. They promote reforms to the voting system within the IMF and propose the creation of global reserve funds in hopes of gradually replacing the dollar. Since they have no interest in abruptly replacing the currency in which they hold the bulk of their reserves, they are banking on drawn-out negotiations.

They might suggest a reform to the Security Council of the United Nations, currently composed of five permanent members with the right to vote. Yet these negotiations are fraught with conflict because many candidates are vying for the new seat under consideration. Among them are the old powers (Germany, Japan) and those on the rise (India, Brazil). Moreover, neither China nor Russia is convinced of the wisdom of this change. Several sub-powers have also shown an inclination to offer troops for UN missions, thereby providing cover for the hypocrisy of humanitarian imperialism. This conduct not only demonstrates the affinity the dominant classes of these countries feel for the global status quo, it also indicates the difficulties they confront in pursuing alternative paths. Some members on this fringe compete among themselves on various economic terrains and others still maintain old border disputes. And, many times, their strategic priorities do not converge.

For example, the BRICS held various summits in order to agree on specific increases in trade, the creation of a reserve fund, and the eventual constitution of a Development Bank. But they have mostly focused on finding agreements about short-term contingencies and have failed to make progress on significant commitments. These attitudes are determined by the close relationship the dominant classes are nurturing with transnational corporations. They are bourgeois, and have discarded the old pretences of the anti-imperial projects of the 1960s and 1970s. A 'Non-Aligned' bloc or a summit like the one celebrated in Bandung is beyond their horizons. They play their part on the neoliberal stage alongside the multi-millionaire elites who are deeply integrated in the global club of the most powerful. We can see these tendencies at work in the four following cases.

Russia

Russia's recovery is plain to see. The Putin era counteracted the social disintegration, economic collapse and loss of international influence which came in the wake of the USSR's implosion. Yet focusing on the contrasts between these two periods may obscure critical continuities. The Russian president consolidated a new capitalist class, which was forged from the old bureaucracy by means of pillaging state property. The brazen sacking of state property during the Yeltsin period led to the collapse of the rouble.[10]

Putin limited the excesses, restoring order, which was required for capitalism to function. He reconstructed the state's power by means of building an authoritarian machine, based on popular exhaustion with the previous chaotic period. He introduced rules for accumulation and consolidated the concentration of energy and finance sectors into the hands of a few wealthy bosses. He also exerted a certain level of state control over investors in order to buttress consumption and investment. This included the imprisonment of several millionaires.

This new vertical political power is based on fraud and the persecution of the opposition, but it has, nonetheless, gained several electoral victories. The flow of stolen votes is used to reinforce the political submission of a working class which has been orphaned from its traditions and practices of self-organisation. The legacy of many decades of bureaucratic totalitarianism continues to obstruct the formation of unions and left-wing groups, despite enormous social inequality and growing disillusionment with capitalism.[11]

Against this background of popular passivity and demoralisation, Putin has recreated a nationalist ideology which exalts provincial leaders and revives the old traditions of Slavic supremacy. He is trying to rebuild Russia's role as a sub-imperialist power over the entire area of the old Czarist Empire. Massacres of Chechens served as a point of departure for these efforts. In these, Russia could count on the implicit support of the West which was perpetrating similar crimes in the struggle against the 'terrorist enemy'. But this complicity did not attenuate the growing tension between Russia and US imperialism, which attempted to take advantage of the collapse of the USSR to exterminate its old rival. The US ringed Russia with NATO missiles in order to force the liquidation of the great Soviet arsenal.

Putin understood that disarmament would make forging a sufficiently solid capitalist system impossible, so he initiated a defensive plan to reconstruct Russia's military power. He intervened in Georgia, deployed troops into Central Asia, intervened in the negotiations with Syria, and annexed the Crimea in a coup against the Ukraine. These actions consolidated a state autonomy which the big capitalists needed in order to secure their investments. These sectors divided their sympathies between the United States and Europe, while they amassed fortunes in Berlin, London or New York. Today, the elite rely on a powerful Soviet tradition of intervening in global affairs and they leverage diplomacy in order to bolster business.

Russia has recovered this space because it maintains an enormous military structure, which is not under the collective supervision of imperialism. This military gravitas, and not its economic expansion, explains Russia's international resurgence. Yet the global crisis affected it more than other emerging economies and it has not rebuilt its previous industrial structure, relying heavily instead on gas and petroleum exports.

India

India also played a role in the emerging economies' rise, owing to the geopolitical place it occupies in the convulsive Asian sub-continent. It is the great power in a region buffeted by a multitude of border disputes, separatist demands and local ambitions. The omnipresence of its army offset the tumult in Sri Lanka, tensions in Bangladesh, conflicts in Nepal, and a wave of Taliban-orchestrated terror. It has been shaped by the unresolved status of Kashmir, four wars with Pakistan, and border disputes with China after the military clash in 1962. There is also the unresolved status of Tibet.

The dominant classes manage a conglomeration of more than one billion people in 28 states and seven territories, speaking 18 official languages, and belonging to several religions and communities, all existing within a caste structure. The state structures are formally secular, but are crisscrossed by a multiplicity of sectarian clashes and by bloody explosions of communalism. This quagmire is habitually glossed over with a celebratory rhetoric which presents India as a stable and multi-cultural democracy.[12]

The biggest change in all this is the pro-US turn taken by the ruling classes who have adopted the neoliberal credo. The collapse of the USSR and the Pakistani military's prior support for the Taliban helped bring about this confluence of interest with the United States. The Yankees have increased investment in India from US$76 million to US$4 billion in less than twenty years. India already belonged to the secret global atomic club, but now it has the support of the Pentagon, which had previously supported its Pakistani rival.[13] Over the last decade, India's economy has recorded higher growth rates and gave birth to several multinational corporations with global status. It has also achieved a certain expansion in the technology sector, especially in software services. But its sub-contracting activities are carried out very far away from the epicentres of the digital revolution. Any comparison with patents or profit rates in the United States only confirms this gap.[14]

As with China, the resurgence of India has been accompanied by a millennial feeling of the rebirth of civilisations that occupied predominant global positions until the 18th century. But India's current growth is not comparable to its neighbour's. Industry continues to operate on a non-integrated, intermediate scale, highly dependent on external inputs and royalty payments. Productivity is low and infrastructure remains very obsolete. Social differences with China are even more pronounced. India has created the largest number of new millionaires and it has a large middle class. But 77% of the population remains in poverty and 40% are underweight. The fight against hunger has failed and 100 000 farmers committed suicide between 1996 and 2003 because of debt or fear of failure. The history of social exclusion persists on a gigantic scale. Four out of ten people cannot read or write and the index of human development places India in 126th place.[15]

On top of all this, the current process of accumulation faces two limits that were not present in prior centuries. India cannot offload its surplus population through waves of immigration (as Europe did to America) and it suffers from unemployment aggravated by technological innovation. These obstacles tend to be accentuated by neoliberalism's pressure to make labour markets more flexible and to privatise public enterprises. But this aggression is beginning to be met by a resistance that might alter all of this.

South Africa

South Africa represents another case of a nation developing a growing geopolitical gravitational pull in the wake of the heroic popular struggle that finally buried the old racist political system. But this feat – symbolised by Mandela – gave way to a managed transition which consolidated the supremacy of enriched minorities. The co-optation of an African elite allowed the dominant classes to project themselves anew across the region and facilitate a certain economic growth. The end of the apartheid regime's isolation allowed for the consolidation of a free trade region and consolidated an industrialised economy which absorbs fully 70% of sub-Saharan Africa's electricity.

This strategic relocation explains South Africa's incorporation in the nucleus of the BRICS. Russia and India have a GDP four times bigger than South Africa, and China's is 16 times as large. Even South Korea, Turkey and Indonesia surpass South Africa on this score. Its geographic territory and population are smaller than those of Argentina or Iran and it has serious competitors such as Nigeria in its own continent. However, the post-apartheid regime is the only one with the necessary structures to provide regional leadership.

During the 20th century, South African business combined regional expansion with militarism and racism. The white settlers were converted into a ruling class and Afrikaners associated with the mining industry took on the role of police. They routinely deployed the military power they built up during a period of import substitution policies.[16] With the end of white domination, South Africa's ambitions for territorial expansion have been extinguished, but not the role it plays as the gravitational centre of the region's economy. The new African elite are promoting neoliberal capitalism under the banner of an 'African Renaissance'.

The historical leader of the mine workers (Cyril Ramaphosa) became the director of major corporations in a country which is no longer repudiated by its neighbours. South Africa has emerged as the darling of the IMF and the World Bank. Its leaders spout progressive rhetoric at the UN, while acting as trustworthy partners for the United States.[17] But this neoliberal turn has torn South Africa apart. Since 1996, the combination of privatisation and trade liberalisation, with the removal of restrictions on the movement of people, generated a chaotic urbanisation which has only deepened social polarisation.[18] Unemployment has doubled and now affects 36% of the population. Inequality ranks at the top of the world index (Gini coefficient of 0.73). Disasters in the provision of water, precariousness of housing, and the degradation of education are major problems. Wages have stagnated alongside the growth of employment agencies which mediate the labour supply. And hidden forms of servitude persist on the 87% of land which is monopolised by white farmers.

The extreme modalities of combined and uneven development which generated apartheid in the first place have not disappeared. That system joined capitalist and pre-capitalist forms together by means of exceptional extra-economic methods. The temporary and migrant labour that connected the modern sectors to the backward sectors of the economy has now been remoulded and is recreating the old fractures.[19] South Africa is also enduring the erosion of its traditional energy-mineral base. This sector has gone international and maintains its economic primacy (23% of GDP and 60% of exports). However, extractive industries are exhausting subsurface resources after several failed attempts at diversification. For all these reasons, the global crisis has impacted South Africa more severely than other similar economies. There has been a level of capital flight in a situation marked by rising social tensions and the massacre of mine workers, which recalled the terrible repression of the past.

Turkey
The case of Turkey also illustrates how a regional sub-power can stand out, based on its geopolitical military weight. Over the last few decades, the dominant classes there have developed a strategy for expansion into the Arab world and the Mediterranean. This policy is based on deploying its military beyond its borders (the occupation of Cyprus) and in reinforcing its internal oppression of the Kurdish minority. The national rights of this section of the population are put down at the point of a gun, disregarding the opinion of the majority of the Turkish people. But after 30 years of resistance, the government had to accept the opening of negotiations when faced with the establishment of Kurdish autonomous regions in Iraq and Syria.[20]

In Turkey, internal coercion and expansionary ambitions are official state policy, currently being carried out by a conservative Islamic administration. Its leaders took office 11 years ago, promising they would not repeat the authoritarian nationalism of Kemalism. In fact, they are especially focused on recreating a sub-imperial project in which they gain regional supremacy over Iran, Egypt and Saudi Arabia. In order to do so, they are preserving the despotic tradition of maintaining a large bureaucracy operating under military tutelage. The end of the dictatorship did not eradicate the vestiges of totalitarianism and the actual power of the Parliament remains very weak.[21]

Neo-Ottomanism has persisted in Turkey as the historic ideology of the ruling sectors across a variety of periods, from the heights of the imperial state to the depths of semi-colonial status. Currently, this tradition is being adapted to serve the project of inserting Turkey into a globalised neoliberal order as a regional power. Based on this strategy, Turkey has joined NATO, tolerates the Pentagon's use of its national territory, and has participated in incursions into Afghanistan, Somalia and Iraq, all the while seeking to act as a partner, and not simply a vassal, of the United States. It was in pursuit of these same goals that Turkey offered support for the Islamists fighting in the Syrian civil war.

The Turkish bourgeoisie has embraced neoliberalism and accepted its geo-political horizons. It has benefited from an 8% annual growth in GDP, lifting the country into the ranks of the intermediate economies with several corporations achieving global status. But the storm clouds which are currently affecting all intermediate economies are now threatening Turkey's ascension.

New Islamic free traders have displaced the old secular protectionists, but all of them have abandoned their focus on development in favour of promoting trade liberalisation. They seek to join the European Union and in this enjoy the media's and the stock exchange's active support. The United States endorses Turkey's membership for the same reasons that it supported the entry of Eastern European states into the EU; however, it has been difficult to achieve a consensus within Old Europe about including an autonomous power characterised by so much repression and so little secularism.[22]

The Islamic government hoped to use the Arab revolts to export its model of rigidly conservative neoliberalism. Yet the commotion that spread throughout the region ended up infecting Turkey itself and the Taksim Plaza in Istanbul was transformed into a mirror image of Tahrir Square in Cairo. A wave of demonstrators occupied this site for weeks, protesting against religiously based political and social restrictions and police brutality.[23] This reaction highlighted dissatisfaction with Turkey's neoliberal surgery in a country burdened by attacks on social freedoms and democratic setbacks. Taksim's challenge eroded the government's ability to project its model of conservative Islam and undermined its pretence at regional supremacy over its rivals Iran, Egypt and Saudi Arabia. Turkey ended up being drawn into the revolt it had hoped to defuse.

Regression in the periphery

The global crisis negatively impacted the classical periphery. It hit hardest economies that export basic goods, import processed products, and suffer the plundering of their natural resources. These countries cannot rely on the shock absorbers that intermediate economies can call on to temper the impact of an unfavourable international context. They remain ravaged by the adverse political conditions imposed by neoliberalism that eliminated any countermeasures which previously limited global polarisation. The collapse of the socialist bloc and the loss of historic gains by workers in the First World have only facilitated the opening of this breach.

The periphery is made up of economies which have suffered the greatest impoverishment. At the extreme end of the poles, abysmal income differences persist. The per capita GDP of the Congo (US$231) or Burundi (US$271) places them light years from Monaco (US$114 232) or the United States (US$48 112). These fractures have grown significantly during the last decades so that the gap which separates per capita income in the richest and the poorest regions has risen between 1973 and 1998 from 13.1 times to 19.1 times. There are many statistics which demonstrate the geometric expansion of the chasm which separates the first 40 countries in the global rankings from the last 40 countries.[24]

The accumulation of capital on the global scale always involves an international division of labour which leads to the transfer of resources from the periphery to the centre. In its neoliberal stage, this polarising dynamic continuously modifies how this process takes root in various localities. The expansion of growth in certain areas is consummated at the expense of others through unequal exchanges and processes which recreate underdevelopment.[25] Polarisation can be verified in a dramatic form by looking at the worsening of hunger. This social tragedy has been on the rise since 2003, powered by a cycle of rising foodstuff prices. Until 2008, shortages were mostly concentrated in grains and certain cooking oils. But it then extended to affect all products. In December 2010, the Food and Agriculture Organisation price index surpassed its all-time high. Hopes for decreasing prices based on a global slow-down have not been realised. Hunger affects around 1.2 billion people, but its threat extends to 2.5 billion people living in poverty. We need only recall that food shortages influenced the opening stages of the Arab uprisings ('an uprising for bread') in order to understand the social impact of this problem.

There are three explanations for the persistence of food-price inflation. The first attributes the upward trend to the formation of bubbles, produced by speculation over future grain prices. This dynamic channels the excess liquidity generated by the lack of investment opportunities in developed countries into the foodstuff markets. Commodity traders in the United States place obscene bets on the prices of basic human needs every day. Before 2000, the futures market for these products was regulated and placed strict requirements on traders to disclose their positions. These regulations were abolished and these markets were opened to short-term investment funds.

Investors arrived en masse and in 2007 total transactions averaged US$9 billion. Financiers later perfected their operations and they no longer even sign futures contracts. They buy and sell commodities according to daily price fluctuations without any intention of ever taking physical possession of them. They simply manage contracts through financial derivatives which, consequently, increased by 600% in this sector between 2002 and 2008.[26] Big banks (BNP Paribas, Deutsche Bank, JP Morgan, Morgan Stanley, Goldman Sachs) specialised in this type of activity to restore profits after the 2008 crash and were directly involved in the abrupt price hikes for the three foodstuffs which comprise 75% of basic global consumption (corn, rice and wheat).[27]

The second explanation argues that the increase in food prices stems from activities which have indirectly affected these basic products. These developments increase the cost of inputs and accentuate soil exhaustion. Food prices also rise along with oil, transportation and irrigation, and the same general effect emerges from the expansion of supermarkets, which inflate demand by introducing new consumer habits.

The final explanation asserts that increasing food costs are a structural problem, driven by demand from new Asian consumers. And although supply has expanded because of productivity improvements, these analysts believe that change in diets for millions of new consumers has impacted all prices.

Taken together, these three explanations point to complementary aspects of the same phenomena. In the coming years, it may become clear which of these three has been the main determinant in causing food shortages. But whatever the most important cause, be it financial manoeuvres, competing activities, or structural gaps between production and consumption, the results are the same: an exacerbation of the tragedy of hunger.

Neoliberal globalisation provides the backdrop for this scourge. It mandated that agriculture be converted to focus on exports at the expense of traditional crops. This transformation benefited agro-business, undermined food security, destroyed the peasantry, and accentuated a rural exodus. Free-trade standards pushed by the WTO forced export specialisation onto many peripheral economies, converting them into net purchasers of basic products. They lost their national food reserves and found themselves unprepared to face the current cycle of rising costs. This vulnerability favoured several developed economies that subsequently offloaded their surpluses onto ruined communities who had previously been self-sufficient. Malnutrition constitutes the sharpest end of the stick when it comes to the regression suffered by the Third World as transnational corporations covet and prey on their natural resources, with oil, minerals, water and forests being the major targets for this theft.

Can Africa withstand the pressure?

Sub-Saharan Africa has been a major site for social tragedies, including the terrible dramas of refugees, mass migrations and ethnic massacres. Bloodletting generated by local wars has cost three million lives. During the 1980s and 1990s, the region suffered a decline in life expectancy from 58 years to just 51 years by 2001. This macabre scene resulted from innumerable disputes over the appropriation of natural resources. Battles between local bosses for control over exportable resources provoked the total collapse of several societies (Rwanda, Somalia, Liberia, Sierra Leone). Others were bled dry for coltan (Republic of the Congo) or by the appearance of diamonds, copper and oil (Ivory Coast, Sudan, Angola). The battle for these prizes reanimated old ethnic, regional and confessional rivalries, which were promoted by the elites and which disrupted the decolonisation process during the 1960s and 1970s.[28]

It is not the case that Africa suffered these disgraces because of its 'marginalisation from the world'. In fact, it is the most integrated and subordinated region in the whole international division of labour. Its rate of extra-regional trade as a proportion of GDP (45.6%) is very high when compared to Europe (13.8%) or the United States (13.2%). The problem stems from the historic form in which this integration has occurred. During slavery, Africa suffered a demographic calamity that dramatically reduced its population. During the colonial period (1880–1960), pillage was generalised and small farmers were forced to cultivate tropical export crops. The brief period of nationalist decolonisation (1960–75) rapidly gave way to neoliberalism, which once again drove Africa back into its position as a producer of primary materials. But the current stage includes various novelties.

In the first place, the formation of a black capitalism has been consolidated. This is made up of the local partners of the multinational corporations who capture a portion of the pillaged resources. In many countries, mining and petroleum regulations have been reformed in order to increase this slice, which also serves to nourish a process of primitive accumulation. This has led, in certain countries, to significant participation by local bourgeoisies. South Africa leads this group, but Nigeria is also strengthening its gravitational pull.

Second, China's arrival has changed the balance of forces between the local dominant elites, on the one hand, and the United States and the old colonial powers on the other. This new player is investing in the continent, purchasing enormous quantities of primary materials and offering infrastructure credits without the conditions attached by the World Bank. The section of the new African bourgeoisie which is more closely linked to the West is contesting those who support developing closer ties with the Asian giant. China, however, has an advantage in that it does not carry the baggage of being a former colonial power.

Third, a significant change in the economic conjuncture has been produced in the last decade. The rate of growth began to recover, reaching an annual average of 5.1%, which beat the world average of 3% and which is an enormous improvement compared to its regression between 1980 and 1990. This rise accompanied strong growth in investments in extractive industries, which jumped from US$7 to US$62 billion, all in the context of a widespread transformation of agriculture. Imports increased 16% per year and the terms of trade improved by 38% compared to 2000–12.[29]

These modifications have changed the ideological climate of 'Afro-pessimism', which presented the tearing apart of the continent as an unavoidable destiny. Now, a version of 'Afro-optimism' is exuded by the neoliberal elites, auguring in a charmed future. If the first theory blamed the recurrent pillaging of Africa on self-flagellation and cynical opportunism, the second only serves to sanction it as the starting point for escaping underdevelopment.[30] This last vision is responsible for disseminating all kinds of fantasies about the imminent appearance of middle classes and forgets the abysmal prevailing social conditions in the highest-growth nations. Sixty per cent of the population in Angola and Nigeria live in poverty. Nigeria has the highest proportion of its citizens living in emergency housing on the entire continent and 80% lack potable water. Moreover, youth unemployment averages 60%. In the countryside, the situation is even worse because of the huge demographic pressure on cultivable land, reduced renewable water reserves, and widespread deforestation.[31]

Arab unemployment, Eastern exploitation

Another example of the periphery's misadventures can be found in the Arab world. The political upheaval which has rocked this region for the past three years emerged from multiple causes. But one thing is for sure, several decades of furious neoliberalism created poverty, stagnation and inequality and this triggered the explosion. The region has suffered record unemployment, partially disguised by its rentier regimes' practice of distributing handouts. But privatisation and labour flexibility have generated large-scale social fractures.[32] Pressures to reduce social spending and eliminate food subsidies pushed millions of youth in the Middle East into losing hope. They could not survive in their own countries and were forced to emigrate to Europe. These dispossessed ignited the revolts when a Tunisian vendor set himself on fire to protest prohibitions on selling in the streets.[33]

Like Africa, this region enjoyed a brief period in which nationalism flourished in the 1960s. This experience ran aground because of the inability of these processes to eradicate the parasitical domination of the big capitalists. Neoliberalism subsequently aggravated an explosive combination of underdevelopment and rentierism.[34]

A third case of regression on the periphery can be found among some Asian nations which have not participated in the expansionary wave generated by China and the intermediate economies. This zone has suffered terrible indices of multi-dimensional poverty as measured by the United Nations Development Programme. Its last report emphasised that 51% of the global population which suffers from extreme misery lives in South Asia and 15% alone live in the east of this continent. Yet such a high level of poverty is becoming a magnet for multi-national companies seeking new supplies of cheap labour, and labour-intensive sectors, such as textiles, are an important barometer of this trend.[35]

In the 1970s, the first wave of offshoring of clothing manufactures settled in Korea, Taiwan, Singapore and Hong Kong. The second move came in the 1980s, landing in Indonesia, Sri Lanka, the Philippines, Bangladesh and Thailand. In recent decades, a third flow has reached Cambodia, Laos, Burma and Bangladesh. The most famous brand names impose frightening levels of super-exploitation on their workers. A major international protest campaign under the banner 'Clean Clothes' is denouncing the atrocities that predominate in these workshops.

An example of this drama came to life in Bangladesh. There, the GDP has grown consistently since the 1990s, converting the country into the third-biggest clothing exporter in the world with 4 000 factories, employing three million workers. These employees work between 12 and 14 hours a day, breathing in dust in small, badly lit rooms without ventilation. The local bosses operate on narrow margins and pass this pressure along to the workers, who suffer repression and even the murder of trade unionists. This situation burst into the international news when 250 people died after a factory lacking labour protections collapsed. Many journalists drew analogies between these current subhuman working conditions and those present in England during the industrial revolution.[36]

Conclusion

China has risen to become a central global economy. The historic leap in industrialisation allowed it to play a previously unimaginable international role in rescuing the financial system. But it has so far failed to make the shift to domestic consumption. Its substitution of commercial reforms with capitalism has generated over-investment, bank speculation and social polarisation. Global economic expansion began to hinder China's defensive geopolitical strategy, accentuating disputes between coastal and interior elites. The restoration of capitalism is extremely advanced, but it has not been completed. Meanwhile, competing tendencies for cooperation and conflict with the United States persist.

The intermediate economies have grown, but are located on a lower rung. Various regional sub-powers with ambitions to become sub-imperialist powers have regained influence, but have not forged common blocs. These countries operate within the neoliberal order and it is wrong to characterise them by using short-term financial criteria. Russia rebuilt its state when faced with oligarchic plundering in order to stabilise accumulation, erecting a contentious obstacle for NATO. India's growth lags far behind, compared to China's development, in a region crisscrossed with military conflicts. In a framework marked by high unemployment and inequality, the co-optation of a post-apartheid black elite has made it possible for South Africa to project itself. Turkey's neo-Ottoman expansionism undergirds its own neoliberal growth.

The global income gap continues to widen, impoverishing the periphery. Malnutrition is accentuated by rising food prices generated by the capitalist restructuring of agriculture. Black capitalism stands out in Africa after a period of bloody wars for the spoils of natural resources. New powers are now intervening and the local elites are enriching themselves. The Arab world continues to suffer high levels of exploitation while in Asia this process can even be characterised as super-exploitation.

Poverty, unemployment, infamously low wages, and super-exploitation mark the periphery with the neoliberal period's deepest scars.

Notes

1. Pierre Salama (2013) Desaceleração econômica: a China na tormenta?, 3 October, www. cartamaior.com.br.

2 Giovanni Arrighi's view is discussed in Claudio Katz (2011) *Bajo el imperio del capital*, Buenos Aires, Luxemburg, chapter 14.

3 Joseph Nye (2013) Dos décadas para barajar y dar de nuevo, www.clarin.com 12/01/2013; Zbigniew Brezinsky (2013) Adiós a las guerras por el poder global, www.clarin.com/o 24/02/2013.

4 Jacques Sapir (2008) *El nuevo siglo XXI*, Madrid, El Viejo Topo, pp 74, 116–120.

5 Hart in the first case and Ding in the second. Martin Hart-Landeberg (2011) The Chinese reform experience: a critical assessment, *Review of Radical Political Economics*, 43, 1. Ding Xiaoqin (2009) The socialist market world economy, China and the world, *Science and Society*, 73, April.

6 Mariano Turzi (2011) *Mundo BRICS: las potencias emergentes*, Buenos Aires, Editorial Capital Intelectual, pp 43–44.

7 Nouriel Roubini (2014) El panorama cambiante del riesgo mundial, 6 April 2014, www.lanacion. com.ar; El problema de la Argentina y de otros mercados emergentes, 31 January 2014, www. project-syndicate.org.

8 Javier Martínez Peinado and Gemma Cairó i Céspedes (2012) El desarrollo de una semiperiferia como necesidad de la transición hacia el sistema capitalista global, Seville, February 2012, www. pendientedemigracion.ucm.es.

9 Immanuel Wallerstein (1988) *El capitalismo histórico*, Mexico City, Siglo XXI; Giovanni Arrighi (2009) The winding paths of capital, *New Left Review*, 56, March–April.

10 Boris Kagarlistky (2005) El estado ruso en la era del imperio norteamericano, *El imperio recargado*, Buenos Aires, CLACSO.

11 Ilya Boudraitskis (2012) Poutine ou le chaos, *Inprecor*, 581–582, February-March-April.

12 Perry Anderson (2007) The Indian ideology, *Counterpunch*, December, www.threeessays.com; Clea Chakraverty (2007) Búsqueda de una identidad para el siglo XXI, *Le Monde Diplomatique*, January.

13 Siddharth Varadarajan (2008) India ávida de reconocimiento, *Le Monde Diplo*, November.

14 Vincent Shie and Craig Meer (2010) The rise of knowledge in dependency theory: the experience of India and Taiwan, *Review of Radical Political Economics*, 42, 1.

15 Martine Bulard (2007) India recupera su jerarquía, *Le Monde Diplomatique*, January.

16 Patrick Bond (2007) South African sub-imperial accumulation, Rosa Luxemburg Political Education Seminar 2006, Johnnesburg.

17 John Saul (2005) Globalización, imperialismo, desarrollo: el nuevo desafío imperial, *Socialist Register 2004*, Buenos Aires, CLASCO.

18 Patrick Bond and Ashwin Desai (2006) Explaining uneven and combined development in South Africa. In Bill Dunn (ed) *Permanent Revolution: Results and Prospects 100 Years On*, London, Pluto Press.

19 Caroline Skinner and Imraan Valodia (2007) Two economies?, Rosa Luxemburg Political Education Seminar 2006, Johnnesburg.

20 Mohamed Hassan (2013) Entrevista, www.luchainternacionalista.org.

21 Elif Çağlı (2009) On sub-imperialism: regional power Turkey, Marksist Tutummarxist. cloudaccess.net, August.

22 Perry Anderson (2009) *The New Old World*, London, Verso, pp 392–472.

23 Olga Rodríguez (2013) Turquía, www.eldiario.es, 6 June.

24 Economía mundial: un abismo de riqueza entre países ricos y pobres, 10 November 2013, www. argenpress.info.

25 Immanuel Wallerstein (1986) *Marx y el subdesarrollo*, Madrid, Zona Abierta, p 38.

26 Jayati Ghosh (2102) Precio, www.pagina12.com, 18 November.

27 Eric Toussaint (2104) La banca especula con materias primas y alimentos, 20 March 2014, www. vientosur.info.

28 Eric Hobsbawm (2000) *Naciones y nacionalismo desde 1780*, Barcelona, Crítica, chapter 5.

29 Jean Nanga (2013) Afrique subsaharienne et ses croissances, *Inprecor*, 592–593, March-April-May; Jean Nanga (2010) Ogre Chinois en Afrique, *Les Autres Voix du plante*, October.

30 Mbuj Kabunda (2013) África y los africanos en el espejo, 21 June 2013, www.alainet.org/active.

31 Jean Batou (2104) Redeploiment de l'imperialisme francais en Afrique, 15 January, www.contretemps.eu.

32 Gilbert Achcar (2013) Le Peuple veut, 29 April, www.contretemps.eu.

33 James Petra (2011) Las raíces de las revueltas árabes y lo prematuro de sus celebraciones, 6 March, www.rebelion.org.

34 Claudio Katz (2013) De la primavera al otoño árabe, Cuadernos de Marte, *Revista Latinoamericana de Sociología de la Guerra*, Facultad de Ciencias Sociales UBA, Buenos Aires, 3, 5.

35 Amin Samir, Houtart François, Tandon Yash, Dierckxsens Wim, Founou-Tchuigoua Bernard, Tablada Carlos, Padilla Mariela (2013) Audacity to build a new paradigm in the face of the contemporary crisis of capitalism, Preparatory document for the South–South Forum 2012/2013, Quito, 5 May.

36 Albert Sales i Campos (2013) Los trapos sucios de la moda global, *Brecha*, 3 May 2013.

References

Aguirre, Rojas and Carlos Antonio (2007) Immanuel Wallerstein y la perspectiva crítica del análisis de los sistemas-mundo, *Textos de Economía*, 10, 2

Amandla, Mandela is immortal: he has lived the fullest of lives, 10 December 2013, www.socialistworker.org

Anderson, Perry (2008) Apuntes sobre la coyuntura actual, *New Left Review*, 48

Ashley, Brian (2012) La gran desilusión, 24 September, www.kaosenlared.net

Boatc, Manuela (2006) Semiperipheries in the world-system: reflecting Eastern European and Latin American experiences, *Journal of World-System Research*, 12, 2

Bond, Patrick (2005) El imperio norteamericano y el sub-imperialismo sudafricano, *El Imperio Recargado*, Buenos Aires, CLACSO

Castro, Jorge (2012) India muestra límites a un modelo de desarrollo, 12 August, www.clarin.com

Dic, L and Yu Zhang (2011) Making sense of China's economic transformation, *Review of Radical Political Economics*, 43, 1

Dowd, Douglas (2007) The dynamics, contradictions and dissent of today's China, *Review of Radical Political Economics*, 38, 1

Dyer, Geoff (2014) China vs the US: is this the new Cold War?, 20 February, www.ft.com

Economist, The (2011) Tiger traps, 17 November

Gelman, Juan (2013) Un macho coreano, 4 April, www.pagina12.com.ar

Halimi, Serge (2013) Give us your money, 1 January, www.Mondediplo.com

Hart Landsberg, Martin and Paul Burkett (2007) *China entre el socialismo real y el capitalismo*, Caracas, CIM

Harvey, David (2013) El neoliberalismo como proyecto de clase, 24 March, www.herramienta.com.ar

Katz, Claudio (2008) La oportunidad del hambre, August, www.lahaine.org/katz

Khor, Martín (2008) ¿Durará el boom de los productos básicos?, 12 February, www.redtercermundo.org.uy

Kurkcigil, Masis (2013) Après la revolte, *Inprecor* 595–596

Lewkowicz, Javier (2012) China, www.pagina12.com, 21 October

Li, Minqi and Chiara Piovani (2011) One hundred million jobs for the Chinese workers, *Review of Radical Political Economics*, 43, 1

Lin, Chun (2009) The socialist market economy: step forward or backward, *Science and Society*, 73

Molero-Simarro, Ricardo (2014) Karl Polanyi in Beijing: Chinese growth model reorientation and China's changing role in the world economy, Third IIRE Seminar on the Economic Crisis, Amsterdam, 15 February

Nanga, Jean (2005) L'Afrique a l'heure du Forum Social Mundial, *Inprecor* 523–524

Reddy, Niall (2012) Sur les traces de la Tunisie?, *Inprecor* 587

Rodríguez, Olga (2012) Yo muero hoy: las revueltas en el mundo árabe, *Editorial Debate*

Rousset, Pierre (2013) Le Pakistán, théatre de guerres, *Inprecor* 573–574

Serfati, Claude (2001) La Mondialisation armée, Paris, Textuel

Sousa Santos, Boaventura de (2014) La novedad que vino de la India, 7 April, www.pagina12.com

Terlouw, Kees (2003) Semi-peripheral developments: from world-systems to regions, www.tandfonline.com

Weil, Robert (2009) Class bases of Chinese Marxisms todays, *Science and Society*, 73

Whitehouse, David (2013) Agresseur ostensible et agresseur futurif, *Inprecor* 592–593

Zhu, Andong and David Kotz (2011) The dependence of China's economic growth on exports and investment, *Review of Radical Political Economics*, 43, 1

PART 2
BRICS 'develop' Africa, Latin America and Eastern Europe

7

BRICS corporate snapshots during African extractivism

BARUTI AMISI, PATRICK BOND, RICHARD KAMIDZA,
FARAI MAGUWU AND BOBBY PEEK

BRICS corporates in Africa (by Baruti Amisi)
The centuries-old looting of Africa, followed by the conference in Berlin that from 1885 began the 'Scramble for Africa', is being repeated now in a predatory attack by BRICS countries on the continent's resources. Large corporations from Brazil, Russia, India, China and South Africa are not committed to development for ordinary people – whether in the homeland or the victim countries. As BRICS penetrate further into Africa, the winners consist of multinational and parastatal corporations, including some based in the industrialised countries – e.g. the Walmart retail empire – which purchase semi-processed inputs or finished goods from BRICS, along with local elites who lubricate the looting through corruption, cost overruns, and access to our cheapest electricity supplies.

Many African countries, if not all, are located at the extreme end of what Immanuel Wallerstein 30 years ago termed the core–periphery relationship, a position which impoverishes them to the advantage of rich and industrialised countries in the core. BRICS countries represent sub-imperialists trying to improve their relative location in the world system, perhaps moving toward imperialist power and thereafter even to imperialist superpower status, as the USSR once enjoyed. These countries have different levels of economic development and political influence, vested interests in the African continent and the DRC in particular, and geopolitical positions in world politics.

But they all share four characteristics. First, all the BRICS countries present important opportunities for foreign direct investment (FDI) which, drawn towards mega-developments like the Congo River Inga Hydropower Project or towards minerals and petroleum extraction, impoverish the same people that they should empower. Impoverishment occurs through dispossession of natural resources with little or no compensation, unequal shares of the costs and benefits of mega-development projects, repayments of debts incurred to build these projects, and structural exclusion from accessing the outcomes of these initiatives.

Second, BRICS countries share the same *modus operandi* at their different stages of imperialism, either as countries that have been active in Africa for a very long time (Russia and China); newly arrived (India); or traditional sub-imperialist countries (Brazil and South Africa). The pattern is similar: accumulation by dispossession is taking place through abuse of local politics, national elites, warlords, and war economies, as in the eastern side of the DRC where, between BRICS and the West as consumers of the resulting mineral outflows, six million or more deaths have been the result.

Third, BRICS countries share the same interests in Africa's natural resources, including but not limited to mining, gas, oil and mega-dam projects for water and for electricity to meet their increasing demands for cheap and abundant electricity. They are also actively involved in the search for new markets, and hence they promote construction of roads, railways, bridges, ports and other infrastructure. But this infrastructure is often indistinguishable from colonial-era projects, meant to more quickly extract primary products for the world market.

Fourth, BRICS countries have poor records of environmental regulation. There is virtually no commitment to mitigate climate change and invest in truly renewable energy, to take environmental impact assessments seriously, and to consult with and compensate adversely affected communities.

With three BRICS countries having crashed in 2013 to join the 'fragile five', and Russia crashing in March 2014 thanks to the implications of its Ukrainian political and Crimean land grab, following China's surprising trade deficit in February 2014 as many of its major industrial companies lowered their production, there is desperation in the air. The prices of important commodities such as copper and iron are falling as a result. The BRICS appear to need new market niches for trade, along with cheap energy through oil, coal and hydroelectricity, which can assist in lower-cost extraction and transportation. But each BRICS country is different.

Brazil

Brazil's approach to Africa's natural resources seems to be characterised by the rhetoric of indigenisation to advance its sub-imperialist interests and those of other imperialist powers. It uses its historical ties with people of African descent to sign lucrative contracts in the continent. In fact, Brazil has the largest population of black people in the world after Nigeria.

Brazil has interests in African mining. Vale, the world's second-largest mining corporation, has exploited coal in Mozambique since 2004. Other mining interests abound in Angola, the Democratic Republic of Congo, and South Africa. In infrastructure, Odebrecht, Brazil's biggest construction company, is building dams, houses and hospitals. There are also growing investments in oil, biofuel, diamonds and the supermarket sector. In energy, Petrobras, a state-controlled energy group, is acquiring further exploration rights and increasing production.

Brazil's imports from Africa are overrepresented by minerals and crude materials (which make up 80%) whereas Africa's imports from Brazil are diversified and include agricultural products (sugar, dairy, meat, cereals), vehicles and parts, nuclear reactors and machinery, ores and ash. Brazil's major trading partners in Africa consist of Nigeria (32%), Angola (16%), Algeria (12%), South Africa (10%), and Libya (7%). These countries make up 77% of Brazil's total trade with the continent.

BRICS scholar Oliver Stuenkel argues that Brazilian economic and commercial interests are becoming much more visible than before. Petronas is present in 28 countries, investing US$1.9 billion in coal, oil and natural gas in Nigeria in 2005. Eletrobras is planning the construction of a US$6 billion hydroelectric power plant in Mozambique, which will most likely be financed by BNDES, the Brazilian Development Bank, which provides more funds than the World Bank. Vale invested US$700 million in coal, oil and natural gas in Mozambique in 2007. Vale recently signed a US$1 billion deal to build a railway in Malawi to transport coal from Mozambique.

Russia

Russia's position in the race for natural resources of the African continent is ambiguous. This country takes advantages of its historical presence, relations, and involvement in anti-colonial wars and its failed attempts to create communist states in the continent to advance its economic and political interests. Some key Russian officials believe that they were left behind in the scramble for Africa's natural wealth. As then President Medvedev put it in 2009, 'Frankly, we were almost too late. We should have begun working with our African partners earlier.'

Russians can use the rhetoric of historical exclusion and exploitation to lobby African leaders to give them lucrative contracts in the exploitation and processing of natural resources, construction projects, and arms deals. Russia–Africa relations reached their peak in the 1960s, which incidentally coincided with the wave of independence in various countries in the continent. Russia–Africa relations then regressed significantly in 1991 when Boris Yeltsin, the first president of the Russian Federation, declared that 'Russia's policy of foreign aid would be halted and that Russia would ask African countries to repay their debts as soon as possible.' This period also coincided with the dissolution of the Soviet Union and the introduction of the market economy in Russia.

Russia–Africa relations are taking a new turn now due to Russia's search for new natural resources, and market niches for Russian goods. Russia also needs the support of developing countries to strengthen its voice in different bodies of the United Nations around pressing issues such as the Chechnya and Crimea crises, international conflicts, violations of human rights, and lack of freedom of expression of individuals who oppose or call for regime change.

The priorities of Russia for its foreign economic strategy in the region include but are not limited to the following: (1) prospecting, mining, oil, construction and mining, purchasing gas, uranium, and bauxite assets (Angola, Nigeria, Sudan, South Africa, Namibia, etc.); (2) construction of power facilities – hydroelectric power plants on the River Congo (Angola, Zambia, Namibia, and Equatorial Guinea) and nuclear power plants (South Africa and Nigeria); (3) creating a floating nuclear power plant, and South African participation in the international project to build a nuclear enrichment centre in Russia; (4) railway construction (Nigeria, Guinea, and Angola); and (5) creation of Russian trade houses for the promotion and maintenance of Russian engineering products (Nigeria and South Africa).

Prospecting and mining represent the first priorities of Russia's foreign economy policy to gain access to a source of supply of key minerals – e.g. zinc, manganese, copper, nickel, and platinum – which are essential for the functioning of a modern economy but will be depleted within the next decade or become difficult to access and costly to develop. Africa is the best destination for the new scramble because of the availability of these resources and the lower costs of exploitation. Russia also has military and arms interests in Africa. Indeed, Russia is the second largest arms exporter, which in 2011 amounted to a total value of US$66.8 billion.

Most of these activities occur through five major Russian companies, alone or in partnership with other MNCs:

- Renova Company deals recently concluded with the South African government;
- RusAl is close to purchasing the still incomplete Aluminium Smelter Company of Nigeria, Alscon;
- RusAl is to participate in the privatisation of a smelter in Tema (Ghana) that, in contrast to the projects in Nigeria and Congo, is operating and supplying primary aluminium to the American market;
- Alrosa owns 32.8% of the stock in the Katoka Mining Society, which manages an industrial complex in Angola;
- The South African Lonmin Company, the third largest platinum producer in the world, may also be of interest to Renova; and
- SUAL and the UK-based investment company Fleming Family and Partners (FF&P)'s assets are concentrated in sub-Saharan Africa (for example, tantalum production in Mozambique).

The commitment of Russia in the extraction and processing of Africa's natural resources is illustrated by four Russian companies – RusAl, Norilsk Nickel, Alrosa and Renova – which plan to invest at least US$5 billion in sub-Saharan Africa over the next five years.

India

India has had historical ties with Africa since the ninth century, more recently based on British colonialism. India has been actively involved in anti-colonial and liberation struggles as well as providing diplomatic support and solidarity to newly emerging African nations. Conversely, there have been limited trade ties as well as episodes of antagonism and neglect in Indian-African relations despite Indians' migration to Africa. Technical support established in early 1970s from India to African countries was modest.

As its economy expanded, India has extended commercial interests, exports, and cooperation beyond Eastern and Southern Africa to include many other African countries. India has trained over 1500 Africans in Indian universities. The presence of India in Africa has been led by entrepreneurs and private business interests.

Indian business interests are mainly dominated by firms such as Tata Motors, Jindal Coal, Vendata Mining (in Zambia's copper industry), Dabur, Marico, the Essar Group, Godrej, Bharti Airtel, Kirloskar, Karuturi Agro Products (in Ethiopia), and several pharmaceuticals. Currently, India is also involved in the Oil and Natural Gas Corporation (ONGC) and steel through Mittal Steel. There is also involvement by the Indian navy in the northern Indian Ocean against Somali pirates' activities. India also has interests in the mining of diamonds in Zimbabwe with an investment of US$1.2 million; and has reserves of uranium in Namibia and Malawi.

Africa supplies some 20% of India's fuel imports. Thirty per cent of India's energy is met by oil with 70% of this commodity being imported. The remaining 70% is met through domestic coal reserves. It is expected that India's demand for energy will double by 2015, pushing India to import 90% of its oil. India is therefore obliged to diversify its energy suppliers through oil exploration and production. This is undertaken by the Oil and National Gas Corporation (ONGC), which has ventured into Africa, e.g. oil exploration in Libya and Nigeria, investment in hydrocarbons in Sudan and offshore drilling in the Ivory Coast.

India's foreign policy is characterised by a readiness 'to cooperate with various international partners, without becoming too strongly bound to any particular partner or possibly entering into a relationship of dependency'. As a result, India maintains strong ties with Russia (its main supplier of weapons). India is also developing positive relations with various Asian partners, including Japan and South Korea – with whom India signed strategic partnership agreements in 2006 and 2010, respectively – as well as the resource-rich Central Asian states.

China

From the 1960s, China was involved in several liberation struggles in Africa through provision of military training and logistical support. It also provided development aid such as the Tanzania–Zambia Railway (TAZARA), which remains the crown jewel of China's assistance. With a US$412 million interest-free construction loan, the TAZARA was designed and built in the 1960s to offer an alternative to South African ports to ship minerals from Central Africa.

In addition, it served an ideological and practical role within Beijing's strategy to oppose Moscow's authority in East Africa. China's interests in Africa were renewed by its increasing need for Africa's natural resources, yet, without a doubt, African political leaders have long appreciated China's presence. Popular opinion has always remained mixed, with South Africans listing fear of China as the second most common political opinion about threats to the country, according to recent Pew surveys.

China has four main interests in Africa: (1) access to raw materials; (2) access to new markets; (3) political influence; and (4) isolation of Taiwan from African states. According to US scholar David Shinn, 'China imports about 90% of its cobalt, 35% of its manganese, 30% of its tantalum, and 5% of its hardwood timber from Africa'. In 2003 China consumed 25% of global aluminium and steel production; 32% of iron ore and coal production; and 40% of the world's cement, figures that have probably risen since. China's imports from Africa are led by Angola, the second-largest single source of Chinese oil, followed by the Sudan and Nigeria, which account for 32% of oil imports.

Similar to Western counterparts, China's economic growth goes hand-in-hand with the need for new markets to sustain its industry. China's exports to Africa have increased by a factor of nine since 2000. But some 60% of Chinese exports to Africa go to just six countries – South Africa, Egypt, Nigeria, Algeria, Morocco and Benin. The export of machinery, automobiles, and electronic products, which now account for more than half of China's exports to Africa, is also on the rise.

In exchange for these exports, China also enforces on Africa's poorest countries its 'One-China Principle' – which insists that all countries must only recognise China, and that Taiwan is part of China. Taiwan remains a thorn in China's flesh. China is consequently using its economic and geopolitical power as well as its veto rights to punish African countries which have diplomatic ties with Taiwan even though the Chinese Communist Party (CCP) tolerates trade relations with Taiwan.

China needs Africa to strengthen its political position in global affairs. It therefore has to use the expansion of economic power – through its first two interests discussed earlier – to seek support from 54 African countries, which now represent over one-quarter of the UN's 193 members in institutions such as the UN Security Council, the United Nations Human Rights Council and the World Trade Organisation (WTO), where there are unending disputes and negotiations.

South Africa
South Africa has two main interests at play in Africa. First, there is its own influence as regional hegemon and its quest for political and economic expansion. This occurs through humanitarian aid and peacekeeping missions in war-torn countries. South Africa uses these missions as stepping-stones for economic conquests of new territories and conquests of territories previously exploited directly by Western countries.

South African capitalists have advanced in Africa via mining, banking, defence, retail and tourism, many of which require a supply of cheap energy. Second, there is the intermediary or sub-imperialist roles that South Africa plays between imperialist economic and military powers, such as the United States, United Kingdom, Canada, and several others in the core, and poor and underdeveloped countries with abundant natural resources in the periphery countries including but not limited to the DRC, Mozambique, Zambia and others.

South African sub-imperialism is invading Africa through both MNC and foreign-owned MNCs with long-term bases in the country, including companies like Anglo American, De Beers and BHP Billiton which used to be domiciled in SA. There are now also black-owned and black-controlled firms such as African Rainbow Minerals, and some smaller initiatives close to the ruling party and president himself.

BRICS in Mozambique (by Bobby Peek)

In Mozambique, there is a new neo-colonial exploitation underway. It is not Europe or the United States that dominates, but rather countries which are often looked at as rivals, such as Brazil, Russia, India, China and South Africa. This is a dangerous statement to make but let us consider the facts.

South Africa has been extracting electricity from Mozambique through the Portuguese-developed Cahora Bassa Dam, which has altered permanently the flow of the Zambezi River, resulting in severe flooding on a more frequent basis over the last few years. In the 2013-14 floods, it was reported that a woman gave birth on the rooftop of a clinic. This follows a similar incident in 2000, when Rosita Pedro was born in a tree during severe flooding that year.

South Africa's failing energy utility Eskom is implicated in the further damming of the Zambezi, for it is likely to make a commitment to buy power from the proposed Mpanda Nkuwa Dam just downstream of Cahora Bassa. Most of the cheap energy generated by that dam is fed into a former South African firm, BHP Billiton, at the world's lowest price – but jobs are few and profits are repatriated to the new corporate headquarters in Melbourne, Australia.

After years of extracting onshore gas from near Vilanculos, the South African apartheid-created oil company Sasol is planning to exploit what are some of Africa's largest offshore gas fields, situated off Mozambique, in order to serve South Africa's own export-led growth strategy.

Brazilians are also in Mozambique. Sharing a common language as a result of colonial subjugation by the Portuguese, business in Mozambique is easier for the Brazilians. The result is that the Brazilian company Vale, which is the world's second-largest metals and mining company and one of the largest producers of raw materials globally, has a foothold in the Tete Province of Mozambique between Zimbabwe and Malawi. They are so sensitive about their operations there that an activist challenging Vale from Mozambique was denied entrance to Brazil last year to participate in the Rio +20 gathering. He was flown back to Mozambique and only after a global outcry was made, led by Friends of the Earth International, was he allowed to return for the gathering.

Further to this, India also has an interest in Mozambique. The Indian-based Jindal group, which comprises both mining and smelting, set their eyes on Mozambican coal in Moatize, as well as having advanced plans for a coal-fired power station in Mozambique, again to create supply for the demanding elite-driven economy of South Africa.

Russia also plays an interesting role in Mozambique. While not much is known about the Russian state and corporate involvement, following the break-up when the Soviet Union collapsed, there is a link with Russia's Eurasian Natural Resources Corporation which has non-ferrous metal operations in Mozambique. Interestingly, the Russian government has just invested R1.3 billion in Mozambique to facilitate skills development to actively exploit hydrocarbons and other natural resources, according to Russian Foreign Minister Sergei Lavrov.

So this tells a tale of one country, in which tens of billions of rands of investment by BRICS countries and companies result in the extraction of wealth. Mozambique will join the resource-cursed societies of our region, with polluted local environments, and a changed structure of people's lives, making them dependent on foreign decisions rather than their own local and national political power. This is not a random set of exploitations, but rather a well-orchestrated strategy to shift the elite development agenda away from Europe, the US and Japan, to what we now term the BRICS.

This positioning means that the BRICS' drive for economic superiority is pursued in the name of poverty alleviation. No matter how one terms the process – imperialist, sub-imperialist, post-colonial, or whatever – the reality is that these countries are challenging the power relations in the world, but sadly the model chosen to challenge this power is nothing different from the model that has resulted in mass poverty and elite wealth globally.

This is the model of extraction and extreme capital-intensive development based upon burning and exploiting carbon, and of elite accumulation through structural adjustment, also termed the Washington Consensus. The agenda of setting up the BRICS Bank is a case in point: it is opaque and not open to public scrutiny. Except for the reality as presented above, these countries are coming together with their corporate powers to decide who gets what and where in the hinterland of Africa, Latin America, Asia and the Caucasus.

It is projected that by 2050, BRICS countries will be in the top ten economies of the world, aside from South Africa. So the question has to be asked: why is South Africa in the BRICS? Simply put, the reality is that South Africa is seen as a gateway for corporations into Africa, be they energy or financial corporations. This is because of South Africa's vast footprint on the continent.

Remember Thabo Mbeki's peace missions? Well, they were not all about peace; they were about getting South African companies established in areas of unrest so that when peace happens they are there first to exploit the resources in these countries. This could potentially be a negative role if South Africa is only used as a gateway to facilitate resource extraction and exploitation of Africa by BRICS countries, as it is now used by the West. The question has to be asked by South Africans: why do we allow this? I do not have the answer.

Returning to poverty alleviation, the reality is that in the BRICS countries we have the highest gap between those who earn the most and the poor, and this gap is growing. Calling the bluff of poverty alleviation is critical. How to unpack this opaque agenda of the BRICS governments is a challenge, for while their talk is about poverty alleviation the reality is something else.

We recognise that what the BRICS are doing is nothing more than what the North has been doing to the South, but as we resist these practices from the North, we must be bold enough to resist these practices from our fellow countries in the South. Thus, critically, the challenge going forward for society is to understand the BRICS and, given how much is at stake, civil society must scrutinise the claims, the processes and the outcomes of the BRICS summit and its aftermath, and build a strong criticism of the BRICS that demands equality and not new forms of exploitation.

BRICS seen from Zimbabwe (by Farai Maguwu)

Zimbabwe's latest economic blueprint, known by its abbreviated form, Zim Asset, identifies BRICS as central to the country's economic revival. There has been an upsurge of Russian, Chinese and South African investments in Zimbabwe's extractive sector over the past decade, but mining has been characterised by environmental degradation, tax evasion, human rights abuses and exploitative labour practices. No one knows whether Zimbabwe stands to benefit from BRICS, nor does the government have clearly stated objectives or a well-defined strategy of getting the most out of BRICS. Even the much celebrated 'Look East Policy' remains more of a political slogan than a coherent strategy.

The biggest dilemma is how to turn around the extraction and externalisation of resources, and generate a patriotic path for capital accumulation arising from diamonds, platinum, gold, chrome and other minerals. In order to achieve ambitious double-digit growth targets for minerals, the Zimbabwe government claims it will establish a Sovereign Wealth Fund, attract FDI, establish special economic zones, continue using the multi-currency system, implement value-addition ('beneficiation') strategies and ensure improved electricity and water supply. This will also require the re-capitalisation of the Minerals Exploration Company, Zimbabwe Mining Development Corporation and Minerals Marketing Corporation of Zimbabwe.

BRICS investments will be needed, but the past decade has seen highly controversial precedents. BRICS corporations make up Zimbabwe's top three investors: China leads with investments of US$375 million approved by Zimbabwe Investment Authority (ZIA) in 2013, followed by Russia with approvals worth US$40 million and, third, South Africa with US$39million. Next door in Mozambique, Brazilian and Indian corporations are not far away – in Tete Province – digging coal and displacing the peasantry on a vast scale.

China

Since 2000, China has been Zimbabwe's biggest foreign investor. ZIA records show that from 2010, investments contributed 72% of total FDI, or US$670 million, from a total of US$930 million worth of projects. In 2012, China's cumulative investments in the mining sector (mostly in gold, diamonds and chrome) totalled US$583 million, or 62% of the total US$688 million FDI approvals for the entire Zimbabwean mining industry last year.

China is unapologetic about the fact that its aid and investment are not tied to political or economic conditions. Such conditions, when imposed by the US or Europe, typically mix liberal democratic provisions with structural adjustment. The latter policy was imposed on Zimbabwe, and in part accepted by President Robert Mugabe's government during most of the 1990s. They failed, as in most of Africa, but unusually, Mugabe bucked the trend of acquiescence from 1997, during a series of social uprisings, and he has since zigzagged between authoritarianism and concessions to the majority.

Like the West, China seeks Africa's natural resources but its investments are not conditional upon achievement of minimal human rights and democratic objectives. There continue to be reports of human rights abuses perpetrated by Chinese employers against their Zimbabwean employees, and the resources from China's co-owned ventures in the diamond mines are reportedly responsible for the war chest that helped Mugabe hire an Israeli firm, Nikuv, to undermine the integrity of the July 2013 elections, which he won handsomely.

China has become a major player in the country's economy through joint venture enterprises like Anjin Investments – involved with the military in the Marange diamond fields – and Sino-Zimbabwe Holdings, which previously had a concession in Marange as well. According to a recent report by Global Witness, Anjin enjoys the most lucrative diamond concessions. One gift, in exchange, was US$98 million for the construction of the army's National Defence College. Sino-Zimbabwe is now conducting chrome mining along the Great Dyke belt.

Russia

There has been a steady increase of Russian companies operating in Zimbabwe's mining sector in the past decade. The frozen relations between Zimbabwe and the West since the early 2000s gave Russia and her BRICS allies the opportunity to penetrate Zimbabwe's mining sector with ease. Although Zimbabwe derives no tangible economic benefits from its strong ties with Moscow, political and military ties between the two countries continue to grow strong.

As a symbol of Russia's growing influence in Zimbabwe, in September 2014 President Putin dispatched a high-powered delegation led by Foreign Minister Sergei Lavrov as well as the Industry Minister Denis Manturov to negotiate several deals, especially in the mining sector with Zimbabwe. The highlight of the tour was the signing of a US$4.8 billion platinum deal, with Russia promising to provide the investment funds. Russian firms Rostec and Vnesheconom Bank are part of a clandestine consortium that involves Russia's defence industries. Rostec is Russia's biggest arms manufacturer, comprising 663 entities that form 13 companies, of which eight operate in the military-industrial complex while Vnesheconom Bank is tasked with financing the deal.

The deal, which stands out as the largest single foreign investment Zimbabwe has had in over a decade, followed a visit to Russia by Zimbabwe's Finance and Economic Development Minister Patrick Chinamasa and Mines and Mining Development Minister Walter Chidhakwa in July 2014. The platinum deal was hailed by both Mugabe and the visiting Russian ministers as a key driver in Zimbabwe's economic recovery. However, it turned out the deal is nothing more than a military relationship whose benefits will entirely accrue to the army. The Zimbabwean government is represented in the deal by Pen East Mining Company, believed to be a subsidiary of Zimbabwe Defence Industries, which falls under the Ministry of Defence. The Ministry of Mines appears to have little control over the deal. Given that Rostec is into arms manufacturing and given the EU arms ban on Zimbabwe, it is apparent that the Darwendale platinum deal is a barter trade to enable the Zimbabwe National Army to acquire military hardware in exchange for platinum.

This means that while Russia will derive massive economic benefits from the deal, it will in turn offer Zimbabwe weapons of repression. Zimbabwe has not had war with its neighbours since independence in 1980, except for a brief intervention to assist the Mozambican government against Renamo rebels in the late 1980s. On the contrary, Zimbabwe is having serious internal threats to human security in the form of hunger, disease, climate change and joblessness. These challenges cannot be defeated by military hardware but rather by sound, consistent and people-centred policies. Instead of allowing Zimbabwe's mineral wealth to contribute to economic recovery for the overall welfare of its people, Russia is ensuring the country remains poor and oppressed by strengthening the military. The Darwendale platinum deposit has been estimated at 40 million ounces of Platinum Group Metals and is among the world's largest PGM deposits.

Another Russian company, DTZ-OZGEO (Private) Limited, is jointly owned by the Development Trust of Zimbabwe (DTZ) and a Russian company, Econedra Limited. This company is involved in gold and diamond mining in Penhalonga and Chimanimani respectively and holds several claims all over Zimbabwe in places such as Shurugwi and the Bvumba. However, DTZ-OZGEO has performed poorly in terms of transparency, environmental management and corporate social responsibility. Mugabe expressed disappointment with the secretive nature of DTZ-OZGEO operations during the ZANU-PF People's Conference held in Mutare in December 2010 and during a meeting with traditional chiefs in Manicaland in 2011. As he bitterly put it,

The company [Development Trust of Zimbabwe], having joined hands with the Russians, approached us saying they wanted to mine gold in Mutare and we gave them the go-ahead. They later moved to Chimanimani. We were told that DTZ and their Russian counterparts are mining gold in Chimanimani and now it is diamonds. We have not realised any real revenue coming from them and they are saying they are having some difficulties. I talked to some of the directors during our December People's Conference here in Mutare and I told them that they were remaining too much in isolation and why don't they become transparent. We will pursue the matter because we want to know what they are doing. We want our people, especially our children, to benefit through this company.

However, three years later DTZ-OZGEO continues with its opaque operations amidst massive environmental degradation. Penhalonga residents are up in arms with the company for destroying the course of the Mutare River. Since commencement of its operations about a decade ago, DTZ-OZGEO has been panning for gold on the banks. For a stretch of over three kilometres, the Mutare River has been reduced to a canal while vegetation on either side of the river has disappeared. Water in the river has become perennially muddy due to panning. Yet the Mutare River is a major source of drinking water for humans, livestock and wild animals further downstream.

In August 2013 the company was temporarily stopped from its environmentally unfriendly mining activities but later resumed operations, doing exactly the same things they had been fined for. DTZ-OZGEO co-director, Ismail Shillaev, speaking during a media tour for journalists from Mutare on 24 June 2011, could not convincingly explain their operations, insisting that they sell their gold to Fidelity Printers. When asked to explain the actual quantities they were getting on a daily basis, he remained silent. Shillaev said they were involved in community development work when approached by local authorities like the Mutasa Rural District Council. He said they had rehabilitated some of the roads in the district, but most roads remain impassable.

A 2013 visit to Tsvingwe Primary School exposed a distinct lack of corporate social responsibility: children were learning in the open even during the dead of winter due to a shortage of classroom blocks. Tsvingwe Primary School is situated about a kilometre from the DTZ operations. Authorities at the school also expressed their disappointment with DTZ-OZGEO, adding that most of their pupils' parents worked for the company. The pupils are also exposed to new environmental hazards such as the increasing occurrence of dust in the air, the disappearance of vegetation and impassable roads due to DTZ-OZGEO's operations. The smash and grab operations of DTZ-OZGEO, coupled with the failure by the company even to construct houses for its employees, reveal a company that has no long-term plans for the community.

South Africa
Due to its proximity to Zimbabwe and close political relations over the past century, many South African companies have invested in Zimbabwe's mining sector. The major players have been De Beers, Gold Fields, Implats, Aquarius Platinum and Anglo American plc. Anglo American and its subsidiary companies have invested in Zimbabwe for 60 years.

While De Beers was fingered in murky underhand dealings in Marange from 1965 to 2006, most South African investors have performed more reasonably in terms of safety, health and environment and literacy levels of employees. Indeed, many researchers remark that South African companies in the platinum sector in Zimbabwe offer higher standards than in their parent companies back home.

Nevertheless the dominance of South African companies in Zimbabwe's platinum sector, especially Implats/Zimplats, reflects South African economic hegemony in Zimbabwe. Until a recent ban on the export of raw platinum, Zimbabwe exported raw ore to South Africa where it was refined. This means South Africa has always had the lion's share of Zimbabwe's platinum by value, and helps explain why SA companies dominate mining.

India

India's investments in Zimbabwe's mining sector have enormous potential, but so far have been hindered by politics. Essar, an Indian global company, emerged as the preferred bidder for Zimbabwe Iron and Steel Company (ZISCO) in 2011 after an international tender had been issued by government. It set up New Zim Steel to revive the steel-making capacity at the currently non-functional ZISCO plant and New Zim Minerals, which would explore beneficiation of iron ore that is owned by ZISCO Steel and create value so that the country becomes a world leader in beneficiated iron ore.

Two years on, operations have not started due to myriad challenges, chief of which is the rights to an estimated US$60 billion worth of iron ore reserves in Chivhu. Essar's Resident Director for Africa, Middle East and Turkey, Firdhose Coovadia, admits, 'Yes there are challenges, in our particular case bear in mind we are dealing with a national asset, it's an emotive asset.'

Another company, India's state-owned National Mineral Development Corporation (NMDC), is reported to have signed a Memorandum of Understanding with a Zimbabwean company, Mosi-oa-Tunya Development Company (MtDC). The MoU paves the way for the formation of a 50/50 joint venture company that will undertake diamond, gold, chrome and iron-ore exploration and mining in Zimbabwe. NMDC, listed on the Bombay Stock Exchange (BSE), is India's largest iron-ore producer. The Mosi-oa-Tunya Development Company is reported to be a special-purpose vehicle under the administrative control of Walter Mzembi's Tourism ministry. It is perplexing why a parastatal under the Ministry of Tourism is signing MoUs for mining deals when this is the prerogative of the Zimbabwe Mining Development Corporation. This is the sort of shady dealing which greatly undermines the long-term investment potential of relationships with BRICS corporations and countries. There is a need to clearly define the functions of all ministries and departments to avoid confusion and corruption in the operations of government.

Brazil

Although not active in Zimbabwe in any major mining investments, just over the eastern border, the Brazilian mining company Vale has a large coal project whose operations have raised serious concern among the affected communities. The company displaced over 700 Mozambican families in Cateme, who are now being controlled by the police after violent repression occurred at a community protest in 2012.

Angered by Vale's failure to keep the promises made before the relocation in 2009, and the lacklustre response by the national and provincial government to their problems, over 700 families living in Cateme gave the company and authorities an ultimatum in December 2011 for them to address their demands by 10 January the following year. Otherwise, they warned that they would mobilise.

On the eve of 10 January, over 600 people blocked the rails and roads of the area. Police responded by violently suppressing the demonstration, resulting in several injuries. In addition, 14 people were arrested, according to the Maputo environmental-justice NGO Justiça Ambiental, and several were tortured while in prison.

Today these Vale victims live without basic services, according to activist Jeremias Vunjanhe, of Justiça Ambiental /Friends of the Earth Mozambique in an interview with Real World Radio. Human Rights Watch noted that 'in many cases the people lost the ability to grow food and ended up relying on the foreign coal companies for handouts'.

Vale is the world's largest producer of iron ore and pellets, a key raw material for the iron and steel industry, and the second largest producer of nickel. Since 2007, the company has owned the concession of a coal extraction project in Moatize, an area considered to be one of the world's largest reservoirs of coal. The project has been severely criticised by some national groups, among other things because 1300 families had to be displaced. In addition to the Cateme relocation centre, the September 25th Centre is home to 500 families.

Vunjane told Real World Radio that Cateme inhabitants lack access to water, to land for agriculture and to transportation to get medical attention. The issue of transportation is extremely urgent as residents regularly need to be transported to the provincial hospital in Vila de Moatize, 40 kilometres away. Cateme's Health Centre can only meet some basic needs.

The population of this area understands that the relocation process was ill-managed and they complain about Vale's broken promises, among them the promise to maintain their homes for the first five years of the project. They also demand the establishment of a water channel system that can ensure access to tapped water. Also, the Brazilian company had promised to give each affected family two hectares of land for agriculture, but the promise has been broken.

BRICS development banking in Africa (by Richard Kamidza and Patrick Bond) Although there are many active development finance institutions associated with BRICS across Africa, and even more suppliers of trade finance and other forms of credit, it is useful to focus on at least one relatively organic institution – the Development Bank of Southern Africa (DBSA) based in Midrand between Johannesburg and Pretoria – for revealing insights into how the corporates might anticipate the availability of financial back-up. The DBSA is wholly owned by the South African government, and is accountable to its board. It is constitutionally mandated to provide financial, technical and other assistance in support of social and economic infrastructure investment inside South Africa as well as in other Southern African Development Community (SADC) countries.

This mandate is carried out by the Bank's International Division, which in 2013 received a R7.9 billion (then nearly US$900 million) capital boost from government, followed in 2014 by another R15.2 billion (then US$1.45 billion). The Bank's level of funding has been increasing annually, although because the rand crashes regularly (at least seven times since 1994 by 15% or more), this may not translate into overall dollar growth. In rand terms, the allocations to the region rose substantially in 2011/12 (to R3.8 billion) and 2012/13 (to R5.6 billion), with a focus on energy and transport. One of its largest loans was announced in mid-2014: US$460 million to the Zimbabwe National Railways for track and vehicle rehabilitation (the inability of the Zimbabwe government to service any of its existing stock of US$11 billion of outstanding foreign debt was not remarked upon).

DBSA funding is mainly directed to strategic projects such as Kinshasa's N'djili National Airport (DRC), the Maseru public hospital and Lesotho Highlands Water Project (Lesotho), the Mozal Aluminium Smelter Plant (Mozambique); the Ohorongo Cement Plant (Namibia); Lunsemfwa Independent Power Producers and Kariba North Bank Hydro Power Extension Project on the Zambezi River (Zambia); and the Beitbridge-Harare-Chirundu road (Zimbabwe).

The DBSA works closely with major corporations in several sites. In Mozambique, it is co-financing the Mozal aluminium smelter and synthetic-fuels giant Sasol's gasfields and processing facilities.

In Tanzania, the DBSA is negotiating future projects, especially the Kilwa energy project and similar projects, valued at US$227 million and US$280 million, respectively. In Angola, the DBSA has been increasing funding in the energy, water, roads and drainage, communications, tourism, social infrastructure and sanitation sectors, and rehabilitating civil war-related infrastructure, and has put US$150 million into the Banco BAI financial services and US$80 million into housing projects. The DBSA is also financing part of the country's increase in electricity-generating capacity from the present 1 200 MW to 8 400 MW by 2025.

In Lesotho, the DBSA disbursed about R740 million to Tsepong, a public–private partnership (PPP) consortium led by South African private hospital and healthcare group Netcare, to construct, upgrade and operate a new public hospital at Botshabelo in Maseru. Netcare, a South African company, led the consortium; in Zimbabwe, the share Netcare held of a similar project was 30%, with 70% reserved for the state-owned enterprise.

A bias to privatisation appears to be growing. In Zambia, the DBSA provided a loan of US$262 million to the Zambian Road Development Fund Agency for the rehabilitation of five priority roads, three of which form part of the Trans African Highways route running from Cape Town to the DRC's Katanga Province and onwards to Kinshasa. DBSA financed the PPP Kasumbalesa Border Post between the DRC and Zambia, which was meant to reduce costly delays of overland freight traffic, but which suffered debilitating implementation crises.

Similar PPP financing of R1.4 billion was provided to Infralink Pty Ltd – a joint venture between the Zimbabwe National Road Administration and Group Five Limited of South Africa – to rehabilitate roads and implement tolling of existing national routes, covering 801.5 kilometres on an east-west axis from Plumtree through Bulawayo to Harare and then Mutare.

Critiques of the DBSA relate partly to its facilitation of corporate takeover of infrastructure. In addition, because of the small portion of funding going to the region compared to South Africa, there is a perception that the bank is only regional in name. In 2012, around 14% of its assets were in the region outside South Africa, with future SADC lending anticipated at US$2.3 billion.

That perception is also restated in South Africa's own National Development Plan: 'SA is critically under-represented in organisations like the African Development Bank and SADC. The latter is critical as South Africa is a major funder of the group ... To fulfil South Africa's obligations in the BRICS and in the region, the DBSA should be strengthened institutionally.'

But did the DBSA deserve the R7.9 billion in new funding in 2013? This was a well-grounded complaint by SADC deputy executive secretary João Samuel Caholo less than a year before: 'There is resentment towards the DBSA in certain quarters because it is in South Africa, and South Africa is the only shareholder. SADC has no say in what the DBSA does and although the bank does work on a bilateral level with SADC countries, we need our own bank ... The name of the DBSA is misleading, as it was established by the apartheid government that saw Southern Africa as consisting of apartheid South Africa and the former homelands.' After leaving his job, Caholo renewed his criticism in October 2013, arguing that the DBSA 'only exists in name', while in contrast, 'A regional bank is supposed to have regional representation of all SADC member states, or at least the participating members in the governance structure. This is still not the case for DBSA.'

Just as it was deployed to become Pretoria's core representative as the BRICS Bank was being conceptualised, the DBSA fell into disrepute within South Africa for recording R430 million in net losses in 2011–12, based on (unspecified) investments. In late 2012, the new DBSA CEO, Patrick Dlamini, announced a 'new restructuring process, staff would be retrenched [from 750 to 300] and corruption would not be tolerated. We can no longer allow the DBSA to be associated with shoddy work.' Dlamini's prior job was as an executive with the Air Traffic and Navigation Services company, and he had no prior development finance experience.

In late 2013, the complaints and confessions were the same. In the *Sunday Times*, Chris Barron interviewed Dlamini: 'We have huge room for improvement. Our job is to fund infrastructure development at municipal level, but if you look at this space you see a serious collapse of infrastructure.' His own infrastructure had also collapsed, for Barron's sources noted 'the departure of staff members with valuable information technology, project management and other skills ... [who] have been snapped up by the big commercial banks, which will be competing with the DBSA to provide infrastructure funding.' As Barron noted, 'Hard-earned taxpayers' money was invested in Sol Kerzner's One&Only hotel ... It lost a fortune on five-star luxury hotels, platinum jewellery and other such projects instead of investing it in boring things like water-treatment plants, roads, schools and hospitals.' The loan and investment amounted to nearly R3.2 billion, or 7% of the portfolio.

Yet in addition to managers of inappropriate investments, the entire social and environmental division was dismissed, including leadership of an important Green fund to promote employment. Moreover, as Carol Paton of *Business Day* remarked in 2013, 'When it comes to project work, the bank will be in the same position as most state departments: it will need to put out to tender. There is also another problem. The business model of the bank remains tenuous ... it does not take deposits and so does not have a source of cheap money, the capital injection provided for in this year's budget being a rare event.'

The man tasked with ensuring the revitalisation of the DBSA in the region was Moe Shaik, who trained as an optometrist but became the leading spy in the Zuma government prior to numerous internal crises in the National Intelligence Agency. One problem was his revelation of important and highly embarrassing political secrets to US embassy officials, which in turn were published by WikiLeaks. Shaik's forced resignation from the security services in 2012 was followed by a brief Harvard executive course, after which he was controversially appointed the DBSA's main liaison to the region.

The overall impression left by the DBSA is that it is blatantly ecologically destructive, privatisation-oriented, hostile to social concerns, and incompetent. These problems should logically disqualify the DBSA from being a core contributor to the BRICS New Development Bank, as is often proposed by leading South African officials, who until mid-2014 even anticipated a potential hosting role.

Conclusion

In short, it is obvious that corporations from the BRICS countries have intensified extractivism in Mozambique, Zimbabwe and other sites in Africa, at a time when the continent's wealth is being rapidly evacuated, in large part due to corporate malpractices. These include tax evasion, transfer mispricing and outright theft of minerals. BRICS elites – both country leaders and corporations – are not allies of ordinary Africans, but rather are pursuing their own agendas. Without a clear strategy of maximising gains and minimising losses, Africa is likely to come out of the BRICS engagement worse off, having lost its valuable assets, seeing the environment destroyed, witnessing debilitating political corrosion, and with a much poorer population.

8

The story of the hunter or the hunted?
Brazil's role in Angola and Mozambique

ANA GARCIA AND KARINA KATO

As long as we are hostages of the story told by the hunters who go hunting and tell us 'Today, I have killed a lion' and do not have the opportunity to listen to the animals' story ..., we will sing the hunter's song ... The hunter here is the mega-project, the great entrepreneurships. So we will wait for the day in which the animals will have the opportunity to tell their own version of the story.[1]

Portuguese-speaking African countries gained unprecedented relevance for Brazilian foreign policy since the early 2000s with the new government of Luis Inácio Lula da Silva (President Lula). His foreign policy agenda was focused on 'South–South Cooperation', including an economic project that articulated the interests of great business groups with policy interests in these countries. Some examples include the initiatives called 'cooperation for development' and the National Bank for Economic and Social Development (BNDES) credit policy. The trinity 'cooperation-investment-financing' expresses to some extent Brazil's own domestic development model based on mega-projects in the areas of oil and gas, mining, infrastructure and agribusiness. This chapter provides a preliminary study, mapping Brazil's incursion in Angola and Mozambique in terms of financing, investment and cooperation. We will focus on three main themes: the identification of the prioritised sector and the institutional arrangements which support them; the state's differentiated role in both countries and the ambiguous (and very often conflicting) relationship between the Brazilian projects and the actors involved; and the new forms of 'South–South indebtedness' that resulted from these transactions and their potential consequences.

The relationships between Brazil and Africa have been studied under different perspectives in areas such as history, culture, ethnicity and language. Our approach will focus on political-economic relations (commercial, finance and business) since 2003. Under Lula da Silva's government, Portuguese-speaking African countries gained unprecedented relevance as a result of interest by multinational corporations with headquarters in Brazil, especially construction, oil and gas, and mining companies.[2] This expansion enjoyed strong political support resulting in the concomitant increase of direct export credit policies and the financing of Brazilian business projects in Africa. Seen not from an isolated but from a mutually related perspective, 'cooperation for development' has direct consequences for new political–business relations. There has emerged a complex field of dispute between political and business interests. In our viewpoint, such recent advances made by Brazil towards Africa can be represented by the trinity of 'investment-cooperation-financing'. Each has distinct characteristics and dynamics, but all of them are articulated by the same political and economic project. This is the core of the contemporary relations between Brazil and Africa, particularly in the Portuguese-speaking countries.

In general, we can point out two main approaches to rebuild and value Brazil's role in Africa. The first one we call 'hegemonic vision',[3] which focuses on the image of Brazil as a 'partner' that establishes horizontal relations with its African counterparts. Celso Amorim's (2011) statement is quite a good example of Brazil's projected image as a model to be followed by African countries. It says that 'for each African problem there [would be] a Brazilian solution'. This viewpoint is also shared by some multilateral financial organisations, such as the World Bank which, together with the Institute of Applied Economic Research (IPEA), claims that 'the new Africa coincides with global Brazil' (IPEA and World Bank 2011:3).

On the other hand, there are some more critical voices of the performance of the 'emerging countries' (mainly China and also Brazil) under a neo-colonialist viewpoint which sees the African continent as a new field of dispute between the traditional and the new, emerging powers over African natural resources and markets.[4] In spite of good intentions, both visions tend to victimise African countries and their governments and underestimate their capacity for action. They usually rebuild the Brazilian presence in Africa from a Brazilian perspective and, though coming to interesting and important conclusions, they end up oversimplifying the established relations in these interactions.

We think that both viewpoints have a common element: the use of 'lenses' from outside the local reality. In this chapter, we make a preliminary attempt to go beyond these approaches. Our starting point was the recognition that, first of all, we need to listen to local actors. Based on their distinct perceptions, we can reconstruct the way the Brazilian presence in Angola and Mozambique is expressed. We interviewed a wide range of governmental actors, scholars, and representatives of private companies, social organisations, trade unions and international bodies. From different areas and opinions, we aimed to identify their insights about the incursion of Brazil into their countries.

Some of the results are briefly reviewed in this chapter, which is organised into three topics: (a) we attempt to identify the main advances towards the Brazilian incursion in Angola and Mozambique, the network of actors and the institutional arrangements involved in it; (b) we aim to reflect upon the state's differentiated role in both countries and the ambiguous, sometimes conflicting, relations established between the Brazilian projects and actors involved; and (c) finally, we problematise new forms of 'South–South indebtedness' and the potential consequences for the country's development. Our investigation points to the need for building instruments for participation and democratisation – and the strengthening of counter-hegemonic projects involving these distinct countries – in order to promote the effective development of Brazilian and African societies. From our perspective, this is a challenge to be faced if we intend to advance towards the strengthening of the South–South cooperation as a project of integration based on solidarity and the promotion of integral development, as announced in the official discourses.

Brazil's political-economic relations in Angola and Mozambique

The most remarkable aspect of the Brazilian presence in Angola and Mozambique is related to the actions of the Brazilian construction companies and extractive industry. Angola leads as the main destination of Brazilian private investment and Odebrecht is the company most mentioned in the interviews. Besides construction, Odebrecht's operation in Angola includes, for example, sanitation services and garbage collection, agricultural production (Capanda Agro-industrial Center–PAC), diamond mining and supermarket management. The company is also notorious for its advertising signs in the streets of Luanda and its entrepreneurial and social accountability actions. Due to its strong presence in several economic sectors and the bonds established with the higher circles of the Angolan political powers, as stated by many interviewees, Odebrecht today is 'almost Angolan'. According to an interviewee, 'the company has already had a consolidated position in the country'[5] and has established direct and solid

119

relations with the Angolan government, most of them without the intermediation of the Brazilian government.

However, the company's arrival in Angola in 1984 was directly associated with the Brazilian government's actions. At the time, the recognition of Angola's independence by the Brazilian government[6] was important to facilitate the company's operation. This is remembered today by the interviewees as a differentiated trace of Brazil's actions in the country, strengthening the bonds between both countries. Brazil also opened a line of credit (US$1.5 billion) for the construction of a hydroelectric plant in Capanda, Malange.[7] With the end of the civil war (1979–2002), Odebrecht's political and economic power in the country was consolidated.[8] The interviewees emphasised the political relevance of the Capanda project for the legitimation of the new government of the Popular Movement for the Liberation of Angola (MPLA). The work started in 1987 and was only concluded in 2004 with the concession of a new Brazilian line of credit, totalling US$580 million from 2005 to 2007. The political relevance of the project seems to overcome its functionality as many interviewees considered the Capanda project a huge 'white elephant' with little social use.[9]

This project became the main vector of Brazilian expansion in the country. In 2008, the Angolan government announced the construction of the Capanda agro-industrial complex in Malange. The complex has 411 000 acres (of which 279 000 were usable); these are meant to host industry, large agricultural and animal farms and small family farms. Odebrecht took part in building the complex in two forms: through partnerships with the Society for the Development of the Capanda Agro-industrial Complex (Sodepac), and the Angola Bioenergy Company (Biocom). The latter will produce ethanol and electricity and will be located in the agro-industrial complex (with grinding capacity of 2 million tonnes of sugar cane per year).

In relation to accountability, the interviews revealed the lack of transparency regarding public contracts entered into by these companies and the national government. In particular, they unveiled the fragility of the bidding processes for public works. Political-business networks with little transparency are the main forms of doing business and signing contracts in Angola and the key factor considered in official decision-making processes. At the same time, the lack of transparency was also associated with the unreliable quality of the services rendered by Odebrecht. According to one local observer, 'There is a road here – Senador Camara and Samba too – which has been rebuilt for the umpteenth time … it's astonishing.'[10]

In Mozambique, the main mark of Brazil's presence is Vale, which has operated in the country since 2004. The Moatize mine opened the doors to the mining company. Vale brought to the country the major Brazilian construction companies Odebrecht, Camargo Corrêa and Andrade Gutierrez. Initially, the project centred on coal mining in Moatize, Tete, with exports through the Beira port. The Moatize mine has already gone through expansions and Vale is also involved in the construction of the Nacala Corridor in the area. The huge project involves the duplication of the railroad to allow iron ore exports through the Nacala port in Nampula and aims at the consolidation of a privileged logistical corridor to African countries and Asia through the Indian Ocean.[11]

Moreover, Vale also has the control of the country's biggest railways owned by the Nacala Integrated Logistics Corridor, a partnership between Vale (80%) and Railroads of Mozambique (20%). The company has already invested around US$1.9 billion in the mining and port complex.[12] Vale investments in the region are backed by the Brazilian cooperation agencies for agriculture, particularly the Program of Triangular Co-operation for Agricultural Development of the Tropical Savannahs of Mozambique (ProSavana). As an interviewee remarked, 'Nacala is the booster of Brazilian agribusiness' internationalisation.'[13]

As opposed to evaluations of Odebrecht's operation in Angola, the Mozambican interviewees revealed that initial expectations of job creation and local development stemming from Vale's operations did not occur. This can be explained by the low capacity of the Mozambican government to negotiate and inspect the actions of a company with the economic power of Vale. As one informant argued, 'the government was taken by surprise by the dynamics and the new projects the company was bringing to the city.'[14] In addition, also contrary to Odebrecht, Vale did not foster social and entrepreneurial accountability, did little advertising and did not assess the qualifications of local workers for its projects. Only recently, after a great deal of negotiation with the Mozambican government, the company was obliged to contribute to a Tete training centre in partnership with Odebrecht and Keltz.

Although in operation more recently than Odebrecht, Vale does not depend on the intermediation of the Brazilian government to promote investments in Mozambique either. The mining company has full access and great bargaining power to negotiate with the government and impose its interests. Facing a population less experienced in formal work, Vale's arrival in Tete has been followed by allegations such as excessive hiring of outside workers (either from other regions of the country or other African countries) and discriminating against local workers in favour of Brazilians. This allegation deepened the company's conflicts with both workers and local communities.

As for aid-financed cooperation initiatives, interviewees pointed to the training of the African workforce (teachers, students and other technical staff) as a remarkable dimension of the Brazilians' contribution. These are accomplished by means of partnerships involving the Brazilian Federal Agency for Support and Evaluation of Graduate Education (CAPES), the National Council for Scientific and Technological Development (CNPQ), the National Industrial Training Service (SENAI), universities, companies and others. In strict collaboration with private actors, the SENAI workforce training centres for the construction industry were most impressive. Although recognising the Brazilians' potential control of their intellectual property, most of the interviewees considered the cooperation both relevant and positive. In Angola, it is worth stressing that the technical training programmes of the Sociedade Naçional de Combustíveis de Angola (Sonangol) has agreements with the Brazilian universities to train its workforce.[15]

With respect to wider technical cooperation, Mozambique is the main target of Brazilian aid (MRE 2010). Between 2010 and 2013, Brazilian cooperation in this country exceeded US$70 million with a focus on the agricultural sector (Chichava 2011). This cooperation involves complex institutional arrangements, including the participation of the Japanese International Cooperation Agency (JICA), the Institute of Agricultural Research of Mozambique (IIAM), the United States Agency for International Development (USAID), the Ministry of Agriculture of Mozambique, the Brazilian Cooperation Agency (ABC), the Brazilian Enterprise for Agricultural Research (Embrapa), the Ministry of Agricultural Development (MDA) and the Food and Agriculture Organisation of the United Nations (FAO). An important dimension of this area is the remodelling of the agricultural and animal research institutions of both countries after Embrapa, a triangular cooperation programme with USAID.

Among the projects, ProSavana stands out most as advancing and increasing the Brazilian agribusiness producers' operations, most of them from the Centre-West, in Mozambique. ProSavana has three components: (a) the improvement of research capacity and technology transfer for agricultural development; (b) the implementation of pilot projects in commercial and family agriculture; and (c) the elaboration of a master plan integrated to agricultural development for the Nacala corridor. Therefore, the Nacala logistical corridor, which also involves Vale, is directly linked to Brazilian cooperation on agriculture.

According to Embrapa, ProSavana aims to incorporate the family farming sector. Embrapa's representative says they will bring to the African savannah Brazilian experience promoting family farms in the South and Centre-West regions. The idea is to promote family farm units on 'the fringes' of the soya export agribusiness chain.[16] However, this is rather small if we consider the whole dimension of the project (in particular if we consider the financial dimension). The region of Nacala is mostly composed of subsistence farmers (80%) involved in very traditional agriculture (*machamba*, in Mozambican Portuguese).

As will be clear, though, the analysis of all these projects and the understanding of their articulations and complex institutional architectures are constrained by the lack of official information in Mozambique. Information available is confused, fragmented and often contradictory. In the opinion of members of the National Union of Peasants (UNAC) of Mozambique, Brazilian involvement in agriculture and rural development encompasses a complex game of interests. They are far from being 'disinterested' or horizontal, as claimed in the official discourses of Brazil's South–South cooperation. The programmes of food security and support to family farming, promoted by the joint cooperation between the MDA and FAO, are very important to rural development and to those working on Mozambican lands. They cannot be seen separately from the large-scale agricultural projects run by Embrapa in cooperation with JICA and the Mozambican government. According to UNAC, cooperation programmes such as the Food Acquisition Programme (PAA) would be the 'good side of the cooperation' though much smaller than the other projects (which would embody the negative side of the cooperation) such as the ProSavana. The Brazilian cooperation evidences traces of a 'new colonialism' by transposing its experience, institutions and public policy instruments to Africa.[17]

The role of the state in conflicts involving Brazilian companies

Angola and Mozambique are two very different countries in spite of some common elements. They experienced Portuguese colonisation, late independence struggles, prolonged civil wars and attempts to build the state under a Soviet socialist model. Colonisation and armed conflicts have left significant marks at the economic, political, social and cultural levels in both countries.

At an economic level, the Portuguese influence is expressed in the still strong power of Portuguese groups and products in the economy,[18] particularly in Angola with the increasing role of the Angolan political elite in Portuguese companies (Santos 2013). At a political level, the ties are visible in a small number of social organisations which are not part of the government circle, and are in a difficult position, having informed popular participation in public decisions and because of the obstacles posed to those who have critical opinions about the government's actions. During the colonial regime, Portugal did not allow independent political activity or organised initiatives such as unions, student and ethnic groups, regional associations or political parties as they were seen as potential destabilisers of power and were thus systematically repressed. On the other hand, the war against the colony, and later on years of civil war, left a feeling of aversion to conflicts which, in the opinion of most interviewees, led to avoidance of confrontation and the promotion of public debates and discussions. All the interviewees questioned the possibility of constructing democratic processes even though the country can now rely on formal institutions, such as elections, parties and a parliament.

However, both countries reveal fundamental differences. One of the most relevant is the way the state intervenes in the economy to organise and plan the economic processes and development. In Angola, we experienced an ever-present and highly bureaucratic state which is the main employer in the country, mainly in the oil sector and the swollen bureaucracy. The state is in charge of the enforcement and control of the streets, the investment management (with control over the companies established in the country and the selection of the priority sectors for investment), and is at the centre of civil society (through community-based organisations affiliated to the party in government, for women, the young and rural people). In many cases, the government is represented at company boards which, according to the interviewees, equates to the possibility of receiving 'commissions' or bribes in each accomplished, authorised or rendered investment. [19] The interviewees also confirmed the impression that the Angolan government is highly capable of intervening and organising the economy in spite of its low level of transparency and social participation in decision-making processes.

In Mozambique, the interviews revealed the ambiguous role of the state. On the one hand, the interviewees stressed its capacity for coercion, repressive actions against protests and uprisings of the population and workers, and control over civil society's critical stances. [20] Nevertheless, many relativised the state's power to lead the ongoing economic process in the country and negotiate and impose conditions on foreign investments. As a hostage of public debt, the Mozambican state was repeatedly associated with a so-called 'incapacity' to attract, control and monitor investments in its territory, particularly concerning labour and environmental issues and community rights. The result of the equation is a state with a seemingly relative fragility in the face of huge multinational corporations and the required flow of resources from cooperation and donations to have the national accounts settled, but present enough in the control of society, communities and workers. This fragility is highlighted by the recent discoveries of mineral resources in its territory, which cannot rely on a bureaucratic and qualified body for their management and control.

This fragility was also mentioned in the interviews, particularly the inability to negotiate and impose conditions on the company. The interviewees talked about labour conflicts concerning safe working conditions and huge pay gaps between national and foreign workers performing the same function.[21] In turn, the resettlements promoted by the company brought many problems and revealed the incapacity of the local and national governments to deal with the situation. In the resettlement '25 de Setembro',[22] residents reported several problems, such as the lack of clear information, compliance with the agreements and understanding of the local culture at the time of the establishment of the settlement projects. Moreover, families were settled in areas where they could not work on traditional crops (*machambas*), had little access to water provision and were very far from the urban centres and districts.[23]

The interviewees also stressed the importance of the government in 'minimising' the conflicts with the mining company: 'There have been many strikes because of wage inequality. Odebrecht and Vale have had police intervention in the past years. The Ministry sends the National Police to calm the situation ... The Ministry has, as its working area, to assist the companies, act to reduce labour conflicts. They listen to the company ... then we pass the company's proposal to the employees.'[24] Because of these events, a representative of the central government in Maputo pointed out the role of the company in the increase of conflicts between the population and the Mozambique Liberation Front (FRELIMO). She said: 'Vale created the conditions for the people to be against their government.'[25]

In contrast, given its huge reserves of mineral resources, mainly oil, Angola has presented impressive economic growth in the last few years in spite of consolidating a society with great economic and social inequality. In the capital, 'two Luandas' overlap: on the one hand, extreme poverty and the lack of access to public services and basic human rights; on the other hand, a small national (and international) elite with investment flows in the global market and consumer and lifestyle profiles similar to that of the main global elites. Therefore, there is the oil Luanda and the Angola Luanda.

The informal market dominates in the country and around 70–80% of the population work informally, with major participation by women who are the heads of their households (Jose 2013). National industry has little diversity, and almost all the consumer goods are imported, from food to bricks, even others with more added value, such as electronics and perfume. Moreover, there are poor systems of education, health, transport, safety and infrastructure as a result of over 20 years of civil war. In the capital Luanda, wealthy areas are crossed by streets and alleys with open sewers and there are daily power cuts, forcing the wealthier families to have private power generators. The buses and *'candogueiros'* (public transportation provided by vans) serve the poorest sectors of the population; they share the capital's chaotic streets with the luxury cars of rich families who have increasingly been living in closed condominiums. In the peripheral areas of the city and in the interior of the country, the situation is even more precarious due to the effects of the civil war and the consequent destruction of the infrastructure.

Mozambique, meanwhile, has been, during the last few years, the target of multilateral financial institutions, such as the International Monetary Fund (IMF) and the World Bank, to implement their liberal economic reforms. After independence and a 16-year civil war, the Mozambican state aims to grow the economy by increasing foreign investments through a development standard based on the export of primary goods, mainly minerals, the import of high value-added goods, and low diversification of the national industry. It is worth pointing out the great dependence on foreign aid to balance the budget. Its infrastructure is better than Luanda's. In Maputo there are more paved streets and basic sanitation and the supply services for power, water and internet are much better structured. The services available to Maputo's population and visitors are also more sophisticated and the city is not as expensive as Luanda.

In both countries, mainly in Angola which intends to become a regional power and leader (rivalling South Africa), the main question for the interviewees was the means available for economic diversification and sustaining economic development. In both contexts, foreign aid and technology transfer by cooperation and foreign investment policies are considered necessary but not sufficient to attain the longed-for 'modernisation leap'. Also, environmental issues were not visible as in the Western countries and its discussion has been overshadowed by the concerns about food security and industrial development.

New forms of South–South indebtedness and its consequences

Based on a quick process of economic growth, the accelerated exploration of its immense oil reserves and mainly taking advantage of easy international credit access, in particular from China, Angola has been increasing its capacity of negotiation and bargaining with European countries and multilateral financial bodies. The interviewees drew attention to the Chinese government loan to Angola in 2004 when it ceased to negotiate with the IMF and got loans from

China without any conditions. This was a 'break point' as, at that moment, the 'Western powers shook ... At first, the OECD countries attacked, saying that the lack of conditions would provoke more corruption. Next, they ran to offer lines of credit not to lose market share for China and others and increasing their action.'[26] However, Angola has recently amended its legislation, establishing a minimum initial level of U$1 million for private investments and imposing the alignment of private investments with the government's goals, whether official or not.[27]

An important characteristic of current international loans in Angola is the use of commodities and raw materials as guarantees for the negotiated credits. It is the so-called 'oil-account.' Therefore, the current Brazilian or Chinese loans do not involve direct conditions concerning macroeconomic and tax policies but rather imply the continuous supply of natural resources. As reported, the BNDES may use in Mozambique the same guarantees adopted in Angola by creating a mechanism of receivables backed by coal.[28] However, up to now, the BNDES's actions in these countries have been small in the face of the magnitude of investments and credit directed towards Africa. Although these actions determine the internationalisation of the Brazilian companies, as mentioned before, they do not constrain the companies' expansion in these countries.

In addition, even if there are no conditions, the macroeconomic and/or tax policies (the traditional credits of the Northern countries) and the credits of the emerging countries (including BNDES) are usually linked to the import and purchase of goods and machinery of the countries granting the credit. With regards to the Chinese credits, they also involve hiring people and, in some cases, carrying out bids in China. As elicited in the interviews, this would be one of the main constraints for its potential development as it would prevent chain effects, technology transfer and training of the local workforce.

So the increase of South–South financial relations has created new forms of indebtedness among the Southern countries, backed by mineral and energy resources. The interviewees pointed out the possible implications of the indebtedness for future generations. This indebtedness can be reinforced with a specific productive route based on primary-export activities and then nullified or minimised with the possibilities of diversification of the productive structure. Moreover, the risk of exhaustion of natural resources (minerals and energy) is apparent in the medium and long term. As commodities, these mineral resources lead to economic instability and are subject to price fluctuations and speculation in the international market, compromising the consolidation of a sustainable development process from the economic, social and environmental viewpoint.

In Mozambique, the situation is different. The country faces another vicious cycle: international donations. Its budget for current expenses depends on about 47% of financial aid from the European countries and the World Bank, the so-called Programmatic Partners (G19).[29] This situation led to a structural dependence on international aid to 'close the accounts' wherein the donor countries interfere directly in their public policies, in particular the macroeconomic and sectorial policies. On the one hand, some interviewees stressed that the conditions of these loans jeopardised the sovereignty of the Mozambican government towards defining the priorities for its development. On the other hand, representatives of the Mozambican government and international cooperation defend the need to impose targets to fight corruption and the creation of mechanisms to improve governance and transparency.

In these dynamics, the economy is little diversified and works on increasing dependence on packages to attract investments based on the concession of big tax exemptions (considered excessive by the interviewees). Companies like Vale have been granted tax exemptions for 30 to 50 years. Some interviewees questioned the need for so many incentives since the natural reserves are already attractive enough. The vicious cycle is formed because the budget is dependent on the donations of central countries while the entry of direct foreign investment and the upsurge in the economy, which could represent higher government revenues and the future budget balance, are cancelled by the increasing tax exemptions granted and the concentration of investments in businesses directed towards export.

Therefore, for most of the interviewees, the activities of multinational companies in these countries are marked by an accumulation process based on the unbridled exploration of the mineral resources and the creation of economic enclaves which do not result in development. In Angola, for example, there is no national productive sector to meet internal market demands (except for the hydrocarbons), which continues to depend on imports. In Mozambique, the situation is similar. In Tete, where the mining companies Vale, Rio Tinto and Jindal are operating, the roads are often disrupted by trucks carrying iron ore, wood and other resources to supply the international market. In contrast, the poorly paved streets, poverty, poor housing, the lack of sanitation and markets for local production, and the high cost of living are evidence of the unequal economic growth and how far this process is from effective economic and social development. We can feel the 'open veins' of Africa.

Conclusion

Much has been said about the contents and the initial goals of the Brazilian transference projects in Angola and Mozambique. However, very little or no visibility is given to the ways these projects are implemented and to the actors and institutional arrangements involved. This chapter tried to fill this gap with an approach on this perspective. The 'new Africa' has been increasingly configured as the major arena for exercising different dimensions of a 'global Brazil'. But how is this 'global Brazil' and all the flows set in motion in the African countries able to effectively meet the problems faced by society in Angola and Mozambique? The consolidation of the mechanisms as 'cooperation for development' in Portuguese-speaking Africa has led to the construction of a hegemonic consensus (in Gramsci's sense) of Brazil's actions regarding the other peripheral regions. And, in this sense, Brazil is in a paradoxical position as both an exploiting and exploited country which subordinates and is subordinated at the same time.

In spite of holding a place dependent on the political, productive, technological and financial global structure, Brazil has been differentiating itself (along with the other emerging countries) from the other peripheral countries and gaining increasing relevance in the global structure of expanded capital reproduction. However, as long as it advances in this process, it increasingly reproduces, in its own peculiar way, an imperialist logic marked by the consolidation of the relations of political-economic domination in other countries and peoples, inside and outside its borders. In this context, the 'new Africa' fits the political and economic strategies of the Brazilian dominant class formed by governmental bodies, large companies and, in some cases, civil society organisations which help to legitimise the actual hegemonic accumulation process. But to what extent does the new 'global Brazil' fit the political and economic strategies of the 'new Africa'?

In our point of view, we should look for answers in the singular role Brazil plays in the global system and in its peculiarities as a national state. In the global context, Brazil is considered one of the main leaders in the emergent bloc and has been widely recognised for its ability to consolidate a development model to match economic growth (mainly driven by the export of natural resources and the internal consumption boost) and the increase of public policies (mainly social ones) of income redistribution and to fight poverty. So Brazil is placed in a privileged position to negotiate with these African countries. On the one hand, it is unquestionable that the Brazilian experience to deal with the local problems of peripheral economies (inequality, poverty, indebtedness, insufficient capacity for national investment, etc.) has much potential to contribute to African governments and societies. Brazil, in this sense, would play an important role in giving more visibility and power to the interests of these countries in political and economic global contexts, to consolidate new forms of cooperation and integration to break with the instruments of domination by the Northern countries, and to give inspiration for social policies, among others. It seems that these factors have been taken into account, at least in part, by the governments and societies of the African countries when structuring their relations with Brazil. On the other hand, however, as a country aspiring to the position as one of global capitalism's powers, we cannot ignore the economic and political interests of the main sectors of the dominant classes in the country regarding Africa, quite often interpreted as a new accumulation frontier.

In Angola and Mozambique, the future prospects of Brazil's activities are mostly associated with the expansion of large-scale export agriculture (including technology transference). In both countries, the advance of Brazilian capital is accomplished particularly in agribusiness expansion, technological transfer, machinery, grain (soya) production and agro-fuel for export. In turn, the priorities of the Angolan and Mozambican governments have turned to the consolidation of large-scale export agriculture. Moreover, the strategy of meeting the internal market demand and the guarantee of food security, though present in the governments' discourses and development plans, does not seem to have priority in the implemented instruments and public policies.

During the research carried out, and beyond the relations already established with the African countries in question, our investigation pointed more and more to what is dreamt about for the future of these societies. Among other internal factors in each country, the relations with Brazil were valued as one of the potential vectors to change the current development projects into reality in the near future. Among other priority themes aimed to increase the cooperation we included education, leadership formation, research interchange and science and technology experience exchanges. The humanisation of the public services and the increase of human capital investments are conditions for increasing citizenship and democratisation in the decision-making processes. Brazil therefore is seen as an inspiration and a country able to develop the 'dialogic technology' as an instrument of negotiation and conflict mediation. Therefore, rather than the outcomes (the so-called 'modernisation leap'), the relationship with Brazil should focus on the processes which enabled the elaboration and implementation of certain public policies essential to the development of the country and adapting them to the local reality. As said by an interviewee, 'We Angolans are the ones who have to look for other *Brazils*.'[30]

This evidences the need for other South–South instruments of interaction and cooperation which (instead of direct transference of public policies from one country to the other) are centred on the construction of interchange processes and the improvement of public policies and incentive processes for development in both countries. A strong position is held regarding the strengthening of channels of participation and the democratisation of decision-making to incorporate popular demands and mechanisms of direct participation, particularly to involve more vulnerable groups who are almost always invisible in the development processes. Moreover, considering the increasing actions of the Brazilian companies in Angola and Mozambique, it is necessary to prioritise projects of mutual institutional strength for social movements and the communities affected by the mega-projects, such as mining, and oil and steel, and to increase the communication between trade union movements and civil society organisations between these countries and Brazil. An interesting example which is already on course is the case of the International Network of People Affected by Vale.[31]

Participation and democratisation are means to advance towards the construction of a counter-hegemonic project to foster effective development in these societies and to strengthen the new South–South solidarity relations. According to an African saying (which inspired this chapter's title), the hunting story is always told from the hunter's perspective and not the hunted. The latter always escapes and, when it cannot escape, it usually cannot talk anymore. The hegemonic discourse, in the African saying, is the hunter who gets stronger by claiming itself as universal. It identifies itself as the unique version of the economic development accepted and recognised by everyone.

Raising and sustaining other contradictory versions to this narrative is crucial to prevent the recurrence of old patterns of domination. In the case of the African saying, the challenge posed is to give voice and resonance to the multiple stories told by those who have been (and still are) persecuted by the hunter but somehow managed to escape and remained strong enough to tell us their stories.

Notes

1. Oral statement by a professor at the University of Lúrio, Nampula, in an interview in Mozambique.
2 Some texts approaching the issue, which may provide a good perspective of the relations between Brazil and Africa in this period, include White (2010), IPEA and World Bank (2011) and Villas-Bôas (2011).
3 Based on Gramsci's (2008) notion, we call this view hegemonic because it is reproduced and naturalised in common sense by most scholars, researchers, and even identity and cultural movements, based on the attempt to build a consensus about the political and entrepreneurial activities of Brazilian actors as mostly 'positive' in African countries, which would be better received than those of other powers, such as China and the European countries.

4 See Vizentini and Pereira (2014), Schlesinger (2012), and Cabral (2011), among others.

5 Oral statement by a representative of the Brazilian Embassy in an interview in Luanda.

6 Brazil was the first country to officially recognise Angola independence.

7 The consortium for the construction of the hydroelectric plant was formed in 1982 by Russia, Odebrecht and Furnas.

8 Oral statement by a representative of the National Agency for Private Investment (ANIP) in an interview in Angola.

9 Oral statement by a representative of the Secretariat of Human Rights of Angola in an interview.

10 Oral statement by a professor at Agostinho Neto University and a professor at the Catholic University of Angola in an interview.

11 Oral statement by professor at the Lúrio University in an interview in Nampula, Mozambique.

12 Vale to invest US$6.4 billion in mine expansion in Moatize [Vale quer investir 6,4 bilhões USD na expansão da mina de Moatize], *O País*, 6 July 2012, http://opais.sapo.mz/index.php/economia/38-economia/21021-vale-quer-investir-64-bilioes-usd-na-expansao-da-mina-de-moatize.html.

13 Oral statement by the Brazilian representative of Apex for Africa in an interview in Luanda.

14 Oral statement by representatives of the Union of Workers of the Construction and Mining Industry (Snticim) in Tete, the Mozambican Debt Group, and the Agency for the Local Development of Tete, in interviews.

15 Oral statement by the dean of the Technical University of Angola in an interview.

16 Oral statement by a representative of Embrapa in an interview in Mozambique.

17 Oral statement by a representative of the National Union of Peasants (UNAC) in an interview in Maputo.

18 Although the Portuguese were progressively losing ground to other countries, mainly China and South Africa.

19 Oral statement by a representative of a Brazilian urban transport company in an interview in Luanda.

20 Information collected in interviews with civil society organisations, scholars and some state members critical of the use of these instruments.

21 Oral statement by a representative of a service security company for Vale, in an interview in Tete.

22 Vale removed a community (around 13 000 rural families) from its lands for the implementation of the mine in Moatize, separating the families in two settlements: Cateme and 25 September. Some of these conflicts are reported in 'Reports on the unsustainability of Vale 2012', http://atingidospelavale.files.wordpress.com/2012/06/relatorio-insustentabilidade-vale-2012-final1.pdf.

23 Oral statement by two residents of the 25 September community in an interview in Moatize.

24 Oral statement by a representative of the Ministry of Provincial Labour for Tete in an interview.

25 Oral statement by a representative of the Ministry of Labour in an interview in Maputo.

26 Oral statement by an economist of the Centre for Scientific Studies and Research of the Catholic University of Angola (CEIC), in an interview in Luanda.

27 Oral statement by a representative of the National Agency for Private Investment (ANIP) in an interview in Luanda.

28 País elabora estratégia para se tornar mais competitivo na África, *Valor Econômico*, 8 November 2011.

29 The G19 is composed of Germany, Austria, Belgium, Canada, Denmark, the European Commission, Spain, Finland, France, Ireland, Italy, Norway, the Netherlands, Portugal, Sweden, Switzerland, the African Bank for Development (BAD) and the World Bank and their associate members, the United Nations and the United States.

30 Oral statement by the representative of the Adventist Development and Relief Agency (ADRA) in an interview in Luanda.

31 See http://atingidospelavale.wordpress.com/.

References

ABC and Embrapa (2011) *Projeto de melhoria da capacidade de pesquisa e de transferência de tecnologia para o desenvolvimento da agricultura no corredor de Nacala em Moçambique (ProSavana – TEC)*, Executive summary

Agencia Brasileira de Promocao da Exportacao e Investimento (Apex) (2010) *Angola: estudo de oportunidades 2010*, www.apexbrasil.com.br

Alem, A and R Madeira (2010) Internacionalização e competividade: a importância da criação de empresas multinacionais brasileiras. In Ana Claudia Alem and Fabio Giambiagi (eds), *O BNDES em um Brasil em transição*, Rio de Janeiro, BNDES

Alem, AC and C Cavalcanti (2005) O BNDES e o apoio à internacionalização das empresas brasileiras: algumas reflexes, *Revista do BNDES*, 12, 24, pp 43–76

Amorim, C (2010) Política externa é uma política pública como as demais: está sujeita à expressão das urnas, *Desafios do Desenvolvimento*, Brasília, IPEA

Amorim, C (2011) A África tem sede de Brasil, *Carta Capital*, 28 May

Amundsen, I and C Abreu (2007) *Sociedade civil em Angola: incursões, espaço e responsabilidade*, Bergen, CHR – Michelsen Institute

Cabral, L (2011) Cooperação Brasil-África para o desenvolvimento: caracterização, tendências e desafios, *Textos CINDES*, 26, December

Carneiro, JD (2011) Angolanos olham para o Brasil, mas brasileiros não olham para Angola, diz escritor, *BBC Brasil*, 9 September

Castro, CM and F Goulet (2011) L'Essor des coopérations Sud-Sud: le Brésil en Afrique et le cas du secteur agricole, *Techniques Financières et Développement*, 105

Chichava, S (2011) As economias emergentes' no sector agrícola moçambicano: leituras, implicações e desafios. In L de Brito et al. (eds) *Economias 'emergentes': desafios para Moçambique*, Maputo, IESE

Chuquela, FJP (2012) Com descoberta de recursos, Moçambique entra numa posição 'privilegiada e de risco', *Verdade*, 16 May

Fellet, J (2011) Laços com presidente e obra durante a guerra marcam atuação da Odebrecht em Angola, *BBC Brasil*, 18 September

Fiocruz (2008) A cooperação internacional desenvolvida pela Escola Nacional de Saúde Pública Sérgio Arouca da Fundação Oswaldo Cruz com a África, *Boletim Técnico Internacional 2008*, Rio de Janeiro

Garcia, A, K Kato and C Fontes (2012) *A historia contada pela caca ou pelo cacador? Perspectivas sobre Brasil em Angola e Mocambique*, Rio de Janeiro, Instituto Politicas Alternativas para o Cono Sul, http://www.pacs.org.br.files/2013/03/Relatorio-Africa.pdf

Garcia, A (2012) A internacionalização de empresas brasileiras durante o governo Lula: uma análise crítica da relação entre capital e Estado no Brasil contemporâneo, PhD thesis, Pontifical Catholic University of Rio de Janeiro

Giugale, M (2012) Who will be Africa's Brazil?, *The Huffington Post*, 21 March

Goulet, F, JJ Gabas and E Sabourin (2012) À l'épreuve du terrain: des pratique brésiliennes et chinoise de coopération technique agricole en Afrique, *Sociologies Pratiques*, 27, pp 75–89

Gramsci, A (2008) *Selections from the Prison Notebooks*, New York, International Publishers

IPEA and ABC (2010) *Cooperação brasileira para o desenvolvimento internacional: 2005–2009*, Brasília, Instituto de Pesquisa Econômica Aplicada and Agência Brasileira Cooperação

IPEA and World Bank (2011) *Ponte sobre o Atlântico: Brasil e África Subsaariana parceria Sul-Sul para o crescimento*, http://www.ipea.gov.br/portal/images/stories/PDFs/livros/livros/111222_livropontesobreoatlanticopor2.pdf

Jose, M (2013) Zungueiras de Luanda causam polémica, *Voz da América*, 29 January

Minsterio das Relacoes Exteriores (2010) *Balanço de Política Externa 2003–2010*, http://www.itamaraty.gov.br/temas/balanco-de-politica-externa-2003-2010/

Portal Nikkei (2012) ProSavana: Brasil, Japão e Moçambique discutem cessão das terras, *Jornal Nippak*, 20 April

Santos, Q (2013) É presidente de Angola que faz da sua filha uma milionária, acusa a Forbes, *Público*, 14 August

Saraiva, JFS (2010) The new Africa and Brazil in the Lula era: the rebirth of Brazilian Atlantic policy, *Revista Brasileira de Política Internacional, Brasília*, 53, pp 169–183

Saraiva, JFS (2012) *África parceiro do Brasil Atlântico: relações internacionais do Brasil e da África no início do século XXI*, Belo Horizonte, Editora Fino Traço

Schlesinger, S (2012) *Cooperação e investimentos internacionais do Brasil: a internacionalização do etanol e do biodiesel*, Rio de Janeiro, FASE

Selemane T (2010) *Questões a volta da mineração em Moçambique*, Maputo, Centro de Integridade Pública

Sennes, R and R Mendes (2009) Políticas públicas e multinacionais brasileiras. In A Almeida and JR Ramsey (eds) *A ascensão das multinacionais brasileiras: o grande salto de pesos-pesados regionais a verdadeiras multinacionais*, Rio de Janeiro, Elsevier and Belo Horizonte, Fundação Dom Cabral

Stolte, C (2012) *Brazil in Africa: just another BRICS country seeking resources?*, Chatham House, November

Villas-Boas, JC (2011) Os investimentos brasileiros na África no governo Lula: um mapa, *Meridiano 47*, 12, 28, pp 3–9

Visentini, PGF and AD Pereira (nd) *A política africana do governo Lula*, http://www.ufrgs.br/nerint/folder/artigos/artigo40.pdf

White, L (2010) Understanding Brazil's new drive for Africa, *South African Journal of International Affairs*, 17, 2, pp 221–242

9

China's geopolitical oil
strategy in the Andean region

OMAR BONILLA MARTINEZ

This chapter discusses China's oil dependency and its effect on the Andean region. My hypothesis is that one of the objective limits to Chinese development is found precisely in its oil dependency. This limitation consequently drives the need to gain access to these resources, which, in turn, has caused changes in the Ecuadorian economy and society, particularly that which is dependent on petroleum. In order to be able to understand how this dialectic arises between the dependency on buying oil and Ecuadorian dependence on its sale, the chapter is composed of two parts: while the first part reviews the characteristics and conditions of Chinese development, the second part considers the case of Ecuador. Consistent with the object of inquiry, I give special attention to the variables of work, environment and economy in analysing both China and Ecuador.

The emergence of China in the international order cannot be explained as marginal to its long history, during which one of its main comparative advantages has been the uncommon development of its workforce. Chinese agricultural systems are among the most ancient on the planet; this can be seen in the use of irrigation, rice cultivation and in the social organisation capable of sustaining a highly skilled population for social production. Huge engineering works allowed China to consolidate the bases of a thriving agricultural society. In order to flood enormous rice fields, the empire and Chinese people were capable of changing the course of the Yellow River. This type of work was repeated on various occasions through the diversion of major rivers. Besides supplying the population, the works were able to integrate a vast and diverse territory in order to create a state and an empire. These deeds made various civilising advancements possible as well as an economy that for many centuries was the most important in the world. Nevertheless this would not have been possible without a strong control over peasants and the workforce due to an iron bureaucracy – in particular, the army – and a generalised civic ideology such as Confucianism able to uphold it. Thus it was that water management permitted rice field irrigation, enabling the workforce to be fed while disciplining it and making it capable of building huge engineering works. This was the case of the Great Wall in whose construction more than ten million people died. Behind this kind of work there was interplay between population control and government involvement.

Past Chinese potency entered into crisis when European powers obliged the empire to open its borders. The most dramatic episode was the Opium Wars in the mid-19th century when England, which controlled the commerce of this drug, used its military to force China to allow drug consumption in its interior. England also forced the import of raw materials, particularly textiles, as well as the use of the Chinese workforce in English factories relocated to China. In this manner Europe turned trade to its advantage at the same time it occupied Hong Kong.

European intervention and the Japanese invasion during World War II that demanded control over natural and human resources caused the traditional system of domination to enter into crisis. The relationships imposed in China became suffocating for the majority of peasants and workers who took part in various revolts (Wolf 1999) that culminated in the revolution led by Mao Zedong with general peasant support. Nevertheless, during the revolutionary era, the Chinese economy had already deteriorated due to colonial pillage, World War II damages, and the very same popular war led by Mao.

It should be noted that the same revolution would turn to disciplining and preparing the population for agricultural and industrial work. In fact, among the measures taken after the triumph of the revolution in 1950 the industrialisation process known as the Great Leap Forward stands out, from the end of the 1950s and beginning of the 1960s. From Mao's perspective, which was absolutely anti-colonial and at the same time admiring of European industrialisation, it was necessary to modernise China at all cost. This implied work quotas that caused famines and the death of millions due to abandonment of the countryside. Once Mao's measures were applied, the country began recovering military power, developing heavy industry and building a strong state able to control the population, to displace traditional elites as well as to ward off foreign powers, including the Soviet Union.[1]

With Richard Nixon, the United States and China achieved the first step in their rapprochement and China was shaped into a strategic partner of the United States. If a capitalist power was being delineated in the Asian interior, at the same time China was transforming into a geopolitical barrier for the United States. It would be able to access the US market and concurrently the US bourgeoisie would have cheap, skilled and disciplined labour at its disposal. With Mao's successor, Deng Xiaoping, a new bourgeoisie appeared under the auspices of the Communist Party and with the advantageous opening of United States markets a reform began favouring exports. China became converted into the workshop of the world thanks to foreign investments. Its manufactured goods exports which were 50% in 1980 reached 95% in 2005 (Durand et al. 2008).

Nevertheless, Chinese development also signified a series of shocks for the workforce and nature. Industrialisation caused famines and destroyed a good part of traditional agriculture in order to be replaced by hydroelectric plants and reservoirs putting an end to many of the centuries-old productive systems. Parallel to this, the work days imposed on the labour force were extremely difficult; despite the control the state exercised over almost every sphere of life, social discontent set off a series of protests across the country in recent years. It would evoke a nightmare that has always weighed upon those in the bureaucracy and the dominant classes: the rebellion of the oppressed.

The immense Chinese population provides millions of labourers who work long hours and days in *maquiladora* plants at the lowest salaries in the world. Without a doubt this is what is behind the wave of strikes China has witnessed in the last few years. Worker strikes and suicides are provoking a wage reform. Remunerations have increased steeply in the last five years. According to the ILO (International Labour Organisation), the rise in salaries has no equal anywhere in the world. This upsurge has caused the economy to decelerate from an annual growth rate of 12% to around 8%. It is said that this rise has encouraged many firms to migrate to such countries as Vietnam or Bangladesh, according to the Chinese government; it will facilitate the creation of a domestic market and a better quality industry.

In spite of this wage increase, problems continue in the Chinese countryside from where it is hoped that tens of millions of peasants will relocate to the cities, in order to fuel the Industrial Reserve Army. The phenomenon can be understood as primitive accumulation. Nevertheless, the problems are also environmental: deforestation has accompanied Chinese capitalist development and the country lacks water because, in spite of the presence of the Himalayas, it does not have large reserves of fresh water. In addition to this, the Chinese energy matrix depends on coal, a greater contaminant than petroleum. At the beginning of 2013 the unprecedented fact could be observed that one-third of China was underneath a carbon dioxide cloud. This was repeated midway through the year when serious samples of pollution forced millions of Chinese to suspend activities.

According to the World Health Organisation (WHO), this level of air pollution has never been known. According to the WHO, half a million people have died from atmospheric contamination since 2008, mainly from respiratory diseases and cancer (Lander 2013). Air pollution has generated unheard-of protests in China, where thousands and sometimes tens of thousands have manifested their rejection of polluting factories, waste incinerators and, above all, the lack of state environmental policies. Besides causing socio-environmental problems, the ecological crisis has forced many industries to stop production on the days of worst pollution.

We see then that Chinese economic growth has been checked by the following limitations: the first consists of the population's resistance to the model of over-exploitation and deprivation, and the consequent demonstrations; the second is the health and other problems arising from pollution; and the third is the genuine lack of hydrocarbons and other strategic resources. Although China recently showed possibilities of resolving some of the social aspects of the crisis temporarily, at least those that have to do with over-exploitation, others remain that do not seem to have solutions, at least in the medium to long term.

Chinese geopolitical oil strategies

One of the best ways to understand the role that China has chosen as an emerging power is to be found in its strategies to guarantee access to natural resources. This begins with studying its policy of alliances and conflicts with Europe and the United States, the other members making up the BRICS countries (Brazil, Russia, India, China and South Africa) as well as those in its sphere of influence and in distant places that have welcomed it, such as Africa.

Since the 2008 crisis, the Chinese economy has continued to develop in absolute terms, making it possible to predict that it may become the next world hegemonic power towards the 2050s.[2] However, there are some constraining factors, among which perhaps the most important is petroleum. Twenty-five years ago China was the major oil exporter to all of East Asia (Ricaurte 2012); today it is an oil importer in second place behind the United States. For China, perhaps more than any other country, petroleum is a fundamental input in manufacturing and construction. Scarcity of this resource has already occasioned the closures and paralysis of giant industrial complexes as well as the rise in price of Chinese products that are increasingly consumed the world over.

In order to access and control petroleum resources, China has created three gigantic multinationals: the China National Offshore Oil Corporation (CNOOC), the China National Petroleum Corporation (CNPC) and the China Petroleum and Chemical Corporation (SINOPEC). In parallel, the National Bank of China has been able to negotiate loans and purchases with countries that are the objects of investment and has often not been able to or wanted to access World Bank or International Monetary Fund (IMF) credits. Nevertheless, control over petroleum is not an easy task. China even faces conflicts over the crude oil reserves in its seas, a controversy aggravated by the United States' efforts to curb Chinese expansion.

China in Ecuador

The Ecuadorian Amazon is an area of important Chinese investment in the construction of hydroelectric dams, in petroleum exploration and in mineral reserves. It is possible to think of a giant Asian enclave that occupies no less than one-third of Ecuador and also extends to a large part of the Peruvian Amazon. The conditions for this land grab have to be looked for in the crisis created by the neoliberal model.

Decades of IMF and World Bank loans to Ecuador facilitated US interference at the national level as economic and social policies were subjected to the conditions laid down by the aforementioned loans. On occasion there were governments that accepted the credit institutions' guidelines and renounced state budgetary planning. Thus Ecuador's economy was hardly autonomous and, moreover, depended basically on the export of petroleum resources. The World Bank and IMF were functional for US oil capital because their guidelines served their oil firms and guaranteed them access to the petroleum reserves.

In contrast to what happens with the United States and the traditional credit institutions, the relationship with Chinese banks and companies, even though they belong to the Chinese state, is openly mediated by the state and their impact is more obvious and direct. Secondly, China's foreign oil policy has few qualms about the type of government it conducts business with. The only thing that interests it is access to petroleum reserves and that expenses are cheaper for the Chinese state. According to official figures, Ecuador's debt with China is more than US$10 billion. Much of this debt forms part of the 'commercial operations' with the State Oil Company. The guarantee of repayment would be the petroleum and the loans often carry high interest rates.

The history of economic and commercial relations between Ecuador and China is recent. Even though a commercial treaty was signed in 1975, diplomatic relations with the opening of embassies took place only five years later. The first petroleum contract with a Chinese firm was in 2003 with the CNPC for Block 11 located in the northeast of the Ecuadorian Amazon. The US Santa Fe Company had explored the block without finding any oil and subsequently it had passed into the hands of the Lumbaqui Oil Company of Ecuador. According to Alexandra Almeida,[3] two things were surprising about the Chinese interest in this petroleum field. The first is that CNPC prospecting took place in two conservation areas, the Sumaco Park and the Cayambe Coca Reserve outside of the projected area; and the second event was that, despite the failure of the search for oil by the two former companies, the CNPC insisted on taking over the field. It did not find oil but it remained operating in Ecuador. During its activity in Block 11, the company had a severe social and environmental impact, according to Acción Ecológica.[4]

The Chinese consortium (CNPC and SINOPEC) also negotiated for Blocks 14 and 17 held by the Encana Company for a sum of about US$1.5 billion. Among the assets for sale were the 36.3% participation that Encana held in the OCP oil pipeline (the principal pipeline in Ecuador) and a future 40% participation in Block 15 and the Edén-Yuturi and Limoncocha oil fields where Occidental was operating. Simultaneously CNCP and SINOPEC acquired five petroleum blocks with an extraction of 75 200 barrels a day and proven reserves of 143 million barrels as well as 36% of OCP (*China Daily* 2005). At the same time, on 30 May 2006, the government authorised the transfer of City-AEC Ecuador's shares and a name change as well as the block known as Tarapoa to the Andes Petroleum consortium consisting of CNPC and SINOPEC International; the same consortium also took charge of the Estación de Transferencia de Crudo (LTF, Crude Oil Transfer Station) in order to become one of the major foreign investors in Ecuador.

Meanwhile, a new consortium of Chinese companies, PetroOriental SA, began operations in Orellana and Pastaza provinces with two blocks in the Yasuní National Park.[5] China's exploitation of the above-mentioned fields occasioned a high degree of social conflict in addition to impacts on nature, as Alexandra Almeida recalls:

In Tarapoa there was a very big strike to avoid drilling, it is possible that subconsciously they wanted to negotiate better but the community was mobilised; they began to have very serious conflicts with the Chinese also in Block 14, the Mawi 1 community that asked for a million dollars as indemnity for environmental damages. Also there was a community called Rodrigo Borja where there had been a walkout for work reasons, apparently the Canadians had paid them double, the people of this community alleged that the Chinese exploited them, that they paid little; the Chinese version was that the Ecuadorians were slow and that if it were up to them they would only bring the Chinese down; the people's version was that the Chinese were disorganised and kept the camps dirty.

In the face of these and other conflicts the firms showed little disposition to negotiate. An example of this fact is found in an anecdote of Alexandra Almeida:

There is a story a friend told me. It appears that they did not satisfy the workers of a community. The people sequestered ten Chinese workers, they grabbed them, this was in Block 7 in Murialba port, the people remained with the Chinese various days and nobody went to complain. They say that the Chinese bosses told them that, if they wanted to keep the Chinese, they would bring more from China where there are millions. A doctor friend who worked for SINOPEC told me this. All the measures that the communities took to pressure them did not work, they worked very long hours all the time with their workers on a very tight schedule.

The companies showed little disposition to deal with those affected or with the workers. This broke with company tendency to seek the sympathy of directly affected local groups through creating clientele relationships: with the Chinese firms there was less willingness to care about their image and they therefore went from having an adequate labour policy to having less good relations with the local communities.

Another ongoing conflict beginning in 2007 resulted in the dismissal of many Andes Petroleum Consortium workers operating in Block 14–17 Shiripuno when labour outsourcing was prohibited. The workers claim that the criteria used to fire them were discriminatory and not work-related and thus demanded payment for the earnings that the firm has not handed over. Their legal representative stated that the firm continues to outsource workers: 'To the south of Dayuma parish there are many oil companies that are outsourcers, the Ministry of Labour Relations of Orellana has not done any supervision, at the end of the day the people work and like this break the labour code. The workers never gain access to a copy of the contracts.'[6]

From the testimony of this worker one can conclude that Chinese firms in Ecuador have operated and continue to operate by violating labour rights. The interviewee added that presently these block workers receive only a uniform and some gloves for tasks that require protection. Also, he reported that the firm does not allow workers to obtain cheap food because in the workplace lunches cost more than eight dollars while they are paid a minimum wage.

In another case deserving attention, one encounters the damages suffered by the Siekopai community (previously known as Secoya) located in the new Block 62. SINOPEC carried out seismic activity within this territory and one of the ways in which it proceeded was to install an encampment where around 500 oil workers passed through and hosted more than 150 on a permanent basis in the Secoya Cultural Centre in the middle of the San Pablo community where, according to censuses, no more than 650 people lived. This was unusual because the majority of companies' rules had traditionally forbidden the installation of campsites within the communities.

One of the community leaders appraised the Chinese presence in this way: 'The Chinese firm, Andes Petroleum, has extended its block, the Tarapoa block, and now the Secoya territory has become a part of this block, which is now called 62. It has already begun to work, to operate there, even putting up a base camp. This is the worst of the worse, the Chinese have done what no one has ever done: neither Petroamazonas nor OXY have done this to the Secoyas.'[7] The leader's commentary explains the social problems that the camp installation caused; there were already ruptures in the group's fabric during the negotiations for its establishment. 'Because really, we the leaders said that the negotiation should not be entered into, that it was not to sign; but instead a group of local young people suddenly said we want to work and want money. Like I already told you, change is now rooted in youth. The youth already think in a different manner, they do not think long-term but bread today and famine tomorrow.'[8]

In addition to the general idea of company deception that spread throughout the Siekopai community, one of the occurrences that shocked the community was the pressure put on women:

> The most serious thing is not to have respect and also the nation's weakness, the weakness of the leaders of the Siekopai nation, to have allowed this to happen on its very doorstep, and still above all that a girl of the Siekopai nation went with an oil company worker, leaving her young husband, leaving a child, she left with an oil worker and they were not punished. They did not castigate the company nor the person who took a Secoya

woman. Can you imagine! I have never seen such a cultural, familial outrage, and the destruction they have left, those who did this, affected the whole family.[9]

In order to tackle the allegations, the Clínica Ambiental (Environmental Clinic) of Ecuador conducted a multi-disciplinary investigation of the psychosocial impacts caused by the Chinese company. Among the report's conclusions, the following stands out:

The presence of workers in the SINOPEC firm triggered the consumption of alcohol among adolescents, adults and women to the detriment of family relations and increased intra-family violence including accusations of jealousy, abandonment, maltreatment and physical and psychological violence. The family fabric, already feeble, underwent fragmentation, mistrust and an increase of fear. The firm just fired some of the workers because they were unable to do their work but did not worry how this would affect the community and never attempted to correct its workers on its own initiative. Given that China and Ecuador are signatories to Convention 169 of the ILO, SINOPEC demonstrated grave irresponsibility in the way it treated this Indian nationality (Clíncia Ambiental 2013).

It needs to be added that, besides attempting to obtain the majority of oil concessions and to save the most possible costs, the Chinese companies showed little respect for the collective, the workforce and the environment. In summary, we read from the official website that 'Andes Petroleum Ecuador Ltd. operates in the Tarapoa Block and in the Lago Agrio Storage and Transfer Station (Sucumbios). PetroOriental SA operates in Blocks 14 and 17 (Orellana). Andes Petroleum Ecuador Ltd. and PetroOriental SA are companies formed with capital coming from state companies of the People's Republic of China. These are: China National Petroleum Corporation (CNPC) whose equity participation is 55% and China Petrochemical Corporation (SINOPEC), which holds the remaining 45%' (Clíncia Ambiental 2013). In addition, CNPC holds 36.26% of the Crude Oil Pipeline (OCP) shares.

To conclude, in November 2013 CNPC, through its subsidiary Andes Petroleum, put itself forward for Blocks 79 and 83 in the XI Round of Petroleum Tenders in the southeast of Ecuador. This is how Chinese oil firms are present in Ecuador, either as direct operators or as shareholders.

China in the Yasuní

The Chinese presence in Yasuní territory is emblematic for at least three reasons: first, as the most biodiverse place in the world, the park contains immense biological and social wealth and is also the territorial space of indigenous peoples among whom the Tagaeri and Taromenane stand out for their voluntary isolation; secondly, because the area has acquired significance both within the country and abroad due to the society's desire to keep crude oil in the ground in one part of the territory, a proposal at first welcomed by the government but later discarded; and thirdly, because of the violent form that exportation from this region has taken.

On 18 March 2007, SINOPEC together with Petrobras and ENAP of Chile signed a memorandum of understanding with the Ecuador government for the exploitation of Ishpingo-Tambococha-Tiputini (ITT, having one-fifth of Ecuador's reserves). The operational plan, developed by SINOPEC, established in eight clauses the requirements 'for the development and production' of the fields in the ITT block.

Two options were put forward: Plan A proposed no petroleum extraction from Yasuní-ITT while Plan B, the oil companies' proposal, was fronted by the then Energy Minister Alberto Acosta and by the head of Petroecuador, Carlos Pareja Yannuzzelli. Led by the President of the Republic, Petroecuador's Administrative Council decided to keep both options open. Although Plan A was declared to have priority, it was decided to go ahead with Plan B's conditions for exploitation. It was pointed out that the option of Plan A would always be considered when the international community contributed at least half of the funds that ITT oil extraction would generate.

The press release from that meeting of 1 April 2007 signalled that the first option – that of not exploiting the fields – was based on the arguments not to disturb an area of extraordinary biodiversity and not to put at risk the existence of the various Tagaeri and Taromenane peoples who were in voluntary isolation. The existence of these two peoples who formed part of the Wuaorani nation had been identified by reports but it was also characterised by violent incidents. The 2008 Constitution protected the territories of these 'voluntarily isolated peoples' and ensured that violation of their rights 'would constitute a crime of genocide'. However, for various sectors of civil and political society the hazards persisted.

Another fact scandalised the country's public opinion: the publication by the English newspaper, *The Guardian,* of a document that proved that the Chinese credit negotiations included conditions for Ecuador favouring Chinese investment in the ITT block and Block 31 (*The Guardian,* 19 March 2014). These negotiations were taking place in periods when the Ecuadorian state was still maintaining that it was necessary to keep this area free from oil companies; more than one analyst speculated that the credit conditions were decisive for the state's choosing the firms' proposal for prospecting in this zone. Because the only company authorised to exploit the ITT block is Petroamazonas, it is important to add to this that it recently incorporated into its Ecuador operations the concept of 'contracting specific integrated services', allowing it to turn over to one company alone practically all petroleum operations (seismic surveys, drilling, crude oil transport, security services, cleaning, etc.), a protocol that could possibly benefit Chinese firms in this block.

Consequences of the new occupation

In this controversial scenario, the Chinese companies' strategy has been to make acquisitions of fields and operations fundamentally in the areas surrounding the Yasuní. The logic of occupying this space and managing these reserves lies in the fact that to exploit them it is necessary to have control over light crude oil reserves, the access roads and the transport required to exploit these areas. These strategies have a double component: on the one hand, the direct purchase of shares and, on the other, the entry into direct contest for fields via direct negotiations with other national companies and via mechanisms that have produced benefits for the Chinese concessions.

Despite the first option of no petroleum extraction, the constant presence of Chinese companies in the Yasuní has lasted. This was patently visible in the change of Block 14's boundaries, which created an oil corridor for the Andes Petroleum company from the potential crude oil storage areas (Eden field) to the ports of the Tiputini. The petroleum companies' operations produced impacts in all its phases. From the actual attendance of community mediators in all stages of the negotiations they created agents of social and environmental pollution. Highways, dirt roads for seismic surveys, and encampments were only some of the problems with which the Amazon peoples have had to cope.

For example, seismic analysis requires the intense and widespread presence of workers. It is an extremely noisy activity since it depends on the use of explosives, motors and chain saws to open dirt roads. The noise drives the fauna away and creates pollution and inconvenience in the zone. For the development of both Block 31 near the ITT and Blocks 14 and 17, complementary surveys have been contracted. Also, in order to exploit the ITT, a new 3D seismic survey would be necessary. Due to the problem of the noise, among other factors, various killings have occurred. The incidents recorded by isolated peoples reveal the pressure their territories suffered. On 26 May 2003 a massacre of the Tagaeri happened under the influence of persons linked to the wood-cutting/oil companies interested in obtaining facilities that would guarantee their economic activity in inviolate areas (Chavez 2003).

On 2 March 2008, the woodcutter Mariano Castellanos was speared to death by the isolated peoples that inhabited the Armadillo region. On 10 August 2009 in the 'Los Reyes' settlement formed by colonists an event occurred that involved the death of a female colonist and her children. These deaths were attributed to the isolated indigenes belonging to the Armadillo clan. The motives for the deaths were presumably the racket produced by the South Hormiguero Platform electricity plant of PetroOriental, operating in Block 14.

On 5 March 2013 the Taromenane people again reacted to the invasion of its territories. According to what the Wuaorani relate, the attackers had warned about their distress due to excessive noise, unrecognised cultivations, many foreigners, tree-cutting and the construction of the petroleum platform and had asked their Wuaorani brothers to deal with this. Not being able to do anything, the Taromenane attacked a pair of Wuaorani elders, killing them with lances. In revenge, the Wuaorani in turn attacked Taromenane settlements, killing at least twenty of them and kidnapping two small girls.

The highways that have invaded the forests, as well as deforestation and the ever-greater pressure on the isolated people's territories, are also problems. Road construction presupposes the concentrated presence of squadrons of workers and is also an incentive for trading in wood and forest species. At present there are Wuaorani families that have come to live next to the motorway built by Maxus, now in the hands of Repsol. This has caused even more conflict among the Wuaorani and the clans that are in voluntary isolation.

The struggle in the Yasuní zone is not a cultural one. It is a conflict generated by the oil and timber companies' presence. It is a problem for which the state is directly responsible because it does not stop the threat to the territories of people who have lived there for millions of years.

Conclusion

The varied Chinese geopolitical oil strategies have achieved access to petroleum sources in the short term. The firms have adjusted rapidly to the Andean region's political changes. Nevertheless, little has been done to respect national and international human rights norms. In Ecuador, the Chinese firms have notably contributed to the expansion of the extractive frontier, principally in the Yasuní, showing little or no interest in the consequences for the well-established peoples and the environment. They show scarce interest in bettering work conditions and in assuming responsibility for their workers and ex-employees. Nonetheless, the Ecuador state shares the blame in all the above-mentioned events.

Notes

1. The tension between the two supposedly socialist countries was the opportunity for the United States to strike a blow at the Soviet Union but, at the same time, it was decisive for China's appearance on the world market.
2 The United States continues to sustain important growth besides its military power and favourable geographic conditions.
3 Interview at Acción Ecológica in Quito, January 2013.
4 Acción Ecológica (2005) *Atlas Amazónico*, Quito, http://www.accionecologica.org/images/2005/petroleo/documentos/10-Atlas-BLOQUE%2011-CNPC.pdf.
5 Personal interview with Alexandra Almeida, January 2013.
6 Personal interview with CV, May 2013.
7 Personal interview with EP, May 2013.
8 Personal interview with EP, May 2013.
9 Personal interview with EP, April 2013.

References

Chavez, G (2003) Muerte Tagaeri-Taromenane: justicia occidental o tradicional, *Revista Iconos*, 17
China Daily (2005) Oil consortium buys EnCana Ecuador assets, 16 September, http://www.chinadaily.com.cn/english/doc/2005-09/16/content_478433.htm
Clíncia Ambiental (2013) Pueblos indígenas y petroleras. 3 Miradas', *Ciencia con Conciencia*, 3, September
Durand, MF, P Copinschi, B Martin and D Placidi (2008) *Atlas de la globalización: comprender el espacio mundial contemporáneo: dosier especial China*, Valencia, University of Valencia Press
Lander, E (2013) *Documento preliminar, China y América Latina*, Fundación Rosa Luxemburg
Ricaurte, BR (2012) *El impacto ecológico del comercio ecuatoriano: flujos de materiales con los Estados Unidos, la Unión Europea y China*, Flacso-Sede Ecuador, http://flacsoandes.org/dspace/handle/10469/5303#.UrrnsLQxueE
Wolf, E (1999) *Las revoluciones campesinas del siglo XX*, Madrid, Siglo XXI

10

The transnationalisation of
Brazilian construction companies

PEDRO HENRIQUE CAMPOS

This chapter attempts a quantitative analysis of the overseas contracts signed by Brazilian heavy civil construction companies from 1969 until the end of the Lula da Silva government.[1] By compiling such information as prices, quantity, geographical distribution, contractors and so on, we see that most contracts are found precisely in regions with priority for Brazilian foreign policy, that is, in South America followed by African countries. On the basis of the research data, we can also establish that movement overseas is extremely concentrated in a few national firms. Thus, we are able to conclude that transnationalisation is a movement typical of large Brazilian capital and depends upon strong state support.

The purpose of the present chapter is to develop a quantitative approach to the international operations of Brazilian heavy civil construction contractors from 1969 to 2010.[2] Since the end of the 1960s, national contractors have been seeking and making contracts for public and private works in other countries, above all in Latin America, Africa and the Middle East and, afterwards, also in Europe and North America. The first international contracts signed by Brazilian construction firms date from 1969. This fact explains our choice for the start of the timeline. As the endpoint of the process, 2010 is justified because it is the end of Lula da Silva's government, a period marked by strong inducements for these companies' operations outside the country.

The introduction of figures and quantitative methods can enrich and facilitate the corroboration of certain interpretations of the historical process and can lend a greater degree of reliability to certain conclusions drawn. But their use comes with some precautions. This is because quantitative data cannot be understood as ends in themselves but rather as the base for firm explanations and interpretations of reality (Cardoso and Brignoli 2002). Also useful is Pierre Vilar's (1965) and Jean Bouvier's (1976) advice. As they remind us, taking into account its historicity and keeping a holistic perspective in view, the use of data should not exclude a qualitative interpretation of the process. Thus, in our analysis of the data, we will relate the internationalisation of Brazilian contractors to such issues as the international system, Brazilian foreign policy and the process of capital accumulation in Brazil and in the world. Regarding the documentation used, it is mainly composed of primary sources derived directly from the object of investigation. The principal body of documents consulted comes from the monthly journal *O Empreiteiro*, from its launch in February 1968 until the end of 2010, a total of 493 issues. In addition to the information culled from the journal, we gained access to other industry sources from company websites that give details about their overseas constructions.[3] Another type of primary source accessed was the memoirs of company heads and agents associated with the firm's internationalisation process containing some information on the subject under discussion. We completed these documents with such subsidiary sources as mass circulation periodicals,[4] news and materials related to the subject as well as secondary sources (mainly master's theses) where we extracted relevant facts on overseas civil construction contracts and contractors' experience with these projects.

The data was processed and certain questions were asked of the sources, which revealed such facts as the country where the contract was signed; the contractor responsible for the construction; other firms present or not in the consortium implementing the build; the name of works; the type of construction; the value of the works; date of the contract; period of execution; financers of the works; source of information. Even so, the data presented is preliminary and does not cover all the characteristics of the process.

With this method, we were able to register a total of 404 signed contracts since 1969 of which 368 were signed by 2010. With this, we had a few interesting results indicating certain tendencies in the movement of Brazilian firms towards internationalisation, such as their principal areas of activity, the degree of concentration of the works abroad in a few Brazilian firms, the dominance of certain types of works at the expense of others, the degree of state support through financing the contracts and the historical path of the transnationalisation process as well as its pace by identifying periods of intensification and periods of withdrawal.

From the quantitative treatment of the data, we verified regular tendencies

Table 1. Contracts established by Brazilian contractors by country, 1969–2010

Country	Number of Contracts	Country	Number of Contracts
Algeria	9	Libya	8
Angola	23	Malaysia	1
Argentina	10	Mauritania	6
Bahamas	1	Mexico	9
Bolivia	22	Mozambique	5
Botswana	1	Nigeria	2
Cameroon	4	Panama	8
Cape Verde	1	Paraguay	13
Chile	29	Peru	24
China	4	Portugal	35*
Colombia	17	Russia	1
Congo	3	Santa Lucia	1
Costa Rica	3	Saudi Arabia	1
Cuba	1	Singapore	1
Djibouti	1	South Africa	2
Dominican Republic	7	Spain	2*
		Surinam	1
Ecuador	15	Swaziland	1
Egypt	1	Tanzania	1
England	3	Trinidad and Tobago	1
Germany	1		
Guinea	2	United Arab Emirates	4
Haiti	1		
India	1	Uruguay	11
Iran	2	USA	40
Iraq	9	Venezuela	16
Laos	1	Zaire	3
	Total: 51		Total: 369*

Source: prepared by the author.
* There are 368 contracts because one of them is a high velocity train between Portugal and Spain and has been accounted for in both countries. For this reason there is one less contract.

Figure 1. Countries with more than ten contracts with Brazilian contractors

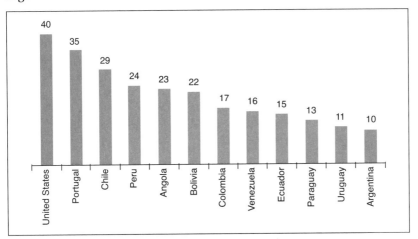

Source: prepared by the author.

in and characteristics of the course of the internationalisation of Brazilian contractors. First, let us analyse the geographical distribution of the contracts.

As Table 1 shows, Brazilian heavy construction companies performed rather vigorously over more than forty years, accounting for 368 contracts in 51 foreign countries in all inhabited continents with the exception of Oceania. In spite of appearing generalised, their activity brings to light a few target countries.

We can see from Figure 1 the countries that were the primary targets of the internationalisation process of Brazilian contractors. It is interesting to note that the American market was the leading target country for Brazilian contractors. This was due to its having the world's largest market for infrastructure projects and its receptivity to other countries' businesses. However, one needs to consider the important presence in this country of Odebrecht, the contractor with a history of success in construction, particularly in Florida and for the American Armed Forces. Odebrecht had 31 of the 40 Brazilian construction contracts in the country.

The Portuguese market, in second place, is also noteworthy. Despite not being a country with a huge volume of infrastructure projects, Portugal's entrance into the European Union, which occurred in 1986, gave rise thereafter to a number of public works interventions in its territory. In this context the Andrade Gutierrez and Odebrecht companies acquired local companies and influence in that market, becoming important agents for the integration of Portuguese infrastructure with European infrastructure. In 1988, Odebrecht absorbed Bento Pedroso

Figure 2. Distribution of contracts per continent/region

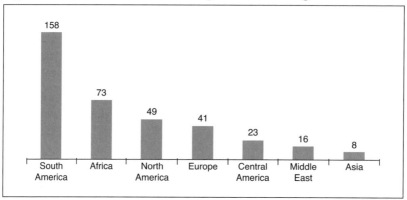

Source: prepared by the author.

Constructions (BPC) and Andrade Gutierrez acquired the Zagope construction company, both having a reasonable portfolio of ongoing works in the country. In this way the presence of Brazilian contractors in the Portuguese market was focused on the activities of their subsidiary companies, which are responsible for 33 of the 35 Brazilian construction contracts in the country. Furthermore, the fact that Portugal is a Lusophone country facilitated the Brazilian companies' entrance; it also accounts for their intense activity in other Portuguese-speaking nations, above all in Africa.

A significant aspect of the geographical distribution of Brazilian contracts is their limited activity, even recently, in the 'emerging' markets of the other BRICS members. Even though, in recent years, China, India, Russia and South Africa have implemented diverse infrastructure projects, Brazilian civil engineering firms have participated little in this process. Thus, up until 2010, there were only two contracts signed in South Africa, four in China, one in India and one in Russia, but none of them were long-term or of great monetary value. The explanation seems to lie in the fact that these markets are relatively restricted to local heavy construction firms or to firms of countries that have traditionally dominated them.

In addition, it is possible to observe that, of the 12 countries with more than ten Brazilian construction company contracts, nine are in South America. Only three countries are outside this region: North America, Europe and one African country. In this sample of 255 contracts (out of the total of 368) in countries with more than 10 contracts with Brazilian firms, 157 or 61.5% are in South American countries. Of these, Chile had the largest number, with 29 projects up until

Table 2. Ratio of the incidence of Brazilian contractors within each continent

Continent	Number of Countries	Countries with contracts with Brazilian contractors	Ratio
Africa	54	17	31.5%
Central America	20	8	40%
North America	3	2	66.7%
South America	12	11	91.7%
Asia	50	8	15%
Europa	46	5	10.9%
Oceania	14	0	0%
Total:	199	51	

Source: *The IBGE website was consulted for the number of countries per continent. http://www.ibge.gov.br/ accessed on 10 March 2014.*

2010. In fact, only the two independent Guyanese countries out of all 11 South American countries had fewer than 10 contracts with Brazilian contractors: Surinam, where there was only one contract up until 2010, and Guyana, where no contracts had been signed.

Thus we find South America predominates in terms of the number of contracts by continent. It is also here that half of all Brazilian civil construction firms' overseas contracts are located. Africa stands out as the second region of preference for Brazilian contractor activity, with a total of 73 contracts or 19.8% of all overseas contracts. North America follows with basically 40 contracts in the United States, nine in Mexico and none in Canada. The European data can also be confusing if one does not pay proper attention to it. This is because of the 41 contracts on the continent, 35 are in Portugal, basically concentrated in the activities of the Odebrecht and Andrade Gutierrez subsidiaries in the country. Thus, Brazilian firms' entrance into the continent is highly limited by barriers and mechanisms impeding their insertion. There are, therefore, no works by Brazilian contractors in the large and important markets of France or Italy, given their protectionist policies and those of other European countries. Another region presenting difficulties for Brazilian contractors is Asia, where their presence is reduced. Despite the somewhat restricted number of contracts in the Middle East, the region is extremely attractive as a market for Brazilian

Figure 3. Overseas contracts signed by Brazilian contractors, by year

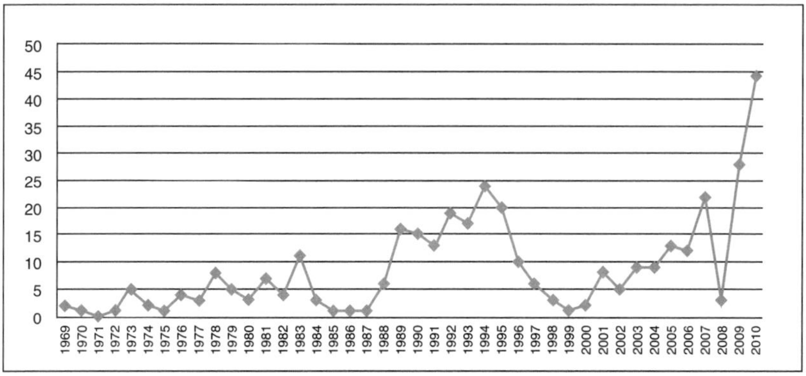

Source: prepared by the author.

contractors as the contracts are usually very lucrative.

With this information, it is possible to observe the ratio of Brazilian firms' incidence within each continent. Thus, from Table 2, one can see how the presence of Brazilian contractors is more generalised among the various countries of South America, North America, Central America and Africa than in Europe or Asia, where their incidence is restricted to only a few countries.

Finally, with this data and according to what one is able to observe, if the Brazilian contractors' internationalisation process is an intense, consolidated and proven movement on various continents and in various countries of the world, it is also marked by a high geographical concentration in a few regions and countries, such as South America, Africa and Central America along with the United States and Portugal. Even though the incidence of Brazilian contractors is significant in these places, its presence in European, Asian and Oceanic markets is practically nil.

Beyond the geography of this internationalisation process, there are a number of questions of a historical order that affect the Brazilian construction firms' performance. Thus, using Figure 3, one can see the trajectory of the quantity of contracts established by them abroad from 1969 to the end of the Lula da Silva government in 2010.

In the first place, it is necessary to highlight that in these cases the data is not totally reliable. In spite of a majority of the 368 contracts having clear indications of when they were signed, we were not able to get this information from the sources consulted for all of them. So we made deductions in some cases since the firms or journals researched did not exactly indicate the year but usually the length of time of the work and the period when the contract was signed.

We can see certain trends from this figure that can be explained by domestic as well international factors. In the first years of transnationalisation, the process was in its infant stage and only a few transnational contracts were signed each year. Thus Brazilian firms made their first investments in foreign markets in that moment and the number of contracts agreed annually was, in general, low. This characterised the first seven years of the period between 1969 and 1975, which also represents the peak of domestic demand for public works within Brazil; even so, Brazilian contractors sought opportunities abroad. In order to understand the beginnings of the construction industry's transnationalisation process, it is important to highlight the Asian and African independence movements on the international scene as well as the lines of credit of the World Bank and Inter-American Development Bank accompanying international tenders for Latin American public works. Driven by these two factors, the Brazilian companies obtained their first overseas contracts.

Nonetheless, with the worldwide petroleum shock of 1973 and the redirection of domestic policies toward incentivising the export of manufactured goods and services mainly through the creation of political-economy mechanisms favouring civil engineering firms acting abroad after 1975, what one notes is that the transnationalisation process gained more vigour from 1976 and was prolonged until 1983. Despite this being a period of stagnation and even retraction of domestic demand for public works, the companies that established overseas contracts were precisely the country's largest, which maintained a moderate level of domestic activity, as they were anchored in the dictatorship's huge ongoing projects, such as the Itaipu and Tucuruí hydroelectric projects, the Angra nuclear power stations and the Carajás project.

Between 1984 and 1987 business activity abroad stagnated.[5] This reality can be explained both by the international recession and the inertia of the Brazilian economy in the face of public works sector failures as well as by diminished state support for these companies' foreign investments. The 1980s were characterised by a global and Latin American recession along with a consequent weakness of demand for public works in those markets where Brazilian contractors had their principal activity.

After this downturn in civil engineering services exports, 1988 saw the beginning of an extremely vigorous period of Brazilian contractors' international expansion; now led by Andrade Gutierrez and Odebrecht – and no longer by Mendes Júnior – they even acquired foreign construction companies and established themselves in such promising markets as Portugal and the United States. Between 1988 and the mid-1990s there was a period in which more than ten contracts were signed each year. This was, therefore, the Brazilian contractors' richest period of international expansion. Accounting for this success were the international economic recovery at the end of the 1980s and beginning of the 1990s, the opening of world markets at the end of the Cold War, the expansion of the regional economic integration process (European Union and NAFTA) and capital globalisation as well as Brazilian government incentives for companies to internationalise and the greater competitiveness of domestic firms. This was a period of low growth for the Brazilian economy and a crisis in the public works sector. In any case, this was not very different from the previous period (pre-1988) and the one afterwards (post-1997). In the final analysis, what seem to explain this cycle of Brazilian contractor expansion abroad in the ten years between 1988 and 1997 are short-term international market conditions associated with the fact of having huge and experienced Brazilian civil engineering firms that had maintained state support even after the dictatorship had ended.

Yet, by the second half of the 1990s, a series of national and international economic shocks occurred. The 1997 Asian crisis followed by the Russian setback in 1998 and the Brazilian one in 1999 checked the international public works market and the momentum of the Brazilian contractors' international expansion. The second half of Fernando Henrique Cardoso government's term was marked by a severe economic recession that affected Brazilian civil engineering firms and their overseas activities. Thus the period 1996–2003 was noted for a certain retraction of the transnationalisation process of Brazilian contractors in the face of deteriorating national and international economic conditions.

The previous era was when Brazilian contractors had signed the greatest number of foreign contracts. In this light, the Lula period (2003–10) was distinguished by the recovery of the Brazilian economy, by the growth of the international economy led by new development centres and by being an era when Brazilian heavy construction firms expanded their activities abroad. If the growth of all BRICS members in this period, especially the Chinese economy, did not directly generate opportunities for public works in them, it did stimulate projects, particularly in logistics, in regions such as Latin America and Africa. Also important were the projects of the Initiative for the Integration of the Regional Infrastructure of South America (IIRSA) and the rise in petroleum prices (due to American wars in the Middle East) that caused a growth of the market for public works in such oil-producing countries as Venezuela, an important area for Brazilian contractor activity. Besides the positive domestic and international scenario, a decisive factor for grasping this expansion was broad state support and favourable public policies. BNDES lines of credit and Brazilian

Figure 4. Brazilian contractors' foreign contracts, by type of works

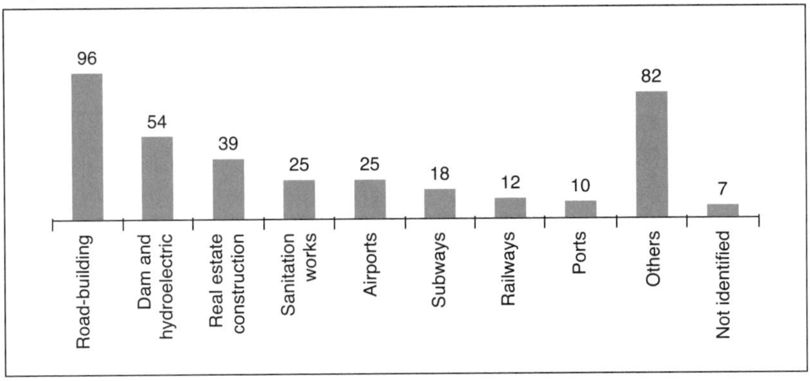

Source: prepared by the author.

diplomatic assistance fortified the capacity of Brazilian contractors to expand abroad. Despite the shock of the 2008 crisis, which had an immediate effect upon the international activity of these firms, what followed was a strong recovery process and continuity in the national construction companies' expansion into other countries including annual records in the number of foreign contracts.

Thus, as already noted, international and domestic factors conditioned the operations of Brazilian contractors between 1969 and 2010. State and diplomatic support as well as market conditions and the international system has to be taken into account to explain the annual number of signed contracts. As we have shown – in opposition to other explanations[6] – the domestic market slowdown was not responsible for companies becoming transnational. On the contrary, as we have observed, when the Brazilian economy boomed these companies extended their overseas activities while periods of retraction marked a diminishing number of their contracts in other countries. As was also highlighted, from the 1980s, when there was already a group of large and experienced contractors in Brazil and active public policies offering protection and incentives for these companies, their even greater success abroad (imperfectly measured by the number of contracts established outside the country) depended upon external more than domestic circumstances. Despite certain differences among them, these firms remained highly capitalised and assisted by the state apparatus, no matter who was in power. In relation to the type of works involved, there were some interesting trends in regard to the Brazilian contractors' transnationalisation process, as one can see in Figure 4.

According to Figure 4, Brazilian civil engineering firms expanded overseas

Figure 5. Brazilian contractor overseas constructions, by firm

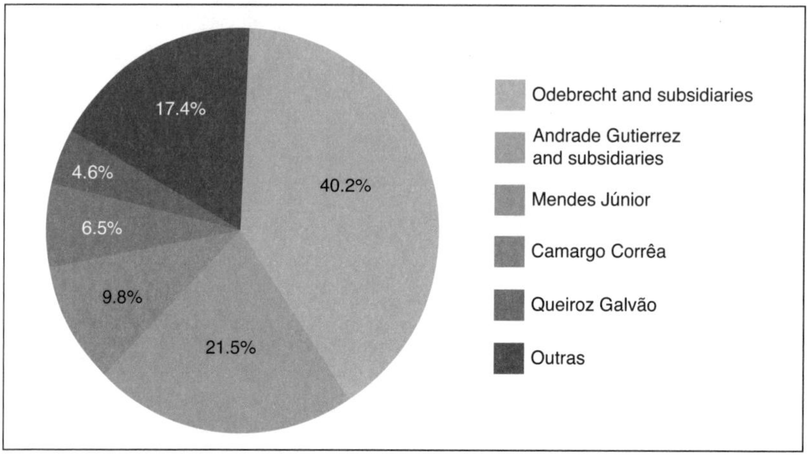

Legend:
- Odebrecht and subsidiaries
- Andrade Gutierrez and subsidiaries
- Mendes Júnior
- Camargo Corrêa
- Queiroz Galvão
- Outras

Values shown: 40.2%, 21.5%, 9.8%, 6.5%, 4.6%, 17.4%

Source: prepared by the author.

precisely in those areas where historically they had greatest domestic experience. Thus they built roads, dams and hydroelectric plants above all; that is, precisely the type of construction they had built domestically and which also corresponded to the type of road transport and energy generation characteristic of the Brazilian economy. In this way, the contractors seemed to export the Brazilian development model effective from the mid-1950s, characterised by the pattern of road transport and the model of electricity generation on the basis of hydroelectric plants. Brazilian contractors did not have the same drive to construct railways, ports or thermoelectric facilities abroad; they did not have the same experience in these niches. Among the works listed in Figure 4 as 'other works', we find diverse types of construction such as urbanisation projects, pipelines, specialised engineering structures (bridges, viaducts and tunnels), stadiums, industrial works, electrical installations, etc.

Finally, to complete this picture of the trends and characteristics of the internationalisation process of Brazilian firms, it is interesting to examine Figure 5 in which the concentration of construction abroad by firm is shown. What one perceives in the process of Brazilian contractor internationalisation is an elevated degree of concentration. Thus, if at least 37 Brazilian heavy construction firms had overseas contracts, only five held 82.6% of the total between 1969 and 2010. One group, Odebrecht and its subsidiaries, held more than 40% of all the contracts that heavy construction companies established overseas. However, at the beginning of the process in the 1970s, various firms were constructing overseas, such as Rabello, Esusa, Ecisa, Affonseca and others that went into bankruptcy and ceased work abroad. In other words, a good number of these firms, corresponding to 17.4% of the civil engineering firms in foreign markets, no longer have activities there and the market has become more concentrated in only five firms, which today take practically all of the overseas contracts.

Therefore, as has been shown, the Brazilian contractors' internationalisation process is not generalised among various-sized Brazilian heavy construction firms. On the contrary, we are dealing with the typical expansion of big capital headed by the firms considered leaders in the domestic public works market.[7]

In search of an explanation

The data treated in the present research has confirmed the hypotheses with which we have been working. Without ignoring such accounts of the phenomenon as the thesis of Brazilian sub-imperialism, we think that the explanation given by Ruy Mauro Marini and his followers is not sufficient to elucidate the internationalisation of Brazilian firms. This is because what explains their overseas activity is the experience and large-scale capitalisation that firms underwent in Brazil before and mostly during the civil-military dictatorship (1964–88), rather than market constriction. Hence these firms were involved in various economic sectors in the domestic market and, because of their size and technical expertise, were able to execute similar works overseas. Assisted by ample state support and favouritism, this expansion occurred above all in such priority regions as South America and especially sub-Saharan Africa where Brazilian foreign policy was able to operate with greatest force and intensity.

Thus, on the basis of the data presented, we reaffirm[8] the following: in Brazil we have monopoly and international capital that not only exports capital but also seems to possess great influence in determining the direction of domestic public policy and foreign policy. Therefore, the international standing of the state and Brazilian capital should no longer be interpreted as within the rules of underdevelopment, of complete dependence or subordination to the contemporary interstate capitalist system. The Brazilian pattern of capital accumulation and the monopolistic size of certain domestic groups point more towards a relative autonomy of the state and Brazilian capital in a situation of complex dependence in which the country stays in a kind of economic subordination in relation to the central poles of the international system. However, the country behaves as an 'imperialist' power over other countries (such as those in South America and, to a lesser degree, those of the African continent), where Brazil presents itself as an exporter of manufactured goods and capital with superior technology and as an active agent of vertical cooperation agreements.[9]

It is important to note that the international expansion of these groups takes place in parallel to and in relation to the extension of their domestic power and areas of activity. Thus, it is precisely during the Lula government that these companies extended their overseas operations and obtained important concessions as well as capital injections and contracts for public works in Brazilian territory. Projects such as the World Cup stadiums, the Olympic Games' installations, the huge hydroelectric plants in Madeira and Belo Monte, the large-scale urban interventions in the principal Brazilian cities and the military projects in this period did not occur to the detriment of these companies' overseas activities. On the contrary, they extended their economic and political power in the domestic environment and in foreign markets simultaneously, guaranteeing them renewed central influence in the direction of the Brazilian polity. The domination of international monopoly capital seems to be altered by the prevalence of these huge private conglomerates that guide domestic policy and, at the same time, the country's international agenda.[10]

Notes

1. This chapter is the fruit of research that had the financial support of Faperi and CNPq.

2 The heavy construction industry is the economic sector that covers firms, commonly known as contractors, engaged in infrastructure works. These companies are responsible for building works preferably contracted by the state apparatus: besides ports and airports, roads, railways, waterways, bridges and viaducts in the transport sector; hydroelectric plants, thermal plants, transmission lines, substations, among others in the energy sector; sanitation works such as water and sewage treatment plants, canalisation, underwater pipelines; urbanisation projects such as public roads, pavements, public parks and others; industrial works including factories, petroleum platforms, etc.; pipelines such as oil and gas pipelines, slurry pipelines and ethanol pipelines. Often, these firms also operate in other engineering branches, executing industrial, electrical and building projects .

3 The websites of Odebrecht, Andrade Gutierrez, Camargo Corrêa, Mendes Júnior, Queiroz Galvão and OAS.

4 *O Globo*, *Folha de S. Paulo*, *O Estado de S. Paulo*, *Valor Econômico* and *Le Monde Diplomatique Brasil*.

5 For the domestic context during the dictatorship, see my forthcoming book *Estranhas catedrais: as empreiteiras brasileiras e a ditadura civil-militar, 1964–1988*.

6 Especially the explanations based on Ruy Mauro Marini's studies. See, principally, his book *Subdesenvolvimento e revolução*.

7 Thus, in *O Empreiteiro*'s 2010 list of major Brazilian contractors, Odebrecht is in first place followed by Camargo Corrêa, Andrade Gutierrez and Queiroz Galvão, precisely four of the major multinational Brazilian civil engineering firms. Mendes Júnior, which went through the bankruptcy process in the 1990s, figures in tenth place.

8 According to what we originally indicated in Campos 2013.

9 See, for example, Ana Garcia's doctoral dissertation.

10 Such as Virginia Fontes pointed out in *O Brasil e o capital-imperialismo*.

References

Bouvier J (1976) O aparelho conceptual em história econômica. In MBN da Silva (ed). *Teoria da história*, São Paulo, Cultrix, pp 135–161

Campos, PHP (2010) A transnacionalização das empreiteiras brasileiras e o pensamento de Ruy Mauro Marini, *Contra a Corrente: Revista Marxista de Teoria, Política e História Contemporânea*, 2, pp 70–77

Campos, PHP (2013) A ditadura dos empreiteros: as empresas nacionais de construção pesada, suas formas associativas e o Estado brasileiro, 1964–1985, *Praia Vermelha: Estudos de Política e Teoria Social*, 21, 1, pp 135–152

Campos, PHP (forthcoming) Estranhas catedrais: as empreiteiras brasileiras e a ditadura civil-militar, 1964–1988, Niterói: Eduff

Cardoso, CFS and HP Brignoli (2002) *Os métodos da história*, Rio de Janeiro, Graal

Fontes, V (2010) *O Brasil e o capital-imperialismo: teoria e história*, Rio de Janeiro, EdUFRJ

Garcia, A (2012) A internacionalização de empresas brasileiras durante o governo Lula: uma análise crítica da relação entre capital e Estado no Brasil contemporâneo, PhD thesis, Pontifical Catholic University of Rio de Janeiro

Guedes, H (c.1995) *Histórias de empreiteros*, São Paulo, Clube dos Empreiteros

Marini, RM (2012) *Subdesenvolvimento e revolução*, Florianópolis, Insular

Mendes, MV and L Attuch (2004) *Quebra de contrato: o pesadelo dos brasileiros*, Belo Horizonte, Del Rey

Vilar, P (1965) Para uma melhor compreensão entre economistas e historiadores: história quantitativa ou economia retrospectiva? In P Vilar and J Marczewski, *Desenvolvimento econômico e análise histórica*, Lisboa, Presença

11

Behind the image of South–South solidarity at Brazil's Vale

Judith Marshall

Brazil's ex-president, Lula da Silva, has made the South–South trajectory to Africa a regular feature of his political life both during and after his two terms in office. Throughout Africa he is held in high esteem as a leader of national liberation, in the pantheon of South Africa's Nelson Mandela or Mozambique's Samora Machel. On his first presidential visit to Mozambique in 2003, Lula got a hero's welcome and gave emotional speeches about South–South solidarity and the strength of Brazil's affinity to Africa. He responded with empathy to the AIDS pandemic and promised Brazilian support for a project to produce affordable AIDS drugs. The Brazilian entourage included Roger Agnelli, the brash banker who while still in Bradesco had played a key role in assessing the value of Brazil's premium state enterprise, Companhia Vale do Rio Doce (Uchoas 2009). The evaluation of assets was carried out in preparation for a privatisation auction which took place in 1997. Agnelli subsequently became Vale's first president and CEO.

Buoyed by the 'commodities supercycle' with average increases of 150% from 2002 to 2012 (NI 2014), the seemingly endless Chinese demand for iron ore to feed its steel industry and the abundant capital available from the Brazilian National Bank for Social and Economic Development (BNDES), Agnelli seemingly had the Midas touch. His era of command in the newly named 'Vale' was characterised by aggressive global expansion and fabulous profits and returns to shareholders. Yet by tracking Vale's trajectory, whether within Brazil itself, in Mozambique where it has embarked on a greenfields investment in a coal mining, railway and port complex, or in Canada where it acquired established nickel operations, a picture emerges of conflicting corporate images. There is also a marked dissonance between the corporate images projected by Vale and the realities on the ground throughout Vale's global operations.

From an institutional location as a staff member in the Global Affairs and Workplace Issues Department of United Steelworkers (USW), the major union representing mine workers in Canada, I have had the opportunity to monitor this dissonance between Vale's images and practices at first hand over the past decade. I have done so both in Canada after Vale's purchase of the operations of a major Canadian mining company, Inco, and in Mozambique, where USW has had long-standing connections supporting union training programmes through the Steelworkers Humanity Fund. Over the last decade, USW has organised four worker-to-worker exchanges, taking Canadian and Brazilian Vale employees to Mozambique to be part of the resource team for week-long union training courses for Mozambican Vale workers. These kinds of worker-to-worker exchanges have characterised the international work of the USW for many years (Marshall 2009).

In 2011, USW, with support from the Canadian International Development Agency, CIDA, organised a study visit to Brazil for 14 Mozambicans and four Canadians, to see Vale's operations in the north of Brazil at first hand and learn how unions and communities in Brazil were impacted by the mega-project of iron mines, railway and port operation in Para and Maranhão states and what their strategies of resistance were. The participants included Vale employees, community leaders and local and provincial government officials from regions already impacted by Vale projects or to be impacted in future. The USW has also been an active participant in the International Network of People Affected by Vale, starting from its initial meeting in 2010. After retiring from USW in 2012, I carried out a small survey, inviting workers in Canada, Brazil and Mozambique to respond to a questionnaire about their experiences of working for Vale. The results of the survey were incorporated into a paper presented at the III International Conference of the Institute of Social and Economic Studies (IESE) in Maputo, Mozambique, in September 2012 (Marshall 2012). This study of Vale in the context of the BRICS is very much shaped by my participant-observer location and the opportunities it has provided to monitor Vale at first hand.

Vale's practices raise questions of whether multinational corporations based in the BRICS actually differ from global mining companies linked to the historical capitalist and imperialist centres. Vale's Department of Communications and Image works hard to project an image of South–South solidarity, with Brazilian mining investments in the Global South touted to bring with them the jobs and economic development that the companies from the imperialist 'North' do not. In its operations in the 'North', Vale works to project the image of corporate management expertise and Wall Street credentials, yet its management of the long-established nickel mines in Canada brought major turbulence. There were 11- and 18-month strikes. The labour–management relationship was stalemated by Vale's insistence on major concessions from the union as a precondition for even coming to the bargaining table. Vale's position flouted all accepted practices in Canadian traditions of collective bargaining and amounted to a frontal attack on the prevailing labour culture.

If Vale's intentions were ever in doubt, the words of Tito Martins, the then Director of Basic Metals, at the end of the 11-month strike, made them crystal clear. The major Brazilian business publication, *Valor Econômico*, published an article entitled 'Vale celebrates reducing the power of the unions in Canada'. Tito Martins claimed in the article that Vale had won everything it wanted from the prolonged arm-wrestle with its Canadian workers. Martins explained: 'What was important for Vale in this negotiation was to get the employees in Canada realigned into the same kind of relationship the company has with its employees around the world. This relationship involved three crucial issues: pension plan, bonus and chain of command between employer and employee without direct intervention of the union' (Durão 2010, my translation).

The 18-month strike in Newfoundland and Labrador, where the largely aboriginal work force is employed in a 'fly-in/fly-out' operation at Vale's Voisey's Bay mine, resulted in a call by the provincial government for a formal Industrial Inquiry (Province of Newfoundland and Labrador 2011). The main recommendation of the Inquiry was 'that government now re-examine the mechanisms by which it facilitates collective bargaining to take account of a) the organisational structure of multinational corporations, b) the need to ensure that such corporations respond to Canadian labour relations values, and c) the relative economic weight of the parties in the collective bargaining relationships (Province of Newfoundland and Labrador 2011).

Vale also has an abysmal record for health and safety since its takeover of the Canadian operations, with five fatalities since 2011, one in Thompson and four in Sudbury, plus two more fatalities in a contracted-out operation at arm's length from Vale. Three of the six fatal accidents occurred in 2014, all in Sudbury. In the words of one Vale worker in the 2012 survey, 'Whether underground or in the smelter and refinery, Vale has made it more dangerous than it was before. Removing accident, incident and concern form 079 [form encouraging any worker to make a report, even if only to register a concern], gutting training programmes and ordering cheap parts from China are three examples' (Marshall 2012).

Vale in Africa

Local lore in Mozambique has it that President Lula introduced Agnelli and Vale to Mozambique, encouraging President Armando Guebuza to reject the Chinese bid for Mozambique's coal deposits because the Chinese would bring their own workers. Be that as it may, Agnelli was invited shortly after the visit to become a member of Mozambique President Armando Guebuza's International Advisory Council and Vale was the first to be granted a licence to develop Mozambique's major coal reserves. Agnelli holds positions on similar international advisory bodies for the government of South Africa, the Mayor of Shanghai and the Sultanate of Oman (*Forbes* 2014).

During his visit to Mozambique in 2012, Lula conveyed the same mixed messages of solidarity on the one hand, and a sales pitch for investment by Brazilian companies on the other. This time, Lula arrived with Agnelli's successor, Murilo Ferreira. The antiretroviral drugs plant was officially opened nine years after the project was officially announced, and only after Vale, with major media fanfare, had topped up the original investment (Club of Mozambique 2011).

While in Mozambique Lula gave a public lecture entitled 'The struggle against inequality' chaired by Graça Machel, widow of Mozambique's first president, Samora Machel, and a well-known public figure in her own right. She introduced Lula as a hero of the people like Samora and Lula lectured on Brazil's experience under Worker Party governance. He characterised it as one of growing and distributing the economic pie at the same time, thus ensuring the jobs and redistributive social programmes that can alleviate poverty. He urged Brazilian companies investing in Mozambique to contribute to this fight against inequality. During his visit, however, Lula also found time to join the new Vale president in lobbying the Minister of Labour, Helena Taipo, to reduce the restrictions on foreign workers in Vale's Mozambique operations. A Brazilian magazine, *Veja*, noted for being critical of Lula and the Workers Party (PT), picked up the story under the title 'Lula lobbies for company in Mozambique':

Vale was one of the sponsors of the tour that Luiz Inácio Lula da Silva did two weeks ago in Africa. The company's president, Murilo Ferreira, travelled on the same jet that carried the former president to Mozambique. There, they met with Labour Minister Helena Taipo, who has been putting barriers to the exploitation of coal by the Brazilian company in Moatize mine, one of the largest in the world. At the meeting, Lula tried unsuccessfully to convince her to reduce the requirement that Mozambicans make up 85% of the manpower employed in Vale's operations (Veja 2012, my translation).

Brazilian pressure to reduce Mozambican controls on foreign workers is not something new. A labour delegation from Canada and Brazil met with the Provincial Director of Labour in Tete Province in 2011 in the context of a tri-national worker exchange. We were told of Vale's constant pressure on Mozambican authorities to allow Vale to exceed the previously negotiated quotas on foreign workers. There was also pressure to give work permits to foreigners without sufficient skills to carry out the training component meant to be carried out by each foreign worker allowed a work permit.

The construction phase of the project included not only large numbers of Brazilian workers but also construction workers from the Philippines. Many of these were hired by Kentz Engineers and Contractors, a company which operates in nearly 30 countries and runs one of the world's biggest nickel-cobalt refineries in the world in Madagascar. In Mozambique, Kentz was subcontracted by Vale. Kentz employs more than 2500 overseas Filipino workers in its global operations. Many of the Filipinos working for Kentz in Madagascar were repatriated to the Philippines at the end of 2010. They filed cases before the Philippines Overseas Employment Administration (POEA) at the beginning of 2011, alleging unfair labour practices by Kentz. These included salary delays, overcrowded barracks, food shortages and inadequate health care (Bulatlat 2011).

On 18 November 2011, the Ministry of Labour in Mozambique announced problems involving Kentz and Filipino workers: 'The labour ministry has just expelled, with immediate effect, 115 foreign workers, mostly of South African and Filipino nationality, who were brought here illegally by the South African company Kentz Engineers & Constructors.' The company is a subcontractor of Brazilian mining giant Vale Moçambique, at the company's coal concessions in Moatize in the north-west of the country. Department inspectors found workers at the construction site who were denied workers' holidays or weekends and proper protective clothing. It also had not registered its Mozambican workers for social security. Kentz Engineers was fined close to 34 million meticals (R9.2 million) and granted 30 days to fix irregularities (*Mail & Guardian* 2011).

The workers based in Tete who participated in the international exchanges indicated that the operational phase of the coal mine today employs not only the quota maximum – or more – of Brazilian workers, but also many foreign workers, with or without legal residence status, from the neighbouring English-speaking countries of Zimbabwe, Zambia and Malawi. Many sons and nephews of powerful Mozambican government and business figures in the national capital, Maputo, also get the coveted jobs at Vale. The numbers of jobs created for people in the local communities around the mine or natives of the chronically underdeveloped Tete Province are few. Yet these are the people who suffer the major impact from the mining boom in terms of pollution, scarcity of housing and other services, traffic, noise and rising cost of living in general. The booming mining operations also bring social problems with prostitution, drugs and AIDS on the rise. These social problems were already much in evidence because Tete is a major junction for cross-border trucking operations to neighbouring Zimbabwe, Zambia and Malawi. Mining has made the social issues even more acute (Selemane 2009).

The few opportunities for employment generated by the mining operations and the dramatic inequalities in salaries and benefits between foreigners and nationals create a generalised sense of resentment. One Vale worker commented, 'I work alongside foreigners but they earn four times more than I do.' Another said: 'Mozambican machine operators work together with Brazilian machine operators, some of whom have less training than the Mozambicans, but the Brazilian is automatically the supervisor.' These sentiments were expressed in a survey conducted in 2012 to determine whether workers' experiences of Vale in Brazil were similar to what Vale workers in Mozambique and Canada experienced (Marshall 2012). These particular comments capture the hollowness of Vale's discourse on contributing to job creation for Mozambicans. They also show the strength of the anti-Brazilian feelings, not so different from anti-American or anti-British sentiments at other times and in other places.

While there are no systematic studies to draw on, the feeling at popular level in Mozambique is that Vale is actually taking away jobs. The forced resettlements to make way for the mines have left rural families from the areas around the mine with no land or water for their agricultural activities and no access to local markets. A recent study carried out by Antonio Jone for the Observatory on the Rural Environment concluded that the families sent to the rural resettlement in Cateme have been adversely affected. Vale's much-touted adherence to all of the World Bank recommendations on forced resettlements turns out to be far from the truth.

Starting from the principles defended both by the operational guidelines of the International Finance Corporation and Mozambican legislation with respect to forced resettlements, what must be guaranteed is complete relocation and support such that those resettled improve or, at a minimum, recover their mode of living or subsistence. In the case of Cateme, there is a need to continue to implement activities with a view to guaranteeing access to land for agriculture for all the families, in quantity (the 2 hectares promised) and quality (fertile and not rocky), with proximity to sources of water not just to irrigate their fields but also to develop fishing. Activities to support clearing of trees and bush, preparation of the land, levelling and stabilisation of the soil and distribution of seeds, fertilisers and pesticides must also be continued. It is important to identify areas where there is less pressure on resources, as a way of avoiding imminent land conflicts and litigation over other resources such as bamboo, saplings, cane and wood, all essential for other income-generating activities. As a final conclusion, and in response to the central objective of this text, as well as other aspects, we can say with certainty that in the case of Cateme, the process of resettlement has had a negative effect on food production (Jone 2014, my translation).

Local artisans in the affected areas such as those making building blocks, have been left with no space to carry out their trade. They have carried out angry lobbying activities in recent years directed both at government and Vale. They are demanding more adequate compensation from Vale than the US$2000 paid to them originally. They have adopted a page from corporate logic and argue that they have suffered a permanent loss of livelihood through which they could have expected a lifetime income more in the neighbourhood of US$350 000. In June 2013, Vale took the position that the matter was closed, with the brick makers and Mozambique government taking equally strong positions:

> According to Ricardo Saad, a director in Vale Mozambique, the process of compensations payments ended last year but the mining company continues to engage with the brick makers in development projects ... Before the start of coal mining operations more than 800 families were removed from their home areas and the company offered and paid ... about two thousand dollars to each family. Today, however, those among the resettled families who lived from making building bricks, consider that the money paid was very little and demand $350 000 each. To express their anger, the brick makers have blocked the Sena railway line used by Vale to transport coal to the port of Beira. The Mozambican government believes that Vale is a strategic partner that participates in the development of the country. (*Jornal de Angola* 2013, my translation)

Over the past year, the situation has not been resolved. Vale has been forced to reopen discussions about compensation, the brick makers have continued to back up their demands by periodically bringing production to a halt, arrests of their leaders notwithstanding, and the government continues to express concern about profits lost by their 'development partner', Vale.

Vale: 'worst company in the world'

In January 2012, Vale had the dubious honour of being voted the 'worst company in the world'. The awards ceremony took place during the World Economic Forum in Davos, Switzerland, which has become in recent years a popular, extra-parliamentary gathering place for powerful business and government leaders to deliberate about corporate-led globalisation. Two Swiss-based organisations, Greenpeace and the Berne Declaration, have used the World Economic Forum to focus on the negative social and environmental practices of global corporate players. For the past eight years, they have given a Public Eye award based on an online competition for the 'worst company in the world'. Vale was awarded the 2012 'Nobel prize of shame', winning 25 000 of the 88 000 votes cast.

The award was presented by Joseph Stiglitz, winner of a genuine Nobel Prize in economics for earlier work he had done problematising the efficacy of market mechanisms. Stiglitz is former head of the World Bank, and now a prestigious dissenting voice in global forums, where he often utters dire warnings about where unregulated globalisation is taking us. In his presentation, Stiglitz mused aloud about how long powerful global players like Vale and Rio Tinto and BHP Billiton could operate with so little regard for the social and environmental consequences of their projects and so little accountability to the '99%' of the population who are excluded from their game plans. Stiglitz went on to say that to protect our planet and our society, we depend not only on government regulations to prevent abuses, but also on a broadening of our concept of self-interest, both for individuals and corporations.

It is in everyone's interest – even the richest 1% – that our planet thrive, that the divide between the haves and the have-nots not be too excessive. For firms, this entails corporate responsibility, going beyond the minimum required by the law to protect the environment. It means treating workers with decency and fairness, not exploiting all the advantages that asymmetries in bargaining might afford (Stiglitz 2012).

Vale and global security

Vale's aggressive expansion in the years since its privatisation has made it the second-largest mining company in the world with operations in 16 Brazilian states and in 33 countries on six continents. Despite its origins as a state company and its closeness to the Brazilian government, including significant Vale shareholder blocks still in the hands of Brazilian government workers' pension funds, Vale's ascendancy to its current global-player status has been characterised by a ruthlessness and singleminded devotion to high profits and generous dividends to its shareholders.

Brazilians are particularly indignant about how this national icon passed into private hands in 1997 as part of the global pattern of privatisation under structural adjustment programmes. BNDES, the Brazilian Bank for Socio-Economic Development, took on responsibility for promoting widescale privatisation of the economy. The sale of Vale is considered to be the most scandalous privatising episode in Brazilian history. The company was sold for only R$3.4 billion in a period of parity between the real and the US dollar. A submission to the Federal Regional Tribunal (TRF) in Brasilia in 2004 made explicit a series of irregularities that proved that Vale was undervalued. Some mines were ignored in the calculations, others undervalued. The forestry sector was also undervalued. Intangible assets of enormous value (technologies, patents and technical knowledge related to geology and mining engineering) were not considered. Vale's stock holdings in Açominas, CSN, Usiminas and CST were ignored. The list of irregularities is enormous. Bradesco, the bank responsible for the evaluation, took over control of Vale one year later. Vale's first president, Roger Agnelli, was an ex-executive director of Bradesco (Uchoas 2009, my translation).

Even a decade later, an informal plebiscite for the renationalisation of Vale organised by unions, students and the Landless People's Movement in 2007 was able to mobilise three million votes. While President Lula seemingly took no heed of the demands of the plebiscite, he did put public pressure on Vale during the ensuing global economic crisis. Vale tried to take advantage of the 2008 crisis as a moment for large-scale lay-offs and reneging on planned investments in the Brazilian steel industry. Lula used the popular anti-privatisation sentiment expressed through the plebiscite to justify a very public scolding of Roger Agnelli. Lula suggested strongly that for a company as close to government as Vale there was an obligation to respond to a moment of global turbulence by playing a stabilising role.

During 2009, the tensions between the Brazilian government's vision of the role Vale should be playing and Agnelli's vision of Vale's role were openly at odds. By September, the Brazilian magazine *Exame* was being quoted by other business media as the source of information on government plans to oust Agnelli. In an article entitled 'Lula criticises Vale and articulates ouster of Vale President', journalist Rafael Souza Ribeiro (2009) writes as follows:

The government's wish to increase its role in the administrative control of Vale did not begin today. President Luiz Inácio Lula da Silva has already stated several times this year that mining needs to invest more in Brazil to provide employment for the population. Since his dismissal of more than 1000 employees last year, attributed to the economic crisis, Roger Agnelli, President of Vale, has fallen into disfavour in the corridors of government. According to *Exame* magazine, there was even a committee created to remove Agnelli from the presidency of the mining company.

Indeed, Agnelli's use of the global crisis to justify laying off 1300 workers and backtrack on investment commitments to produce steel in Brazil came back to haunt him when his term of office expired in 2011. Brazil's new President, Dilma Rousseff, orchestrated the Vale shareholder blocks close to government to bring about a change of leadership in Vale. The Brazilian daily *O Estado de São Paulo* captured the dilemma in its coverage of the inauguration of a huge new Vale ore carrier in 2011. Agnelli, whose departure had already been announced, presided over the event to which government leaders had been invited. The ship had been specially commissioned in Korea and was designed to carry the massive loads of iron ore from the mines in Carajás in the Amazon, which have been exporting unprocessed iron ore to world markets since the 1980s. In recent years, the largest volume of exports has gone to China.

Agnelli's departure was driven by pressures from the government, a shareholder of the company, by way of state pension funds. The problems started with the orders for ships to be purchased outside of Brazil (the one presented yesterday was from Korea). It deepened with the decision to sack 1300 workers at the peak of the financial crisis and to delay promised investments in domestic steel production. Yesterday, Agnelli said that Vale was committed to efficiency and has different visions and missions than those of government, though he did not consider them to be in conflict. 'Each has a vision, each has a mission. The company's mission is to generate profits in order for the company to grow in capacity and invest more. The vision, the mission of the government is different from that of a company, totally different,' said Agnelli (Valle 2011, my translation).

The change of leadership from Roger Agnelli to Murilo Ferreira and Vale's promises of a more humane management and a reduction of tension brought hopes for change. Ferreira took office as new President in 2011 and shortly thereafter began a round of visits to Vale operations throughout the world. The raised expectations were dashed by Vale's pointed snubbing of union leaders throughout his inaugural tour of Vale's global operations. In response to criticisms he did, however, agree to meet with the 14 presidents of Vale operations linked to mining in Brazil on 23 September 2011.

According to a report by Valerio Vieira, President of Metabase Inconfidentes union, which represents two Vale mines in the Minas Gerais state, most of the union leaders present were happy to buy into Ferreira's notion of a kinder, gentler Vale and praised his readiness to dialogue with them. They lauded his visible emotion during the discussion on workplace fatalities. Vieira, who had worked for Vale on and off for 25 years, was not convinced. In his report to Metabase, shared with Vale activists in other countries, Vieira recounted saying to Ferreira that it would take a great deal more than three months for him to change the course of Vale after a decade under Agnelli's leadership. Moreover, it would take a level of political will not yet demonstrated.

> I said to him [Murilo Ferreira] and to those present that every time we have a meeting with the company management we are told that things are getting better, but there is a contradiction. What is said in Rio is contrary to what happens on the ground in Minas. Workplace accidents continue and they are being covered up. The harassment by managers has never been so intense. The unjust punishments and dismissals are of such proportions that it will be difficult to convince the union in Metabase Inconfidentes and our members that things are going to change. Mr President, you will have to convince us because up to now, nothing has changed (Vieira 2011).

Vieira's report on the meeting identified eight characteristics of working for Vale in Brazil: (1) Vale is noted for being very anti-union; (2) A Vale worker tends to earn less than workers in similar workplaces; (3) Vale managers engage in constant bullying of workers; (4) Vale imposes unrealistically high production goals, thus creating the atmosphere of permanent stress which Vale promised to eliminate; (5) Vale workers live with the constant threat of being fired without due cause; (6) Vale supervisors impose arbitrary disciplinary measures with great frequency; (7) To work at Vale means to work in dangerous conditions because Vale puts production above all else and often covers up health and safety incidents; (8) Vale regularly tries to buy union and government leaders by offering them vehicles, travel, credit cards, etc.

In 2012, a small sample of Vale workers in Canada, Mozambique and Brazil were asked whether these eight characteristics of working for Vale identified by Vieira were applicable to their situations. While the situations in each country are completely different, the overwhelming response to the survey was that Vieira's characterisation of working for Vale resonated profoundly in the other countries (Marshall 2012).

Mining companies competing within the neoliberal world order

Vale's rapid ascent to become a major global player in the mining sector occurred within a consolidated neoliberal world order. While Vale wrapped itself in the Brazilian flag and adopted the elevated language of the Global Compact, its operations at home and abroad were characterised by relentless implementation of production targets, even at the cost of security in its mines and safety along its export corridors. It showed a callous and widespread disregard for human rights and assumed only as much responsibility for the damages its operations inflicted on workers, communities and the environment as the law – or adverse publicity – forced it to do.

Vale showed no hesitation in benefiting from just the asymmetries of power alluded to by Joseph Stiglitz when he awarded the 'worst company in the world' prize to Vale. This is evident in relation to the indigenous, ex-slave or traditional farming and fishing villages in northern Brazil, already negatively impacted by the original 890-kilometre transport corridor linking the Carajás iron mines to the São Luis port and now facing massive expansion of that line (Faustino and Furtado 2013). It is equally true in relation to the 1300 families in traditional peasant farming communities in Mozambique who lost their lands and livelihoods because they were in the way of Vale's new coal mines in Mozambique (Mosca and Selemane 2011).

The neoliberal world order in which Vale has emerged as a major player creates daunting challenges for Vale workers and communities and, indeed, for all those caught in its wake as the company forges ahead to realise its dreams of global dominance. Whether working for Vale in long-established mining cultures like Canada or Australia or working for Vale in its new mega-projects in Mozambique or Guinea or Indonesia, workers are faced with a company that epitomises all the worst of the current trends in global mining.

What are these contemporary practices of big mining companies based in the old imperial centres that Vale has so readily espoused? An analysis of these current trends was the main theme of an International Mining Conference organised by the United Steelworkers union in Toronto in June 2012. Andrew Vickers, Mining and Energy Sector Secretary of the Australian union CFMEU, made a major presentation with his take on the state of global mining viewed from Australia and the Pacific region. The general consensus of the conference delegates was that big mining companies were following a common strategy in both the Global North and Global South. This is the world in which Vale is excelling, far from the image it projects of South–South solidarity and a pillar of the national economy in Brazil.

The first characteristic common to big mining companies today is a strong desire for no third-party, i.e. union, intervention, with companies going out of their way to ignore unions. In Australia the mining union has waged – and won – a fight against Rio Tinto's push for individual contracts, but, even so, Rio Tinto has succeeded in union-busting in Australia's iron mines.

Vale's labour relations epitomise this anti-union stance. The actions during Roger Agnelli's presidency to reduce the unions' role in its Canadian operations have continued under Murilo Ferreira, despite Ferreira's protestation to the contrary. In June 2012 Ferreira gave a lengthy interview to the Brazilian business journal *América Economia* to mark his first year as CEO of Vale. When queried about the troubled relationship with the Vale union in Canada, and whether it was 'possible to seek a rapprochement with the opposition', his reply was: 'I found a very tense situation with the union when I arrived in Canada. I had lived for two and a half years in that country when I was Vale executive director. At that time I had an extraordinarily good relationship with the union. Upon returning to Vale as president I met with trade unionists and hope to do so again shortly. Where I go, I talk to them. I am planning to go to Canada to talk to the union in July, at which time I hope to see my union friends again' (*América Economia* 2012).

Ferreira's fine words about 'union friends' in Canada were somewhat belied by the words of Myles Sullivan, a USW staff member interviewed for the same article when he was in Brazil for the Vale Annual General Meeting and the launch of the Vale Unsustainability Report (AV 2012). Sullivan said at the time: 'For the situation to improve, Vale has to recognise and respect the USW as the bargaining agent of the employees whom we represent. Our members who carry out the work know what creates the best conditions for the work environment. If Vale stopped working against us and, on the contrary, supported us, it could benefit tremendously' (*América Economia* 2012).

Ferreira's self-congratulatory stance is even more problematic when it is juxtaposed with Sudbury local union president Rick Bertrand's memory of his first meeting with him. This came about after several Ferreira visits to Sudbury as CEO during which there was no union contact whatsoever. Bertrand opened the meeting with Ferreira by commenting that it was a pity it had taken four workplace fatalities in 11 months in Vale's Canadian operations to prompt the Vale CEO to engage directly with the union.[1]

In Canada, the union historically has played a major role in the day-to-day management of workplace relationships. The 200-page collective agreements include language to cover virtually every area of possible contention, with a mutually recognised set of steps for grievance procedures according to the seriousness of the infraction. Vale's desire, however, to marginalise the role of the union has included upping the ante in the grievance process, slapping step four grievances on what formerly were seen as minor infractions worthy of a step one, thereby creating huge backloads of cases needing formal arbitration procedures for their resolution. Anecdotally, workers mock the foolishness of the new management style which goes on the offensive even in the face of obvious company faults. A worker who tripped and had a minor arm injury in a darkened stairwell, unlit because management had not changed the light bulb, is given a formal reprimand for 'lack of awareness of his surroundings'!

Another characteristic of the big mining companies today is their preference for projects in remote areas, often 'fly-in, fly-out' enclaves. This serves as a way of keeping the intrusive nature of the mining project and their negative community and environmental impacts out of view of the general public. It is also a way of keeping workers separate from union organisers. Vale is using the enclave nature of its 'fly in, fly out' Voisey's Bay operation in Canada as a way to isolate its largely inexperienced workforce from participating in broader union events, like the international mining conference and the opportunity it provided to debate global trends. The National Office of USW is told frequently that Vale is using strict adherence to the rotations of the shifts, flying crews in and out every two weeks, as reason for not allowing its employees the leave for union activities stipulated in their collective agreements.

The delegates to the conference concluded that throughout the world big mining companies are showing a general tendency to push for health and safety as purely a management task with no recognition of workers' rights to participate. Vickers spoke of having left behind in Australia a huge dispute with BHP Billiton about the company's introduction of new policies to house all safety matters with supervisors. Ged Kearney, President of ACTU, a sister union in Australia, took up this question at a United Mineworkers Federation Memorial Day.

Contractors are increasingly favoured by some mining companies over permanent employees because they are cheaper and many contractors are not union-oriented and are less likely to raise safety concerns. Safety standards for some contractors have been found to be lower than other workers, as they received less training and induction.

At the core of the CFMEU's dispute with BHP Billiton-Mitsubishi Alliance in the Bowen Basin is management's insistence on appointing health and safety officers who do not represent a workforce that is increasingly contract driven (CFMEU 2012).

Canadian Vale workers come from a tradition of very strong union action in health and safety. The right to know, the right to participate and the right to stop production are strongly held principles. The right to know means being informed of products and processes that represent safety hazards. The right to participate means active union participation and joint structures. The right to stop production means a worker's right to bring production to a halt in the face of a perceived danger. In bigger mines, some of the worker-elected members are freed from production jobs to do full-time health and safety. The worker health and safety representatives are fully trained by both multi-level courses offered in labour schools run by the unions and company training. These representatives act as trainers for the rest of the workforce, as well as playing a proactive role in the day-to-day monitoring of all health and safety issues. They participate fully in all inspections and accident or fatality investigations. All of the Canadian Vale workers participating in the survey were in agreement that their new employer's approach to health and safety was highly problematic, a view that was exacerbated by the reality of five fatalities in the Thompson and Sudbury operations since 2011. In the Canadian context, this statistic is truly shocking.

In Canada, joint health and safety committees are mandated by law, as are mine rescue teams, first response teams and full health and safety training for all workers. The person in command of the first response team can be from either the management or union side. In the event of an emergency, this person takes charge with orders that supersede the hierarchies in place for normal production routines. All of the other levels of security available in the community, from firefighters to ambulance services to police forces, can also be called on, depending on the scale of the emergency.

One of the first bilateral exchanges between Canadian and Brazilian Vale workers took two Canadian health and safety workers to visit Vale mining in Carajás and railway and port workers in São Luis. They wrote reports when they came back, but the big question posed for them by talking with Vale workers in Brazil was: 'How can Brazilian Vale workers fight for health and safety when they fear for their jobs?' The common Vale management practice of dismissing workers without due cause meant that all bets were off. Why put your head up to fight for a safe workplace if doing so can cost you your livelihood?

While visiting Vale's largest iron ore mine in Carajás, in the Amazon jungle, we were shown a 'state of the art' central control where operators can monitor the performance of equipment, from bearing and engine temperatures to speeds of hauling trucks, all designed to improve productivity. This all looked great until we toured the mine site and saw employees wearing paper dust masks, like those banned in Canada because they offer little or no protection. When talking to our union brothers, we found that they were not aware of basic programmes, such as Work Place Environmental Monitoring or ensuring respirators are appropriate for the task and properly fitted. This leads one to ask where Vale's priorities are, which must be production over safety (Anderson 2006).

The post-conference trip to Sudbury for the international delegates gave the Sudbury Vale workers an opportunity to explain how the company actually took advantage of the lengthy strike situation in Canada to introduce a new top-down health and safety programme, with language making it even more 'behaviour-based', i.e. with the explicit assumption that workers' behaviour – ignorance, carelessness, inattention and the like – is the main cause of workplace accidents and fatalities. Policies were introduced to give management an even stronger disciplinary hand. Mechanisms that had built up serious worker involvement and responsibility were gutted, like Form 079, which allowed and encouraged any worker anywhere, at any time to report on concerns, incidents and accidents. Another change that shifted the dynamic in a negative way was a new rule that made bonus pay calculable only for 'face time', i.e. time spent actually in production working on the rock face. Down time because of a safety concern or a safety incident meant that people were not getting those hours included in their bonus calculations, a guaranteed mechanism to encourage workers themselves to become more lax.

The USW report on the double fatality at the Frood-Stobie mine in Sudbury on 8 July 2011 captures all of the problems with Vale's approach. Two young workers, one in a supervisory role, were fatally injured while working on an ore pass about 900 metres below the surface. Management had been alerted several times previously of the danger of a build-up in that area. When the workers opened the door to check the flow from one level to another, they were buried in an avalanche of wet muck (*Sudbury Star* 2011).

After the accident, Vale said that it wanted a joint investigation – but it also wanted full control, the right to lead the investigation, the right to limit the scope of the investigation, the right to have Vale lawyers review the report, the right to set boundaries on who could be interviewed during the investigation and the right to limit the release of the investigation results to government, union and families.

After five days of negotiation, and with all of those red flags signalling danger, the union reluctantly said no, and took on doing an independent investigation, a right enshrined in the Ontario Health and Safety Act. Members were released to head the investigation. Vale tried to limit the time and resources, but again the Act offered protection. Vale then tried to force the investigation members back to work.

In the end, a carefully documented 206-page report was produced entitled *Double Fatality Investigation Report Frood/Stobie Complex* (USW LU6500 2012). It found Vale guilty of culpable negligence. The supervisor who was killed had written memos alerting more senior management of dangerous conditions. He had physically set up barriers to prevent dumping of material that could further block ore passes but these were removed. He and another young worker died, suffocating in a slide of wet muck triggered by opening a door to check the ore pass. The report included 20 recommendations to Vale and three recommendations to the Ministry of Labour. The Ontario government report has since been released and fully corroborates the findings of the USW report. However laudable the labour and government reports, and whatever the fines or prison sentences imposed, nothing can change the wilful negligence of Vale and the loss of two workers' lives.

The analysis of current mining strategies during the conference included lengthy discussion about how the big players in the world of mining have launched a major propaganda initiative to sell the idea that modern mining can be sustainable and that modern mining companies can and should self-regulate. The mining companies advocate such instruments as Corporate Social Responsibility programmes and adherence to bodies like the Global Compact and the ICMM with their voluntary global reporting initiatives. Yet the information supplied by the company in its voluntary reports often shows marked inconsistencies with what happens on the ground.

For example, in the official Vale Sustainability Reports as well as in Vale's PR videos, the resettlements in Mozambique become models of excellence. In the alternative Vale Unsustainability Report prepared by the International Network of People Affected, the voices of the resettlers themselves tell of no land, no water, houses with wall cracks and crumbling foundations after the first rainy season (International Network of People Affected by Vale 2012). More recently, Antonio

Jone's study of 'food security' in the Vale resettlement corroborates that it has been anything but a success story, and has actually left peasant producers much worse off than they were prior to having been resettled (Jone 2014).

While the shocking inadequacy of the resettlement programme may be the most immediately visible negative impact of the contribution of Vale's mining operations to Mozambique's development, this is confirmed by the scathing comments of Portuguese sociologist Boaventura de Sousa Santos in his reflections on Mozambique and the ways in which the mining boom is shaping the patterns of economic, social, political and cultural development.

> The risks of this conditioning are, among others, growth of the GNP instead of social development; generalised corruption of the political class that defends its private interests by becoming increasingly authoritarian as a way of holding onto power, now seen as the source of primitive accumulation; increases rather than reductions in poverty; growing polarisation between a tiny, super-rich minority and a huge majority of beggars; environmental destruction and uncounted sacrifices of the population in areas where the resources are to be found, all in the name of a 'progress' which they themselves will never know; creation of a consumer culture which is available only to a small urban minority but imposed as an ideology on all of society; suppression of critical thinking and protest actions by civil society under the pretext that civil society represents obstacles to development and is a prophet of doom. In summary, the risks are that, after this cycle of resource orgy, the country will be economically, socially, politically and culturally poorer than it was at the beginning. That is what the 'resource curse' is all about (Sousa Santos 2012, my translation).

One of the most cogent analyses of mining within the logic of the prevailing economic model can be found in James Ferguson's *Global Shadows: Africa in the Neo-Liberal World Order* (2006). Ferguson argues that we should put aside any discourses about big mining investors needing stable democracies and good governance as preconditions for their operations. In Africa, they have happily invested in countries with raging wars and governments of notorious instability and corruption such as Angola, the DRC and Equatorial Guinea. He sees trends that began with oil companies now spilling over into mining. The model is that of capital-intensive enclaves, effectively insulated from the local economy, guarded by private armies and security forces. Angola's off-shore oil with production virtually unabated during endless years of war was the perfect project, with neither the oil itself nor the wealth it created ever touching African soil.

African governments have not found the means or the political will to use mega-projects in mining as the strategic pillar for a broader industrial strategy, part of a plan for diversification, articulation and broadening of the productive base. Mining projects have tended to become simply enclaves, articulated globally but unconnected in the host country. According to Ferguson:

> it is worth noting how such enclaves participate not only in the destruction of national economic spaces but also in the construction of 'global' ones. For just as enclaves of, say, mining production are often fenced off (literally and metaphorically) from their surrounding societies, they are at the same time linked up, with a 'flexibility' that is exemplary of the most up-to-date, 'post-Fordist' neoliberalism, both with giant transnational corporations and with networks of small contractors and subcontractors that span thousands of miles and link nodes across multiple continents ... (Ferguson 2006:13).

Viewed from within Mozambique, Carlos Nuno Castel Branco posed the same question in this way:

> A Vale, a SASOL, a Kenmare, a BHP Billiton, an Anadarko, an Artumas etc., etc., generate billions of US dollars each year for their global strategies. Each one of these companies has an annual liquid profit many times higher than the annual budget of Mozambique. For them, Mozambique is a source of resources and profits. This is what we can rationally expect from a multinational company under global capitalism. The question is how can the state and the citizens in our Republic guarantee a rational and sustainable use of these resources in a way that benefits our country and its people, and not just the national and international economic and political elites (Castel Branco 2009:4, my translation).

Vale behind the images

The Brazilian corporations understood to have reached the status of 'global challenger' status, with Vale in the lead, project an image of themselves as a 'motor of development' both in Brazil and in the countries where they invest, generating employment and economic growth, a symbol of 'global Brazil'. This is well documented in a recent study of Brazilian investments in Angola and Mozambique (Garcia, Kato and Fontes 2012).

The government of Brazil attaches high importance to support for companies like Vale. The large amounts of credit conceded by BNDES and other public policies set up to support and facilitate the global investments of Brazil's multinationals are seen as fully justified. The activities of these companies are portrayed as advantageous for Brazil as a whole. The argument is that through these 'global challengers' Brazil increases the entry of foreign exchange (through deposits of profits), increases its exports, broadens its insertion into chains of global innovation, as well as the effects on suppliers to these companies, who also increase their production (Alem and Madeira 2010).

This narrative is squarely within the neoliberal paradigm. A country that wants to gain a hegemonic position globally is in need of big companies. Despite their ownership by private interests and notwithstanding their open espousal of high profit levels that guarantee good returns to their directors and shareholders as their main objective, Brazil's big companies and their global expansion are treated as synonymous with Brazil's 'national interests'. Worker or community or citizen resistance to the operations of these companies, whether at home or in global operations, is readily categorised as criminal action (Garcia and Fontes 2014).

Does this much-heralded ascent of the BRICS to the elite club of global powers really encompass the national interests of all citizens of Brazil? Do all Brazilians experience Vale's success as a 'global challenger', as cause for celebration? Does every Brazilian think that Vale's ability to enter the vicious competition between the global giants in the world of big mining means that Brazil has 'arrived', that it can now stand tall, hold up its head, proudly taking its place in the G20 with the 'developed' countries of the North?

To assume Vale's success and Brazil's national interests as synonymous is to operate within an old discourse about development that sees the transition of the nation-state from agrarian to industrial societies as the task, with the state as the main actor, the national society as the main target of development planning, and foreign direct investors as the key source of capital for these development goals of employment, modernisation and economic growth to be realised.

Perhaps multinational corporations from the BRICS are better understood by stepping outside this old development discourse based on territories and situating them instead as players in a new global discourse based on flows. This is a world where there is a fully articulated transnational economy with flows of capital, information, technology, equipment and even land, labour and private security forces (Sikor 2013). All of this global economy operates outside the logic and largely outside the regulation of national jurisdictions. A big mining company takes minimum responsibility for the territory – and citizens – in which its mining operations happen to be located, operating instead through global supply chains and the highly articulated flows that now characterise the global economy.

Corporations use 'branding' instruments to 'green wash' their images with strong language about sustainability, or 'blue wash' them, wrapping themselves in the legitimising language of the Global Compact and the United Nations. What is gilded for the public as the need for a 'social licence to operate' is put into internal company practice more as 'security risk management'. Companies are driven fundamentally by their concern for 'damage control', seeing any person or policy or institution that gets in their way as a security risk and, consequently, an 'enemy' of the corporation.

André Almeida, a former director in Vale's Department of Intelligence and Corporate Security, recently handed over large numbers of documents to Brazil's State Prosecutor. They point to Vale's involvement in widespread spying and infiltration focused on people and organisations deemed by Vale to be its enemies. These include well-respected journalists, lawyers and human rights activists, as well as organisations such as Justice on the Rails and the International Network of People Affected by Vale (Marshall 2013). The expanded vision of corporate self-interest expounded by Stiglitz seems to be very far from Vale's corporate game plans.

The elite social forces in Brazil and other BRICS countries that are intent on making their countries competitive in the global economy are part of the new transnational class of winners produced by globalisation. They are members of the 50% of the transnational consumer class that resides in the Global South, many with aspirations to be part of the '1%'. Through their multinational corporations like Vale, they aspire to industrial modernity and world-class consumption.

The aspirations of the government and business leaders in the BRICS to attain global status, measured by triumphs like hosting the Olympics or the World Cup, may genuinely include a component of recuperation of pride, dignity and respect after centuries of colonial and imperial humiliation. The vision pursued, however, offers no alternative to the current world order of production and consumption. The vision is not inclusive of the poor within their own nations and takes little cognisance of the impact of the growth model they aspire to on the long-term wellbeing of the planet. The strongly felt aspirations of the BRICS to be players in the current global system and 'world-class' consumers only serve to exacerbate existing rich–poor disparities and to inflict further damages on the environment, making them major perpetrators of ongoing global instability and injustice.

As Wolfgang Sachs argues in a brilliant essay entitled 'Liberating the world from development':

the competitive struggle of the global middle classes for a greater share of income and power is often carried out at the expense of the fundamental rights of the poor and powerless. As governments and businesses, urban citizens and rural elites mobilise to forge ahead with development, more often than not the land, the living space and the cultural traditions of indigenous peoples, small farmers or the urban poor are put under pressure ... The shiny side of development is often accompanied by a dark side of displacement and dispossession, which is why economic growth has time and again produced impoverishment next to enrichment (Sachs 2013:25).

However much the emergence of the BRICS as new global powers after centuries of imperial subjugation and humiliation may carry with it a deeply felt sentiment of national liberation, the practices of emerging Brazilian or Indian or South African or Chinese players in the world of big mining are little distinguishable from the pillage of their global competitors linked to old imperial centres in Europe and North America.

Note
1. Private conversation with Rick Bertrand, Sudbury, June 2012.

References
Alem, AC and R Madeira (2010) Internacionalização e competitividade: a importância da criação de empresas multinacionais brasileiras. In Ana Claudia Alem and Fabio Giambiagi (eds) *O BNDES em um Brasil em transição*, Rio de Janeiro, BNDES
América Economia (2012) Murilo Ferreira reage, www.americaeconomiabrasil.com.br/artigo/edicao-412/negocio/murilo-ferreira-reage
Anderson, Perry (2005) *Brazil*, Unpublished report to USW
Bulatlat (2011) *The slaves of Madagascar: abused OFWs repatriated for fighting for their rights*, http://bulatlat.com/main/2011/01/16/the-slaves-of-madagascar-abused-ofws-repatriated-for-fighting-for-their-rights/
Castel-Branco, CN (2009) Comentários no lançamento do relatorio 'Alguns desafios da indústria extrativa em Mocambique', http://www.iese.ac.mz/lib/publication/outras/ComentáriosdeCastelBranco-RelCIP.pdf
CFMEU (2012) http://cfmeu.com.au/the-growth-of-insecure-work-is-making-australian-workplaces-less-safe-warn-unions
Club of Mozambique (2012) *Brazilian mining company – Vale – pursues corporate social responsibility projects in Mozambique*, http://www.clubofmozambique.com/solutions1/sectionnews.php?secao=mining&id=25960&tipo=one
Durão, Vera Saavedra (2010) *Vale comemora redução do poder do sindicato no Canadá*, www.relacoesdotrabalho.com.br/profiles/blogs/no-valor-economico-vale

Faustino, Cristian and Fabrina Furtado (2013) *O Projeto Ferro Carajas S11D, da Vale S.A.*, Acailandia, DhESCA Brazil

Ferguson, J (2006) *Global Shadows: Africa in the Neo-liberal World Order*, Durham, NC, Duke University Press

Forbes (2014) Roger Agnelli profile, http://www.forbes.com/profile/roger-agnelli/

Garcia, Ana and Virginia Fontes (2014) Brazil's imperial capitalism, *Socialist Register 2014*

Garcia, Ana, K Kato and C Fontes (2012) *A historia contada pela caca ou pelo cacador? Perspectivas sobre Brasil em Angola e Mocambique*, Rio de Janeiro, Instituto Politicas Alternativas para o Cono Sul, http://www.pacs.org.br.files/2013/03/Relatorio-Africa.pdf

Jone, Antonio (2014) Produção alimentar nos reassentamentos: o caso de Cateme em Moatize, *Destaque Rural*, 2, January, www.omrmz.org/images/publicacoes/D.R.2.pdf

Mail & Guardian (2011) Mozambique expels SA workers, http://mg.co.za/article/2011-11-18-mozambique-expels-sa-workers/

Marshall, Judith (2009) Learning democracy from North–South worker exchanges. In Linda Cooper and Shirley Walters, *Learning/Work*, Cape Town, HSRC Press

Marshall, Judith (2012) Mining mega-projects and labour: working for Vale, the 'worst company in the world, Unpublished paper presented at the III Conference of the Institute for Social and Economic Studies (IESE), Maputo, Mozambique, 4–5 September, www.iesse.ac.mz

Marshall, Judith (2013) Secret surveillance targets civil society, Canadian Centre for Policy Alternatives Monitor, December, https://www.policyalternatives.ca/publications/monitor/secret-surveillance-targets-civil-society

Mosca, João and Thomas Selemane (2011) El Dorado Tete, Maputo, Centro de Integridade Pública

New Internationalist (2014) Commodities and dependency: the facts, *New Internationalist*, 470, March

Portal de Angola (2013) Vale refuses to pay more to the brick makers, http://www.portaldeangola.com/2013/06/mocambique-vale-recusa-se-a-pagar-mais-a-oleiros/

Province of Newfoundland and Labrador (2011) *Report of the Industrial Inquiry Commission in a Matter Between Vale Newfoundland and Labrador Limited and United Steelworkers*, USW Local 9508

Ribeiro, Rafael de Souza (2009) Lula criticizes Agnelli and articulates his ouster from Vale presidency says magazine, http://www.infomoney.com.br/mercados/noticia/1676402/lula-critica-agnelli-articula-iacute-presidente-vale-diz-revista

Sachs, Wolfgang (2013) Liberating the world from development, *New Internationalist*, 460, March

Selemane, Thomas (2009) Alguns desafios na indústria extractiva em Moçambique, Maputo, Centro de Integridade Pública

Selemane, Thomas (2010) Questoes a volta da mineracao em Mocambique: relatorio de monitoria das actividades mineiras em Moma, Moatize e Sussundenga, Maputo, Centro de Integridade Pública

Sikor, T, G Auld, AJ Bebbington, T Benjaminsen, BS Gentry, C Hunsberger, A-M Izac, ME Margulis, T Plieninger, H Schroeder and C Upton (2013) Global land governance: from territory to flow?, *Current Opinion in Environmental Sustainability*, 5

Sousa Santos, Boaventura de (2012) *Moçambique: a maldição da abundância?*, http://correiodobrasil.com.br/mocambique-a-maldicao-da-abundancia/491145/

Stiglitz, Joseph (2012) Speech at Public Eye Awards Ceremony, 27 January, www.publiceye.ch/en/news/press-release-27th-january-2012

Sudbury Star (2011) A devastating loss, http://www.thesudburystar.com/2011/06/09/a-devastating-loss

Uchoas, Leandro (2009) Imperialismo brasileiro: Vale explora trabalhadores no Canadá, *Brasil de Fato*, 27 August 27 – 5 September

USW LU 6500 (2012) *Double Fatality Investigation Report Frood/Stobie Complex*, www.uswlocal6500.ca/news.php?extend.142.

Valle, Sabrina (2011) Roger Agnelli sai da Vale e critica PT, 'O governo e a Vale têm missões diferentes', http://www.jogodopoder.com/blog/economia/rogner-agnelli-sai-da-vale-e-critica-gestao-do-pt-o-governo-e-a-vale-tem-missoes-diferentes/
Veja (2012) Lula faz lobby para empresa em Moçambique, http://veja.abril.com.br/blog/ricardo-setti/politica-cia/lula-faz-lobby-para-empresa-em-mocambique/
Vieira, Valério (2011) Report of a conversation with Murilo Ferreira, President of Vale, Unpublished

12

Rio's ruinous mega-events

EINAR BRAATHEN, GILMAR MASCARENHAS AND CELINA SØRBØE

In the last decade, all the BRICS countries have invested enormous financial resources and political prestige in hosting mega-sports events: the 2008 Summer Olympics in Beijing, the 2010 Commonwealth Games in Delhi, the 2010 FIFA World Cup in South Africa, the 2014 Winter Olympics and the upcoming 2018 FIFA World Cup in Russia – the latter replicating Brazil's 'double' approach of FIFA World Cup (2014) and Olympic Games (Rio de Janeiro 2016). It is also nearly certain that South Africa (Durban) will host the Commonwealth Games in 2022 and will bid for the 2024 Olympics, and that Beijing will bid for a Winter Olympics.

In other words, there is a trend whereby mega-sports events and so-called 'emerging economies' grow closer. These countries combine three crucial elements: availability of resources; an ambition to strengthen their image as an emerging power worldwide; and relative weakness of institutions which protect the environment and human rights. The combination of these elements enables host cities to abide by the 'package' of interventions that international organising committees such as the Fédération Internationale de Football Association (FIFA) and the International Olympic Committee (IOC) require.

This chapter will start with describing the 'global city' – the importance for cities today in making themselves present on the global stage to compete for investments. Then it will show how mega-sports events have become a central strategy for cities in the South branding themselves as 'global cities'. The inherent characteristics of hosting such events, which demands flexible planning to respond to the demands of private investors, challenges existing institutional frameworks and democratic governance. Our main case is Rio de Janeiro. The chapter will finish with the counter-reactions that are growing in host cities against these developments.

Our argument is that the mega-sports events are increasingly aligned with large private interests, strengthen neoliberal city management practices in terms of 'urban entrepreneurship', and suppress the demands and rights of ordinary citizens. In this way, host cities such as Rio become 'cities of exception'. The question the chapter tries to answer is: how do popular forces react to these developments, and why? Will the mass protests that took Brazil and the world by surprise during the 'rehearsal' FIFA World Cup in June 2013 set new standards and bring new types of 'exceptions' to host cities?

Mega-sports events and the 'global city'

In today's globalised world, there is growing interurban competition for international flows of capital and visitors. In order to produce an image of a city that can compete for these resources on the international market, publicity strategies of 'branding' the urban space gain importance (Mascarenhas 2012). Hosting international mega-sports events has recently been adopted as a 'branding' strategy by cities in the Global South. Mega-events like the FIFA World Cup and the Olympics bring with them international capital, tourists and investors, and place the host city in the world's spotlight. The host cities are using the arena of the mega-events to mark themselves as up-and-coming 'global cities' to be reckoned with.

Brazil and Rio de Janeiro's successful bids for the 2007 Pan-American Games, the 2014 FIFA World Cup, and the 2016 Olympics crown the country's remarkable rise after decades of underachievement to becoming an economic and diplomatic heavyweight. Just as the Beijing Olympics of 2008 marked China's revival as a world power (Broudehoux 2007), the 2016 Rio games may be seen as a stamp of approval on the South American giant's coming of age.

Rio de Janeiro's successful bids for these events have been attributed to a fundamental shift in the municipal leadership's strategy during the 1990s. Local scholars point at the rule of the populist-turned-neoliberal mayor, Cesar Maia, as the turning point (Vainer 2000). In 1993, Maia invited the Rio de Janeiro Trading Association (ACRJ) and the Federation of Industries of the State of Rio de Janeiro (FIRJAN) to join the municipality in elaborating a Strategic Plan for the city. A key urban planner from Barcelona, Dr Jordi Borja, was the main consultant. Inspired by the 1992 Barcelona Olympic Games, the plan emphasised the big potential of large projects and mega-events, such as the Olympic Games, in branding Rio de Janeiro as a destination for tourists and foreign investors and transforming Rio de Janeiro into a 'global city'. In 1994, the municipality, private companies and business associations came together and created a Strategic Plan of Rio de Janeiro, which was approved without democratic channels of participation (Vainer 2000:106). In 1996 the city sent its first bid to host the Olympic Games and in 2009 it won the bid for the 2016 games (Mascarenhas, Curi et al. 2011). The Strategic Plan is steered by business demands and interests with the aim to make the city more 'attractive' on the international market (Braathen et al. 2013:9).

Business and business opportunities are essential foundations for the new city and the new urban planning. In business, efficient management relies on the ability to take advantage of opportunities faster than the competitors. In the view of strategic planning, the city itself should function as a company. Political control and bureaucracy, such as responding to the institutional rights and guidelines of the Constitution or the Master Plan, erode a city's capacity to take advantage of business opportunities and, consequently, come across as efficient and competitive (Vainer 2011:5). The hosting of mega-sports events intensifies these processes, as they demand flexibility in order to fulfil the requirements of FIFA or IOC.

In their critical assessment of the 2010 FIFA World Cup in South Africa, Bond et al. (2011) show that the results were dubious priorities, overspending, loss of sovereignty and human rights, and broken trickle-down promises. Mega-sports events bring in multinational corporate sponsors, for whom exclusive rights to the sport venues and other public spaces are demanded (Klauser 2011; Mascarenhas et al. 2012). As existing institutional frameworks are overruled to respond to the needs of international sponsors and private interests, the Olympic bid books become the *de facto* urban planning documents in host cities. The close cooperation between a municipality and private sector leaders has been depicted by David Harvey as an international trend of transformation of urban governance towards 'urban entrepreneurship' (Harvey 1989). Others have termed this new strategic planning either 'ad hoc urbanism' (Ascher 2001) or *cidade empresa* – 'company city' (Vainer 2011).

According to Vainer (2000), the overriding of institutional guidelines and the implementation of a neoliberal regime can only happen by unifying the city around a common project. In Rio, the Olympic Games have served as the pretext, and two elements have been instrumental in legitimising the transformation of Rio into a host city. On the one hand, the city's patriotism led to a profound sense of pride among the inhabitants at the prospect of hosting a global mega-event. On the other, there was a generalised sense of an urban crisis stemming from the escalating violence that has characterised the city since the 1990s. The urban crisis authorised and demanded a new form of power in the city. Drawing on Giorgio Agamben's theories of the state of exception, Vainer claims that the preparations for these events have led to cities such as Rio becoming 'cities of exception'.

Cities of exception: the case of Rio de Janeiro

Inspired by the works of Foucault on biopolitics and governmentality, and also the reflections of Walter Benjamin, Hannah Arendt and Carl Smith, Giorgio Agamben has written about the state of exception. Agamben (1995) shows how the effects of the decisions made by the state (or whoever has the sovereign power) can lead to the exclusion of people from the political community and the protection provided by its laws and rights. In situations of crisis or war, exceptional actions are justified by the exceptional circumstances, leading to the acceptance of measures outside the legal framework. This permits the physical elimination of not only political opponents, but also of entire categories of citizens that are perceived as external and non-integral to society (Foucault 2003; Agamben 2005).

The notion of 'civilising' Rio has been a running theme in the city's history, with the upper classes attempting to control the activities, dress code and behaviours of the masses to serve their interests. Local elites have long fantasised about Rio being a First World city, and they have worked hard to maintain this illusion (Broudehoux 2001). As Brazil's capital of culture and tourism, Rio de Janeiro has been known as the *cidade maravilhosa* – the 'marvellous city', since the end of the 19th century. Parallel with the production of the image of the city as a tropical paradise, the urban informal settlements known as favelas sprang up as aberrations on the modern city. Throughout their history, the favelas have been rejected by the 'formal' city and have continually been threatened with destruction (Perlman 2010:26).

During the period of the military dictatorship (1964–85) the vast majority of the favelas of Rio de Janeiro were targets of public removal policies. The residents were moved to new housing estates in areas distant from the city centre – both to 're-civilise' these populations and to beautify the city. With the re-democratisation of Brazil in the 1980s, policies towards the favelas were revised. As they had proved incapable of solving the housing deficit in the city, the removal policies came to an end, and the public debate shifted to concentrating on the necessity of integrating the favelas in the city (Oliveira 2012:47). Programmes such as Favela-Bairro, launched by the municipality in 1993 to upgrade all of the city's favelas, led to the notion that 'the favela has won!' in the late 1990s (Zaluar and Alvito 1998). One of their arguments was that favelas were no longer at risk of removal and most people defended their urbanisation instead. Was Rio de Janeiro about to become an 'exception from the exception' – a city for the dispossessed masses?

With the supposedly pro-poor policies of the governments after 2003, when Inácio Lula da Silva from the Workers Party (PT) became president, one may presume that the old divides between the 'favela' and the 'asphalt' are being erased. The federal government is investing unprecedented amounts on large-scale programmes for slum upgrading, social housing and improved infrastructures. The main references are the federal Programme for Accelerated Growth (PAC) and My House My Life (MCMV). In Rio de Janeiro, these programmes are tightly connected with the mega-events.

There are ample opportunities for host cities to use mega-sports events like the World Cup and the Olympics, and the capital and investments coming with them, as a concrete tool for social change. The massive public spending required to be able to pull off such events often faces local opposition. Leaving a positive legacy is therefore one of the recent concerns of the 'Olympic system' as a way of legitimising itself (Horne and Whannel 2012). Cities in the bidding process present a legacy plan on how they will use the event to address the city's social, economic, infrastructural and planning challenges as a central aspect of their candidacy, often going beyond what is strictly necessary in order to stage the Games. The last Olympic Games to be hosted, the 2012 London Games, were applauded for a legacy plan that emphasised the urban regeneration of selected underprivileged neighbourhoods. Rio de Janeiro also has an ambitious plan to use the Olympics for citywide transformation. Legacy plans range from housing improvements to crime reduction, social inclusion, regeneration, and communications infrastructure combined with an attempt to revive the city's national and international image (Girginov 2013:301). The Morar Carioca Programme pledged a social legacy from the Olympic Games in terms of com-prehensive upgrading of all the favelas in Rio de Janeiro by 2020 (Prefeitura do Rio de Janeiro 2010; Bittar 2011). In the Sustainability Management Plan of the Olympics (SMP), developed by the municipality of Rio de Janeiro, the city government states that one of the strategic objectives of the municipal planning department is to 'organise an all-inclusive Games, leaving the city's population with a positive social balance'. No wonder that in a soccer-crazy country such as Brazil, the prospect of hosting the FIFA World Cup initially had wide support.

Sport, once viewed as a form of entertainment, has now emerged as an important political, social and economic force (Hiller 2000). Sport also plays an important cultural or cultural-hegemonic role. It can be used, or abused, to strengthen national identities. These different roles of sport are played out in powerful ways in the mega-sports events (Tomlinson and Young 2006). The official slogan of the 2014 Brazil World Cup was 'All in one rhythm'. According to the web pages of FIFA, the Slogan is more than a tagline. 'It represents the underlying mindset and theme running through all aspects of the tournament organisation ... Brazilians are invited to join together and celebrate the immense sense of pride in their country's position on the global stage and their role as hosts of the 2014 FIFA World Cup.'[1] The 2016 Olympics slogan is 'Live your passion'. These slogans capture the powerful sentiments that sports embody.

Broken promises

What was observed in South Africa in connection with the FIFA 2010 World Cup can be expected on an even larger scale in Brazil. The many delays, budgets exceeded, corruption scandals, and human and civil rights abuses that have plagued the construction works in Rio de Janeiro have already led to a sobering-up process. Growing numbers of people are questioning the true intentions of the authorities and the ultimate consequences for ordinary residents.

In spite of a decade of economic growth and poverty reduction under the PT administrations, Brazilian cities still have the dubious reputation of being the world's most unequal. People's increased income has enabled the growth of consumption. It has, however, not automatically resulted in an improved quality of life, as indicators of crime, violence and levels of education and health remain poor. Neither has it addressed the socio-spatial segregation that characterises cities such as Rio de Janeiro. According to the Brazilian Institute of Geography and Statistics (IBGE), 22% of the population of Rio de Janeiro lived in favelas in 2010. While not all living in the favelas are poor, a range of socio-economic, political, racial and cultural markers still work to exclude favela residents from many of the citizen rights enjoyed by residents of the formal city – what Holston (2007) has termed 'differentiated citizenship'. With the preparations for the mega-events, these differences are becoming more evident.

Carlos Vainer (2011) argues that the preparations for the mega-events have authorised, consolidated and legalised practices of legal exception in order to abide by the demands of private sponsors and the organising committees. The forms of illegality and exceptions to the institutional order have been multiplied, making Rio a city of permanent exception. Contracts and case-by-case negotiations have become more important than the law, and bargaining power has more weight than the application of the majority's decisions and the citizens' rights. Previously acquired rights enshrined in the Constitution, such as the right to housing, are progressively being eroded on the grounds that they impede the freedom of the market and therefore restrict economic development and modernisation (Dagnino 2010). This is especially evident in the city's favelas. The word *remoção* ('removal') which was broadly used during the military dictatorship is once again back on the agenda. Forty thousand are threatened by removal in Rio alone because of large-scale construction projects connected to the mega-events. The majority are poor favela residents.

Vila Autódromo, a fishing village which developed into a working-class neighbourhood in the upper-middle-class boomtown Barra de Tijuca in the western zone, serves as an example of the conflictual relationship between local residents and the government because of the upcoming mega-events. It is threatened by collective relocation because of the construction of the main sports arenas and accommodation centres for the 2016 Olympic Games (see Braathen et al. 2013). While the government, after massive pressure from residents and civil society organisations, has promised to consider an alternative plan where part of the community can remain, civil society actors claim the municipality is still using extra-juridical measures to force residents to accept relocation. Another community impacted by the ongoing city 'improvements' is the favela complex Manguinhos, located in abandoned factory areas. Since being selected for the PAC programme in 2008, a brutal, drawn-out eviction process has affected the community. The authorities have strategically employed an expulsion tactic where they demolish some houses and leave the ruins and, with them, garbage, rats and hazardous conditions behind. This makes life unbearable for those residents who remain, while sending a strong message that their eviction is imminent (Braathen et al. 2013).

These cases exemplify clearly how the 'benefits' and 'legacy' of the mega-events that the constructors promote can be imposed at the expense of poor communities and residents located near the sports facilities and the main access roads. Replacement housing being constructed through the federal housing programme MCMV has overwhelmingly been located in the distant northwest of the city, where land values are cheap, employment opportunities are limited and transport connections are poor. Studies by urban planners indicate that the MCMV programme reproduces the logic of older 'housing estates' where the poor end up being pushed to locations far from job opportunities and without a system of transportation (Braathen et al. 2013). These people's institutional rights have had to give way to the prosperity of society in general, defined within a neoliberal discourse of economic development. In the words of Agamben, this 'bare' or 'naked' life represents persons or groups of persons that 'others, with impunity, can treat without regard for their psychological and physical wellbeing' (Agamben 1995).

Securitisation

Recent image-making efforts in Rio exemplify the relationship between space, power and social justice in a society inundated with free-market ideology and intensified social polarisation. Increased deployment of security forces and policing is also part of this picture. According to Samara (2010, 2011), urban governance in a neoliberal environment is often driven by security concerns over protecting public order and economic growth, especially in highly unequal cities. As with Cape Town before the 2010 World Cup, Rio de Janeiro's quest to position itself on the global stage has resulted in two conflicting agendas. On the one hand, the reputation of Rio de Janeiro as one of the world's most unequal cities demanded the implementation of pro-poor strategies to address the legacy of social and spatial inequalities. The PAC, MCMV and Morar Carioca programmes upgrading the favelas are supposedly leaving a 'lasting legacy' to the city after the mega-events. On the other hand, the desire to reach global-city status in terms of attracting international investment, economic growth and tourism in order to demonstrate (Western) goals of urban achievement demanded that the city deal with the notorious insecurity that has given it a reputation for being a dangerous place to visit.

In the 1980s the international drug trade came to Rio de Janeiro, and drug traffickers found a stronghold in the favelas where the state presence was weak. The police took a militarised approach to combating drug trafficking, and the social conflict in the city became formulated as a 'war'. The violence associated with the drug trafficking grew in frequency and intensity throughout the late 1980s and 1990s, and assaults, robberies, kidnappings, shoot-outs and *balas perdidas* ('lost bullets' striking innocents caught in the cross-fire) became everyday security issues. The rising trend of poverty and insecurity tarnished the national and international identity of Rio de Janeiro, and portrayed an image of a city incapable of handling its security issues. In order to secure peace in the city as a whole, improving Rio's reputation and thereby securing investments, a new policing programme called UPP (Units of Pacifying Police) was developed. The programme relies on the permanent placement of UPPs in strategically located favelas, reclaiming a monopoly of power over favelas that have 'threatened' the sense of security in the city. The UPPs depend on PAC for their budget, which is also the principal fund for infrastructure associated with the World Cup and Olympics. The link to the mega-events is evident.

The pacification programme has changed public security policies in the favelas from pure military interventions to proximity policing combining security and developmental measures. While less violent than earlier police interventions, the UPPs establish a permanent militarised regime in the pacified favelas that goes beyond combating the drug traffickers. In order to neutralise the threat these territories are seen to pose to the sense of security in the city as a whole, the UPP security regime controls and manages the life of *all* favela residents (Sørbøe 2013). The ways this is done are many, such as discourses, regulations, administrative means and police activity that represses behaviour that is not considered civilised (Leite 2000:384). While promoted as a programme to spur an approximation process between the favela and the asphalt, the UPP's practice in the favelas can be seen as a 'differentiated policing of space' (Samara 2010, 2011). The pacification represents a police mechanism that is exercised according to the spatial configuration of the city. The UPPs are only stationed in favelas, while the other neighbourhoods of Rio de Janeiro fall under the jurisdiction of the civil police. The unequal treatment of the favela residents by the UPPs by the civil police can be seen as a 'differentiated management of illegalities', in the words of Foucault (Foucault and Miskowiec 1986).

'Rebel cities': the June 2013 protests

Rio, like other cities in Brazil, has a strong institutional framework demanding popular participation and transparent governance. With the re-democratisation of Brazil, the 1988 Constitution established the legal basis for some of the world's most progressive democratic institutions, and incorporated innovative proposals for an alliance between the state and civil society. When Lula won the elections in 2001, many civil society organisations and activists believed it represented an historic opportunity for significant change in Brazil. In response to the demands from social movements, Lula's administration created institutions such as the Ministry of Cities and the Council of Cities, stimulating public participation in local, state and national housing and sanitation projects (Rolnik 2011). These structures were seen as spaces where the state and civil society were expected to work together to ensure that priority-setting matched the public interest and to secure accountability in the definition and delivery of social policies (Heller and Evans 2010). The last years have, however, seen a procedural and substantive disillusionment with the existing spaces and mechanisms to institutionalise citizens' participation in public decision-making (Baiocchi et al. 2013). The initial approval has given way to a growing sense of disappointment with how Lula and PT manage the challenges of governing Brazil (Hochstetler 2008; Rolnik 2011).

In this situation, the hosting of 'world-class' sports events draws in many people and increase their political engagement. In Brazil, the popular culture around sports (soccer) and festivals (carnival) has always been linked to politics or possible political abuse (DaMatta 1991; Wisnik 2006). People react with contempt at corrupt politicians who usually exploit public investments in the events for private gain.

In the process of political and urban change that has accompanied the construction of Rio de Janeiro as an Olympic city, it has been turned into a space for business, and no longer a space for political and democratic debate. Massive investments have been made over a short period, and ad hoc decisions have prevailed in order to develop binding plans. The prospect of the benefits that will come with hosting international mega-events has legitimised this depoliticisation of host cities. Basic democratic rights are put on hold, and the demands and rights of ordinary citizens are suppressed. These transformations have catalysed growing politicisation and social mobilisation in host cities and created an arena of conflict between actors associated with the state, the market and civil society.

As a response to the last decade's transformation in urban governance, millions of Brazilians took to the streets in June 2013 in what became the largest street demonstrations in recent history. What started as a protest against a price hike in public transportation in São Paulo quickly escalated to mass mobilisations against the massive public spending on stadiums and infrastructure related to the mega-events while the quality of public services remains precarious. They also revolted against the violence used by the police force to quell the demonstrations (Maricato 2013).

The June demonstrations raised issues in the public debate in Brazil regarding citizenship – how to listen to the 'voice of the street', take grievances of ordinary people seriously, and improve the quality of democracy. These manifestations did not come from nowhere: they represent the culmination of years in which a new generation of urban movements has formed. Organisations such as the Movimento Passe Livre ('movement for free transport'), student movements, urban resistance movements, favela residents' associations and the homeless workers' movement Sem Teto (those without a 'roof'/house) have, through occupations and demonstrations, issued in broader networks challenging the existing emptied-out, top-down spaces of participation. This new generation of urban movements and civic networks anticipates an 'insurgent citizenship'

(Holston 2007). As opposed to a statist citizenship that assumes the state as 'the only legitimate source of citizenship rights, meanings and practices' (Holston 1998:39), this alternative conceptualisation of citizenship is active, engaged, and 'grounded in civil society' (Friedmann 2002:76). It moves beyond formal citizenship to a substantive one that concerns an array of civil, political, social and economic rights. These demands include the right to housing, shelter, education and basic health. As such, it incorporates the notion of the 'right to the city' (Lefebre 1967), which recognises all city residents as 'rights holders' in the city, defending the needs and desires of the majority and affirming the city as a site for social conflict.

While 'the right to the city' has been recognised by the institutional framework in Brazil, the hollowing out of the functions of the institutional spaces for citizen participation by neoliberal reforms has left many of the promises unfulfilled (Santos Junior et al. 2011). The new generation of civil society movements has claimed the concept of the right to the city for its own, and it was frequently seen on banners and posters during the June protests. As emphasised by David Harvey, the right to the city is 'far more than a right of individual or group access to the resources the city embodies: it is the right to change and reinvent the city more after our hearts' desire' (Harvey 2012:4).

The right to the city has become a slogan for movements worldwide who fight against the manifestations of many modern cities in which public processes and utilities have been privatised and where development is driven primarily, if not solely, by corporations and markets. In protesting these tendencies, practices of insurgent citizenship have become the means through which the urban margins negotiate and contest their right to universal inclusion (Holston 2007:22). The Comitê Popular da Copa e das Olimpíadas – People's Committee of the World Cup and Olympics – is one example. The committee links established NGOs and social movements with favela communities that are threatened by evictions because of public works linked to the mega-sports events. Also, within the favelas residents have found ways of taking part in local decision-making processes. Residents' associations in several favelas have been revitalised by threats of removal, and local actors have been able to link up with external political events such as the Rio+20 conference and the People's Summit in June 2012 and other public legal forums dedicated to the defence of citizens' rights. The June protests sparked a new wave of social mobilisation, allowing local communities' struggles over localised issues to connect to a wider discourse of urban development conflicts in Rio de Janeiro and globally.

On the edge of an urban revolution?

Through the use of social media networks, the June protests gained size and strength, recruiting students and middle-class residents who had little prior experience of activism but were fed up with the ongoing processes. The sheer size of the mobilisations forced politicians to respond, and President Dilma Rousseff, Governor Sérgio Cabral and Mayor Eduardo Paes quickly responded by giving in to some long-standing demands from civil society in Rio. President Rousseff promised massive federal investments to improve the urban systems for collective transport. In a rush she also tabled a bill, approved by the Congress, ensuring that 75% of the future oil revenues were to be earmarked for the health and education sectors. Governor Cabral of Rio de Janeiro put on hold the demolition of public sports and school facilities adjacent to the Maracanã stadium. Mayor Paes declared a truce in his war against some of the communities resisting removal, such as in Morro da Providência and Vila Autódromo, and started negotiations with the community leaders. However, in a public statement on 8 August, the People's Committee stated that 'The recent retreats of the state government ... are nothing more than reactions to the popular mobilisations. People taking to the streets have sent a clear message to politicians: we will not accept living in a city for sale! We will not accept a city managed for private benefit!'

This statement is most likely correct. The retreats of the state and municipal governments came after persistent public demonstrations and protests. Both Governor Cabral and Mayor Paes are facing demands for their impeachment, and they and others are feeling the pressure coming from the streets. However, the recent promises have been interpreted by some as mere reactionary fire-extinguishing politics; as a populist compliance with some of the demands of a population with a short memory. Civil society gained some small victories with the protests, but there have been no profound changes in the urban regime. The 'Olympic project' continued to dominate the city governance. The history of Vila Autôdromo, which has gone through numerous threats of removal and guarantees of permanence, shows that a promise today might very well be challenged in the future. Civil society will have to keep up the pressure to guarantee that the politicians stick to their promises.

'Rebel cities' are, according to David Harvey (2012), places where the right to the city is translated into 'the urban revolution'. In Brazil this urban revolution has but begun.

Note
1. http://www.fifa.com/worldcup/organisation/officialslogan/.

References
Agamben, G (1995) *Homo Sacer: Sovereign Power and Bare Life*, Stanford, Stanford University Press
Agamben, G (2005) *State of Exception*, Chicago, University of Chicago Press
Ascher, F (2001) *Les Nouveaux Principes de l'urbanisme: la fin des villes n'est pasà l'ordre du jour*, La Tour-d'Aigues, Éditions de l'Aube
Baiocchi, G, E Braathen, et al. (2013) Transformation institutionalized? Making sense of participatory democracy in the Lula era. In K Stokke and O Törnquist (eds) *Democratisation in the Global South: The Importance of Transformative Politics*, Basingstoke, Palgrave Macmillan
Bittar, J (2011) Morar Carioca, Speech delivered 11 November 2011 at a public meeting organised by Clube de Engenharia, Rio de Janeiro
Bond, P, A Desai and B Maharaj (2011) World Cup profits defeat the poor. In B Maharaj, A Desai and P Bond (eds) *Zuma's Own Goal: Losing South Africa's 'War on Poverty'*, Trenton, Africa World Press
Braathen, E, T Bartholl, AC Christovão and V Pinheiro (2013) Rio de Janeiro. In E Braathen (ed) *Addressing Sub-standard Settlements*, Bonn, European Association of Development Institutes
Broudehoux, A (2001) Image making, city marketing, and the aestheticisation of social inequality in Rio de Janeiro. In N Alsayyad (ed) *Consuming Tradition, Manufacturing Heritage: Global Norms and Urban Forms in the Age of Tourism*, London, Routledge
Broudehoux, A (2007) Spectacular Beijing: the conspicuous construction of an Olympic metropolis, *Journal of Urban Affairs*, 29, 4, pp 383–399
Dagnino, E (2010) Citizenship: a perverse confluence. In A Cornwall and D Eade (eds) *Deconstructing Development Discourse: Buzzwords and Fuzzwords*, Oxford, Practical Action Publishing
DaMatta, R (1991) *Carnivals, Rogues, and Heroes: An Interpretation of the Brazilian Dilemma*, Notre Dame, University of Notre Dame Press
Foucault, M (2003) *Society Must Be Defended: Lectures at the Collège de France 1975–1976*, New York, Picador
Foucault, M and J Miskowiec (1986 [1967]). Of other spaces, *Diacritics*, 16, 1, pp 22–27
Friedman, J (2002) *The Prospect of Cities*, Minneapolis, University of Minnesota Press
Girginov, V (2013) *Handbook of the 2012 Olympic and Paralympic Games. Volume 1: Making the Games*, New York, Routledge
Harvey, D (1989) From managerialism to entrepreneurialism: the transformation in urban governance in late capitalism, *Geografiska Annaler B*, 71, 1, pp 3–17
Harvey, D (2012) *Rebel Cities: From the Right to the City to the Urban Revolution*, London, Verso
Heller, P and P Evans (2010) Taking Tilly south: durable inequalities, democratic contestation, and citizenship in the Southern metropolis, *Theory and Society*, 39, pp 433–450
Hiller, H (2000) Mega-events, urban boosterism and growth strategies: an analysis of the objectives and legitimations of the Cape Town 2004 Olympic bid, *International Journal of Urban and Regional Research*, 24, 2, pp 449–458
Hochstetler, K (2008) Organized civil society in Lula's Brazil. In P Kingstone and T Power (eds) *Democratic Brazil Revisited*, Pittsburgh, University of Pittsburgh Press
Holston, J (1998) Spaces of insurgent citizenship. In L Sandercock (ed) *Making the Invisible Visible: A Multicultural Planning History*, Berkeley, University of California Press
Holston, J (2007) *Insurgent Citizenship*, Princeton, Princeton University Press
Horne, J and G Whannel (2012) *Understanding the Olympics*, London, Routledge
Klauser, FR (2011) Interpretative flexibility of the event-city: security, branding and urban entrepreneurialism at the European Football Championships 2008, *International Journal of Urban and Regional Research*, 36, 5, pp 1039–1052
Lefebvre, H (1967) *Le Droit à la ville*, Paris, Anthropos

Leite, MP (2000) Entre o individualismo ea solidariedade: dilemas da política e da cidadania no Rio de Janeiro', *Revista Brasileira de Ciências Sociais*, 14, 44, pp 73–90

Maricato, E et al. (2013) *Cidades rebeldes: Passe Livre e as manifestações que tomaram as ruas do Brasil*, São Paulo, Boitempo Editoral

Mascarenhas, G (2012) Globalização e políticas territoriais: os megaeventos esportivos na cidade do Rio de Janeiro. In SMM Pacheco and MS Machado (eds) *Globalização, políticas públicas e reestruturação territorial*, Rio de Janeiro, Letras

Mascarenhas, G, G Bienenstein et al. (2012) The 2016 Olympiad in Rio de Janeiro: who can/could/ will beat whom?' *Esporte e Sociedade*, 7, 19, pp 42–61

Mascarenhas, G, M Curi et al. (2011) The Pan American Games in Rio de Janeiro 2007: consequences of a sport mega-event on a BRIC country, *International Review for the Sociology of Sport*, 46, 2, pp 140–156

Oliveira, F de, et al. (2012) *Grandes projetos metropolitanos: Rio de Janeiro e belo horizonte*, Rio de Janeiro, Letra Capital

Perlman, J (2010) *Favela: Four Decades of Living on the Edge in Rio de Janeiro*, Oxford, Oxford University Press

Prefeitura do Rio de Janeiro (2010) *Morar Carioca: plano municipal de integração de assentamentos precários informais*, Rio de Janeiro, Rio2016 and Prefeitura do Rio de Janeiro

Rolnik, R (2011) Democracy on the edge: limits and possibilities in the implementation of an urban reform agenda, *International Journal of Urban and Regional Research*, 35, 2, pp 239–255

Samara, TR (2010) Policing development: urban renewal as neo-liberal security strategy, *Urban Studies*, 47, 1, pp 197–214

Samara, TR (2011) *Cape Town after Apartheid: Crime and Governance in the Divided City*, Minneapolis, University of Minnesota Press

Santos Junior, O, AC Christovão et al. (2011) *Políticas públicas e direito à cidade: programmea interdisciplinar de formação de agentes sociais e conselheiros municipais*, Rio de Janeiro, Letra Capital

Sørbøe, C (2013) Security and inclusive citizenship in the mega-city: the pacification of Rocinha, Rio de Janeiro, Master's thesis, University of Oslo

Tomlinson, A and C Young (2006) *National Identity and Global Sports Events: Culture, Politics, and Spectacle in the Olympics and the Football World Cup*, New York, SUNY Press

Vainer, C (2000) Pátria, empresa e mercadoria. Notas sobre a estratégia discursiva do planejamento estratégico urbano. In O Arantes, C Vainer and E Maricato (eds) *A cidade do pensamento unico: demanchando consensos*, Petrópolis, Editora Vozes

Vainer, C (2011) *Cidade de exceção: reflexões a partir do Rio de Janeiro. XIV Encontro Nacional da Anpur*, Rio de Janeiro, Anpur

Wisnik, JM (2006) The riddle of Brazilian soccer: reflections on the emancipatory dimensions of culture, *Review: Literature and Arts of the Americas*, 73, 39, 2, pp 198–209

Zaluar, A and M Alvito (1998) *Um seculo de favela*, Rio de Janeiro, Fundação Getulio Vargas Editora

13

Modern Russia as semi-peripheral, dependent capitalism

RUSLAN DZARASOV

The main aim of this chapter is to provide an analysis of the nature of modern Russian capitalism from the perspective of how the specific methods of capital accumulation affected state development and evolved over the last 20 years. My approach is based on a reinterpretation of the world system analysis from the perspective of Marxian surplus value theory.

After great enthusiasm and expectations raised 20 years ago by Gorbachev's perestroika, it seems that all parties – both Russians and the West – are severely disillusioned. Russians suffer plummeting living standards and the pitiable condition of the Russian state; the West suffers challenges posed by Putin to some aspects of Western domination in the post-Soviet area.

Marxism and world system analysis

World-System Analysis (WSA) provides a vision of capitalism consistent with so-called 'orthodox Marxism'. Surplus value theory is equally applicable both to national capitalist economies, including theoretically possible closed economies, and to the world system. Marx's *Capital* and the world system approach correlate as the abstract and the concrete. The ascent from abstract to concrete lies at the heart of the Marxian method; and the essence of core–periphery relations, which are at the heart of WSA, could be (and should be) interpreted from labour value and surplus value perspectives. The very nature of the phenomenon of peripheral capitalism lies in the transfer of a significant part of the labour value fund created by the population of a dependent nation, to the core countries. The lack of this theoretical underpinning deprives WSA of a sound foundation. On the other hand, reconsideration of WSA from the perspective of the surplus value approach makes it a powerful tool of analysis of the modern world.

Working along the lines of Marxian methodology, the modern Russian school of critical Marxism was developed at Moscow State University, the Academy of Sciences and a number of other universities. It focuses on different features of the political economy of dependent development peculiar to modern Russia, with a focus on class interests and class conflicts shaping social change in modern Russia.

Genesis of modern Russian capitalism

The deficiency of the mainstream account of so-called 'transition' is its purely technical approach to market reforms, lacking any account of the social, class interests as their major driving forces. There are two principal formative forces which shaped modern Russian capitalism: the degeneration of the Stalinist bureaucracy and the impact of global financialised capitalism. The first manifested itself in growing privileges and informal command over resources, giving private gains on the basis of state property. The second manifested itself in the growing dependence of the core capitalist countries on exploitation of the periphery of the world system, with financial capital increasingly replacing productive capital. In the course of the radical market reforms of the early 1990s these two factors mixed to produce nascent capitalism in Russia. From the standpoint of WSA, Russia belongs to the semi-periphery, which, on the one hand, is dependent on the core, but, on the other, aspires to control its own regional periphery in the area of the former USSR.

Big business and the deficient accumulation of capital in Russia

To give an account of Russian capitalism as a social system, one needs to define the concrete form of surplus value characteristic of this society. Such an approach provides an opportunity to use the logic of capital, where all major economic relations are derived from the notion of surplus value. The present chapter argues that the main features of modern Russian capitalism, including its accumulation of capital, pattern of development, political system and position in the world economy and in the system of international relations, can be explained from the perspective of the concrete of surplus value. The latter is treated as the dominant social interest shaping all aspects of Russian capitalism.

The specific Russian model of corporate governance (which is a euphemism meaning the methods of capitalist control over assets) is of an authoritarian type. Dominant owners developed a whole infrastructure of control including informal, corrupted ties with state functionaries and the suppression of hired labour. Under this term is a set of partially formal, but predominantly informal, relations securing control over assets on the part of dominating groups. External elements of this infrastructure assume corrupted ties with state functionaries, which provide protection of 'property rights'. Internal elements secure control over hired labour, including informal means of coercion.

This control is highly unstable and can always be challenged. Instability of 'property rights' engenders short-term managerial strategies. This, in turn, conditions the main type of income appropriated by Russian capitalists. I call it 'insider rent', by which I mean short-term income, derived from control of the firms' financial flows. The most widespread way of withdrawing funds from Russian firms includes establishing figurehead trade houses registered in offshore sites. The controlled enterprises sell their products to these companies at prices lower than the market level. Later these products are sold at market prices and money is accumulated in the private accounts of the dominant owners. In fact, these are finances withdrawn from investment, wage and salary funds, among other sources. Insider rent is appropriated at the expense of unpaid labour and, thus, constitutes a concrete form of surplus value, peculiar to a Russian type of 'accumulation by dispossession', as argued by David Harvey.

Insider rent extraction leads to a number of intra-firm conflicts between the dominant owners and workers, rank-and-file managers and minority share-holders. To suppress these conflicts and defend their 'rights' against rival business groups, Russian owners had to increase their infrastructures of control. Rent withdrawal and expenditure on infrastructure undermine both the supply of and the demand for investments in productive capacities. From the inferior investment strategies of Russian big business come corporations which often ignore potentially profitable investment projects because of their long payback periods. On the other hand, Russian big business systematically withdraws funds through off-shore sites to save them in the West, another manifestation of its semi-dependent, comprador status. Despite the great expectations raised at the dawn of the market reforms, Russian big business failed to become a vehicle for technical progress and modernisation.

Growing inequality and crippled economic growth

Insider rent extraction as a concrete form of appropriation of surplus value determines not only capital accumulation but all other socio-economic processes as well. First of all, it shapes the distribution of the national income, causing growing inequality. The share of Russian labour within GDP shrank compared to Soviet times, and living standards deteriorated sharply. Sociologists observe the new poverty phenomenon, which means such types of dispossession can't be remedied under the current social conditions. Impoverishment of the population sets powerful limitations on the domestic market, which further decreases profits and undermines incentives for investment.

Moreover, the distribution of insider rent extraction between industries is reflected in the price structure of the national economy. The export-oriented sector, composed mainly of energy producers and metallurgy, enjoys higher rates of price indices than manufacturing oriented to the domestic market. This price disparity in favour of exporters of products with a low degree of processing, and to the detriment of manufacturing, reflects the semi-peripheral position of the Russian economy in the world system. Price disparity, in turn, determines the redistribution of financial flows among industries in favour of exporters.

Inflating the costs of manufacturing production, exporters appropriate part of their financial flows, withdrawing further these funds from Russia and saving them in the West. The monetary policy of Russian government is fully oriented to supporting exporters. Since Russia has great net exports (export revenues minus import revenues), it enjoys an active trade surplus. The inflow of foreign currency into Russia leads to an appreciation of the national currency, which undermines the competitiveness of Russian exports. In order to avoid this, money is printed to buy excessive dollars so as to save them in the West. The current undervaluation of Russia's currency is beneficial to exporters and detrimental to importers, which puts manufacturing and the population at a disadvantage. Thus, insider rent extraction reflects and strengthens the semi-peripheral position of Russia in the world economy, preventing it from modernising, despite all the lip service paid to innovations by the government.

Putin's authoritarianism and his challenge to the West

The authoritarian nature of Russian capitalism has some of its roots in the radical market reforms of the 1990s. Since the peripheral nature of Russian capitalism means systematic transfer of a significant part of the country's labour value fund to the core, one needs strong extra-economic means to coerce people into submission. It is not surprising that the Supreme Soviet – the first democratically elected Russian Parliament, opposing privatisation – was shot at by tanks in October 1993 and an authoritarian constitution was imposed on the demoralised society. The need to coerce people, determined by the nature of semi-peripheral capitalism, is the eventual reason both for the authoritarian model of corporate governance and for the authoritarian model of the state itself. Insider rent can elucidate much in this respect as well.

Russia's nascent capitalist class is divided into separate groups which aim to extract short-term incomes in Russia so as to accumulate abroad. The deficiencies of big business, which stems from its comprador nature, prevent true bourgeois class consciousness from coming into being. Fragmented businesses with short-term interests, oriented to the core, simply cannot develop common interests in the long run and a common vision for the future of Russia. As a result, they are unable to come to terms with subordinated classes, and this power relationship therefore excludes genuine democracy.

Since corrupt ties with the state are essential to survival in Russia, state functionaries are involved in the activities of different business groups. As a result, they have two affiliations: formally they belong to the state hierarchy and informally they belong to business groups. The second affiliation is stronger. As a result, Russia's state apparatus is fragmented. The power vacuum was filled by powerful oligarchs in the 1990s. The ensuing anarchy threatened to dismantle the very fabric of society and the state, putting in danger the capitalist order itself. In the 2000s Putin severely persecuted particular oligarchs who challenged his personal power. Others were smart enough to get the message: if they didn't meddle in high politics, they were free to enrich themselves. That is how Putin filled the power vacuum that the increasing authoritarian character of the state created. Using windfall profits from skyrocketing oil revenues, Putin partially restored the functions of the state neglected under Yeltsin.

In foreign policy, Putin followed in the steps of Yeltsin's 'Yes' diplomacy. However, by the late 1990s both the Russian government and the wider public had become disillusioned with the rapprochement with the West. Russia was far from being accepted in the 'family of civilised nations' of the core. It was systematically marginalised by the West. In the course of the Chechen war, elements of the national-liberation movement among the Chechen people were subjugated by the expansion of Islamic extremism. For decades this expansion was strongly supported by the West politically, economically and militarily. In 1999 NATO started so-called 'humanitarian interventions' in Yugoslavia, completely ignoring Russian protests and defeating pro-Russian Serbs.

In the 2000s, a number of 'revolutions' were staged in the former Soviet republics to install anti-Russian governments. Despite Western assurances given to Gorbachev that NATO would not move 'an inch' to the East, the aggressive Western military bloc embraced the former East European allies of the Soviet Union. In addition, the US unilaterally quit the anti-missile treaty and initiated a new anti-missile defence system in Eastern Europe on the borders of Russia. The New Great Game – the contest of Russia, the USA, the EU, China and militant Islam for control over the oil resources of the Caspian region and Central Asia – started. As if all this was not enough to undermine Russia's national security, the West announced its plans to include Ukraine and Georgia in NATO. This would effectively make Russia permanently insecure and threaten its very existence.

The essence of Western policy is the struggle to deprive Russia of its semi-peripheral status and make the country another purely peripheral society. By starting the second Chechen war, defeating Georgia in 2008 and then returning Crimea to Russia in 2014, Putin met the Western challenge. Another aspect of his policy was the project of Eurasian reintegration, which already involves Belarus and Kazakhstan. His aim was not to revive the Soviet Union or to start a new Cold War. Instead Putin simply seeks to secure the position of Russia as a regional power or as a semi-peripheral state.

In all of this, the Putin era does not represent a disjuncture with Yeltsin's. They relate as processes of becoming and being. Putin's strategy objectively involves him in deeper and deeper confrontations with the West. Up until the present, he has managed to use oil revenues and play on contradictions among Western countries. But in the long run, the fundamental weaknesses of Russia's semi-peripheral status will increasingly tell. Russia's comprador capitalist class is very vulnerable to Western pressure. A weak economy with a ruined manufacturing sector dependent on world markets cannot provide enough resources for the military strength necessary to withstand a serious, full-fledged confrontation.

Conclusion

WSA, reconsidered in the light of Marxian theory, with its focus on surplus value creation and distribution, explains the phenomenon of modern Russian capitalism as a coherent social system. Insider rent as a concrete form of surplus value explains the aims of Russian firms, their mechanism of capital accumulation, social conflicts, economic development and the place of Russia in the world arena. The Western challenge makes all the weaknesses inherent in the new social order apparent. The only real way for Russia to survive and revive as a viable society is to completely abandon capitalist development and move to democratic socialism. Only a mass radical left party imposing social control over big business and introducing national planning would be able to meet the historical challenges that Russia is facing today.

14

Russia's neoliberal imperialism and the Eurasian challenge

GONZALO POZO

According to the BRICS story, first told over a decade ago by research analysts at Goldman Sachs, four emerging economies were set to become the engine of capitalism in this century. The bottom line (based on specific assumptions about development and demographics, on multiple economic projections and on a rather massive *ceteris paribus* assumption) was that Brazil, Russia, India and China had the potential of reaching an average GDP level higher than the individual growth rates of the world's six richest nations by 2040. Effectively, and provided that the 2001–03 'growth policy-settings' were maintained, the broader BRIC prediction was that the political and economic contours of the international system were undergoing a kind of great transformation (Wilson and Purushothanam 2003:2–4; in one of his projected scenarios, O'Neill 2001).

More than a decade later, forecasts originally made about BRICS would look very different and would have to be formulated in a more nuanced, even circumspect way – *The Economist*, for instance, declared that a general deceleration after 2012 marked 'the end of the first dramatic phase of the emerging-market era' (2013). Additionally, the analytical usefulness of a 'BRICS category' (the acronym now expanded to include South Africa) looks even more questionable in 2015 than in the early 2000s. And yet, the formula has stuck, and the broad questions it poses (particularly the ominous sense that the world system's balance was shifting East) have become a mainstream subject of debate (to cite but one example, see Rachman 2010). Animated by the very strong growth prospects which began visiting their economies particularly in 2006–07, BRIC countries assumed Goldman Sachs' script as their own: very quickly, they began positing themselves (particularly in Moscow and Beijing) as a geopolitical counter to Western hegemony or, at least, as the potential platform for something like a new concert of nations in an increasingly multipolar world order. Indeed, by 2009, the international summits held on social and developmental agendas by Brazil, India and South Africa, and those held since 2006 by the governments of the BRIC countries at Russia's initiative, merged. Since then, BRICS refers both to a category and to an actual international forum, comprising a group of five emerging/emerged powers, representing just under half of the world's population and about a third of global economic activity (Larionova 2012; Lukov 2014). The older the BRICS forum gets, the more diverse the profile and trajectories of its members become. For this reason, a useful starting point is to ask what defines and unites the group, and what is Russia's standing in it.

Now, as in 2001, the BRIC(S) formula was problematic, temptingly offering an illusion of internal consistency between its economies, and helping to hide the extreme differences in productive structure, demographic outlook, developmental strategy and political regime which still distinguish its members (Cassiolato 2014:74; Armijo 2007; BRICS 2014). There are, nevertheless, at least two discernible unifying elements within the acronym. Firstly, and especially if one considers the intellectual aims of Jim O'Neill (then a leading researcher for Goldman Sachs' Global Economics), the BRICS category was a useful way of identifying the best mid- and long-term opportunities for capitalism's big investors. BRICS were, in this formal sense, a cogent group for economic strategists to pore over. Secondly, today, as in 2001, the BRICS remain recognisably unified as proponents of several regional variations on Western neoliberalism, keen on becoming integral (if differentiated) elements of the contemporary capitalist system. Indeed, as O'Neill has recently pointed out, 'in 2001, what particularly interested me about Brazil, Russia, India and China was that they all appeared increasingly eager to engage on the global stage' (2011).

Beyond these two considerations, almost everything within the BRICS is different – even their growth potential, central to their very definition, varies drastically. And meantime, although each of the BRICS is exceptional and has largely taken its own path over the years, in its own way Russia is arguably more exceptional than the others – its inclusion in the mix by Jim O'Neill certainly proved the most controversial. While each BRICS had its own particular legacy and set of challenges to face, the Russian Federation seemed economically much more vulnerable to turns of fortune, decidedly appearing to be the group's paper tiger (Boris Kagarlitsky has labelled it an 'empire of the periphery', 2008).

At the same time, it is not just its relative weakness but also its international assertiveness which set the Russian Federation apart from the others. Russia is now digging its heels into the first year of a conflict over influence in Ukraine. The crisis, fruit of a diplomatic slide which has been in the making for years, is likely to dominate European security for decades. Russia, today, constitutes the first line of inter-imperial rivalries in the system between emerging powers, on the one hand, and Europe, the US and its allies, on the other. Its role in the BRICS group thus gains relevance, not just for itself but in terms of the key questions of power relations in the system it raises. What follows is an attempt to frame and tentatively answer these questions as well as offer an examination of something we could call the 'Eurasian' challenge, both galvanising and explaining some of the specificities of Russian neoliberal imperialism after the collapse of the Soviet Union and particularly under Putin.

BRICS or BICS?
Can Russia legitimately be called a BRICS country, then? Does it offer the hallmarks of an emerging power, as the fulfilment of its BRICS potential should imply? Commentary and tentative answers to these questions can lead to some confusion, since they vary widely depending on the specific year in which they are formulated (betraying, I think, a slight anxiety about the end of the Cold War). I come back to the volatile evolution of Russian capitalism since 1991 below, but its ups and downs have frequently altered the perceptions of Russian power and wealth. In the mid-2000s, for instance, and although Russia had already left behind the worst of the disastrous 1990s, the country seemed to fall short of its BRICS status: 'Russia', wrote S Neil Macfarlane in 2005, 'is more properly seen as a state which has recently experienced substantial damage and is attempting to stop the bleeding' (2006:43). Macfarlane, using data from 2004, rightly pointed out that Russia's baseline growth (filtering out the increase in international hydrocarbon prices) was still very low, and that in GDP terms, Russia was more commensurable to Holland, representing only a third of the size of the Chinese economy. But already in 2007, as the growth trends of the early 2000s seemed to intensify, the European Council on Foreign Relations argued that Russia had clearly become a rising power (Leonard and Popescu 2007). Not only observers but also the Russian elite would soon become infused with the same enthusiasm; and suddenly the prospects blackened once again after 2008–9, with the turbulence induced by the war in South Ossetia, the burst of the commodity boom, and the arrival of the global economic downturn in Russia. In 2012, Russia was certified as 'post-BRIC' (Judah, Kobzova and Popescu 2011). The outspoken

analyst Nouriel Roubini, in a piece called 'Another BRIC in the wall?', wondered whether Russia was not in fact 'more sick than BRIC' (Roubini 2011).

Clearly, the health of the Russian economy has gone through extreme variations. In Russia, the decade after the collapse of the Soviet Union closed with a grim balance: an abysmal contraction of the economy (about 50% of GDP was wiped out only between 1991 and 1994) and a situation in which all main economic and social indicators nosedived (for an exceptionally clear and synthetic overview, see Pirani 2010, chapter 7; see also Cook 2012). Much of that story is not particular to Russia, and indeed horrific (often higher) levels of poverty and inequality have plagued and continue to plague the development prospects of China and, more directly, Brazil, India and South Africa. What is key in the case of Russia is that poverty and inequality – for the most part, the consequence of 20 years of harsh neoliberal reforms – exacerbate an essential element of negative contrast to the other BICS beyond economic metrics: population decline – and remember that demographics was one of the main methodological pillars in the original definition of a BRICS according to Wilson and Purushothanam (2003, Appendix III). In demographic terms, Russia clearly stands out. According to Simon Pirani:

> The death rate [in Russia], having hit an all-time high in the early 1990s, fell temporarily in the late 1990s, but in the 2000s increased. Mortality among men of working age is three to five times higher, and among women twice as high, as in other countries at similar levels of economic development. Those living on the verge of poverty, and suffering high levels of alcoholism, poor nutrition, lack of healthcare, and psychological stress, are most prone to dying young … High death rates have combined with a constantly falling birth rate to produce a sharp decline in Russia's population, and demographers expect this to continue in the coming decades (2010:134).

So back in 2000, as O'Neill was working out his first BRIC formulation, Russia's death rate soared over its birth rate, with a further decline in the fertility rate between perestroika and 1999 of close to 50%. Taken together, these figures mean that the number of Russian women of childbearing age has fallen sharply, which in turn works to dampen Russia's future demographic prospects even more. Although fertility rates have recovered since Putin first took office, the overall size of the Russian population is down by three million people since 1991, and this decline, even when it has substantially decelerated, will remain a feature of Russian development, exacerbated by ongoing health blights such as deeply eroded social networks, illness and alcoholism. It seems clear that there will continue to be fewer Russians, and they will be less healthy, and this last predicament overwhelmingly affects those closest to the poverty line. Nicholas Eberstadt, who conducted a systematic demographic study in 2010, reached even more drastic general conclusions: 'Russia today is in the grip of an eerie, far-reaching and in some respects historically unprecedented population crisis. Since the end of the Soviet era, the population of the Russian Federation has fallen by nearly seven million. Apart from China's paroxysm in the wake of Mao's catastrophic Great Leap Forward, this is the largest single episode of depopulation yet registered in the postwar era' (Eberstadt 2010:281).

Though O'Neill, reassessing the validity of his BRIC concept in 2011, fully acknowledged this population collapse, he flatteringly referred to the efforts by the Putin and especially the Medvedev administrations to revert it, and stated his hope that the country might yet rise to fulfil the economic predictions he had made a decade earlier: 'Russia doesn't need dramatic growth rates, it just needs to avoid crises', no less (2011). The comment is worth pointing out because it reveals a critical indifference to the effects of neoliberalism on the lives of the Russian people, as well as betraying a naïve faith in the officially stated priorities of the Russian elite. As one finds out, O'Neill reserves a similar treatment for an additional condition obviously afflicting Russia today: a binary made up of political authoritarianism and economic corruption. These blots set Russia apart from the other BICS in important ways (both issues being singled out as primary by O'Neill and the Kremlin regime alike).

On corruption, Putin himself has spoken of it as an 'intractable' condition of the Russian state. So widespread is the problem that clinical metaphors abound: 'corruption is the most serious disease affecting our society', said President Medvedev on taking office (Holmes 2012:235). To the degree that it can be quantified accurately, Medvedev also pointed out that known levels of corruption were likely to represent 'only the tip of the iceberg' (Medvedev 2010). Undeniably, the actual yearly toll exacted by corruption on the Russian economy is extremely difficult to gauge and estimates range widely between 5% of GDP (Rosstat 2012) and 25%, according to a recent partisan report (Milov et al. 2011; see also Saratov 2012). In the meantime, Russia's indices of perceived corruption – according to Transparency International – have plateaued in the last two years, putting it around position 130 in the rankings (133 in 2012 and 128 in 2013) – generally well below those of China, Brazil or India. Where the money goes, corruption follows. In Moscow, the city's Prosecutor General Sergei Kudeneyev reported that in 2012 'the number of registered crimes against the interests of the service in commercial and other organisations has almost tripled', while the detection rate for fraud committed by business executives had increased by a staggering 74% (Interfax 2012). Meantime, corruption in Russia is not only associated with activities such as embezzlement or bribes (worth as much as US$300 billion yearly), but, much more worryingly, relates closely to the penetration by organised crime of every level of the state administration (Dawisha 2014:8).

To give but one example from the Russian capital, a cable dispatched from the US's Moscow embassy recounted how 'criminal elements enjoy a *krysha* [literally meaning 'roof' – crimespeak for 'protection'] that runs through the police, the Federal Security Service, the Ministry of Internal Affairs and the prosecutor's office'. According to the document, the then mayor of Moscow (Yury Luzhkov, unceremoniously sacked by President Medvedev shortly after the leak, though not because of it) oversaw the whole criminal structure (Chanche 2010; see also WikiLeaks 2010; Pozo-Martin 2013). Even beyond Moscow, corruption in Russia is ubiquitous and, according to Shlapentokh (2012:157), is largely accepted by ordinary citizens as normal; by now they would only expect a clear and stable sense of how these unwritten rules work.

Russia's population crisis and the effects of corruption might offer enough gloom on their own, but they must still be considered alongside a further element setting Russia quite apart from the other BICS (and also dampening its future): the economy's high degree of dependence on hydrocarbon and, to a certain extent, on other mineral resources, which underscores its 'peripheral' status and its vulnerability to cycles of boom and bust in commodity prices. The years 2000–8 (those of Putin's first two terms as president) saw an almost continuous rise in international oil prices (from just over US$20 a barrel to the historic record price of US$140). At the same time, the Russian economy recorded a miraculous economic recovery. GDP grew in 2000 by 10% (of course, the economy had just come from a drastic slump – the rouble crisis – in 1998), and continued to expand by an average of 4–5% until 2008. Living standards followed the same trend (average GDP per capita rose from US$1778.7 in 2000 to US$9062 in 2008; while unemployment fell from 10.5% to 6.3% in the same period).

By 2008 the Russian state had fulfilled its debt obligations with the West, accumulated over half a trillion dollars in foreign reserves and overseen the creation of two sovereign wealth funds which would, it was hoped, guarantee social coverage and economic stability through periods of hardship. Even more importantly, the good years saw positive developments beyond the hallmarks of an oil boom: there was also a sharp increase in consumer spending, a surge in productivity and shift in GDP towards goods and services produced inside Russia, so the signs looked promising. Putin was able to deepen the comprehensive neoliberal crusade begun in the 1990s, but also reinforced, as we shall see, the capacity of the state to intervene in the economy and control the political scene. That said, other structural weaknesses never went away, and the contradictions of this period can be seen, perhaps more than anywhere else (aside from social inequality and population decline), in the volatility of capital net flows during this period. As with other BICS (though behind China, India and Brazil), Russia saw voluminous net inflows, in this case worth over US$100 billion dollars in just the two years before the global financial crisis broke out. However, as Simon Pirani has noted, 'capital flows during the oil boom were almost all in the form of loans, rather than investment':

> In 2005, debt accounted for more than three-quarters of the total inward flow; by early 2008, it accounted for more than five-sixths, economists at the World Bank reckoned. So while the Central Bank and government, following best market practice, accumulated nearly $600 million in foreign exchange reserve accounts – the world's largest such cash pile after those of China and Japan – Russian companies and banks built up foreign-currency debts on nearly the same scale (Pirani 2010:98).

The result was a surge in private debt which ripples on today, affecting the capacity of the Russian economy to make productive investments and grow sustainably, while its vulnerability to oil shocks continued. Russia is thus extremely fragile (in 2009, the first year of the crisis, GDP fell by 8.9%), and nothing shows this better than capital flight. With the outbreak of the global financial crisis, net inflows were surpassed in value by capital flight in the last quarter of 2008 alone – in other words, the net gains of the previous two years disintegrated in just weeks. Capital flight, the worst effects of which Moscow is only just able to control through a recourse to foreign reserves and surgical forced shut-downs of the stock market, has brought turbulence to the Russian economy time and again since 2008 (with the war in Georgia, the global crisis and, more recently, the conflict in Ukraine and sinking international prices for oil). Officially, since the global downturn, capital flight has reached US$335 billion; in the region of US$80 billion had left the country by 2014 alone, and the continued effects of sanctions and the current drain in the value of the rouble mean we can expect even higher levels into 2015 (Dawisha 2014:8).

Russia, as an emerging economy, remains exceptional within the BRICS. Its geopolitical prowess guarantees it a global presence higher in profile than what its economic capacity would normally reflect. Russia retains, as the inheritor state of the USSR, a seat at the international table more by virtue of its diplomatic assets (veto power at the UN Security Council and nuclear weapons) than by economic prowess. And yet this international clout remains key. The Kremlin's overall foreign goal is thus a double and mutually reinforcing one: to integrate into the global economy, on the one hand, but to do so on its own terms, attempting a restoration of its 'great power' status in the system from which to try and build a new 'concert of powers' and a stable multipolar world. Russia seeks to become a global player, safe from the vicissitudes of Pax Americana and solid in its acknowledged role as regional hegemon. The international aspirations of Russian capitalism, therefore, appear contradictory and, in its difficulties, potentially dangerous. Additionally, the relative weaknesses of a state which challenged the US during much of the 20th century, which has seen bouts of impressive industrial development and which can boast an intensely skilled and educated population to take it forward, appear clearly as the results of political choices, elite projects imposed over the last two decades after the collapse of the USSR. The Russian political economy today in part responds to a design, shared unevenly between international and domestic actors. What then, in broad strokes, is the class nature of Russian neoliberalism, and how does it condition Moscow's international behaviour?

Neoliberal imperialism à la Russe

There is a story which, aside from illustrating the different spatial manifestations of Russian neoliberalism, captures quite well the basic contours of the Putin regime. In September 2005, Gazprom consolidated its position as a global energy behemoth (and Russia's largest firm) with the purchase of a 72.6% stake in the oil company Sibneft, at the time part of a holding company (Millhouse Capital) owned by Roman Abramovich. The operation marked the largest corporate takeover in Russia's history, even when the agreed price had only reached US$13 billion. On the day of this historic garage-sale, however, Sibneft's market value was approximately ten times that amount: if Sibneft had been sold in an international tender it would have gone at a much higher price. The takeover was followed by some important changes: Sibneft would now act as Gazprom's oil branch, and was duly renamed Gazprom Neft (Upstreamonline 2005). The new firm, hitherto based in Moscow, was quickly registered in St Petersburg. In November that year, Gazprom's CEO, Alexei Miller, accompanied by the governor of St Petersburg, Valentina Matviyenko, currently speaker of Russia's

Federation Council, unveiled a joint plan to build the Okhta Business Centre, or 'Gazprom City', where Gazprom Neft was due to relocate permanently after the works were finally completed (Kommersant 2006). It was a project of Babylonian proportions, and its phallic centrepiece was a super-tall skyscraper, which, when erected, would rise over 400 metres into the air, tearing deep into the skyline of a city in which regulations limited the height of any building to a fourth of that. In the place of an appropriate compensation for the inconvenience, Sibneft/Gazprom Neft pledged to pay the local authorities an annual sum of RUB20 billion in local taxes for the citizens' inconvenience. The sum amounted to roughly half of the annual budget for the Leningrad Oblast. By contrast, building the Okhta Centre was expected to cost well over RUB120 billion (almost US$5 billion). The property rights were to be distributed accordingly, once the exact dues of the city administration and gas company are established (Novaia Gazeta 2009). Local residents continued to protest against the development. During 2009 and throughout 2010, pressure mounted on both Gazprom Neft and Matviyenko, until finally, in December 2010, Matviyenko announced that at least the skyscraper would be relocated to some other part of the city (Shakirova 2010).

The story, in itself anecdotal, speaks of Russia's official geopolitical resurgence, built with the energy profits lying at the heart of its new-found (long-sought) great-power status and through the 'power vertical' erected by Putin at home. Just as the old Sankt-Peterburg was the vision and legacy of Peter the Great, a 'Gazprom City' on the Neva testified to Putin's successful restoration programme, very much in the same way as the postmodern monumentality lifted at Sochi for the Winter Olympics in 2014 – including, in this last case, losses through embezzlement perhaps worth as much US$30 billion, according to the assessment offered by the erstwhile deputy Prime Minister turned opposition figure, Boris Nemtsov, murdered in Moscow as this book was going into press (see Nemtsov 2014). The Okhta Centre, just like Sochi or the more recent 'greater Moscow' projects, was meant to showcase Russia's confident entrance into the 21st century not only as a global power but as an international business hub (Golubchikov 2010; see also Pozo-Martin 2013). But what they display, and this remains particularly true of the Okhta Centre, is of deeper significance. Indeed, Gazprom's takeover of Sibneft, the economic event behind the architectural project, was the very embodiment of Putin's wide-ranging programme for the political and economic reorganisation of Russia along clear corporatist lines. His ambitious plan included a new federal set-up able to bring the regions under direct control from the Kremlin, the crackdown on independent media (television in particular), a substantial shake-up of the electoral and party systems, and finally, the deployment of the old Soviet energy infrastructure (especially pipelines) to strengthen and extend Moscow's international standing – energy seen as the 'geopolitical weapon'.

Putin pursued his reforms while aiding, and being aided by, the political ascendancy of the so-called *siloviki*, a term which refers to a political clan whose members originated in the KGB/FSB universe. The usefulness of this label is contested (see for instance Renz 2006), but broadly the *siloviki* were nationalist in outlook, and keen to restore the strength and security of the Russian state, seeing Russia's natural-resource wealth as central in obtaining this goal. The term *siloviki* also included those among Putin's allies and associates whose political or business careers took off somewhere within the old KGB apparatus. Another powerful group, known as the Leningrad faction and exemplified by such prominent figures as Alexei Miller (CEO of Gazprom), or Dmitrii Medvedev himself (Gazprom's Chairman of the Board of Directors since June 2002, before he became Russian President in 2008), was made up of men mostly born in the 1950s and 1960s, who at one point or another would have met Putin when he was cutting his political teeth as head of the city administration's Committee of External Relations. The Gazprom City project thus represented the fusion of authoritarianism and corporatism which characterises Russia's version of neoliberal capitalism (see Ilarionov 2006; Wood 2007; Pirani 2010; and Dawisha 2014; for the specific role of Gazprom see Rosner 2005; Lucas 2008, 35–38; Benton and Buckley 2008; and Sixmith 2010).

But whatever the contrast with Yeltsin, Putin's ascent to the Kremlin represented a consolidation and a recomposition of the Russian ruling class; it was not, as has sometimes been argued, a comeback of the state against the economic elite and, equally, not a bureaucratic crackdown against the first generation of Russian oligarchs, the almighty Berezovskis and Gusinskis of the 1990s. This is true even of his own outlook. Putin is a product of the Soviet Union, of its cynical and pragmatic attitudes towards official ideology; and he is also a product of the Soviet defeat by international capitalism and the humiliation and trauma of the 'transition' to the market. In this worldview, shared by many in the generation which now controls the country, regaining lost Russian greatness means beating capitalists at their own game. As Gleb Pavlosky (until 2011 a close adviser to the President) has put it: 'Putin's idea is that we should be bigger and better capitalists than the capitalists, and be more consolidated as a state: there should be maximum oneness of state and business' (Pavlovsky 2014:57).

The point, then, is that the transformation of Russian politics and society since 1991 has largely revolved around three interrelated elements. Firstly, it involved a violent process of forced privatisation from above, which was the key characteristic of the economic transformation after the fall of the Soviet Union during the 1990s. In its most dramatic episodes, and especially during the loans-for-shares programme, the process, termed the 'sale of the century' by the economic journalist Chrystia Freeland (2006), consolidated the rise of a capitalist system based to a large degree on the power of a handful of business magnates from the middle cadres of the old Soviet nomenklatura (Fortescue 2006:8–9). During 'loans for shares', hitherto state-owned key assets of the Russian economy were leased out by the state through gerrymandered auctions for money to key players in the financial sector. In most cases these assets ended in the hands of Russia's business tycoons or oligarchs (Hoffman 2003:318–320). One of the resources in question was precisely Sibneft, which was acquired in a series of auctions in 1996–97 by Boris Berezovskii and Roman Abramovich to the tune of US$100 million (Jack 2005:175). The neoliberal zeal which animated Russia's transition to a market economy, and the political short-termism, lack of transparency and unbridled greed which framed the reforms, not only exacerbated social inequalities, but crucially perpetuated the relation of close proximity and, in the case of big business concerns, symbiotic interdependence between big business and the Russian state (Bunin 2004). The perverse story of the liberalisation of Russia's economy that was largely overlooked, or in some cases actively encouraged, by Western governments and business also ensured that a full institutional development to accompany the privatisation rounds would never be completed (Mukhin 2001). The 1990s thus laid the foundation of a political and economic set-up in Russia defined by informal sinews of restricted corporatist/authoritarian power, weak political and legal institutions, and extreme forms of capitalist accumulation and exploitation, with the attendant fractures between rich and poor and also often along a pervasive geographical urban–rural divide (UNDP 2009:175–177).

A second, equally important, phase in Russia's post-Soviet development is the meteoric ascent of Vladimir Putin, from an obscure local official in the St Petersburg administration to the highest levels of power, first through the posts of Deputy Chief of the Presidential Staff (March 1997), then, in May 1998, head of the FSB, Deputy Prime Minister in August 1999, Prime Minister later on that month, and finally, after Yeltsin's sudden resignation on 31 December 1999, Russian President until 2008. With Putin's election as President in March 2000 came a wide-ranging process of political reforms aimed at building a 'power vertical', a partial reconfiguration of the relation between state and business and an important reorientation of the main vectors driving policy abroad. Putin was also able to locate himself and the Kremlin at the centre of a more clearly nationalist, more authoritarian, more assertive set of official ideologies which proved successful, not just in terms of his enduring popularity, but also as regards the (often forceful) unification of key sectors of the Russian political system (for a comparison with other forms of right-wing politics see Motyl 2007 and Umland 2009:5–38).

This ideology (we can call it Putinism), at once a political project and a particular vision of Russia's path to prosperity and order, was predicated on the re-emergence of Russia as a powerful international actor, and on the reconstitution of order and economic growth (Gryzlov 2007; Edinaia Rossiia 2007). One of the key virtues is a deliberate ambiguity, designed to fit myriad hues of pragmatism and nationalism into a highly concentrated, neoliberal and statist doctrinal umbrella. This is an important advantage of Putinism, and it explains why Yedinaia Rossiia (United Russia), the only successful Kremlin-backed party since 1991, continues to dominate Russian politics today. Putinism, thus understood, has essentially resolved the ideological instability which characterised Yeltsin's terms of office and, critically, makes Putin himself a guarantor of the political balance between different factions of the Russian ruling class. And of course, Putin's very rise demanded a new class balance since it launched the *siloviki* into the Russian administration, while simultaneously trying to keep business in tight proximity to the state, introducing staple neoliberal economic measures (for instance a flat income-tax rate, introduced in 2001 at the high level of 13%; or to give another example, the New Labour Code of 2001) and redistributing key economic assets into the hands of politically reliable businessmen (Sakwa 2004:96–104; Kagarlitsky 2001; see also Sakwa 2011:131–132).[1]

A third important element of the high degree of authoritarian/corporatist fusion which characterises neoliberalism in Russia concerns Russia's foreign policy, and particularly its imperial – in other accounts 'neo-imperial' or even 'trans-imperial' – character (for an overview of these different categories see especially Colás and Pozo-Martin 2011; on the neo-imperial see in particular Bugajski 2004; on the trans-imperial, see Wallander 2007; for more critical takes for and against, see Tsygankov 2006:677–679; see also Suny 2007). The formation of a bourgeois–bureaucratic amalgam described above is right at the heart of the Kremlin's international agenda and its engagement with the West. In a geopolitical context defined by ethnic fragmentation, political instability, concerns over European energy security, and NATO/EU enlargement, events such as the current conflict in Ukraine reflect something deeper than merely one-dimensional commercial, territorial or diplomatic rows (Nygren 2008, especially

11; Colás and Pozo-Martin 2011; Pozo-Martin 2014).

These disputes, and other instances of friction and conflict such as the war over South Ossetia in August 2008 and the annexation of Crimea in March 2014, are, to put it in terms reminiscent of Lenin, the condensed expression of all the different antagonisms and contradictions which underpin the development of Russian neoliberalism and its complex process of global integration. The first point to make here is that, as can be gleaned from the above discussion, the Russian ruling class is constituted by an amalgam of blurred, interdependent business and bureaucratic interests. The two are, in the words of Tony Wood (quoting the *Financial Times*, and writing on the eve of the global financial crisis), extraordinarily intertwined. There are several noteworthy examples of this beyond Medvedev: there is, for instance, the case of Deputy Prime Minister Igor Sechin, also chairman of Rosneft, the company which engulfed most of the expropriated assets at YUKOS. Sechin is a walking knot of state–capitalist synergies at the highest level: the White House in Washington knows this full well, and has unsurprisingly made an example of him in the sanctions against 'Putin's circle' after the annexation of Crimea.

In the mid-2000s, and taking the presidential administration as a whole, 11 members chaired 6 state companies and had 12 further state directorships; 15 senior government officials held 6 chairmanships and 24 other board seats. Many members of the government are also known to have significant, undisclosed business interests (Wood 2007:60–61). State and business are so closely linked that it is often hard to plot the function, target and character of many policy decisions. In a pervasive legal vacuum, the limits between private ownership and political control not only remain unclear, but must continue to do so. Russian capitalism has thus emerged as a particularly violent, exclusive and authoritarian kind of neoliberal formation.

Further, the outlook of this highly concentrated group has historically appeared as essentially short-termist and mostly ravenous, concentrating more on profit through expansion and less on productive investments in the long term (for instance, see Kagarlitsky 2008:309). The economy's overall reliance on hydrocarbons and the tight symbiotic relation of the Russian state and Russian business (their mutual economic and political reliance) are what makes the Kremlin's foreign policy imperial. It directly calls to mind Harvey's definition of imperialism as a fusion of two distinct logics of power (capitalist and territorial), except that the relation between the two, which Harvey tends to leave under-theorised, appears structural in the Russian case (Harvey 2003:33–34; I return to this point below). In opposition to a pure instrumentalist theory, where individual players and their choices generate and explain foreign policy outcomes, Russian neoliberalism and the social reproduction of its elite provide the broad frame for the Kremlin's international stance.

A key element here is the 'energy weapon' (as we saw, so central in Putin's plans for a restored Great Russia). If the view proposed here is right, the energy weapon is not only a diplomatic instrument, but a source of economic value and political stability essential if Russian neoliberalism, in its current form, is to survive and reproduce. Critically, the imperialist character of the Russian neoliberal state is not only discernible in the assertive and at times aggressive character of Russian foreign policy (particularly in what is called its 'near abroad'), but it is also now recognised as such by its competitors in the system – and this is one of the key political lessons from the Ukrainian conflict. Indeed, let's ask ourselves what the West's overall reaction to the annexation of Crimea has been, and how the US and its allies have applied their punitive measures to the Russian state. Revealingly, the answer is that the West has explicitly targeted the Russian ruling class (or, as the preferred media formula has it, 'Putin's circle' – needless to say that the broader economic pain will be felt by all Russians, especially the most economically vulnerable). As Karen Dawisha puts it:

> [after Crimea] individual Russian citizens would be subjected to asset seizures and visa bans. The Sixth Fleet was not called into action; exports to Russia as a whole were not banned; cultural and educational exchanges were not stopped. Rather, individual elites close to 'a senior Russian Government official' – Vladimir Putin – were targeted. Probably the most serious international crisis since the end of the Cold War, and the White House targets individuals. Why this response? Because at last, after fourteen years of dealing with President Vladimir Putin as a legitimate head of state, the U.S. government has finally acknowledged publicly what successive administrations have known privately – that he has built a system based on massive predation on a level not seen in Russia since the tsars (2014:7).

And, we might add, this Russian 'system' is in no way a hostile entity threatening Western capitalism from the outside, but only one of its instantiations. It cannot be understood but as a partial product of Western intervention in the 1990s (in particular by both Clinton administrations), during the transition to the free market.

The Eurasian challenge

The relative weaknesses of the Russian economy – all the elements that threaten Moscow's global projection and cast a shadow on the prosperity of the Russian state and its people – are, paradoxically, entirely coherent with the rise of Russia as the most direct contender with US imperialism today. A merely quantitative approach to international rivalry will usually overlook the accumulation and class dynamics behind this contemporary form. This is an important point, particularly since much of the literature considering Russia's emerging power status generally maps the relative strength of the Russian economy directly onto its international assertiveness. Such an analytical strategy might make considerable sense at first sight, but it can also prove misleading. S Neil Macfarlane, for instance, argued that Russia's problems led it to pursue a 'mixed approach of partnership or acquiescence on matters of vital interest to the hegemonic power, and more competitive behaviour on issues deemed central to Russia but peripheral to US interests' (2006:42).

The conflict over Ukraine offers a comprehensive refutation of this point: here is an obvious 'issue' (an area of economic and strategic overlapping interests), which, because it is deemed central by both Russia and Western imperialism, can easily morph into a major security conundrum and a geopolitical fault line, quite regardless of the relative balance of strength between any of the contenders. A similar argument would apply for those who, in view of Russia's troubles after 2009, identified a wholesale downscaling in Moscow's foreign policy, and a more sober attempt to build a low-cost sphere of influence, and look for a 'lily-pad empire' (after Donald Rumsfeld's 'lily-pad army' concept): 'In its version of a "lily-pad" empire, Russia seeks to get the benefits while minimising the costs. As one Russian expert says: "We would like to choose the best bits of the CIS" – that is, energy infrastructure, key sectors of the economy and the right to station our military bases abroad – "and leave the rest to go to hell"' (Judah, Kobzova and Popescu 2011:28).

The confluence of state and business interests in pursuing precisely this kind of expansionism (avoiding longer-term investment and development in the Russian economy, and seeking energy and other economic assets abroad) is something we've already examined. Additionally, Russia maintains more than 30 000 military personnel in its 'near abroad' and has also obtained majority stakes in the gas transit systems particularly in Armenia and Moldova, while pushing hard to make gains in Ukraine (Naftogaz as the prize), Belarus and even Eastern Europe.[2] The lily-pad thesis, therefore, is questionable: there is no obvious monetary benefit for Russia in singlehandedly sustaining South Ossetia,

Abkhazia or Crimea. The costs of Russia's imperialist aspirations grow even more if we consider that the main geopolitical proposal offered by Putin since 2012 has been the launch of an Eurasian Economic Union (EEU), which might, at least, provide solid institutional trappings for a closer economic and political integration of the post-Soviet region and, at most, could match Putin's grand vision for a Russian-led reorganisation of that space (Putin 2012). Implementing this plan and consolidating it as the preferred alternative to the EU in the post-Soviet space has become a priority, whatever the costs (and they will be high).

The EEU is, since 1 January 2015, an official working reality, comprising Russia, Kazakhstan and Belarus, with Kyrgyzstan set to join in coming months. Unlike the Commonwealth of Independent States (CIS) before it, the EEU has a clearer institutional structure and builds from several other organisations such as the Eurasian Economic Union, the Customs Union and, more recently, the Eurasian Economic Commission. Modelled loosely on the EU (replicating the morphology of some of its organs, with the obvious exception of a Eurasian Parliament), the EEU seeks to provide a more inclusive, efficient and articulate integration between its members, but, in so doing, it will ensure that its members continue, as much as possible, within Moscow's orbit (Popescu 2014; on the emphasis on parallelisms with the EU, see Putin 2012). Moscow's proposals for the EEU are in this sense quite novel. The use of coercion or direct violence in what it regards as its sphere of influence has proven risky and counterproductive (it has already derailed previous attempts at unifying the post-Soviet space), so the EEU is presented with the reassurance that each member will retain its full sovereignty. This move also reflects a further change in Russian foreign policy thinking: the foreign policy documents of 2000, 2008 and 2013 all highlight the importance of cooperation with the 'near abroad', and the last two gravitate away from the emphasis on security and towards deeper economic integration (for a useful comparative review, see Ruiz Gonzalez 2013).

This new attempt at creating an economic space offers clearer collective benefits (though the main beneficiary is of course Russia) around an institution which proceeds from parliamentary ratification of the founding treaty by each of its members and which offers a rotating frame for decision-making operating by consensus (Popescu 2014:11–13). Through the EEU, Russia also hopes to begin clawing back its commercial position in the region, threatened increasingly by both the EU and China – Russia is currently the biggest trading partner only for Belarus and Uzbekistan. Further, the EEU abolishes internal barriers to trade and sets a common external tariff at a level agreed upon by Russia and the WTO on the former's accession (10%). Critically, this move benefits Russia to the detriment of all other players, since their tariff levels are often twice or three times lower than Russian ones: in joining the EEU they agree to forgo beneficial commercial links with Russia's direct rivals. In compensation, Russia paradoxically accepts an added cost, offering easier labour market access for the region's migrants and also cheap energy exports, advantageous loans and other forms of economic assistance. Importantly, Russia has also offered to front the bill should the WTO impose penalties on other members for raising tariffs (Popescu 2014:11–12).

These points illustrate Russia's willingness to do everything possible to attract members into the Eurasian Union and indicate beyond ambiguity that Russia is ready to put its money where its mouth is, at a time when economic sanctions, capital flight and the rouble devaluation question the viability of the EEU and have already begun hurting all EEU economies. Moscow needs to step up its support for the EEU and make sure its regional influence does not further dissipate. The ostensible political benefits for Russia go well beyond economics. Firstly, the EEU solves the angst which engulfs the Kremlin when it pictures a post-Lukashenko or post-Nazarbayev future in the region (Ukraine's violent Westward drift is something that Moscow is loath to see happening elsewhere). Additionally, the EEU not only integrates the region, but protects it from the increasing penetration of NATO and the EU, and reduces and subdues the political scope of action of local elites. Putin's Eurasian project is meant to represent post-Soviet states with an existential choice: in or out (with all their consequences). The unfolding of the Ukraine conflict over the last few months further reinforces the diametrically opposed nature of the choice offered to states between the EU and the EEU (Cadier 2014).

The EEU's chances of success are critical for Russia also in terms of its essential relations with the most powerful of the BRICS, China. In the 2000s, China and Russia were able to come together on a number of platforms and present an alternative to US/NATO unilateralism and Western hegemony. From these years emerge the Shanghai Cooperation Organisation (2001), constituted by Russia, China, Kazakhstan, Kyrgyzstan and Uzbekistan, and the first formal BRICS summit itself; also in these years the commercial relations between both countries grew. According to Bobo Lo, during the mid-2000s Russia became China's dominant arms supplier, including high-tech aviation equipment – more recently China reduced these imports, which it could now produce domestically (Lo 2008:79).

In the 2000s, China also became Russia's largest trading partner, surpassing Germany, in 2010 – at the same time, the differences between the two of them were already becoming obvious. While China dominated Russian trade, Russia currently accounts for only 2% of China's total exports and represents 1.9% of China's imports. The growing disparity, exemplified in this imbalance fuels Russian concern that, more than a partner, it has now become China's *pridatok* (appendage). More importantly, China has become a presence to reckon with in Central Asia, building transport infrastructure in the region, sending workers, loans and aid, and now striking bilateral energy deals which, for the first time, have broken Russia's transit monopoly. China is mildly supportive of Russia's current role in Ukraine (in November 2014 Russian obtained a central bank liquidity swap line and a commitment of further financial help to contain the depreciation of the rouble).

But this is not so much solidarity as interest. For years Chinese negotiators have been able to get extremely favourable conditions for Russian energy exports, consistently imposing supplies under market price – the recent US$400 billion energy deal between the two parties attests to this loss of leverage, since the baseline gas prices finally agreed on (lower than those already paid in Europe) might not even cover the costs of laying down the pipeline which will deliver the commodity. While Russia digs in its heels to its west, it slowly gives way to China's energy security needs. Once more, Russian imperialism is contradictory and uneven, but ready to maintain its status whatever it takes.

Conclusion

My argument attempts to outline the real, often contradictory role of the Russian Federation as an 'emerging power' and member of the BRICS club, which embodies some of the most common aspects of contemporary capitalism at home (including an important level of elite integration and collaboration abroad). Simultaneously, Russia is the state most clearly opposed to the West on geopolitical lines. These lines of conflict over Ukraine are a central part of the argument here, as they not only confirm the imperialistic character of Russian foreign policy, but, in its latter stages, also showed the West's own understanding and awareness of the nature of Russia's imperialist contestation, whatever specific terminology they reserve for it. The clash of rival imperialist agendas now blown open in Ukraine offers a number of key lessons both in terms of Russia's 'emerging power' status, and the potential of the BRICS to really shift the global balance of power in coming years.

Firstly, and apart from any other distinctions which might set it apart from China, India, Brazil or South Africa, Russia ironically helps confirm that the BRICS do not pose an alternative to neoliberalism, but are rather, and like variations on a theme, different individual developments of it. To follow with a conceptual thread running through this volume, Russia, like the other BRICS, acts as a transmission belt of global capitalism. At the same time, the many differences between BRICS sustain and help intensify a logic of competition between them, and also potentially intensify points of pressure and friction with the West. What this points to is that inter-imperialist rivalries are inter-capitalist rivalries, all arising from the same global system. These rivalries, therefore, occur not across geo-temporal boundaries separating the old geopolitics from the new, the territorial expansionism from the cosmopolitanism – but across the lines drawn by overlapping state–class interests. And in this process, national states still play a central role in articulating such rivalries. The specificity of Russia, then, both in terms of its relations with the other BRICS and of its current opposition to the West in Ukraine, is that it shows, more clearly than any other case, that geopolitical fractures in the system are as integral to contemporary capitalism as its globalising tendencies; the open conflict in the Donbass area of the Ukraine is no mere 'flashpoint' but a determinant crisis with an unclear resolution. Globalising tendencies of their own cannot undo the potential for interstate competition on a large scale. In such conditions, movements of opposition from below in the BRICS might not only offer an essential stepping stone for a renewal and reinvigoration of the global left but, critically, represent a most necessary platform against the dangers of imperialist barbarism.

Notes

1. The precise composition of the ruling elite, and their character is a hotly debated point in the literature. I have only provided broad strokes here drawing on previous work, but for an essential starting point see Kryshtanovskaya and White 2003, 2005a and 2005b; and critical interventions in Rivera and Rivera 2006 and Wood 2007. Once again, the most recent forensic report (but one which elides a full notion of class) is Karen Dawisha's excellent, if controversial, *Putin's Kleptocracy* (2014).
2. Naturally, the official position of the Russian Federation is that it does not have troops in Ukraine, though the annexation of Crimea and the violence in the Donbass would surely increase the overall figure by several thousands.

References

Armijo, Leslie Elliot (2007) The BRICs countries (Brazil, Russia, India and China) as analytical category: mirage or insight?, *Asian Perspectives*, 31, 4, pp 7–42

Benton, Catherine and Neil Buckley (2008) Friends in high places?, *Financial Times* (London), 15 May

Borogan, Irina and Andrei Soldatov (2010) *The New Nobility: The Restoration of Russia's Security State and the Enduring Legacy of the KGB*, London, Public Affairs

BRICS (2014) *BRICS Joint Statistical Publication 2014*, http://brics.ibge.gov.br/downloads/BRICS_Joint_Statistical_Publication_2014.pdf

Bugajski, Janusz (2004) *Cold Peace: Russia's New Imperialism*, Westport, CT, Praeger

Bunin, Igor' (2004) Vlast' i biznes v novoi Rosii, Politcom.ru, 11 June, http://www.politcom. ru/2002/aaa_c_b3.php

Cadier, David (2014) Eurasian eonomic union and eastern partnership: the end of the EU–Russia *entredeux*, LSE IDEAS report, http://www.lse.ac.uk/IDEAS/publications/reports/pdf/SR019/ SR019-Cadier.pdf

Cassiolato, José (2014) BRICS and development. In Vandana Desai and Robert Potter (eds), *The Companion to Development Studies*, London, Routledge

Chanche, Matthew (2010) WikiLeaks: U.S. saw Moscow mayor atop corrupt 'pyramid', CNN, 2 December, http://edition.cnn.com/2010/WORLD/europe/12/01/russia.wikileaks/index.html

Colás, Alejandro and Gonzalo Pozo-Martin (2011) The value of territory: towards a Marxist geopolitics, *Geopolitics*, 16, 1, pp 211–220

Cook, Linda (2012) The political economy of Russia's economic Crisis. In Neil Robinson (ed), *The Political Economy of Russia*, Plymouth, Roman and Littlefield, pp 97–120

Dawisha, Karen (2014) *Putin's Kleptocracy: Who Owns Russia?* London, Simon and Schuster

Eberstadt, Nicholas (2010) *Russia's Peacetime Demographic Crisis: Dimensions, Causes, Implications*, National Bureau of Asian Research Project Report, http://nbr.org/downloads/ pdfs/psa/Russia_PR_May10.pdf

Economist, The (2013) The great deceleration, 27 July, http://www.economist.com/news/ leaders/21582256-emerging-market-slowdown-not-beginning-bust-it-turning-point

Edinaia Rossiia (2007) Chto takoe Plan Putina?, 2 November, http://er.ru/text.shtml?2/1569

Ellman, Michael (2000) 'The Russian economy under Yeltsin, *Europe-Asia Studies,* 52, 8, 2000, pp 1417–1432

Fortescue, Stephen (2006) *Russia's Oil Barons and Metal Magnates: Oligarchs and the State in Transition*, Basingstoke, Palgrave Macmillan

Freeland, Chrystia (2006) *Sale of the Century: The Inside Story of the Second Russian Revolution*, Croydon, Abacus

Frye, Tymothy (2002) Capture or exchange? Business lobbying in Russia, *Europe-Asia Studies*, 54, 7, pp 1017–1036

Golubchikov, Oleg (2010) World-city-entrepreneurialism: globalist imaginaries, neoliberal geographies and the production of new St Petersburg, *Environment and Planning*, 42, 3, pp 626–643

Gryzlov, Boris (2007) Plan Putina – dal'neishego razvitiia strany, 17 September, http://er.ru/text. shtml?2/6793

Harvey, David (2003) *The New Imperialism*, Oxford, Oxford University Press

Hoffman, David (2003) *The Oligarchs: Wealth and Power in the New Russia*, New York, Public Affairs

Holmes, Leslie (2012) Corruption in post-Soviet Russia, *Global Change, Peace and Security*, 24, 2, pp 235–250

Illarionov, Andrei (2006) Russia, Inc., *New York Times*, 4 February

Interfax (2012), Corruption detection rates soar in Moscow, Russia Beyond the Headlines, 5 August, http://rbth.ru/articles/2012/08/05/corruption_detection_rate_soars_in_moscow_17050.html

Jack, Andrew (2005) *Inside Putin's Russia*, London, Granta Books

Judah, Ben, Jana Kobzova and Nicu Popescu (2011) Dealing with a post-BRIC Russia, European Council on Foreign Relations, http://www.ecfr.eu/page/-/ECFR44_POST-BRIC_RUSSIA. pdf

Kagarlitsky, Boris (2001) *Russia under Yeltsin and Putin: Neoliberal Autocracy*, London, Pluto

Kagarlitsky, Boris (2008) *Empire of the Periphery: Russia and the World System*, London, Pluto

Kommersant (2006) Parus im v ruki: Valentina Matvienko i Aleksei Miller vybrali novyi simbol Peterburga, *Kommersant*, 2 December, http://www.kommersant.ru/doc.aspx?DocsID=726850

Kramer, Andrew (2007) Former Russian spies are now prominent in business, *New York Times*, 17 December

Kryshtanovskaya, Olga and Stephen White (2003) Putin's militocracy, *Post-Soviet Affairs*, 19, 4, 2003, pp 289–306

Kryshtanovskaya, Olga and Stephen White (2005a) Inside the Putin court: a research note, *Europe-Asia Studies*, 57, 7, pp 1065–1075

Kryshtanovskaya, Olga and Stephen White (2005b) The rise of the Russian business elite, *Communist and Post-Communist Studies*, 38, 3, pp 293–307

Larionova, Marina et al. (2012) Sotrudnichestvo dla obespecheniya globalnogo rosta. Problemy yprableniya global'nymi riskami i vosmozhnosti 'gruppa dvatsati', 'gruppa vos'mi' i BRICS, http://iorj.hse.ru/data/2012/10/08/1244264531/4.pdf

Lo, Bobo (2008) *Axis of Convenience: Moscow, Beijing, and the New Geopolitics*, London, Chatham House and Washington, Brookings Institution

Leonard, Mark and Nicu Popescu (2007) A power audit of EU–Russia relations, European Council on Foreign Relations, November, http://www.ecfr.eu/content/entry/commentary_pr_russia_power_audit

Lucas, Ed (2008) *The New Cold War: How the Kremlin Menaces Both Russia and the West*, London, Bloomsbury

Lukov, Vadim (2014) A global forum for a new generation: the role of BRICS and the prospects for the future, http://www.brics.utoronto.ca/analysis/Lukov-Global-Forum.html

MacFarlane, S. Neil (2006) The 'R' in BRICs: is Russia an emerging power?, *International Affairs*, 82, 1, pp 41–57

Medvedev, Dmitrii (2010) Stenograficheskii otchet o zasedanii soveta zakonodatelei, President Rossii, 14 July, http://kremlin.ru/transcripts/8343

Milov, Vladimir, Boris Nemtsov, Vladimir Ryzhkov and Olga Shorina (2011) Putin: corruption. An independent expert report, http://www.nemtsov.ru/old.phtml?id=706613

Motyl, Alexander (2007) Is Putin's Russia fascist?, *The National Interest*, 3 December, http://nationalinterest.org/commentary/inside-track-is-putins-russia-fascist-1888

Mukhin, Aleksei (2001) *Biznes-elita i gosudarstvennaia vlast': kto vladeet Rossiei na rubezhe vekov?*, Moscow, Tsentr Politicheskikh Informatsii

Nemtsov, Boris and Leonid Martiniuk (2014) Zimniaya olimpiada v subtropikakh. Nezabisimiy ekspertnyi doklad, http://www.putin-itogi.ru/cp/wp-content/uploads/2013/05/Zimniaya OlimpiadaVSubtropikah-Nemtsov-Martyniuk.pdf

Novaia Gazeta (2009) Peterburg ne khochet umirat, *Novaia Gazeta* (Moscow), 25 May

Nygren, Bertil (2008) Putin's use of natural gas to reintegrate the CIS region, *Problem of Post-Communism*, 55, 4, pp 3–15

O'Neill, Jim (2001) Building better economic BRICS, Goldman Sachs Global Economic Papers No. 66, http://www.goldmansachs.com/our-thinking/archive/archive-pdfs/build-better-brics.pdf

O'Neill, Jim (2011) *The Global Growth Map: Economic Opportunity and Beyond*, London, Penguin

Pavlovsky, Gleb (2014) Interview with Tom Parfitt, *New Left Review*, II, 88, pp 54–66

Pirani, Simon (2010) *Change in Putin's Russia: Power, Money and People*, London, Pluto

Popescu, Nicu (2014) *Eurasian union: the real, the imaginary and the likely*, Paris, EU Institute for Security Studies

Pozo-Martin, Gonzalo (2013) Crime and no punishment: money, violence and the neoliberal transformation of Moscow. In Simona Talani et al. (eds), *Dirty Cities: Towards a Political Economy of the Underground in Global Cities*, Basingstoke, Palgrave Macmillan, pp 43–62

Pozo-Martin, Gonzalo (2014) LeftEast, http://www.criticatac.ro/lefteast/gonzalo-pozo-in-ukraine-clash-of-two-opposed-imperial-agendas/

Putin, Vladimir (2011) Novyi integratsionnyi proekt dlya Evrazii: budushee, kotoroe rozhdaetsya segodnya, Izvestiya, 3 October, http://izvestia.ru/news/502761

Rachman, Gideon (2010) *Zero-Sum World: Politics, Power and Prosperity after the Crash*, London, Atlantic

Renz, Bettina (2006) Putin's militocracy: an alternative interpretation of siloviki in contemporary Russian politics, *Europe-Asia Studies*, 58, 6, pp 903–924

Rivera, Sharon and David Rivera (2006) The Russian elite under Putin: militocratic or bourgeois?, *Post-Soviet Affairs*, 22, 2

Robinson, Neil (ed) (2012) *The Political Economy of Russia*, Plymouth, Roman and Littlefield

Rosner, Kevin (2005) *Gazprom and the Russian State*, London, GMB Publishing

Roubini, Nouriel (2011) Another BRIC in the wall?, Project Syndicate, 15 October, http://www.projectsyndicate.org/commentary/roubini18/English

Ruiz Gonzalez, Francisco J (2013) Russia's foreign policy concept: a comparative approach, IEES, 06/2013, http://www.ieee.es/en/Galerias/fichero/docs_marco/2013/DIEEEM06-2013_Rusia_ConceptoPoliticaExterior_FRuizGlez_ENGLISH.pdf

Sakwa, Richard (2004) *Putin: Russia's Choice*, London, Routledge

Sakwa, Richard (2011) *The Crisis of Russian Democracy: The Dual State, Factionalism and the Medvedev Succession*, Cambridge, Cambridge University Press

Saratov, Grigorii (2012) Korruptsiia v Rossi i Mire, http://www.anti-corr.ru

Shakirova, Karina (2010) Okhta' na vynos, Kommersant (St Petersburg), 9 December 2010, http://www.kommersant.ru/doc.aspx?DocsID=1554493&ThemesID=147

Shlapentokh, Vladimir (2012) Corruption, the power of state and big business in Soviet and post-Soviet regimes, *Communist and Post-Communist Studies*, 46, 1, pp 147–158

Sixmith, Martin (2010) *Putin's Oil: The Yukos Affair and the Struggle for Russia*, London, Continuum

Suny, Ronald (2007) Living in the hood: Russia, empire, and old and new neighbours. In Robert Legvold (ed) *Russian Foreign Policy in the 21st Century and the Shadow of the Past*, New York, Columbia University Press, pp 35–76

Tsygankov, Andrei (2006) Projecting confidence not fear: Russia's post-imperial assertiveness, *Communist and Post-Communist Studies*, 50, 4, pp 677–690

Umland, Andreas (2009) Rastsvet russkogo ul'tranatsionalizma i stanovlenie soobshchestva ego issledovatelei, *Forum Noveishei Vostochnoevropeiskoi Istorii i Kul'tury*, 6, 1

UNDP (2009) *National Human Development Report, Russian Federation 2008. Russia Facing Demographic Challenges*, Moscow, UN

Upstreamonline (2005) Gazprom swallows up Sibneft, Upstreamonline.com, 28 September, http://www.upstreamonline.com/live/article99244.ece

Wallander, Celeste (2007) Russian transimperialism and its implications, *Washington Quarterly*, 30, 2, 2007, pp 107–122

WikiLeaks (2010) Moscow, Luzhkov and the other Mafia, Cable of the US Embassy in Moscow, http://inmoscowsshadows.wordpress.com/2010/12/03/wikileaks-3-moscow-luzhkov-and-the-other-mafia/

Wilson, Dominic and Roopa Purushothanam (2003) Dreaming with BRICS: the path to 2050, Goldman Sachs Global Economics Paper No. 99, http://www.goldmansachs.com/our-thinking/archive/archive-pdfs/brics-dream.pdf

Wolosky, Lee (2000) Putin's plutocrat problem, *Foreign Affairs*, 79, 2, pp 18–31

Wood, Tony (2007) Contours of the Putin era, *New Left Review*, II, 44, pp 53–68

Yakovlev, Evgenii and Ekaterina Zhuravskaya (2005) State capture: from Yeltsin to Putin, Center for Economic and Financial Research (CEFIR), Working Paper 52, http://www.cefir.ru/papers/WP52.pdf

PART 3
BRICS within global capitalism

15

BRICS and transnational capitalism

WILLIAM ROBINSON

The BRICS (Brazil, Russia, India, China and South Africa) countries are what world-systems and other theorists refer to as semi-peripheral countries, or countries that occupy an intermediary position between core and peripheral states within a world hierarchy of nation-states, and are presumably attempting to move up in this hierarchy into the core. The BRICS came together as a group in 2006, have held regular summits since 2009, and exercise growing political and economic clout in the international system.

Nonetheless, a fundamental distinction we want to make in the social sciences, one essential to understanding global capitalism, is between surface phenomena and underlying essence. We must move from the surface-level dynamics of interstate political relations in order to get at the underlying meaning of G7/BRICS dynamics. We must not overemphasise political jockeying in the arena of international relations. The relationship between politics and economics is complex. Latin American Marxists have understood a number of left-populist revolutions in that region in the 1960s and the 1970s, such as that led by Juan Velasco Alvarado in Peru in 1968, less as anti-capitalist challenges than as movements to bring about more modern class relations in the face of the tenacity of the antiquated, often semi-feudal oligarchies, and thus to renovate and free up capitalism from atavistic constraints on its full development.

In a similar way, the BRICS politics aim to force those elites from the older centres of world capitalism into a more balanced and integrated global capitalism. China repeatedly proposed in the wake of the 2008 collapse not that the yuan become the new world currency but that the IMF issue a truly world currency not tied to any nation-state. Such a move would help save the global economy from the dangers of continued reliance on the US dollar, an atavistic residue from an earlier era of US dominance in a world system of national capitalisms and hegemonic nation-states.

There is nothing in BRICS politics and proposals that have stood in any significant contradiction to global capitalism. On the contrary, by and large the BRICS platform pushes further integration into global capitalism. Brazilian and Southern opposition to the subsidy regime for agriculture in the North constituted opposition not to capitalist globalisation but precisely to a policy that stood in the way of such globalisation. BRICS politics sought to open up further the global system for elites in their respective countries. Some of these efforts do clash with the G7, but BRICS proposals would have the effect of extending and contributing to the stabilisation of global capitalism and, in the process, of further transnationalising the dominant groups in these countries. This is not a case of the old anti-colonialism and cannot be explained in the context of earlier First World–Third World contradictions that do not capture the current dynamics. Prashad misreads the economic and political protagonism of BRICS elites. Far from indicating a polarised confrontation or antagonistic interests, this protagonism has for the most part been aimed at constructing a more expansive and balanced global capitalism.

Let us look at this matter further. Brazil led the charge against Northern agricultural subsidies in several international forums in the first decade of the 21st century. Its argument was that such subsidies unfairly undermined the competitiveness of Brazilian agricultural exports. Brazil was seeking more, not less, globalisation: a global free market in agricultural commodities. Who in Brazil would benefit from the lifting of Northern agricultural subsidies? Above all, it would benefit the soy barons and other giant agro-industrial exporters that dominate Brazilian agriculture. And who are these barons and exporters? A study of the Brazilian economy reveals that they are agribusiness interests in Brazil that bring together Brazilian capitalists and land barons with the giant TNCs that drive global agribusiness and that themselves, in their ownership and cross-investment structures, bring together individual and institutional investors from around the world, such as Monsanto, ADM, Cargill, and so forth. Simply put, 'Brazilian' agricultural exports are transnational capital agricultural exports. Adopting a nation-state-centric framework of analysis makes this look like a Brazilian national conflict with powerful Northern countries.

If Brazil got its way it would not have curtailed but have furthered capitalist globalisation and would have advanced the interests of transnational capital.

(Brazil, in fact, took its case against US farm subsidies and EU sugar subsidies to the WTO, which ruled in Brazil's favour, suggesting that the WTO, far from an instrument of US or European 'imperialism', is an effective instrument of the transnational state.) What appear as international struggles for global hegemony or struggles of the South against the North are better seen as struggles by emerging transnational capitalists and elites outside of the original transatlantic and trilateral core to break into the ranks of the global elite and develop a capacity to influence global policy formation, manage global crises, and participate in ongoing global restructuring. The BRICS' national economic strategy is structured around global integration. Nationalism becomes a strategy for seeking space in the global capitalist order in association with transnational capital from abroad.

Those who posit growing international conflict between the traditional core countries and rising powers in the former Third World point most often to China and its alleged conflict with the United States over global influence. Geopolitical analysis as conjunctural analysis must be informed by structural analysis. The policies of the Chinese (as well as those of the other BRICS states) have been aimed at integration into global production chains in association with transnational capital. Already by 2005 China's stock of FDI to GDP was 36%, compared to 1.5% for Japan and 5% for India, with half of its foreign sales and nearly a third of its industrial output generated by transnational corporations. Moreover, the giant Chinese companies – ranging from the oil and chemical sectors to automobiles, electronics, telecommunications, and finance – have associated with TNCs from around the world in the form of mergers and acquisitions, shared stock, cross-investment, joint ventures, subcontracting, and so on, both inside China and around the world. Inside China, for instance, some 80% of large-scale supermarkets had merged with foreign companies by 2008.

There is simply no evidence of 'Chinese' companies in fierce rivalry with 'US' and other 'Western' companies over international control. Rather, the picture is one of competition among transnational conglomerates, as discussed earlier, which integrate Chinese companies. That Chinese firms have more secure access to the Chinese state than other firms does not imply the state conflict that observers posit, since these firms are integrated into transnational capitalist networks and access the Chinese state on behalf of the amalgamated interests of the groups into which they are inserted. Similarly, these same observers point to a growing US trade deficit and an inverse accumulation of international reserves by China and then conclude that the two states are locked in competition over international hegemony. But we cannot possibly understand US–Chinese trade dynamics without observing that between 40% and 70% of world trade in the early 21st century was intrafirm or associational, that some 40% of exports from China came from TNCs based in that country, and that much of the remaining 60% was accounted for by associational forms involving Chinese and transnational investors. These transnational class and social relations are concealed behind nation-state data. When we focus on the production, ownership structures, class and social relations that lie behind nation-state trade data, we are in a better position to search for causal explanations for global political and economic dynamics.

The international division of labour, characterised by the concentration of finance, technology, and research and development in traditional core countries and low-wage assembly (along with raw materials) in traditional peripheral countries, is giving way to a global division of labour in which core and peripheral productive activities are dispersed as much within, as among, countries. Contrary to the expectations of nation-state-centric theories, TNCs originating in traditionally core countries no longer jealously retain their research and development (R&D) operations in their countries of origin. The United Nations Conference on Trade and Development (UNCTAD) dedicated its 2005 annual World Investment Report to the rapid internationalisation of R&D by transnational corporations. Applied Materials, a leading solar technology company headquartered in California, shifts components for its solar panels all over the world and then assembles them at distinct final market destinations. The company decided in 2009, however, to open a major R&D centre in western China that is the size of 10 football fields and employs 400 engineers. Moreover, many companies that previously produced in the traditional core countries are investing in new facilities in these 'emerging economies' in order to achieve proximity to expanding local markets.

This does not mean that there are no political tensions in international forums. These forums are highly undemocratic and are dominated by the old colonial powers as a political residue of an earlier era. But these international political tensions – sometimes geopolitical – do not indicate underlying structural contradictions between rival national or regional capitalist groups and economic blocs. The transnational integration of these national economies and their capitalist groups has created common class interests in an expanding global economy. And besides, as I have already observed, capitalist groups from these countries form part of transnational conglomerates in competition with one another. The inextricable mixing of capitals globally through financial flows simply undermines the material basis for the development of powerful national capitalist groups in contradiction to the global capitalist economy and the transnational capitalist class. Interstate conflict in the new era is more likely to take place between the centres of military power in the global system and those states where nationally oriented elites still exercise enough control to impede integration into global capitalist circuits, such as in Iraq prior to the 2003 US invasion or in North Korea, or in those states where subordinate classes exercise enough influence over the state to result in state policies that threaten global capitalist interests, such as in Venezuela and other South American countries that turned to the left in the early 21st century.

Breaking with nation-state-centric analysis does not mean abandoning analysis of national-level processes and phenomena or interstate dynamics. It does mean that we view transnational capitalism as the world-historic context in which these play themselves out. It is not possible to understand anything about global society without studying a concrete region and its particular circumstances – a part of a totality, in its relation to that totality. Globalisation is characterised by related, contingent and unequal transformations. To evoke globalisation as an explanation for historical changes and contemporary dynamics does not mean that the particular events or changes identified with the process are happening all over the world, much less in the same ways. It does mean that the events or changes are understood as a consequence of globalised power relations and social structures. As each country transforms its social relations and institutions, it enters a process conditioned by its own history and culture. Thus uneven development determines the pace and nature of local insertion into the global economy. The key becomes their relationship to a transnational system and the dialectic between the global and the local. Distinct national and regional histories and configurations of social forces as they have historically evolved mean that each country or region undergoes a distinct experience under globalisation.

16

BRICS at the brink of the fossil bonanza

Elmar Altvater

One outcome of the global turmoil after the collapse of active socialism in 1989 and the disappearance of the Soviet Union two years later is the emergence of the USA as the 'only superpower'. The bipolar world since then is over, and the 'unipolar moment' (to quote the US neo-conservative Charles Krauthammer) the triumphant alternative. But the USA at the beginning of the 21st century is not a hegemonic power because its political elites follow a monopolar logic of power. They are far from working on a global consensus, from trying to convince people around the world of the historical meaningfulness of US leadership.

The 'only superpower' therefore only succeeds in stabilising the dominant position by use of military forces, secret services, the available technologies of geo-engineering and technological and economic superiority, not by establishing a world-wide consensus. In the long run this display of power is not sufficient to hold a hegemonic position because of the lack of acceptance and cooperation. This is the lesson to be learnt not only from Antonio Gramsci's *Prison Notebooks*, but also from experiences in the contemporary conflicts from Iraq to Syria, from Georgia to Somalia.

The lack of cooperation on a global level is a reason why the world today is structured by (macro) regional free trade areas, custom unions and common markets even though the WTO is intending to create a global free market order. Some of the regional trading blocs negotiated bilateral trade and investment agreements (BIT) with less powerful nations. The number of BITs is high, thus displaying that free trade is more an ideology than a reality. The recent attempts to establish a transatlantic trade and investment partnership (TTIP) and a similar agreement in the Pacific rim, always with the USA at the centre of the project are, on the one hand, harsh blows against the globalism of the WTO and its partners and, on the other hand, a challenge for all the other nations that are not invited to participate in these gigantic trading and investment blocs.

This is a fairly messy situation consisting of (1) one nation-state as a unipolar superpower, (2) extensive free trade and investment areas where the most powerful agents are big private transnational corporations, (3) regional economic communities like the EU or the Mercosur and (4) new 'informal' state alliances entering the stage of global politics. BRICS is such an informal alliance without an elaborated formal institutional infrastructure. But as social science studies of informal labour clearly show, informality is not a static but a highly dynamic condition.

There are tendencies in the direction of further formalisation of the informal alliance, as well as other forces pointing in the opposite direction. The informality of the BRICS alliance is, so to say, a postmodern state of indecision in a global situation characterised by hard economic, financial, social and, above all, ecological constraints for political action. Hard planetary boundaries (Rockström et al. 2009) in the long run do not allow for soft arbitrariness.

A world in disorder

The tsunami of market liberalisation, of privatisation of public goods and services, of a wild deregulation of politics already began in the 1970s. It has proudly been called by Milton and Ruth Friedman (1980) 'the neoliberal counterrevolution'. It prepared the ground for the emerging new neoliberal world order which experienced, less than two decades later, a decisive political impulse from the fall of the Berlin Wall in 1989. Now the 'new' American century followed the 'old' one. The latter began at the end of World War II. It became determinant for global power relations for the next 40 years. It was the era of confrontation between the capitalist market economy ('the free West') and active socialism ('the authoritarian East'). The decisive difference between the old (before 1989) and the new (after 1989) American era was that the new, after the disappearance of active socialism, contained no place for a social system other than the market-capitalist one. The 'short 20th century' (Eric Hobsbawm 1995) ended without the perspective of an alternative system in the cul-de-sac of a history with a past and a present, but without a future. The socialist world (in the East) since then turned from the present and the future into a past history, as did the 'Socialism of the West', the Keynesian interventionism of the nation-states, and the 'Socialism of the South', i.e. of the development state which had its origin in Latin America.

In 1989 socialism was over as a project for a better future which previously had inspired (and also disappointed) many generations. The new generations after active socialism were worse off; they had no alternative. As Margaret Thatcher triumphantly declared: 'There is no alternative beyond the neoliberal promise of "freedom, democracy, wealth".' This was true only of a happy minority of the world population, not for the majority. History came to an end.

The last decade of the 20th century therefore became a period of the 'unipolar moment' of the US, of global governance under the 'benign' leadership of the USA and of new conflicts, some of them, like the wars in former Yugoslavia, in Afghanistan or in Iraq, very brutal ones. The end of this period came abruptly on 11 September 2001. In its aftermath, the consequences, drawn by the Bush administration in responding to the attack on the World Trade Center and the Pentagon, reshaped the world. The unipolar moment of a benign hegemon changed into the domination of the world by a predatory hegemon: the war on terror dragged the world into a series of military conflicts in many regions. It transformed the political landscape of the Near and Middle East, including parts of Central Asia, of Africa and of the former Soviet Union.

Moreover, the political chaos has been enforced by economic factors. The monetary and fiscal policy of the USA after 2001 triggered the global financial crisis which broke out in 2007/2008 and which has since then affected the second power-house of the capitalist world system, the European Union. The massive trade deficit of the USA has an even longer history. It is destabilising the capitalist world system and reshaping the global political power structure.

Birth and baptism of BRICS
This became obvious at the G8 summit of Heiligendamm (Germany) in 2007 when the G8 were forced to open their elitist meeting and to accept some newcomers, Brazil, India, China and South Africa, as partners. They treated the BRICS – Russia already was a member of the G8 – as subaltern partners but they had to take their new political importance into consideration, for the traditional G8 was not able to find a solution to global imbalances, caused by the trade deficit of the USA and the resulting exploding external debt of the superpower, without including the new creditor countries in a political solution. This was especially true for China, but also for the other BRICS countries. Their trade surpluses and the resulting credit position in financial markets made the solution to the crisis of the global economic and financial system only viable by including the new powers in an agreement. The political leaders of the BRICS still had the experience of the debt crisis of the Third World in the 1980s in mind,

and therefore knew about the necessities of cooperation.

This might be the reason why shortly after Heiligendamm in May 2008 Brazil, Russia, India and China formed the BRIC bloc at a meeting in Yekaterinburg. Two years later South Africa joined the group. BRICS was born; the informal alliance received a more formal structure. It now was much more than a mere name invented by Jim O'Neill, a finance manager of Goldman Sachs. Obviously he was fascinated by the sheer weight of the BRICS countries in the world economy: 43% of the world population, 20% of world production, high current account surpluses and therefore, for most of the BRICS nations, a comfortable creditor status on global financial markets. So he hastily baptised the new powers BRIC and later, after South Africa had joined them, BRICS, even before this alliance existed. It is one of the rare cases in history in which an historical event had a name before it really happened.

NSA and informational geo-engineering

One of the premises of the new American world order was the stability of markets. But market stability does not exist in a capitalist system, mainly – as Karl Marx, John Maynard Keynes and Hyman Minsky and many others convincingly showed – due to inherent financial instabilities. This was apparent already years before the outbreak of the world financial crisis in September 2008. Since finance necessarily is bridging the gap from the *present* to the *future* using the values produced in the *past* as collateral, economic relations in time and space are by their very nature insecure and thus risky and characterised by instability. This is the basic reason for the necessity of state interventions in economic market processes in order to avoid the outbreak of a financial crisis. This also is the reason why there always must be an alternative, why a Thatcherite world cannot be stable. Without an alternative there is no space for a political choice and thus no necessity to intervene in a destabilised market system. In the imagination of neoliberals this is no mistake because mankind is always living in a Leibnizian world that is 'the best of all possible worlds'. Political institutions set up in order to stabilise the economy are redundant in a world without alternatives.

The ideologically founded negation of multilateral solutions to new global ecological, economic and social challenges prohibited the establishment of agreements and institutions in the areas of energy, climate, migration and human rights policy. It was also not possible to set up institutions and rules to stabilise unstable financial markets. Interventions in the labour market in order to foster employment opportunities became dogmatically forbidden with the argument of the 'natural rate of unemployment' or with the Phillips curve or with the arguments of the rational choice behaviour of economic agents.

Last but not least, in their new world order the USA, on the one hand, made the private sphere partly public and, on the other hand, privatised public information and knowledge by using their secret service apparatus (NSA) and depriving other individual citizens or governments of their privacy protection, i.e. of fundamental citizens' rights. The USA 'socialised' completely, in contradiction to their dominant liberal ideology, private knowledge and information; but it was not 'socialisation' of left-wing parties and movements in the traditional sense of the 19th and 20th century. It was dispossession in favour of the 'only' superpower and the globally operating big corporations under the protection of the superpower. This is a very clear sign of shameless US-American monopolarism, of a new approach of 'informational geo-engineering' which fits into other endeavours of finding solutions to global challenges by technical and organisational measures of geo-engineering by powerful nation-states, not by the global community and the existing weak institutional infrastructure.

It should be noticed that for the assault on the privacy of the world population not only the USA but also other Anglophone countries bear responsibility. Their alliance has long been called UKUSA, owing to the initials of the two leading powers, the UK and the USA, and at the same time the so-called 'five eyes coalition', because three other countries are participating in this 'gang of five': Canada, Australia and New Zealand. The coalition has its origin in the years after World War II and results from the collaboration of secret services in times of the 'Cold War'. The leaked documents of Edward Snowden show that this strange coalition – not of complete and thus sovereign nation-states, of democratically controlled governments, but of the most secret *arcanum* of these states, the secret services – obviously has been revitalised in times of the internet and of the war on terror in order to steal information on a global scale. The official justification of these criminal acts is – insofar as they are admitted – the defence of national security. But the data is also stolen to get a competitive advantage. Theft is in contrast to free trade because trade is based on private property rights. Therefore the establishment of new informal powers and of new informal state alliances with the intention of stealing private information is in opposition to a free trade order which the governments of the 'five eyes' are preaching. The traditional world of nation-state diplomacy at the beginning of the 21st century is disappearing in a morass of political amorality.

A world ruled by disembedded markets

Instead, a parallel world is in the making. On the one hand there are powerful forces pushing the world towards a global free-trade system. The WTO calls it 're-globalisation' after the 'first age' of globalisation before World War I and a period of 'de-globalisation' between the First and the end of the Second World War (WTO 2013:46–55). Re-globalisation, according to the understanding of the representatives of the WTO, is the return to a quasi-natural state of affairs which already began during the 'first American century' and ended successfully with the dissolution of the socialist alternative so that the whole world can work like a single market. This can be seen in the creation of several regional integration schemes in all parts of the world from Western Europe (EU) to South-East Asia (e.g. ASEAN) or South America (e.g. Mercosur). At the same time tariffs and non-tariff trade barriers have been removed to a remarkable extent. In the year 1995 the WTO inherited from its predecessor the GATT, a nearly (i.e. not completely) tariff-free global trade system.

But it still is not perfect in the understanding of the free trade proponents. They not only want free markets, but disembedded markets. Karl Polanyi (1956) published *The Great Transformation,* a book warning about disembedded markets, especially about those of labour, money and finance and pieces of nature, e.g. real estate markets. His analysis was extremely clear: when the market economy becomes disembedded from society (and, we have to add, from nature) then they work like a 'satanic mill' destroying the commodities traded in the respective markets, i.e. labour power, money and nature. This is a discourse which fits into the Marxian one where the question of commodity – and money fetishism – is a crucial one. Hence, the liberalisation of trade relations not only has consequences for the economic performance of a nation but also a considerable impact on the social system, on political participation and on the natural environment.

New trade agreements covering the Atlantic as well as the Pacific areas are in the making. The new transpacific and transatlantic trade agreements are basically investment agreements tailored to widen the scope of still-existing regulations in the interests of private corporations (so-called investors) against the interests of the people concerned. It may be admitted that free trade is perhaps not only profitable for the corporations but also beneficial for consumers. In any case it is harmful for many of the workers worldwide because of the weakening of the social welfare system and the connected undermining of social security. It also caps opportunities and rights of democratic participation in decisions which concern the common interest. Lastly, it is bad for the natural environment.

The latter is unavoidable because the establishment of a free (or, better, freer and disembedded) trade zone between the USA and Europe and parts of Asia is always linked to expectations of *more* trade, i.e. of *more* production of goods and services, of *more* finance. Thus, free trade is translated into higher economic growth. That is the promise given by the negotiators of the agreement on the Transatlantic Trade and Investment Partnership (TTIP), although it is ridiculously modest: the growth stimulus is calculated to be 0.48%. Nonetheless, it means more growth prerequisites, more consumption of fossil energy, of mineral and agricultural raw materials, more extension of human activities in space, more acceleration in time. This means that at the 'planetary boundaries' (Rockström et al. 2009) which mankind has in some respects already exceeded, free trade triggers growth and, due to the double character of the capitalist accumulation process, not only value production but also the transformation of matter and energy, which inevitably harms nature. The global system of market liberalisation and trade creation is not in balance with the requirements of nature and thus violates the limits of the use of natural resources as well as the carrying capacity of ecosystems. Capitalist dynamics are overshooting the limits of the living and the natural resources of Planet Earth.

Global free trade and the ecological world system

The free trade order comes into existence by removing physical, technical, economic, financial and legal trade barriers. In this process natural obstacles to the free circulation of commodities are also dismantled, due to the double character of economic processes: at the same time commodities have immaterial value but they also represent material and energy transformations. Natural limits, however, are flexible ones and they can therefore be temporarily neglected without sanctions on those who disregard the limits. The neglect and even the violation of limits temporarily has a highly positive but perverse economic welfare effect. The growth rates of GNP in the world are remarkably high since the industrial-fossil revolution in the second half of the 18th century, so that real GNP per capita doubled from one generation to the other. That would be misinterpreted as a quantitative increase only. It was, and still is, a qualitative change, if not a revolution. Dialectics of nature therefore matter, as Friedrich Engels (1983) showed.

It is not always taken into consideration that this economic miracle for human beings has an ugly, seamy side: the negative effects on nature, the much too large 'ecological footprint' of economically rich humans. But the negative effects are understood as market externalities. Therefore they are traditionally beyond the focus of the mainstream discipline in economic (market) theory. Externalities, many economists say, either do not bother or should be internalised in order to make them calculable and thus to improve the economic rationality of market decisions. Externalities are an inevitable result of joint production, and there is on Earth no non-joint production – due to the law of entropy. Thermodynamic physics clearly shows that the output of a production process is, on the sunny side, values, and on the dark side emissions in the atmosphere, the waters and the ground. Economists have an eye on the bright side, but they are very reluctant to shed light on the dark side. The question comes up: How can one internalise a process and its effects economically which physically cannot be internalised?

The double character of all economic processes offers a helpful suggestion. The physical and thus material external effects must not be internalised, nor the positive and the negative ones. It is, however, possible to internalise the transactions on the value side of the economy by making use of the money form of market processes. It is possible to give environmental damages a price, although its meaningfulness is more than doubtful. What is the price of an extinguished species, how can one calculate the costs of the heatwave in 2005 in Europe with some ten thousand people dead? There is no rational answer to this question.

Nonetheless, financial market agents invented financial market innovations which are apt to internalise externalities and thus to calculate the incalculable: securities and other forms of payment for so-called ecosystems services, certificates on pollution rights, etc. New financial instruments are on the political agenda (TEEB – The Economics of Ecosystems and the Biosphere; PES – Payments for Ecosystem Services; REDD – Reducing Emissions from Deforestation and Degradation). The consequence is that natural limits seem to disappear in a monetary calculation where the complexity of nature is simplified to a cost-benefit comparison. Natural limits in this discourse are transformed into market opportunities and sold in booming global financial markets. Organised in such a manner, environmental policy perfectly fits into the market system. Due to financial innovations, the harm done to nature by crossing the limits of growth (and thus of nature) can be monetised and traded in financial markets. The disembedding of the capitalist market economy from society and nature is nearly perfect. The natural nature disappears, the monetised nature arises. If it were not for the material aspect of the externalities, the capitalist trajectory could be a perennial success story.

However, the planetary boundaries are resistant to the neoliberal attempts of internalisation. The world is facing an exhaustion of natural resources. Peak oil is a permanent threat which cannot be reduced by exploring non-conventional fossil fuel in the deep sea, e.g. off the Brazilian coast or in the rain forests of the Amazon, in the polar ice of Siberia and the Arctic Ocean or in the tar sands of Venezuela or Canada. Also with regard to mineral and agricultural raw materials, the natural limits are losing their horror because unconventional resources are found and new conventional reserves are located, such as rare metals and soil in China, or coal in India, or non-conventional plants for the production of bio-energy in Brazil and in South Africa (sugar cane, soya, palm oil, etc.). This means that the limits of resources are indeed flexible ones and that it is possible, as green protagonists promise, that 'the limits grow' and therefore the 'limits of growth', which the Club of Rome first mentioned in 1972, can be neglected.

This flexibility is welcomed as a chance for development by many governments and social movements everywhere in the world. BRICS governments now can opt for the application of a neo-extractivist strategy. It is different from the traditional, colonial and imperialist extractivism, because the extracted mineral ores or agricultural products or riches from the rain forests are not simply robbed by the metropolises of the imperialist world system. Instead, the whole chain of commodification and monetisation of natural resources in the world market remains under the control of strong and mostly left governments. Therefore the neo-extractivist strategies also have been called 'development extractivism' (Bolivian Vice-President Linera). This strategy can be successful so long as the resources do not come to an end, so long as the terms of trade are favourable for primary goods, and so long as the governments concerned are not corrupt and do not play to the tune of transnational corporations. But although natural limits are flexible, they are not nonexistent. On the contrary, they matter and therefore a development extractivist strategy from the very beginning must aim at an alternative, a non-extractivist development model. Even a middle-range development extractivism strategy can be trapped in the economic grinder of the 'resource curse', in the dilemma of the 'Dutch disease', and in the contradictions between internal and external terms of trade.

Moreover, the global 'sinks' (storage) for emissions react less flexibly than the limits on resource availability, given the demand for energy, mineral and agricultural resources. The planetary boundaries with regard to many resources have already been surpassed. It is possible to disregard them, but flouting these natural limits surely will provoke sanctions, perhaps with a time lag, perhaps immediately. Therefore natural limits at the end of the fossil era indeed matter everywhere and for everybody on Earth. They require common action in a world which is – as already shown – divided into strong, but not hegemonic, nation-states which are using methods of geo-engineering (in information politics as well as in climate policy), trading blocs which more and more are transformed into disembedded markets that function as protectorates of big global corporations against the world citizen, more or less informal alliances such as BRICS and, last but not least, many small nations whose influence in the contemporary world is small.

References

Engels, F (1983) *Dialectics of Nature*, http://www.marxists.org/archive/marx/works/1883/don

Friedman, M and R Friedman (1980) *Free to Choose*, New York, Norton

Hobsbawm, E (1995) *The Age of Extremes*, London, Abacus

Polanyi, K (1956) *The Great Transformation*, Boston, Beacon Press

Rockström, J, S Rodhe, PK Sorlin, R Snyder, U Costanza, M Svedin, L Falkenmark, RW Karlberg, VJ Corell, J Fabry, B Hansen, D Walker, K Liverman, P Richardson, JA Crutzen and A Foley (2009) A safe operating space for humanity, *Nature*, 461, pp 472–475

World Trade Organisation (WTO) (2013) *World Trade Report 2013*, Geneva, WTO

17

Scramble, resistance and a new non-alignment strategy

SAM MOYO AND PARIS YEROS

In what way is imperialism today different from the imperialisms of the past? And what strategies are capable of undermining it?

The most basic elements of contemporary imperialism have been analysed extensively. They consist in the formation of a collective imperialism, an unprecedented event, the ongoing internationalisation of production, the re-financialisation of monopoly capital, and continuous military aggression, long after the end of the Cold War.

The economic changes underway have now sapped collective imperialism of its economic vitality and its domestic social peace, obliging it to escalate its military project externally and its class offensive internally. The concrete result today is a new wave of natural resource grabs and new military interventions in the peripheries, accompanied by the demise of social pacts in the centres of the system.

It is clear that the great systemic rivalry of the Cold War had no real winners among the superpowers. The Soviet Union may have been the first to succumb, but disaster is now looming in the centres as well. The only concrete advance of the last half-century has been decolonisation and the emergence of the South. This marked the beginning of the end of the system born in 1492.

The emergence of the South has produced a new set of challenges. During the Cold War, the Bandung movement outlined a coherent set of objectives, comprising total decolonisation, economic development, and 'positive non-alignment'. The latter meant, specifically, non-participation in the military blocs

246

of the superpowers and capacity to judge every external relation on its own merits, in accordance with national interests.

The emergence of the South has also produced a new set of contradictions. The internationalisation of production has continued to differentiate the South among peripheries, semi-peripheries, and now 'emerging' semi-peripheries. One of the key questions is what role the semi-peripheries, and especially the 'emerging' ones, play in the system. Semi-peripheries have in the past been seen as systemic safety valves, by which monopoly capital outsources its production to areas with cheaper labour and natural resources.

During the Cold War, the safety-valve policy gained geo-strategic expression in the Nixon-Kissinger Doctrine, whose purpose was to select Southern partners as proxies in regional economic expansion and political-military stabilisation. Rarely did the policy fail, as indeed it did in Iran. The most precious proxy, then as today, was Israel, but there were other important ones, like Brazil, where the phenomenon was termed 'sub-imperialism', that is, an attempt to go beyond semi-peripheral conveyor-belt functions.

The term called attention to a new contradiction, not only between peripheries and semi-peripheries, but also between centres and the emerging semi-peripheries of the time, regardless of their ideological orientation (Brazil was under a right-wing dictatorship). The contradiction remained non-antagonistic, until the military regime overstepped its boundaries. It negotiated a nuclear accord with West Germany and recognised independent Angola. Thus, the dictatorship was abandoned by the United States, at a time of swelling internal mass mobilisation. The transition was controlled by financial and other political means, leading to the eventual 'reconversion' of this semi-periphery to a de-nationalised neoliberal financial playground.

The term also called attention to the fact that whatever emergence occurred under monopoly capitalism, and its financial and technological domination, it could only be based on the super-exploitation of domestic labour (not the social pacts characterising the centres of imperialism). It was this internal relation that intensified external dependence, creating the need for export markets for semi-peripheral manufacturers and the exertion of regional political-military influence, so as to resolve its chronic profit realisation crisis.

The subsequent 'reconversion' of semi-peripheries generally has produced contradictory effects, whereby a process of privatisation, enhanced extroversion, and de-nationalisation has accentuated internal class conflicts, but also led to the formation of new giant blocs of domestic capitals, which are once again vying for a place in the sun.

They are no longer simply looking to export manufactures but also capital. The 're-emerging' semi-peripheries are even engaged in the 'new scramble' for land and natural resources in Africa. Of course, they are also being scrambled, which is no paradox, given their persisting incorporation into external monopolies.

The question has been raised as to whether the newly 'emerging' semi-peripheries are essentially subservient regional stabilisers, or a force antagonistic to imperialism. Some have argued that the collective emergence of these semi-peripheries implies a system-changing diversification of economic partners in the South.

Should we conclude that the semi-peripheral bourgeoisies have become, inadvertently, anti-systemic? Others have argued that the simultaneous emergence of a handful of big semi-peripheries, and especially of China, marks the inadvertent but terminal systemic contradiction from which the capitalist world system will not recover. Should we similarly conclude that the system is on a progressive historical course?

We can pin our hopes neither on the newly shining bourgeoisies nor on inexorable historical laws. The immediate question is political, and it concerns the type of alliances that are necessary to oppose imperialism, especially as it escalates its military project. Thus, we should also be asking: are all emerging semi-peripheries equally subservient or antagonistic to imperialism? Do they have structural differences which manifest different political tendencies?

In fact, they differ significantly from each other. For example, Brazil and India are driven mainly by private blocs of capital, with strong public financial support, in conjunction with Western-based finance capital. China has much heavier and more autonomous participation by state-owned enterprises and banks. Meanwhile, in South Africa it is increasingly difficult to speak of an autonomous domestic bourgeoisie of any sort, given the extreme degree of de-nationalisation and reconversion that the country has undergone in the post-apartheid period.

The degree of participation in the Western military project is also different from one case to the next, although a 'schizophrenia' – one might say typical of sub-imperialism – is inherent in all this. Ironically, the most reconverted state, South Africa, has signed up to a regional mutual defence pact, effectively against Western military interference in Southern Africa, while continuing to serve as a conveyor belt for Western economic interests on the continent.

India has increasingly fallen into line with US strategy, especially in the nuclear field, but internal resistance remains significant. Brazil, no less schizophrenic than its peers, denounces coups in South America while zealously leading the post-coup invasion of Haiti under US auspices. Russia has remained a blocking power in the UN Security Council, increasingly alienated from NATO. China is the clearest counter-force to the West, consistently exercising full strategic autonomy, despite its evident dependence on external markets and monopolies.

Their modes of engagement with Africa are no less diverse or contradictory. To be sure, all are beneficiaries, including China, of the neoliberal prying open of African economies, conducted since the 1980s under the aegis of the West and its multilateral agencies. Yet they all maintain a higher sensitivity to matters of national sovereignty, even though there remains an unresolved race question everywhere, with paternalist tendencies towards Africa. Moreover, there is potential for the breaking of monopolies in certain sectors – and, by extension, the Western stranglehold – especially by China and its trade finance and oil-for-infrastructure strategies.

Given the tendencies and counter-tendencies of this current conjuncture, it is necessary to rekindle the strategy of non-alignment on new terms. In so doing, it is imperative to avoid the highly ideological 'equivalence' between Western imperialism and the emerging semi-peripheries, whose clearest expression is China-bashing.

Whatever one makes of the new semi-peripheries, they are certainly not the main agents of imperialism, nor are they militarising their foreign policies. Nor, for that matter, are they cohesive nations internally, given the ongoing super-exploitation on which their extroversion is based.

The first principle in a new non-alignment should undoubtedly be non-participation in the military project of the remaining superpower, that is, the United States, as well as its junior partners in NATO and its AFRICOM initiative. The second is the devising of a strategy with respect to both the established and the aspiring scramblers to enable a larger degree of manoeuvre for national development.

Few countries in Africa have used the existing room for manoeuvre in the current conjuncture in the interest of social and economic progress; and when they have, they have typically been labelled 'corrupt' or 'tyrannical' by the West. Zimbabwe, the country that has gone the furthest in breaking up monopolies and devising a pragmatic non-alignment policy (actually named 'Look East'), has been one of the most despised for doing so.

The new non-alignment implies not only resisting the West militarily and 'looking East/South', but also setting conditions on all external relations. Such resistance can only be effective by collective strategies on the continental and sub-regional levels.

Establishing mutual defence pacts, as in Southern Africa – a pact which has shielded Zimbabwe's radicalisation – would constitute a fundamental building block, as would new forms of regional integration, beyond rule-based, commercial integration, which are yet to emerge.

18

The BRICS' dangerous endorsement of 'financial inclusion'

SUSANNE SOEDERBERG

Coinciding with the 5th Annual Meeting of the BRICS in South Africa in March 2013, the United Nations Development Programme (UNDP) released their flagship Human Development Report, *The Rise of the South: Human Progress in a Diverse World.* The latter is a celebration of the BRICS and their 'striking transformation into dynamic major economies with growing political influence'. The Report emphasises how this change is having a 'significant impact' on 'human development progress', as measured by the Human Development Index.

Armed with the recipe for development success, the UNDP recommends several neoliberal strategies that all countries in the South should pursue to ensure that progress be made available to everyone.

First, the South needs to ensure a tighter embrace of global markets. Aside from governments and private enterprises, financial liberalisation involves a new subject: the poor, who have over the past decade been rebranded as the bottom of the pyramid or the unbanked/underbanked. The poor still compose a considerable segment of the population, despite the 'Rise of the South'.

Second, the South needs to adhere to the rules of global governance, i.e. transparency, accountability and rule of law – all of which have been defined by the IMF, World Bank, World Trade Organisation and the G20. The focus on global financial market access and global governance comes together most strikingly in the G20 Principles for Innovative Financial Inclusion of 2010 (hereafter, G20 Principles). In their capacity as members of the G20, leaders of the BRICS countries have been endorsing the financial inclusion agenda as a way to socially include the poor in order to reduce poverty.

Financial inclusion refers to increasing broad-based access for approximately 2.7 billion poor adults to formal or semi-formal financial services ranging from banking to micro-credit to housing loans. In the wake of the 2008 crisis, itself triggered by financial inclusion strategies gone awry in the US and Europe, G20 leaders embraced financial inclusion as a core development strategy for overcoming the global recessionary environment.

The G20 Principles were drafted by the G20's Access Through Innovation Sub-Group and the Financial Inclusion Expert Group, which involved three key implementing partners – Alliance for Financial Inclusion (funded by the Bill and Melinda Gates Foundation), the Consultative Group to Assist the Poor (CGAP), and the World Bank's International Finance Corporation. From this heady mix of pro-market 'experts', the Principles for Innovative Financial Inclusion were drafted and later approved by G20 leaders at the Summit in Seoul in 2010.

The G20 Principles entail a regulatory framework based on (individualised) responsibilisation and voluntary guidelines. The G20 Principles represent extensions of, as opposed to a departure from, the neoliberal development project. The Principles act to legitimate, normalise and consolidate the claims of powerful, transnational capital interests that benefit from the status quo.

The primary way this is achieved is through obscuring and concealing the exploitative relations and speculative tendencies involved in financial inclusion strategies. This trend, which is best described by David Harvey's notion of 'accumulation by dispossession', has also led to the growing dependence on, and increased vulnerability to, the volatile nature of global finance, which has been historically marked by speculation, panics and crises – all of which run counter to the aims of the pro-poor growth and poverty alleviation goals of the financial inclusion agenda.

A good example of the rise of speculative tendencies in global development is asset-backed securitisation (ABS). Securitisation describes a process of packaging individual loans and other debt instruments, transforming this package into a security or securities, and enhancing their credit status or rating to further their sale to third-party investors, such as mutual and pension funds. ABS began to increase dramatically in use in the US during the late 1990s before expanding to Europe and eventually to the South. In the wake of the litany of financial crises in emerging market economies in the late 1990s and the subsequent scarcity of low-cost, long-term loans, the IMF touted the virtues of securitisation as a means for private and public sector entities in the Global South to raise funds.

The ability of micro-finance institutions (MFIs), for instance, to turn to securitisation to raise capital means that more 'financially excluded' people, who in Western terms could be designated as sub-prime borrowers, are brought into the market. ABS in the Global South is quite small in comparison to US markets. Nonetheless, the use of ABS in a wide variety of financial inclusion initiatives has been growing rapidly, albeit unevenly, since the late 1990s.

Yet it is important to grasp that, despite its technical and thus seemingly neutral language, securitisation is neither an apolitical nor a win-win scenario for creditors and debtors alike, but instead is characterised by unequal and exploitative (i.e. predatory lending) relations of power. While securitisation may raise cheap capital for originators (e.g. MFIs) and serve to reduce financial risk for foreign investors engaging in ABS transactions in the Global South, it does so at a social cost by transferring both risks and extractive levies onto the poor.

ABS has done little to deliver on the neoliberal promise of growth and progress through investments in production and thus the creation of stable and sustainable wages and, by extension, poverty reduction. Indeed, the increased frequency and intensity of financial debacles has made the South, and especially the poor therein, more susceptible to the aftershocks of speculative-led accumulation.

Notwithstanding the historical experience of neoliberalism since the 1980s, the solution to the latest crisis has been to include more poor people into a volatile, speculative, and highly interconnected financial system, so that they may, in the words of the G20, 'manage their low, irregular and unreliable income'.

This is a class-based strategy to continually search for more outlets for speculative credit money by creating debtors linked to the global casino and it cannot possibly replace a social wage, decent and affordable housing, education and health services. The 'financial' should be rejected as a means and end-goal of being socially included.

19

China and the lingering Pax Americana

Ho-fung Hung

Accompanying the economic rise of China, many commentators have argued that the global political centre of gravity has been shifting from West to East and from developed countries to developing ones. The book by British writer Martin Jacques, *When China Rules the World*, is just an example. Roger Altman, a veteran investment banker and former Deputy Secretary of Treasury of the US, published 'The Great Crash, 2008: the geopolitical setback for the West' in *Foreign Affairs* in the wake of the global financial crisis, arguing that the financial distress of the West and the continuous robust economic performance of China are accelerating the waning of America's global power and the waxing of China's. Journalist Fareed Zakaria even titled his 2009 bestseller *The Post-American World*, seeing the rise of China at the expense of the US as a global power shift comparable to the rise of the West during the Renaissance and the rise of the US in the 20th century.

Many see China as the most powerful BRICS country, the one that has the actual capability of leading other emerging powers to topple US domination and foster a new and more egalitarian order. But unfortunately that talk about falling US global power and the rise of China as a new superpower leading humanity out of Pax Americana is greatly exaggerated, just as talk of the rise of Germany and Japan as challengers to the US back in the 1970s and 1980s was exaggerated. The decline of US dominance in world politics, while true, has been slowed and delayed. US share of global GDP has been stable above 20% and it continues to be the world's largest economy with a comfortable lead, as measured in current US dollars. The US also continues to be the world's leading military power, with all other military powers trailing far behind.

The persisting economic and military power of the US is attributable largely to the ongoing status of the US dollar as the most widely used reserve currency and international transaction currency in the world during the last 30 years. The internationally dominant status of the dollar, which many refer to as the 'dollar standard', allows the US to borrow internationally at low interest rates and print money to repay its debt as the last resort.

This capability to borrow in its own currency has been allowing the US to solve many of its domestic economic malaises and maintain the most enormous, active war machine in the world through external indebtedness, while avoiding the kind of debt crises that have wreaked havoc on many developing economies which borrowed in creditors' currency. Ironically, the persistence of the dollar standard is now being maintained by the rise of China as the biggest foreign holder of US-dollar-dominated assets, mainly in the form of US Treasury bonds.

The post-World War II global hegemonic role of the dollar was sealed in the Bretton Woods Conference of 1944, which established the gold convertibility of the dollar under the promised rate of US$35 for one ounce of gold. The stability of the resulting global monetary order in the 1950s and 1960s was warranted by America's sizeable gold reserve, current account surpluses, and its unparalleled competitiveness in the world economy.

The collapse of this Bretton Woods order in 1971 can be traced back to the rising productivity of Europe, West Germany in particular, and Japan, following their full recovery from the world war in the late 1960s. Increasing international competition, coupled with the rising wage demand of domestic organised labour and the escalating fiscal and current account deficits incurred by the US's troubled involvement in Vietnam, led to a run on the dollar and the outflow of gold reserves from the US. It left Nixon with few choices but to suspend the gold convertibility of the dollar in 1971, forcing other major capitalist economies to undo their currencies' peg from the dollar. The abolition of gold convertibility allowed the US to attempt reducing its current account deficit and reviving its economic competitiveness through dollar devaluation.

Upon the collapse of the Bretton Woods system, many predicted the end of dollar hegemony and the rise of a multipolar global economic order grounded on more or less even domination of multiple major currencies such as the yen and Deutschmark. What is puzzling is that this predicted multipolar moment never came, and the dollar hegemony continued for four more decades until today. Even with the formation of the euro as a competitor, the dollar remains the most widely used reserve currency in the world. The same can be said regarding the use of the dollar in international transactions.

Figure 1. Shares of currencies in official holdings of foreign exchange, 1976–2011

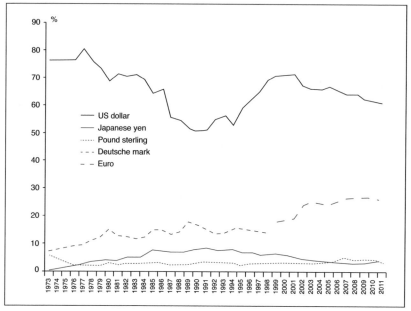

Source: IMF COFER dataset

While the dollar hegemony under the Bretton Woods system was a manifestation of the US's overwhelming economic might, the lingering dollar hegemony after the Bretton Woods collapse was the most significant lifeline that the US relied on to slow its economic decline. The post-Bretton Woods continuation of the hegemony of the dollar after 1971 lasted even longer than the dollar hegemony under Bretton Woods.

The dollar's lasting prowess was first made possible by the exchange between the US and its military allies during the Cold War period, when the former provided a security umbrella and weapons in exchange for the latter's support of the use of dollars in trade and foreign-exchange reserves. The role of the US global military domination in warranting the dollar standard was well illustrated by numerous episodes at the height of the Cold War, when governments of America's European allies were requested to support the dollar by increasing their purchase of dollar instruments and US military supplies, paid in dollars, under the explicit threat of reduction of US troops stationed in their countries.

This dollar-security nexus ensured that the dollar would remain the dominant foreign reserve currency in Western Europe and Japan. It also ensured that the

Table 1. Currency distribution of forex market turnover (percentage, total=200)

	1998	2001	2004	2007	2010	2013
US dollar	86.8	89.9	88.0	85.6	84.9	87.0
Pounds sterling	11.0	13.0	16.5	14.9	12.9	11.8
Deutschmark	30.5	--	--	--	--	--
French franc	5.0	--	--	--	--	--
Japanese yen	21.7	23.5	20.8	17.2	19.0	23.0
Euro	--	37.9	37.4	37.0	39.1	33.4
Mexican peso	0.5	0.8	1.1	1.3	1.3	2.5
Chinese yuan/RMB	0.0	0.0	0.1	0.5	0.9	2.2

Source: BIS Triennial Central Bank Survey

monarchical and authoritarian oil-producing states, which needed US protection even more, would invoice their oil exports in dollars. Large-scale governmental purchases of dollar instruments among key capitalist powers and the use of dollars in oil and arms trade accounted for the vast market liquidity of the currency, motivating private enterprises and other governments to use it for their reserves and trade settlement.

This geopolitical support of dollar hegemony remained unchallenged until the end of the Cold War, in the 1990s. With the Soviet bloc as a common security threat gone, regional powers used to being held hostage by the US security umbrella tried to break free of the US dollar-security nexus. The rise of the euro represented an explicit attempt to create a new currency rivalling the dollar. But Europe's continuous dependence on the US to defend its geopolitical interests, as shown by the Kosovo War in 1999, as well as the lack of centralised monetary authority and fiscal integration in the eurozone, has been undermining the ascendancy of the euro as a true alternative to the dollar.

In 2000–08, the dollar's credibility seemed to be threatened by an unprecedented simultaneous deterioration of the dollar value and US current account deficit. This simultaneous fall is largely attributable to the rise of China as a formidable low-cost exporter to the US. The rise of China's export sector was unleashed by a series of policy changes in the mid-1990s that precipitated an expanding stream of low-wage rural migrant labourers. Such an export-oriented path of growth was also facilitated by China's currency peg with the US that keeps Chinese exports competitively cheap in the world market.

While China's export expansion led to the deterioration of the US current account deficit, its large trade surplus enabled China to accumulate substantial foreign-exchange reserves. It devoted most of these reserves to the purchase of US Treasury bonds, turning itself into the largest creditor to the US. Their financing of the US fiscal deficit allowed the US government to expand expenditures while cutting taxes. It fuelled the American appetite for Chinese exports, and the resulting increase in China's trade surpluses led to yet more purchases of US Treasury bonds. These constituted two mutually reinforcing processes of increasing Chinese exports to the US and increasing Chinese holdings of US public debt, continuously deepening the market and the financial dependence of China on the US. China's massive investment in low-yield US Treasury bonds is tantamount to a tribute payment through which Chinese savings were transformed into Americans' consumption power. In 2008, China surpassed Japan as the biggest foreign holder of US Treasury bonds, and its holding continued to escalate despite the financial crisis that broke out in Wall Street in 2008.

Many expect that China's hoarding of US Treasury bonds made the US increasingly vulnerable to China, which enjoys geopolitical autonomy from Washington and does not rely on US military protection as earlier leading Asian purchasers of US debt have done. China is theoretically capable of dumping its dollar assets anytime to induce a run on the currency, financial collapse, hyperinflation and fiscal crisis in the US. This, if it happens, would spell the final disintegration of the dollar standard.

But upon closer examination, we will be able to see that China's purchase of US Treasuries has become a compulsion generated by its export-led model of development. China's dumping of Treasuries out of its geopolitical rivalry with the US is unthinkable. The vested interests of China that propagated export-oriented growth in the 1990s, composed of coastal provincial governments, export manufacturers and their lobbyists, plus officials from the Ministry of Commerce, were keen on perpetuating such a model, preempting China's transformation to a more balanced developmental model driven by domestic consumption and depending less on the US. China's entrenched export-oriented growth makes the Chinese economy vulnerable to any major contraction of consumption demand in the US and Europe. The large incentive of the Chinese government to employ its foreign reserves to purchase US debt is not only a result of the vast liquidity and presumably stable safe return of the US Treasury bonds, but also an effort to secure the continuous increase in US demand for their own exports.

China's addiction to US Treasury bonds is attributable to China's trade structure too. Under its reprocessing export model, China has become a nodal

Table 2. China's and Hong Kong's holding of US Treasury Securities before and after the crisis outbreak (billion dollars)

	China	Hong Kong	China & HK as share of total foreign holding	China & HK as share of total outstanding	Fed holding as share of total outstanding
End of Sept 2008	618.2	65.5	24.5%	11.8%	8.3%
End of Feb 2013	1 222.9	143.2	24.1%	12.0%	15.5%

Source: US Treasury, Major Foreign Holders of U.S. Treasury Securities database

point where raw materials, machines and components from Asia and other developing countries are put together into finished consumer goods to be exported to the US and Europe. While China's overall trade surplus has been mounting, it has been running a rising trade deficit with the whole world if we take out the US and Europe. This means that the growth in value of China's exports to Asia, Latin America and Africa has not caught up with the growth of China's imports of manufactured components, machineries, and raw materials from them. The US and Europe are the two sole sources of China's trade surplus. China's exports to the US, needless to say, are settled in US dollars. Even China's exports to Europe are settled in US dollars instead of euros. As long as China's rising trade surplus comes mostly in dollars, the Chinese central bank has few choices other than investing these dollars into the most liquid and relatively safe dollar-denominated asset, that is, US Treasury bonds.

Recently, there have been a lot of reports about China's activities in using its foreign exchange reserves for 'buying the world' through outward foreign direct investment. Chinese companies' acquisition of Volvo Cars from Ford Motor and Chinese SOEs' inroad into mining and energy sectors in other developing and developed countries from Zambia to Canada attract a lot of media attention. But despite these high-profile cases, China's outward foreign direct investment is so far of negligible aggregate size, in comparison with other major sources of FDI in the world. The Chinese official statistics show that the stock of China's non-financial outward FDI by the end of 2010 amounted to US$298 billion (US$317 billion if financial investment is included). This amount is even smaller than the outward FDI from Singapore, a city-state with a much smaller economy than that of China. China's outward FDI looks even more insignificant if we take into consideration that 63% of that amount was actually FDIs that land in Hong Kong.

The stock of China's outward FDI in places other than Hong Kong is less than US$118 billion, which is less than a tenth of the Chinese holding of US Treasury bonds. After all, no other market except the US debt market has liquidity deep enough to absorb China's mammoth reserves. Paul Krugman was not exaggerating when he claimed that China had been caught in a 'dollar trap', in which it had few choices other than to keep purchasing US Treasury bonds, helping to perpetuate the hegemonic role of the dollar.

Though China has the geopolitical autonomy that theoretically enables it to end its dependence on the dollar and even end the dollar standard, in reality it has been helping perpetuate the standard, and hence US geopolitical dominance, through its insurmountable addiction to US Treasury bonds caused by its export-driven growth. Compared to China's $1.2 trillion holding of US Treasuries, the BRICS bank forex reserve pool of $100 billion and China's pledged contribution of $400 billion are little more than a drop in the ocean.

The Chinese government has been recently emphasising its ambition to internationalise the RMB into a major reserve and international transaction currency as a way to maintain its export-oriented model while reducing its holding of US dollars, hence curbing its addiction to US public debts. But in actuality, the Chinese RMB, which is not yet a fully convertible currency, has a long way to go to become a major international currency. Its share in international currency use is minuscule, falling way behind the British pound and the yen, and even the Mexican peso (see Table 1). The RMB's rise to the status of a significant international currency will require RMB's full convertibility, which in turn needs China's financial liberalisation. This process will take time, even if the reluctant CCP finally agrees to take the very risky step of fully opening up its banking sector to the global economy. This step is far from an easy choice for the party-state, as such opening up would be a blow to its command of the economy via its control of credits. Before such radical shift on the part of China, the talk about the death of the global dollar standard and US global dominance under a China challenge will remain little more than a fantasy.

Reference

Ho-fung Hung (2015) *The China Boom: Origins, Global Impacts, and Demise*, New York, Columbia University Press

20

The future trajectory of BRICS

Achin Vanaik

What potential does BRICS have and what are its future prospects? Can it really emerge as a collective that will reject the current neoliberal order and seek to promote a much more social welfarist form of capitalist development that might at least unleash a dynamic much more conducive to the emergence of more progressive social and political forces whose pressures from below can then take a more radical anti-capitalist direction? Will it seriously challenge the existing world order where the imperialist behaviour of the US continues to be highly, sometimes decisively influential in shaping the course of events? Or are these governments headed by elites whose principal preoccupation is forging a more cooperative system of global management of a world capitalist order in which their voices will be more seriously listened to and in which their own ranking in the global pecking order of elites rises much more significantly?

In this regard there have been two contesting views. One has been marked by considerable enthusiasm about its potential. The very fact of regular summit meetings with an 'escalating consensus' is thought to bode well for the body's future and its ability to reshape the institutions and practices of global governance. The fact that the G7 gave way to the G8 which in turn has now given way to the G20 (incorporating the BRICS countries as well as other emerging economies) as the main international grouping undertaking to steer the world economy, is taken as testimony of the growing relevance of the emerging powers in general, and BRICS in particular. Others are more sceptical. Here, the BRICS countries are viewed not so much as major reformers of the current global neoliberal order but as new members happily included in a still hierarchical 'world steering committee' because they too will play by the basic rules. BRICS countries account for 42% of the world's population, 18% of its GDP, 15% of world trade and 40% of its currency reserves. (It is often ignored that the states comprising the Gulf Cooperation Council, namely Oman, UAE, Bahrain, Qatar, Kuwait and Saudi Arabia, which are all politically subordinate to the US and more obedient towards its economic needs, have in total more dollar reserves – official, sovereign wealth and other government funds – than does China.)

The main importance of BRICS lies in the fact that it accounts for more than half of the world's GDP growth rate. But there is no indication that there will be a real challenge to the neoliberal order and no interest in promoting an NIEO (New International Economic Order) of the kind that was once discussed by the Non-Aligned Movement (NAM) during the 1970s. Indeed, neither Brazil, which has observer status in the NAM, nor China, which achieved this in 1992, has shown interest in becoming full members of the NAM or in reinvigorating it as a mechanism for transforming global governance. Whether it is being part of the G20 or being aspirants to permanent status in the UN Security Council for those who are not yet permanent, or playing a bigger role in the WTO's Green Room decision-making, the emerging powers have shown more interest in joining the 'big boys' club'. They use their membership of the G77 and similar larger groups to project themselves as representatives of the interests of the majority of the poorer developing countries, the better to leverage pursuit of their national interests in negotiations within that club. This is a balancing act of sorts but not one whose primary purpose is to strengthen the South as a whole or prioritise the interests of the most vulnerable and poorest member countries within the South.

The reality is that a basic political-economic incompatibility rather than organisational handicaps limits the collective's capacity to function as a powerful and innovative new force in the realm of global politics and governance. The South African super-wealthy, mostly white, park much of their wealth and investments in Europe and Australia, creating a domestic balance of payments problem because of repatriation of profits and dividends to parent companies set up abroad. Given this powerful elite force, until 2013 when it crashed, South Africa maintained a strong rand, unlike the other four who are nowhere near as committed to maintaining a strong real, rouble, renminbi or rupee (Gentle 2012).

By demography (50 million) and total GDP, South Africa might not be in the same league as the other four or even as significant as Mexico, South Korea, or Turkey, but it is far and away the biggest investor in Africa, dwarfing the US, EU, China, India and Brazil, and it alone accounts for 40% of all African investment and 80% of all investments in the Southern African Development Community

(SADC) countries. In foreign policy it is more obsequious than the others to US foreign policy except on Palestine. India is pursuing ever closer relations with the US despite hiccups and is part of the US's China containment policies. Brazil is paying more attention to its intra-continental economic activities as well as showing more foreign policy independence from Washington. But outside Latin America this is more a way of asserting a greater self-confidence as an emerging power than actively seeking to put serious spokes in the functioning of US foreign policy. Russia and China, however, are both much more perturbed by US behaviour globally than the other three and thus seek greater political-economic cooperation.

In the BRICS grouping, South Africa and Brazil are among the most unequal societies in the world, while China's Gini coefficient has steadily risen, Russia's too, while India's Gini coefficient (calculated as it is on surveys of consumption expenditure and not on more reliable income data) is widely recognised to be a serious underestimate. In any case, rising inequalities of income and wealth have been characteristic of India's lopsided growth pattern over the last five decades, accelerating after the neoliberal reforms of 1991. It is hardly surprising that the number of dollar millionaires and billionaires is growing rapidly in the South. To make matters worse, Brazil, China and India are major land grabbers in Africa, and South Africa is itself involved in such activities. So much for BRICS 'leading the charge' against Northern exploitation of Africa. The BRICS' share in the continent's FDI stock and flows reached 14% and 25%, respectively, in 2010. This trend is likely to be reinforced in the future.

The members of BRICS, with the exception of Russia, have today a greater proportion of youth than in the advanced countries, but by 2050 it is projected that this gap will disappear, or in the case of South Africa and India be much reduced. But does this mean that between now and 2050 the fast-growing number of yearly new entrants into the national job market is going to prove an economic asset? Not necessarily; indeed, there are reasons to worry about the future performances. Per capita income levels of BRICS and some of the other 'emerging powers' like Indonesia are currently way behind those of the OECD countries. South Korea, Mexico and Turkey have entered the OECD club. In fact, it is simply not ecologically or materially possible (in terms of resource and energy use) for the per capita levels of even the BRICS and other 'high-flyers' to come anywhere close to average per capita levels of the most prosperous OECD countries as measured by actual international exchange rates, which give a truer picture of *global* purchasing power than PPP rates.

This means, given that the per capita figures are averages hiding gross inequalities, that their relatively lower level in the future implies the persistence of mass discontentment and impoverishment in a world where the communications revolution has now made it possible for even the world's poor to know how deprived they are, despite the presence of great wealth in their own societies. It was comparative dissatisfactions rather than absolute levels of economic deprivation that helped fatally undermine the Soviet system. In the South, both relative deprivation and absolute immiseration are in all probability going to persist widely enough, thereby making possibilities of intra-South cooperation more difficult, as well as being a source for anger to erupt against ruling elites – witness the 'Arab uprisings' of recent times.

The historical pattern of capitalist industrialisation in the West and Japan was accompanied by the kind of urbanisation and employment generation there that led to the decline of the rural population to the point that it constitutes, at most, between 2% to 8% of the overall population in the advanced countries. For countries like Brazil, India, China and Mexico the rural population is currently a majority. In due course this may well become a minority, but a significant one well above the proportions now prevailing in the earlier industrialising countries. Even in those countries of the South where urbanisation has been proportionately greater than in the above-mentioned four, what has emerged and will in all likelihood continue, if not deepen, is the rise of an informal sector comprising a very large part of an urban slum population, itself growing. The ICT revolution has been a major factor in reducing the employment elasticities of output worldwide. Rising capital intensity even in agriculture means higher levels of unemployment everywhere and of low productivity, low pay employment, of more part-time work, longer working hours, greater job insecurities and thus a greater proportion than ever of the working poor.

The history of the development of an organised and unionised labour force in Western Europe as the accompaniment of its particular pattern of capitalist modernisation, and even the lower levels of such organisation of the labour force in North America and Japan, are unlikely to be replicated in BRICS, let alone elsewhere in the South. The objective conditions for much greater worker unrest in this part of the world are being laid. Grassroots organisation in slums and in local communities rather than simply at the workplace will become more important and, with this, the necessity of taking up a diversity of issues such as race, ethnicity, gender and skills difference to generate more composite forms of unity in action. While urban-based struggles over the 'right to the city', i.e. the right of the majority of urban residents to shape their lives in ways that promote meaningful cooperation and control over daily existence, are going to become ever more important, given the persistence of the peasantry in much of the South, the land and 'agrarian question' will also remain of great importance.

It is difficult then to see just what the BRICS countries can point to – economically, politically, culturally, strategically – that can serve as the kind of cement that could make the collective a unified and powerful force for significant change on the world level (Ladwig 2012). The most perhaps that can be said is that a serious weakening of US global hegemony and influence would raise – by default more than anything else – the importance of BRICS as a collective unit.

References

Gentle, L (2012) The root of all evil? The dollar, the BRICS and South Africa, *Deccan Chronicle*, 29 March

Ladwig, W (2012) Why BRICS has no force, *Indian Express*, 28 March

21

Does the South have a possible history?

VIJAY PRASHAD

Matters are bleak in the Global South. The locomotives of the South – the BRICS (Brazil, Russia, India, China, South Africa) – splutter as commodity prices drop. Some of this is attributable to the long-running credit crunch from 2007. Old Western fantasies to encage adversaries – whether China or Russia or indeed Iran – drive other problems. Sanctions against this country or that produce extra-economic blockades that are somehow immune to World Trade Organisation challenges – barriers to protect producers are illegal, but barriers to punish countries deemed to be outlaws are encouraged. The rouble spirals out of control, as US$30 billion goes to bail out Russia's Trust Bank.

What locomotives are able to leave the station do not have enough carriages to carry their populations. So inequality rates remain steady in Brazil, India and South Africa, all of which have seen 'orthodox' mechanisms take hold of their financial policy regardless of the temperament of their political leadership.

With certain exceptions, the slow decline of the trade unions and of membership in the mass fronts of the socialist and communist parties is a global problem – leaving many millions of people outside the influence of the Left. Jingoism of the Right pits the working class against itself – on the terrain of anti-immigrant politics, typically. Fellow workers become dry tinder, cowering in the corner as the lit match of jingoism flies around them. The explanations from the Left are more sober – more determined to show how the economic and political system in place pits workers against each other as capital sits back, smirking in its carefully crafted liberalism. But too many ordinary people are isolated from these sober explanations – now reliant as consumers for their theories on television, the internet and of course the political class in each country.

The return of the great leader who promises to solve all problems – to take a stagnant economy and make it purr, to take joblessness by the throat and make it cough out jobs. This is a tradition that seeks its emotions in will, distracting from the terrible conditions of everyday life, the perils of miners or the futility of farmers. Argument is considered a waste of time, only action is valued. Democracy is given lip service but its constraints are mocked. National glory makes its return, but careful not to mimic fascism – an embarrassment for the elite. Justification for military rule has made a comeback after a brief moment in the 1990s when the West promoted 'democracy' above all else. The rhetoric of counter-terrorism and of social instability has allowed the army to leave the barracks from Egypt to Thailand – with liberal elites taking refuge in the Generals.

Turkey's Recep Tayyip Erdogan and India's Narendra Modi are powerful examples of free market or authoritarian populism. They portray themselves as the sharp swords to cut the knots that bind progress. It is acceptable for them to call for austerity – not as a means for personal virtue, but as the suffering of the people for a greater good (in effect, for the greater good of large business linked to their political parties). The long arm of the law, even short of outright military dictatorship, can smash workers' protests and political protests and arrest critical journalists for sedition.

Behind doors, the Masters of the World – the G7 states – continue their shenanigans, most notably through trade agreements. Policy space for the South continues to be constrained by them in international institutions, allowing them to subsidise their own big business but allowing the Global South little freedom to protect their economies. The pressure on the Global South to dismantle their food security systems in the World Trade Organisation is one such example. Another is the Trade in Services Agreement (TISA) pushed by the US and the European Union and their 'Really Good Friends' (a strange term used by the US and the EU to refer to the bloc they have put together). The bulk of the Really Good Friends involved in the TISA negotiations are from the upper-income countries, with only two lower-income states (Pakistan and Paraguay) in the process. The TISA pushes for the turbo-charged privatisation of public services.

Alongside the TISA is the Trans-Pacific Partnership (TPP), a mechanism to export the North American Free Trade Agreement outwards across the Pacific Ocean and down into South America. The TPP has been negotiated utterly in secret and, if not for WikiLeaks, the entire content of the discussion would be unknown to the public. Domestic laws would be overridden by the TPP, in which the Northern elites would set an agenda for the rest. One of the leaked documents suggests that the US is applying 'great pressure' on the countries to cut through the divergence of opinion on questions of intellectual property, forcing Southern countries to bow the knee before Western patents. In the debate around 'investment', one of the documents shows, 'the United States has shown no flexibility on its proposal'. The outcome of these 'negotiations' is typically a victory for the West, whose pressure continues to be overwhelming, and thereafter economies of the South are subordinated by rules to Western advantage.

The record of hope is mixed. On the one side there is the collapse of the Arab Spring – it has devolved into the desolation of Egypt and the bloodletting of Iraq–Syria. Elections in Tunisia are no antidote to the victory of the counterrevolution across the Arabic-speaking lands. On the other side there remain the experiments in Latin America where, despite great challenges, popular democracy continues to be incubated. The weakened US embargo of Cuba and the possibility of a ceasefire in Colombia are only the latest indicators of the continued ebb and flow of the Pink Tide.

The most positive outcome of the Pink Tide was the creation of an alternative trade structure, the Bolivarian Alternative for the Americas, ALBA. Its 2004 declaration contained important principles for a just world trade order – solidarity, cooperation, respect for sovereignty and uneven development. These ideas emerge out of a half-century of struggle by the South to forge a more just alternative to the Western-driven 'development'.

But the undue optimism of the BRICS states that they would be able to diversify the world order simply by their presence has fallen short and pressure to forge an alternative order has been blocked. Instead, the powerhouses of the BRICS set aside the ALBA-type approach to secure the mere entry of themselves into the 'international' institutions. China might occasionally propose a 'mutual benefit' approach, but it is unlikely to push for radical ideas when it takes its seat at the World Bank or World Trade Organisation. There, neoliberal orthodoxy rules. Old ideas such as South–South cooperation have come to mean Southern multinational corporations 'cooperating' with Southern countries, rather than the formation of a trade and development regime that privileges wellbeing over profit.

The real alternative, of ALBA, promises human and environmental wellbeing above profit. But the South American states need the BRICS bloc to put their heft behind such a proposal on the global stage. The politics of such a manoeuvre is currently nowhere to be seen.

22

Whose interests are served by the BRICS?

Immanuel Wallerstein

The world system is in serious trouble and it is causing pain to the vast majority of the world's population. Pundits and politicians grasp at straws. They magnify every momentary, and usually transitory, occurrence of slight improvements in the various measures we are accustomed to using.

In late 2014, we were suddenly being told that the market looked much better in the United States, even if it looked worse in Europe, Russia, China, Brazil and many other places. But as the New Year began, there was a serious decline in both stocks and bond prices in the United States. It was a quick and sharp turnaround. Of course, the pundits immediately had explanations, but they offered a wide gamut of explanations.

The real question in any case is not the prices of the stock and bond markets in any given country. It is the picture of the world system as a whole, which doesn't seem to me to look very good at all. Let us start with the principal measure utilised by Establishment thinkers – 'growth' rates.

By growth rates, we tend to mean prices in the stock market. Of course, as we know and as is obvious, many things can lead to a rise of stock prices other than an improved economy, first of all speculation. Speculation has become so easy and so entrenched in the everyday activity of large operators in the world market that we have begun to assume that this is not only normal but more or less desirable. In any case, we tend to argue that there is nothing anyone can do that can stop it, should we wish to do so. This last assumption is probably correct, which is precisely the problem.

In my view, the only figure that measures the wellbeing of the world economy and the wellbeing of the vast majority of the world population is employment rates. As far as I can tell, unemployment has been abnormally high for quite a while now if one looks at the world as a whole. Furthermore, the rate has been creeping up steadily, rather than the reverse, for the last 30–40 years. The best we seem to be able to anticipate is that the rate will stabilise where it is. Reversing the trend does not seem likely. Of course, if you measure employment rates country by country, they vary and they oscillate. But worldwide, the rate of unemployment has been rather regularly rising.

The reality is that we are living amid a wildly oscillating world system, and this is very painful. Employment rates are not the only measures that oscillate. They simply measure the most immediate source of pain. Exchange rates between major currencies are also a visible source of pain for persons at all levels of income. At the moment, the dollar is rising rapidly vis-à-vis most other currencies. A rising currency rate favours cheap imports and lowers inflation. But it hurts exporters, as we know, and risks longer-term deflation.

Energy costs are also wildly oscillating. The most obvious example is oil. The price was first on a sharp rise across the world during most of 2014, giving enormous income and political power to countries which were producers (as well as to states within North America that were producers). Then, seemingly all of a sudden, there was said to be a glut on the market, and the prices of energy began catapulting downward to a quite low level. Those political structures that had profited from the upswing now face both a rise in sovereign debt and unhappy citizens.

To be sure, there is a political factor involved in these wild swings. But the ability of even large producers, such as Saudi Arabia or Texas, to affect the price swings, should they want to do so, is vastly overstated. These swings are like tornados ripping open houses in their way. In the process, banking institutions that had bet on the direction of prices (either way) find themselves in radical trouble, and no longer with a guaranteed back-up from their governments.

Geopolitical alliances are almost as unstable as the market. The United States has lost its unquestioned hegemony of the world system and we have moved into a multipolar world. US decline started not recently but in 1968. It was for a long time a slow decline, but it became precipitate after 2003 as a result of the disastrous attempt to reverse the decline by the invasion of Iraq.

Our multipolar world has perhaps 10–12 powers strong enough to pursue relatively autonomous policies. However, 10 to 12 is too large a number for any of them to be sure their views can prevail. As a result, these powers are constantly shuffling alliances in order not to be outmanoeuvred by the others.

Many, if not most, geopolitical decisions are impossible to control, even by stronger powers, because there are no good options available. Look at what's happening in the European Union. Greece is about to have elections, in which it seems that Syriza, the anti-austerity party, may win. Syriza's policy is to demand a revision of the austerity measures that were imposed on Greece by a coalition of Germany, France, the International Monetary Fund, and indirectly the US Treasury. Syriza says that it does not wish to leave the euro and will not do so.

Germany says it will not be 'blackmailed' by Greece into altering its policy. Blackmailed? Little Greece can blackmail Germany? In a sense the Germans are right. Greece under Syriza would be playing hardball. The eurozone has no treaty provision either for withdrawal or for expulsion. If the strong powers try to expel Greece from the eurozone, a large number of countries may rush to withdraw for good and bad reasons.

Soon the eurozone might not exist at all, with Germany the single biggest loser. So, from Germany's (and France's) point of view, the Greek demands are a lose-lose proposition. Germany at the moment sticks to its position but has softened the threat of expulsion. France has said that it is against expulsion. This serves Syriza's objectives. That Germany in particular loses whichever stance it now chooses is one of the political consequences of chaos.

The world system is self-destructing. It is in what the scientists of complexity call a bifurcation. This means that the present system cannot survive, and that the real question is what will replace it. While we cannot predict what kind of new system will emerge, we can affect the choice between the substantive alternatives available. But we can only hope to do this by a realistic analysis of existing chaotic swings and not hide our political efforts behind delusions about reforming the existing system or by deliberate attempts to obfuscate our understanding.

In this context, what role do the BRICS play?

In 2001, Jim O'Neill, then chair of Goldman Sachs Assets Management, wrote an article for their subscribers entitled 'The world needs better economic BRICs'. O'Neill invented the acronym to describe the so-called emerging economies of Brazil, Russia, India and China, and to recommend them to investors as the economic 'future' of the world economy.

The term caught on, and the BRICs became an actual group that met together regularly and later added South Africa to membership, changing the small 's' to a capital 'S'. Since 2001, the BRICS have flourished economically, at least relative to other states in the world system. They have also become a very controversial subject. There are those who think of the BRICS as the avant-garde of anti-imperialist struggle. There are those who, quite to the contrary, think of the

BRICS as sub-imperialist agents of the true North (North America, Western Europe and Japan). And there are those who argue that they are both.

In the wake of the post-hegemonic decline of US power, prestige and authority, the world seems to have settled into a multipolar geopolitical structure. In this current situation, the BRICS are definitely part of the new picture. By their efforts to forge new structures on the world scene, such as the interbank structure they are seeking to create, to sit alongside and substitute for the International Monetary Fund, they are certainly weakening still further the power of the United States and other segments of the old North in favour of the South, or at least of the BRICS themselves. If one's definition of anti-imperialism is reducing the power of the United States, then the BRICS certainly represent an anti-imperialist force.

However, geopolitics is not the only thing that matters. We will also want to know something about the internal class struggles within BRICS countries, the relations of BRICS countries to each other, and the relation of BRICS countries to the non-BRICS countries in the South. On all three issues, the record of the BRICS is murky, to say the least.

How can we assess the internal class struggles within the BRICS countries? One standard way is to look at the degree of polarisation, as indicated by Gini measures of inequality. Another way is to see how much state money is being utilised to reduce the degree of poverty among the poorest strata. Of the five BRICS countries, only Brazil has significantly improved its scores on such measures. In some cases, despite an increase in the GDP, the measures are worse than, say, 20 years ago.

If we look at the economic relations of the BRICS countries to each other, China outshines the others in rise in GDP and in accumulated assets. India and Russia seem to feel the need to protect themselves against Chinese strength. Brazil and South Africa seem to be suffering from present and potential Chinese investing in key arenas.

If we look at the relations of BRICS countries to other countries in the South, we hear increasing complaints that the way each of these countries relates to its immediate (and not so immediate) neighbours resembles too much the ways in which the United States and the old North related to them. They are sometimes accused of not being 'sub-imperial' but of being simply 'imperial'.

What makes the BRICS seem so important today has been their high rates of growth since, say, 2000; rates of growth that have been significantly higher than those of the old North. But will this continue? Their rates of growth have already begun to slip. Some other countries in the South – Mexico, Indonesia,

(South) Korea, Turkey – seem to be matching them.

However, given the world depression in which we continue to exist, and the low likelihood of significant recovery in the next decade or so, the possibility that, in a decade, a future Goldman Sachs analyst will continue to project the BRICS as the (economic) future is rather dubious. Indeed, the likelihood that the BRICS will continue to be a regularly meeting group with presumably common policies seems remote.

The world system's structural crisis is moving too fast, and in too many uncertain ways, to assume sufficient relative stability to allow the BRICS as such to continue to play a special role, either geopolitically or economically. Like globalisation itself as a concept, the BRICS may turn out to be a passing phenomenon.

23

BRICS after the Durban and Fortaleza summits

NIALL REDDY

Unlike in Durban in March 2013, the conclusion of the BRICS summit in Fortaleza was greeted with massive international media attention. The ostensible source of this renewed interest, following months of bad press for emerging markets, was the birth of the New Development Bank (NDB) and a US$100 billion Contingent Reserve Arrangement ('CRA') between member nations. Suddenly BRICS seemed to be more than a catchy acronym for investors and challenging critics who charge that the alliance is contentless and largely incoherent.

BRICS also started to appear as a geopolitical presence during the Syria crisis when the US threatened a bombing of the Assad regime, the Ukraine crisis, acting against Western attempts to punish Russia through sanctions and its eviction from the G8 and G20. China's growing dominance of world trade and the increased assertiveness of Brazil and India, leading a coalition of developing countries, together seem to have disrupted the ability of the US and its allies to shape the global trade regime. US and EU bickering caused the collapse of the Doha round of agreements at the WTO. Taken along with international investment, trade and GDP figures, there seems to be ample evidence of a shift in the coordinates of global power. BRICS nations have tended to embrace the narrative of emerging powers, often adopting the grammar of post-war Third Worldism with talk of a 'new world order'.

But on closer examination, the agreements actually inked at Fortaleza hardly represent a radical challenge to the existing state of affairs. The CRA, touted by many as an important step in freeing developing nations from dependency on the IMF, actually replicates the latter's control – requiring borrowers to prove an 'on-track arrangement with the IMF' in order to access anything over 30% of the credit disbursement. Both the NDB and CRA require swap arrangements denominated in US dollars that completely contradict the stated intention of weakening dollar hegemony. Buried within the millenarian phraseology are some more frank admissions of this conservative approach: the BRICS declaration styles its new institutes as a 'complement to existing arrangements'.

The states of today's putative 'emerging powers' are fundamentally different from their radical predecessors whose language they have appropriated, operating in a fundamentally different international context. Some insist that their rise signifies the return of the state in a developmental capacity after its retreat from the economy during neoliberalism. It's hard to see this in the case of South Africa or Russia. India has had some experimentation with heterodox economics but even this limited interventionism looks set to end – aside from a corrupted crony-capitalist incarnation as in the Gujarat model – with the coming to power of Modi, a market fundamentalist. China certainly represents a different case. Its dramatic economic boom would have been unthinkable without the strong guiding hand of the Communist Party and significant state-owned sector. But extreme exploitation and ecological devastation are the prices paid for this version of export-led growth. China and Russia seem to have finally disproven the old liberal axiom that freer markets and democracy are congenitally entwined. In India, Modi's election stands to deepen the systemic oppression and social stratification that facile celebrations of the 'largest democracy in the world' have always found easy to ignore.

In Brazil, Lula's Workers Party combined neoliberal macroeconomic fundamentals with strong industrial policy underpinned by the state bank BNDES, with some downward redistribution through family-support grants and minimum wage increases and subsidies for soya and other commodity exporters. Defying the trend within BRICS, the Gini coefficient has come down in Brazil, although it remains one of the most unequal nations in the world. Despite these progressive linings, Brazil is party to one shared feature of all the BRICS – strong and growing authoritarianism. Its brutal, militarised police force, inherited from the dictatorship, competes with South Africa's for the annual civilian body count.

Whatever their differences in economic policy, the nature of their political system or the ideology of their ruling parties, the foreign policy of BRICS nations is determined by the same set of laws. They are all capitalist societies, whose states are driven to accumulate their own geopolitical power and advance the interests of the corporations and elites on which they depend. With varying degrees of success they are competing in capitalist globalisation and its existing institutions.

Leaving aside an ideological or geopolitical common end, the cohering factor of the BRICS bloc is an attempt to bend the rules of those institutions slightly in their own favour – but not really to replace them. Their growing incursion across the Global South will not by any magic touch open up developmental pathways out of poverty and dependency. We see this most clearly in Africa.

The voracious appetite of China, India and increasingly Brazil for cheap resources is behind the GDP figures that have triggered the business media's sudden rebranding of the region from a 'hopeless continent' to 'Africa Rising', no matter that in reality this means intensified looting and Africans *up*rising. Trade between the BRICS bloc and Africa jumped by more than 70% between 2008 and 2012 to US\$340 billion (more than between BRICS nations themselves). The growth is based almost entirely on primary exports, overwhelmingly oil, giving it an extremely uneven geography that only includes certain countries. Once resource depletion, environmental degradation and other factors are netted out of notoriously sketchy GDP estimates, the optimism seems misplaced – with negative per capita wealth accumulation. The World Bank estimated that by 2007 Africa was losing 6% of its annual income, with these corrections, and that doesn't include the illicit capital flight that accompanies extraction industries.

On top of this we must factor in broader political-economic effects of resource-curse-driven growth – the undergirding of a parasitic elite, a state–corporate revolving-door relationship replete with brutal policing, ecological devastation, rampant inequality and de-industrialisation. In South Africa we have a word that signifies this resource curse: *Marikana.* The rush of BRICS corporates and states for land grabs, financial gaming and resource extraction has generated talk of a new 'scramble for Africa' reminiscent of the one launched at a Berlin conference 130 years ago, when the continent's irrational borders were drawn. BRICS are helping to reproduce Africa's traditional role as a peripheral supplier of cheap labour and resources and an outlet for selling manufactured goods, and not transcending that role.

South Africa has had a crucial part to play in this, justifying its seat at the table, despite its dwarfish size, by its position as the 'gateway to Africa'. The foreign policy that Thabo Mbeki pioneered is mainly geared to opening the continent to penetration by Western and non-Western multinationals through financial and trade liberalisation. South Africa relates to its hinterlands in a similar fashion to other BRICS – with over 80% of imports composed of minerals and energy but still running a trade surplus from its exports of manufactures. South African retail, cellphone, banking and mining corporates are rapidly fanning out across the continent. Sandton's sophisticated financial institutions are positioned as the hub for ingoing investment as well as massive outgoing legal and illicit capital flight.

A similar situation prevails in Latin America. Brazil's affiliations with the progressive governments of the so-called 'Pink Tide' haven't prevented it from pursuing an aggressive programme of transnationalising its biggest firms – securing resources and markets across the continent. The vanguard of Chinese and Brazilian capital's penetration of the Global South has been the national development bank – both of which at this point are larger than the World Bank in terms of lending. Unlike the case of Western-dominated institutions, Chinese lending hasn't come with 'structural adjustments' – demands for pro-market economic policy to ensure repayment. Instead it is typically attached to agreements to source inputs and labour from other Chinese companies. China gets a double deal – interest payments and the biggest share of the economic activity generated by the loan. The benefits and multiplier effects for loaning nations are typically limited. The victims are African and Latin American citizenries whose authoritarian leaders now have more staying power. As China grows in size and developing economies become increasingly dependent on its markets and exports, there are signs that Chinese demands are growing increasingly onerous and starting to impinge on the sovereignty of lending nations in the same way that Washington's Bretton Woods institutions have historically done.

There is little reason to see why a BRICS NDB dedicated to infrastructure lending wouldn't be instrumentalised in the same way and directed to lubricate the extraction of minerals and oil, or to engage in other dubious, destructive mega-projects that even the World Bank no longer touches as a result of civil society protest. There is also little evidence that peripheral nations are absorbing technologies or other developmental assets from these burgeoning exchanges with emerging powers. In short, Eastern and Southern exploitation often looks little different from Northern, except that we have to work much harder to establish solidarity relations as a counterbalance, given oppressive regimes in China and Russia which brook no complaining.

BRICS claims to talk for the Global South in a historical vision of 'convergence' under a 'new world order' are thus rather hollow. The logical end point of the current trajectory is that new imperialist powers will stalk the globe and compete for its resources, not an alternative to capitalism's extremely uneven development – if it gets that far, that is. The literature on shifting power balances is filled with confident predictions about the exact point that East overtakes West (2030? 2050?) as the economic centre of the world. Recall how Japan was going to be the next hegemon – until it crashed in 1990, never to stand up straight again.

So some sobriety and a greater awareness of the fragilities and uncertainties of these historical processes are called for. In the first place we need to escape misleading aggregations. China's growth has been nothing short of a miracle, but without it the whole picture changes. South Africa can't be said to be 'emerging' in any sense. The other members have had varying rates of more moderate accumulation – but all are facing difficulties with the US's attempts to manage the ongoing global crisis and the tapering of easy money (the US$ 'Quantitative Easing' printing press) in the wake of a major commodity price boom.

In a more globalised world, macro-statistics on GDP and trade mask a great deal. The Chinese boom is still deeply dependent on value chains that run through Western markets and are controlled by Western multinationals, which are still technological power-houses retaining ultimate controls through intellectual property and branding power. US military 'hard power' may be receding after its disasters in the Middle East and Afghanistan, plus recent spending cuts, but it still dwarfs the combined might of the BRICS. US military bases still cover the globe, and the rise of AFRICOM is a genuine threat to African self-determination. The dollar's position as world money also appears impregnable in the short run – having become the global safe-haven commodity during a crisis generated in the US itself. China now faces the daunting challenge of redirecting its economy from export production for debt-fuelled US markets to internal demand-driven growth, against the grain of entrenched political and economic interests.

BRICS nations also provide no solution to the most serious looming crisis – global warming – having collaborated with Western powers in Copenhagen and Durban UN summits to scupper any legally binding international convention on climate change. These caveats in mind, it is important to affirm that the shift in the economic structure of the world and the distribution of power is real and significant. It appears to be interfering with the ability of the US to manage global capitalism collaboratively with its traditional allies, the EU and Japan.

There may be something inherently progressive to this, and indeed to a greater geographic, national and racial diffusion of wealth and power. But the opportunities provided by a more multipolar world order will not be delivered from above. Only a 'new world order' that changes rather than spreads capitalist logics of power and profits can truly overturn global geographies of inequality.

24

Building BRICS from below?

ANA GARCIA

The Sixth Summit of the BRICS Heads of States, in Fortaleza, was accompanied by three others: the Business Meeting of BRICS, the Third Trade Union Summit and NGO movements' 'Dialogues on development: the BRICS from the perspective of peoples'. They are composed of actors from very different fields. They also represent projects that sometimes converge and sometimes are in dispute regarding the development model, sustainability, social participation, equality and democracy, among other topics. These actors seek to be part of either the hegemonic or counterhegemonic discourse, along and beyond the state. However, these 'summits' are far from equal in terms of the ability to influence the way BRICS governments take their projects forward.

The first one took place one day before the meeting of presidents and was attended by approximately 700 businessmen and women.[1] The BRICS Business Meeting is the space where large companies from the five countries gather to attempt further integration of their business. They offered a series of recommendations aimed at the government summit, seeking to place the pro-corporate trade and investment position on the agenda. The following recommendations were made: visa facilitation for businessmen; reduction of non-tariff barriers; elimination of dumping and subsidies; creation of a 'BRICS Business Portal' dedicated to information exchange; support for trade fairs, exhibitions and forums within the BRICS countries; a special section in the website of each country for commercial proposals to bring together potential business partners and joint ventures, among others.[2] Business actors also strongly support the creation of the BRICS New Development Bank, aimed at facilitating trade, business and investment, in addition to the potential increase in transactions in local currency (not the US dollar), with the support of central banks for settlement of these currencies.[3] In these respects, the business agenda broadly coincides with the government's one, as we see in the final declaration of Fortaleza and the agreement on the creation of the New Development Bank (NDB) and the Contingent Reserve Arrangement (CRA), which contemplate these recommendations.

At this point there is convergence between the governments of BRICS, businessmen and trade unions. Trade union federations from the five countries, which met in Fortaleza the same day as the business meeting, declared their full support for the NDB as an instrument for the transformation of the global economic architecture. From the point of view of these unions, the BRICS represent a key step towards democratisation of international relations and multipolarity.[4]

The business meeting also engaged in a formal networking session, where 600 companies from agribusiness, mining, infrastructure, pharmaceuticals, information technology, energy, green economy and finance did deals estimated to be worth US$3.9 billion.[5] Finally, another area of business activity, created in Durban in 2013, is the BRICS Business Council, with direct and formalised dialogue with the governments of these countries.

A very different situation arises for unions, social movements and NGOs from the BRICS countries. In their declarations, unions expressed their claim to recognition of the BRICS Trade Union Forum as an institutional space within the formal structure of the group, as it is recognised for the Business Council. They also expressed their intention to participate in working groups and in the NDB in order to open space for social participation in the BRICS.[6]

Other movements, networks and NGOs joined the 'Dialogues on development: the BRICS from the perspective of the people', from 14 to 16 July, which I was able to attend. It was organised in conjunction with local movements in Fortaleza, one of the host cities of the World Cup, which saw a series of protests and social struggles in 2014.[7] The environment in Fortaleza had been radicalised prior to the World Cup, and we can imagine that if the BRICS Summit occurred in March, as planned earlier, we would have had very large protests. However, as it took place immediately after the World Cup, the atmosphere was one of relative exhaustion. The BRICS are not a topic of concern to Brazilian social movements, which have their own agendas, and thus would not attract a large mobilisation. International issues are always distant from local movements' agendas. The last breakthrough was the continental struggle against the Free Trade Area of the Americas ten years earlier, in bringing international issues to everyday life. The mobilisations around the meeting of the Inter-American

Development Bank, held in Fortaleza in 2002, was another event that local social movements protested against.

This time, civil society was led by the World March of Women, the Landless People's Movement, the union federations CUT and CSP-Conlutas, Jubilee South, the Organisation of Brazilian Women, the Popular World Cup Committee, the Brazilian Network for the Integration of People, in addition to local organisations such as Instituto Terramar, Research and Advisory Centre, and collectives of media, women and youth. Representatives of movements and NGOs from Africa, South America, Europe, Asia and the USA also participated. There were leaders from communities affected by mining in South Africa, academics and NGOs from China and India, as well as large international NGOs such as ActionAid. Support came especially from Germany's Heinrich Boell Foundation (which provided two days of debate on the new BRICS bank, bringing together academics and activists from China, India and South Africa) and the Friedrich Ebert Foundation, as well as ActionAid. Brazilians were obviously in the majority, but we could also feel a great presence from South Africans, a lesser presence of Chinese and Indians and, regrettably, almost no Russian activists.

The topics under debate varied widely: socio-environmental conflicts and inequalities, extraction, criminalisation of social movements, social participation, human rights and transnational corporations, in addition to the central theme of the official summit, infrastructure and the New Development Bank (NDB). For this session, Ambassador Carlos Cozendey, the representative of the Brazilian government's foreign ministry in NDB negotiations, entered into a dialogue with movements and NGOs.

It is important to remember that Fortaleza was preceded by the meeting of social movements and organisations in Durban, South Africa, in 2013, which was called 'BRICS from below'. This was sponsored by the Centre for Civil Society at the University of KwaZulu-Natal, the South Durban Community Environmental Alliance and the NGO groundWork. It brought together grassroots social movements, NGOs and academics. Between Durban and Fortaleza, however, there were very few moments of articulation between the social bases of the BRICS countries. Indeed, a 'BRICS from below' concept is a very recent process and its pace is slower than that of governments and business. The social realities in each country differ greatly, and language remains a problem (the common language is English, but it is inaccessible to communities and grassroots movements outside India or South Africa). What is understood as 'civil society' (a concept that applies to business, if we follow the category of

Gramsci), and how it relates to the state, is very different in each country.

There are many difficulties for Brazilian movements and NGOs to find common ground for dialogue with Chinese and Russian organisations, for example. The latter tend to be very close to their governments, and they differ on issues such as the green economy, extraction or social participation. A dialogue with the South Africans is in some ways easier, and, in some cases, it had already been set in place by international campaigns and protests for decades prior to the BRICS.

Interestingly, the theme 'BRICS' is being explored in a more systematic way by agencies and NGOs 'from the North' rather than 'from the South'. For the latter, the group is still somewhat abstract; it is not realised in the struggles and social processes in the territories. What we see, rather, are South African, Brazilian, Chinese, Indian and Russian multinationals, mainly in the extractive sector, which have been generating negative impacts in the territories and, in such cases, generating processes of resistance.

Despite the differences, we can identify some similar experiences of impact, confrontation and resistance, plus themes that are common to the peoples of the BRICS. There are, for example, experiences with mega-events and related violations of rights (the World Cup and Olympics in Brazil, China, South Africa and Russia, and the Commonwealth Games in India). In the five countries, there are many instances of socio-environmental conflicts involving mega-projects of oil, gas and mining, and also rights violations around mega-infrastructure projects involving funding by national development banks. These will all very likely be amplified by the future NDB. In other words, international solidarity and the articulation and strengthening of societies in the BRICS will occur in processes of struggle, insofar as these countries move forward in the development model that they follow today.

One difficulty for the cohesion and articulation of these social movements today is the fact that they have different views on the meaning of the BRICS in the world order. Some movements and organisations are closer to the positions of governments. They tend to characterise the BRICS more optimistically, as a possible alternative pole, balancing with Western powers, leading to a democratisation of the world order. Other movements and organisations are critical of their governments from various points of view, especially of development strategies with high socio-environmental risk and little or no channel for effective social participation. Their view is that the BRICS are 'more of the same', that is, a strengthening of global capitalism and the predatory accumulation of capital, not generating a real alternative to US and global power.

This is reflected in distinct strategies towards the BRICS. Some demand an official space for the participation of civil society, trying to generate channels of influence from within. Others consider this strategy a lost game, given the disadvantageous correlation of forces within the BRICS, since governments have previously outlined their strategies. This position also points to the high risk of co-optation of these spaces of formal participation.

The NDB poses a major challenge to social movements and other civil society organisations. Only now is it possible to speak of the 'BRICS' as a relatively coherent group, with an institution that identifies them. The NDB is still not in operation, but it is necessary to do a thorough analysis of the current capitalist order, in which the bank is situated, as well as of the strategies of these countries in the international financial architecture. The Brazilian government has insisted that the new financial mechanisms (NDB and CRA) are complementary to, not competing with, the IMF and World Bank. Countries have the right to recall 30% of the US$100 billion they have allocated to the CRA, in case of problems in the balance of payments, but if they want to access the rest, they will have to rely on the approval of the IMF.

The NDB, in turn, will focus on infrastructure projects and sustainable development. But it is important to remember that the World Bank had already created, in 2013, the Global Infrastructure Facility (GIF), with strong support from Brazil, India and South Africa. The GIF proposal is to launch bonds in the international market to finance mega-projects.[8] If we take as an indicator the projects funded by the national development banks of the BRICS, such as Brazil's BNDES, we see that the projects prioritised major infrastructure (power plants, highways, ports), and not those that meet basic needs such as water and sanitation. The main beneficiaries are the big construction companies, in addition to giant mining and oil corporations. Thus, it strengthens a monopoly capitalism that concentrates wealth within and outside the BRICS. How does the bank define 'sustainable development'? Which criteria will be used for evaluating social and environmental impacts and which mechanisms of transparency decide which projects are to be financed with public funds? These questions need to be seriously addressed, since governments do not give answers to them.

We cannot yet expect a unified position from social movements and other organisations towards the BRICS. Previous experiences, which were accumulated after numerous confrontations and dialogues with the World Bank, were very different. There are also a number of different relationships with the national development banks, which will reflect different strategies in confronting the new bank.

Some groups propose a dialogue and demand greater space to influence the bank's policies. Oxfam, for example, has made recommendations to the bank, stating that 'another bank is possible'.[9] In discussions in Fortaleza, some groups argued the need for guidelines and socio-environmental safeguards as criteria in projects financed by the NDB, in order to ensure the minimum of safeguards already achieved in the World Bank, IDB and elsewhere. A step back in the normative sphere would be a setback in the fight for human rights.

Yet it seems necessary to consider the previous experiences more systematically and judge where and when, for example, safeguards and guidelines for projects funded by the World Bank really did guarantee human, social and environmental rights in the territories. It is also important to base strategies upon accumulated experience of struggle over influencing national development banks. In Brazil, NGOs and social movements have carried out for many years the 'BNDES Platform'. Strategies of action and influence against financial actors are not new. The challenge ahead is forging unifying strategies within BRICS around the NDB.

BRICS governments, financial institutions and major economic groups (the *BRICS from above*[10]) progress according to the convergence between the state and capital, as they take forward accumulation strategies that worsen the concentration of wealth. It is necessary to build a true *BRICS from below*, with common strategies to fight for rights and international solidarity from the bases in BRICS countries. It will be successful only if built upon processes of social struggles and common experiences. Fortaleza is still a beginning.

Notes

1. http://www.portaldaindustria.com.br/cni/imprensa/2014/07/1,41230/mais-de-700-empresarios-do-brics-buscam-integracao- economica.html.
2. http://www.portaldaindustria.com.br/cni/imprensa/2014/07/1,41222/grupo-empresarial-propoe-medidas-para-ampliar-negocios-entre- paises-do-brics.html.
3. http://www1.folha.uol.com.br/mercado/2014/07/1485787-empresarios-dos-brics-querem-usar-moeda-local-em-transacoes-comerciais.shtml.
4. Declaração de Fortaleza, http://cut.org.br/sistema/ck/files/DECLARACAO%20DE%20FORTALEZA_FINAL%20(1).pdf.
5. Empresarios dos BRICS querem usar moeda local para transações. *Folha de São Paulo*, 14 July 2014.
6. Declaração de Fortaleza.
7. We can cite, among them, the popular demonstrations against the transport price increases and then the World Cup more generally, struggles against sex tourism, the struggle to preserve the Coco Park (including occupation of the park for weeks), the fight against the construction of an aquarium without an environmental permit, etc.
8. http://www.brettonwoodsproject.org/2014/05/world-bank-push-ahead-global-infrastructure-facility/.
9. The presentation by Oxfam pointed in that direction at the seminar on the bank organised by the Heinrich Boell Foundation in Fortaleza. On recommendations for the New Development

Bank: Simon Ticehurst (2014), O Banco dos BRICS e a inclusão, *Valor Economico*, 12–14 July, p. A11.

10. See the introduction by Ana Garcia and Patrick Bond (2014) Critical perspectives on the BRICS, *World Tensions*, 10, 18–19, http://www.tensoesmundiais.net/index.php/tm/issue/view/16/showToc.

References

Andes Info (2013) Banco Sur initiates operations in Caracas, Agencia Publica de Noticias del Ecuador y Suramerica, www.andes.info.ec/en/economia/banco-sur-initiates-operations-caracas.html

Bond, P (2013) Should Brazilians foot the bill so Blatter can foot the ball? *Daily Maverick*, 23 June, www.dailymaverick.co.za/opinionista/2013-06-23-should-brazilians-foot-the-bill-so-blatter-can-foot-the-ball

Bond, P (2014) *Elite Transition: From Apartheid to Neoliberalism in South Africa*, London, Pluto Press

Creamer, M (2014) Nene optimistic first BRICS bank disbursement will be to Africa, *Creamer Engineering News*, 17 July, www.engineeringnews.co.za/article/nene-optimistic-first-brics-bank-disbursement-will-be-to-africa

Davis, L (2008) *Obsession*, New York, Random House

Economic Times (2014) Israel threatens major offensive into Gaza Strip, *Economic Times*, 23 July, http://articles.economictimes.indiatimes.com/2014-07-23/news/51931968_1_israeli-embassy-gaza-conflict-gaza-strip

Fossil Free USA (2014) Go Fossil Free, http://gofossilfree.org/usa

Kasrils, R (2013) The ANC's Faustian pact was Mandela's fatal error, *The Guardian*, 24 June, www.theguardian.com/commentisfree/2013/jun/24/anc-faustian-pact-mandela-fatal-error

Mandeng, O (2014) Does the world really need a Brics bank?, *Financial Times*, 15 July, http://blogs.ft.com/beyond-brics/2014/07/15/guest-post-does-the-world-really-need-a-brics-bank/

People's Daily Online (2014) BRICS bank helps stabilize global order, *People's Daily Online*, 16 July, http://en.people.cn/business/n/2014/0716/c90778-8756136.html

Pew Research Global Attitudes Project (2013) Climate change and financial instability seen as top global threats, www.pewglobal.org/2013/06/24/climate-change-and-financial-instability-seen-as-top-global-threats/

Russian Government (2015) Civic BRICS, http://civilbrics.ru/en/links.php

South African Reserve Bank (2014) *Quarterly Bulletin* 2, www.resbank.co.za/Publications/QuarterlyBulletins/Pages/Quarterly-Bulletin.aspx

Stuenkel, O (2013) Towards institutionalization: the BRICS Contingency Reserve Arrangement (CRA), Post-Western World, 12 May, www.postwesternworld.com/2013/05/12/the-politics-of-the-brics-contingency-reserve-arrangement-cra/

United States Department of State (2013) Diplomatic Mission to South Africa, Pretoria, http://southafrica.usembassy.gov/press-releases-latest/joint-u.s.-south-african-military-exercise-showcases-bilateral-security-cooperation

VI BRICS Summit (2014a) Fortaleza Declaration, 15 July, http://brics6.itamaraty.gov.br/media2/press-releases/214-sixth-brics-summit-fortaleza-declaration

VI BRICS Summit (2014b) Treaty for the Establishment of a BRICS Contingent Reserve Arrangement, Fortaleza, 15 July, http://brics6.itamaraty.gov.br/media2/press-releases/220-treaty-for-the-establishment-of-a-brics-contingent-reserve-arrangement-fortaleza-july-15

Weeks, J (2014) The BRICS bank, Russia and beyond, *Open Democracy*, 15 July, www.opendemocracy.net/od-russia/john-weeks/brics-bank

25

Co-dependent BRICS from above, co-opted BRICS from the middle, and confrontational BRICS from below

PATRICK BOND

There is enormous confusion about how the BRICS relate to the world order, as roughly ten different ideological and practical political stances appeared, ranging from adoration to profound hostility. These ten categories were described in this book's Introduction, and they appear to be sufficiently cemented so that, although we can expect movement between them, the very nature of BRICS – especially its leaders' potential to talk left so they can walk right – will continue to bedevil the work of analysis. The standpoint of critical anti-capitalism has informed the prior pages, but with Washington's hostility to Moscow just as intense, there will continue to be a frisson of anti-imperialism whenever the BRICS make pronouncements about global injustices, or launch new institutions that allegedly offer 'alternatives' to the existing system of power.

To make matters worse, Russia's hosting of the BRICS heads of state summit in mid-2015 appeared to have three overarching objectives: continue building Vladimir Putin's diplomatic support base in the context of ongoing war on its Ukraine border; finalise plans for the 2016 launch of the BRICS New Development Bank; and initiate (for the purposes of co-optation and legitimation) a 'civic BRICS' structure tightly controlled by the five governments (i.e. conjoining BRICS from above with the status quo-oriented forces within BRICS from the middle). From these political-diplomatic, financial and social control processes, we can conclude this anti-capitalist critique of BRICS and consider where resistance might lead in coming years. The geopolitical tensions rising so quickly thanks to Russia's 2014 Crimea land grab and referendum not only led to rapid financial sanctions, to preparations for extreme shifts in energy pipeline routings and to Moscow's eviction from the G8. They also called forth the full-fledged operation of a diplomatic bloc, which was first evident in St Petersburg at the G20 meeting in 2013 when the other four BRICS took Putin's lead in preventing the US from bombing Syria. The bloc was apparent in 2014 in preventing the G20 (hosted by Australia) from becoming a G19. Excitement grew in some leftist and Third World nationalist quarters, given the impression that finally the Washington superpower was experiencing counter-power.

But these moments aside, how much will BRICS-from-above actually threaten the capitalist world order? In Brazil in mid-2014, the BRICS heads of state and finance ministers clearly confirmed they would avoid challenging the unfair, chaotic world financial system. Reporting from the Fortaleza summit on 15 July, *China People's Daily* (2014) bragged that the BRICS 'are actually meeting Western demands'. The point is 'to finance development of developing nations and stabilise the global financial market'. Indeed, if BRICS subservience continues, remarked financier Ousmène Jacques Mandeng (2014) of Pramerica Investment Management in a *Financial Times* blog, 'it would help overcome the main constraints of the global financial architecture. It may well be the piece missing to promote actual financial globalisation.' Applause for the 'alternative' BRICS financial initiatives thus came logically from both Jim Yong Kim at the World Bank and Christine Lagarde at the IMF, and in 2015 both Bretton Woods institutions and more than 40 countries became founder-members of China's Asian Infrastructure Investment Bank, foiling Obama's sabotage diplomacy.

As for the shallow *sturm und drang* occasioned by BRICS' rhetorical challenges to Washington's political or economic power, the deeper, more vital task of progressive intellectual work is to consider big-picture problems. For not much structural insight can be drawn from unpredictable geo-military conjunctures such as Russia in Ukraine, China in the South China Sea, Brazil in Haiti, India in Kashmir, or South Africa in several African war zones, aside from vague assertions about sub-imperial territorial imperatives which sometimes hold up and sometimes don't. The fact that in each of these sites there is so much effective resistance – often by irregular guerrilla forces of the sort that defeated both Washington and Moscow in Afghanistan, or Pretoria in the Central African Republic – suggests that even as regional deputy sheriffs, the BRICS have their work cut out for them. The fine art of geopolitical analysis should find surer moorings than these conjunctures and the gunboat diplomacy that necessarily arises when BRICS states and capital assert their agenda of expansion.

Pollution and speculation

Instead, it is worth dwelling on the two most widely recognised problems of our time, as the most recent Pew global public opinion survey (Pew Research Global Attitudes Project 2013) confirms: climate change and systemic global financial instability. In both, the BRICS suffer what in psychology is termed 'co-dependency'. The word 'comes directly out of Alcoholics Anonymous, part of a dawning realisation that the problem was not solely the addict, but also the family and friends who constitute a network for the alcoholic', according to Lennard Davis (2008). The BRICS are friendly-family *enablers* of Western capitalists, who are fatally addicted to speculative-centric, carbon-intensive accumulation. The most fatal long-term Western obsession facilitated by the BRICS is the emission of greenhouse gases at whatever level maximises corporate profits, future generations be damned to burn. In November 2014, this was confirmed when Barack Obama and Xi Jinping agreed to continue carbon emissions at a level that will lock in a 4 degree temperature rise. In contrast, recall the last time the world's 1% seriously kicked the pollution habit – and genuinely, albeit momentarily, succeeded with what is termed global governance – which was in 1987. With the Montreal Protocol, CFCs were banned so as to halt ozone hole expansion. But since that successful cold turkey episode, neoliberal and neoconservative fetishes took hold. Half-hearted efforts at the UN and other multilaterals to address global-scale environmental, economic and geopolitical disasters have conspicuously failed.

That addiction is just one of the Western afflictions which the BRICS enable. Undeniably, self-destructive financial/monetary policy is another. Suffering what increasingly appears to be the neurological impairment of a junkie, officials in Washington, London, Brussels, Frankfurt and Tokyo continue helter-skelter pumping of zero-interest dollars, euros and yen into the world economy, mainly feeding asset bubbles. This is a hopeless drug-addict's fix: maintaining policies of economic liberalisation that lower national economic barriers and generate huge gains for already wealthy elites holding property or stock market shares. BRICS elites are *not* enemies of the Western economic hedonists, as revealed in the 2014 Fortaleza Declaration (VI BRICS Summit 2014a), which provided exceedingly gentle advice to the West: 'Monetary policy settings in some advanced economies may bring renewed stress and volatility to financial markets and changes in monetary stance need to be carefully calibrated and clearly communicated in order to minimise negative spillovers.' (This refers to currency crashes suffered by most BRICS when the West began reducing 'Quantitative Easing' money-printing in May 2013 – yet another example of co-dependency.)

In short, scanning the world since the major financial and climate policy shifts were taken in 2008–2009, it is evident that BRICS from above repeatedly enable the West's most self-destructive habits during times of acute crisis:

- the April 2009 G20 bailout of Western banks via consensus on a $750 billion IMF global liquidity infusion;
- the December 2009 Copenhagen Accord in which four of the five BRICS did a deal to continue emitting unabated (they 'blew up the UN', according to Bill McKibben of 350.org);
- the 2011-12 acquiescence to the (s)election of new European and US chief executives for the Bretton Woods institutions (for despite a little whingeing, the BRICS couldn't even decide on joint candidates); and
- the 2012 agreement to pay over another $75 billion to the IMF even though it was apparent Washington wasn't going to change its undemocratic ways (the US Congress has refused to allocate the BRICS a higher IMF voting share).

Washington's co-dependants in Delhi and Pretoria are the most blindly loyal. Bharatiya Janata Party (BJP) reactionaries and African National Congress (ANC) neoliberals have regular economic, political and even military dalliances with Washington (United States Department of State 2013), and the BJP is so irretrievably backward that it won't countenance even a parliamentary debate about Israel's Gaza terrorism (*Economic Times* 2014). Playing the role of a frosty, distant relative, the other BRICS elites in Moscow, Brasilia and Beijing occasionally fulminate against Washington's internet snooping and, to Putin's credit, thank goodness the US whistle-blower spy Edward Snowden is at least safe in Russia. But it's likely that BRICS promises to establish new internet connectivity safe from US National Security Agency data-thieves will be broken, and as China's constant internet surveillance and censorship show, conjoined with 2015 revelations about Spy Cables linking Pretoria's spy agency to Israel's Mossad, the BRICS are as bad as, if not worse than, Washington, in terms of maintaining the most vital public good society has yet created: the internet. Another Fortaleza political let-down: the refusal by both Moscow and Beijing to support the other three BRICS' ascension to the UN Security Council in spite of their repeated requests for UN democratisation, because that would lead to dilution of Russian and Chinese power.

The greatest heartbreak, however, will be the passing of sub-imperialism's financial costs to BRICS citizenries and hinterlands. Before the Fortaleza summit, economic justice activists hoped the BRICS would decisively weaken and then break dollar hegemony, especially given the inevitability of rising Chinese yuan convertibility and the Moscow–Beijing (non-$) energy deal a few weeks before Fortaleza. But revealingly, both the New Development Bank (NDB) and 'Contingent Reserve Arrangement' (CRA) (VI BRICS Summit 2014b) have this feature: 'The Requesting Party's [borrower's] central bank shall sell the Requesting Party Currency to the Providing Parties' central banks and purchase US dollars from them by means of a spot transaction, with a simultaneous agreement by the Requesting Party's central bank to sell US dollars and to repurchase the Requesting Party Currency from the Providing Parties' central banks on the maturity date' (VI BRICS Summit 2014). That represents ongoing dollar addiction: a retox, not detox. The dollar is an inappropriate crutch in so many ways, but aside from University of London radical economist John Weeks (2014) writing on the eve of Fortaleza, few analysts acknowledge that genuinely 'inclusive sustainable development' finance would not require much US dollar (or any foreign currency-denominated) credits. Hard currency isn't needed if BRICS countries – or even future hinterland borrowers – want to address most of their vast infrastructure deficits in basic needs housing, school construction and teacher pay, water and sanitation piping, road building, agriculture support, and the like. The US dollar financing hints at huge import bills for future mega-project White Elephant infrastructure entailing multinational corporate technology (like most of South Africa's 2010 World Cup stadiums).

Who, then, will likely benefit? Weeks continues, 'The suspicion uppermost in my mind is that the purpose of the BRICS bank, as a project funding bank, is to link the finance offered to the construction firms and materials suppliers located in the BRICS themselves.' Certainly, the Chinese Government is notorious for doing this; a $5 billion loan from the China Development Bank to the South African transport parastatal Transnet announced at Durban's 2013 BRICS Summit resulted in $4.8 billion worth of locomotive orders from Chinese joint ventures a year later. As Weeks (2014) also observes, 'the voting proposal for the BRICS bank follows the IMF/World Bank model: money votes with shares, reflecting each government's financial contribution. The largest voting share goes to China, whose record on investments in Africa is nothing short of appalling ... The warm endorsement of the NDB by the president of the World Bank suggests enthusiasm rather than tension.'

But isn't the CRA a $100 billion 'replacement' for the IMF, as was widely advertised? No, it *amplifies* IMF power. If a BRICS borrower wants access to the final 70% of its credit quota, the founding documents insist, that loan can only come contingent on 'evidence of the existence of an on-track arrangement between the IMF and the Requesting Party that involves a commitment of the IMF to provide financing to the Requesting Party based on conditionality, and the compliance of the Requesting Party with the terms and conditions of the arrangement' (VI BRICS Summit 2014b). The neoliberal BRICS bureaucrats who laboured over that stilted language – and over the (self-obfuscating) name of the CRA – may or may not have a sense of how close global finance is to another meltdown, in part because of relentless IMF austerity conditionality. But it does reveal their intrinsic commitment to 'sound banking' mentality, by limiting their own liabilities to each other. Current quotas are in the range of $18–20 billion for the four larger BRICS and $10 billion for South Africa (though the latter will only contribute $5 billion, and China $41 billion).

Will it matter? According to São Paolo-based geopolitical analyst Oliver Stuenkel (2013), 'arrangements similar to the BRICS CRA already exist and have not undermined the IMF. The BRICS' CRA is closely modelled on the Chiang Mai Initiative signed between the Association of Southeastern Asian Nations countries as well as China, Japan and South Korea in May 2000.' The initiative is useless, Stuenkel observes, for no one has borrowed from it since. Likewise, he argues, 'The CRA is fully embedded in the IMF system!' What might that mean in future? The last BRICS country default managed by Washington was when Boris Yeltsin's Russia – with US$150 billion in foreign debt – required a US$23 billion emergency loan in 1998. Fifteen years later, four of the five BRICS suffered currency crashes when the US Federal Reserve announced monetary policy changes, and with higher interest rates, hot money flooded back to New York. An emergency bailout may soon be necessary in South Africa, where foreign indebtedness has risen to more than US$140 billion, up from US$25 billion in 1994, when Nelson Mandela's ANC inherited apartheid debt and, tragically, agreed to repay. Measured in terms of GDP, foreign debt is over 40% and even the neoliberal South African Reserve Bank (2014) warns that we are fast approaching 'the high of 41% registered at the time of the debt standstill in 1985'. That crisis and an accompanying US$13 billion default split the white ruling class, compelling English-speaking big business representatives to visit Zambia to meet the exiled liberation movement (Bond 2014b). Less than nine years later, capital had ditched the racist Afrikaner regime, in favour of bedding down with the ANC in what Mandela's key military strategist Ronnie Kasrils (2013) termed the 'Faustian pact'.

South African Finance Minister Nhlanhla Nene predicted that the first NDB borrowers would be African, to 'complement the efforts of existing international financial institutions' (Creamer 2014). But since Nene's own Development Bank of Southern Africa is rife with self-confessed corruption and incompetence (as Chapter 7 above shows), and the two largest NDB precedents – the Chinese and Brazilian banks – epitomise destructive extractivism, is this really to be welcomed? After all, the largest single World Bank project loan ever (US$3.75 billion) was just four years ago, to abet Pretoria's madcap emergency financing of Medupi (Bond 2014), the biggest coal-fired power plant anywhere in the world now under construction, which will emit more greenhouse gases (35 million tonnes/year) than do 115 individual countries.

In 2013, as Medupi came under intense pressure from community, labour and environmental activists (thus setting back the completion several years behind schedule), World Bank president Jim Yong Kim could no longer justify such climate-frying loans. He pledged withdrawal from the Bank's dirtiest fossil fuel projects. That, in turn, is potentially the gap for an NDB: to carry on filthy-finance once BRICS countries issue securities for dirty mega-projects and can't find Western lenders. For in even the most backward site of struggle, the United States, a growing activist movement is rapidly compelling disinvestment from oil and coal firms and projects (Fossil Free USA 2014). Of course there is a need for a genuinely inclusive and sustainable financial alternative, such as the early version, prior to Brazilian state sabotage, of the Banco del Sur that was catalysed by the late Venezuelan President Hugo Chávez. Launched in Caracas with $7 billion in capital, it has an entirely different mandate and can still be manoeuvred not to 'stabilise' world finance but instead to offer a just alternative (*Andes Info* 2013).

Shaky ground on which to build BRICS from the middle and below
To help BRICS elites end their addiction to the Western model of exclusionary, unsustainable capitalism, a revamped 12-step programme will be necessary. The first two steps of the classic Alcoholic Anonymous programme are obvious enough: 'We admitted we were powerless over alcohol, that our lives had become unmanageable and came to believe that a Power greater than ourselves could restore us to sanity.' The cleansing power of political-economic sanity absent in the BRICS elites comes from only one place: below, i.e. social activism. Against that kind of activism, BRICS from above needs BRICS from the middle: the Civic BRICS strategy Putin adopted in early 2015. The project was banal, and attracted such status quo groups that the Brazilian NGO network Rebrip dropped out entirely. In the Russian government's (2015) own words:

> Civic BRICS is the innovative political process, for the first time to be implemented within BRICS Summit in 2015 ... The civil society, rep-

resented by non-governmental organizations, the academic community, independent experts and merely concerned citizens contribute significantly to the transparency, monitoring and evaluation, as well as supervision over the performance outcomes and fulfillment of the commitments undertaken by the Member States. Involvement of the civil society in the discussion of BRICS agenda is extremely important not only to provide the leaders with an opportunity to look at the problems from the viewpoints of different groups of the population and, consequently, to make decisions based on their views and interests, but as well to make decisions made at the Summit more legitimate and ... from the point of view of an adequate retranslation of both decisions and commitments made by the leaders as well as BRICS performance deliverables to the international community.

Civilised society will thus support BRICS monitoring, evaluation, legitimation, 'retranslation' – but have nothing to do with expression of grievances and demands. (The same was true of the management of the BRICS Academic Forum and the association of civilized society think tanks, whose ideas and constituencies would not rock any boats.) Yet in the real world of the BRICS countries, there was an exceptional level of discontent as the BRICS came into being.

• Brazil hosted the BRICS Summit in July 2014, two days after the World Cup ended and just over a year after millions of protesters expressed rage about, first, public sector transport fare increases, and then, increasingly, about Sepp Blatter's politically destructive relationship with Workers Party president Dilma Rousseff (Bond 2013). Police repression was extreme, and after a while far-right forces used the opportunity to mobilise political attacks on the Workers Party and indeed on many protest participants of the left.

• Challenges also come from Russia, as a result not only of expansion into Ukraine (which, though popular in polling terms, did attract a small anti-war movement), but repression of protests. Civil society has been courageous in that authoritarian context: a democracy movement in late 2011, a freedom of expression battle involving a risqué rock band in 2012, gay rights in 2013 and at the Winter Olympics, and anti-war protests in March 2014.

• In India, activists shook the power structure over corruption in 2011–12, a high-profile rape-murder in late 2012, and municipal electoral surprises by a left-populist anti-establishment political party in late 2013 and early 2015.

- In China, activists protest an estimated 150 000 times annually, at roughly equivalent rates in urban and rural settings, especially because of pollution, such as the early April 2014 protest throughout Guandong against a paraxylene factory. But just as important are labour struggles, such as the current long strike against Nike and Adidas.
- In South Africa, multiple resource curses help explain what may be the world's highest protest rate; certainly the labour movement deserves its World Economic Forum rating as the world's most militant working class the last two years. Its militancy is on the rise, what with huge strikes in 2014 generating a 20% increase for platinum workers after five months and 10% for metalworkers after five weeks (at a time inflation was 6%). The labour movement's split between socialists led by the metalworkers ('class struggle') and residual corporatist leadership in the public sector and mining unions ('class snuggle') had the immediate effect in 2014–15 of pulling rhetoric further leftwards. But South Africa's diverse grassroots and labour protesters, including those who on 1882 occasions in 2013 and 1907 times in 2014 turned violent, still fail to link up, notwithstanding the metalworkers' sponsorship of a United Front to do just that. Indeed, many community activists have localistic and xenophobic tendencies, which allow structures of power to stay in place through divide-and-conquer.

These conditions in all the BRICS reveal a degree of reliance for mass movements on civil and political rights, and show how difficult it is for grassroots activists in all the emerging powers to move from conditions of 'IMF riot'-type socio-economic protests to more lasting revolutionary movements. The BRICS-from-below activists are not alone, because these conditions prevail across the semi-periphery, including the MINTs, which are meant to replace the BRICS as the next decade's economic engines. The MINTs-from-below challenges are similar, as are accomplishments.

- Leftists were active in 2014 in Mexico, where mass anti-privatisation protests addressed energy and education. A frightened *Newsweek* reporter in October 2013 reported from Mexico's 'streets of fire', that protests 'have become more frequent, volatile and violent, analysts say, a response to major domestic policy shifts and growing alienation among the young and unemployed'.
- Indonesia witnessed two million protesting workers in late 2013, demanding 50 percent wage increases.
- In Turkey, activists competed with Brazilians and other 'occupiers' for the

largest takeover of public space in major cities in 2013, in order to halt the potential destruction of Istanbul's Gezi Park.

- In Nigeria, the most intense social activism – not including the Boko Haram Islamic terrorist network – came from the oil extraction zone, especially as a result of the Movement for the Emancipation of the Niger Delta (MEND), which in 2008 was at its peak, preventing more than half the oil from being extracted at that stage. However, the most successful was the Occupy Nigeria national uprising against the doubling of the petrol price in January 2012, which drew millions out to protest.

High levels of turmoil have bubbled up regularly since 2011 in Egypt, Thailand and a few other stressed countries: not yet 'emerging powers' but crucial semi-peripheral locations in the world system. In southern Europe, both Syriza and Podemos are markers of social movements maturing into political parties. And there cities in the poorest African countries – Burkina Faso, Togo, the DRC, Burundi – which also witnessed mass civic battles on difficult urban terrain in 2014–15. And in the US belly of the beast itself, the 2011–12 Occupy movement was replaced by Black Lives Matter in taking semi-liberated space. In all these examples, are there new potentials for civil society internationalism? Parallels can be identified in many of the conditions faced by activists, especially human rights abuses and lack of democracy, and these have motivated the largest protests in the BRICS (India in 2011 witnessed 90 million protesting corruption) and elsewhere (Egypt in 2013 had 13 million on the streets against the Islamic government).

To make these links, can civil society organisations continue to develop their *own* foreign policy, bottom up? Some work along these lines has been forged through historic processes that date to earlier 'internationals' (the first global labour movement formed in London in 1864) or, even earlier, campaigns such as the late-18th-century democratic revolutions and the abolition of slavery. Subsequently in the 19th century, South Africa hosted extraordinary examples of settler-colonial and anti-colonial combat (e.g. in 1880–81 and 1899–1902 between whites) and myriad rebellions by black Africans, as well as the 1913 *Satyagraha* movement led by Mahatma Gandhi midway between Johannesburg and Durban – all of which had important international ramifications and hinted at future solidarity, e.g. the 20th century's Pan-African conferences and anti-colonial liberation movement linkages. More recently, South Africans benefited from an anti-racist internationalism that, from the late 1950s, chose a formidable global campaigning approach: boycotts, divestment and sanctions (BDS). The campaign targeted firms active in South Africa, with the argument that the profits made from apartheid (especially the migrant labour system, which was responsible for super-profits) were immoral, that the taxes they paid to Pretoria kept the oppression going, and that even though the firms' South African workers would be adversely affected by BDS, those workers and their organisations mainly supported this non-violent strategy. By the mid-1980s when anti-apartheid BDS peaked, by all accounts it contributed substantially to South Africa's 1985 economic crash, and the campaign kept up pressure until finally it was possible to declare an irreversible victory: the 'one-person one-vote in a unitary state' election on 27 April 1994.

In turn, such memories renew our confidence in international solidarity, especially when BDS is being applied today to Israel (in this case supported by the South African government due to historical relations with the Palestinian Liberation Organisation) and fossil fuel corporations with repeated reference to South African victories. South Africa also has hosted extensive civil society campaigning on behalf of Zimbabweans, Swazis, Tibetans and Burmese struggling for liberation, although rising xenophobia in 2015 reversed all that solidarity work. The global 'Climate Justice' movement sees South Africa as a key site, dating to the 2002 World Summit on Sustainable Development and the 2011 UN Climate Summit. A variety of other global justice projects, especially for access to AIDS medicines and the fight against water privatisation and carbon trading, have had critical groundings in South Africa.

All of these provide varieties of experience for international solidarity – but not yet the coherent overarching internationalist commitments and post-capitalist, anti-racist, feminist and ecological strategies needed for the complex times ahead. BRICS offers one site to compare analysis, strategies, tactics and alliances for what might become a crucial corrective to destructive tendencies by these countries' corporations, as they take the baton from Western multinational corporations, both within the BRICS and across the hinterlands. In this extraordinary context, we academic critics are hoping to open up two crucial debates: first, is BRICS anti-imperialist as advertised, or potentially inter-imperialist as the Ukraine battleground portends, or merely sub-imperialist where it counts most: in the ongoing global financial and climate meltdowns? Second, if the latter (as most of our authors agree), how can the struggles of BRICS from below intensify and link? The detox of our corrupted politics, a sober reassessment of our economies and fortification of our ecologies – all catalysed by re-energised civil societies – rely upon clear, confident answers to both.

Index

Abramovich, Roman 213

accumulation by dispossession 19–21, 98, 202, 252

ActionAid 281

African National Congress (ANC) 19, 289, 291

Agamben, Giorgio 189, 193

Agnelli, Roger 162, 165, 170, 174

Alvarado, JV 231

American Empire 62–3, 67

American Era 237

Andrade Gutierrez 121, 151, 152, 153

Anglo American 19, 104, 110

Arab Spring 268

Argentina 16, 33, 34, 39, 82

Asian Infrastructure Investment Bank 3, 287

asset-backed securitisation (ABS) 252

Association of Southeast Asian Nations (ASEAN) 66, 241, 291

BHP Billiton 104, 169, 175, 176, 180

Bolivarian Alternative for the Americas (ALBA) 268

bourgeoisies, national 11, 25, 29, 32–36, 39, 41, 42, 50, 54, 55, 57, 63, 84, 88, 137, 248

Brazil 22, 28, 31–4, 36–42, 248, 275, 277; and Africa 99; and agricultural subsidies 232–3; and agribusiness 232; and civil discontent 293; and Vale 162–83; and Zimbabwe 112–13; as sub-imperialist 159; in Angola 117–31; in Mozambique 117–31; mega-events 186–97; multinational companies 148–60; World Cup 280

Bretton Woods institutions 3, 6, 23, 48, 55, 255, 256, 277, 287, 289

BRICS 45–6, 50, 55, 58, 65, 206–7, 239, 263; and Africa 97–104, 276; and global capitalism 232; and multinationals 181–3; regional hegemony 17–18, 22–3; and Zimbabwe 106–13; as anti-imperialist 15, 272; as democratising world order 4, 5, 282; as enablers of capitalism 288; as geopolitical power 274; as imperialist 272; as informal alliance 237; as part of neoliberal order 207–8; as sub-imperialist 3, 15–25, 97–8, 104; foreign policy 275; from above 6, 11, 284, 287; from below 4, 5, 7, 11, 67, 281, 284, 294–6; from the middle 6, 11; prospects 261–5, 266

BRICS Business Council 280

BRICS New Development Bank 1, 65, 79,